Rebel Power

*Why National Movements
Compete, Fight, and Win*

PETER KRAUSE

Cornell University Press

Ithaca and London

First published 2017 by Cornell University Press
First printing, Cornell Paperbacks, 2017

Printed in the United States of America

Library of Congress Cataloging-in-Publication Data

Names: Krause, Peter, 1979– author.
Title: Rebel power : why national movements compete,
    fight, and win / Peter Krause.
Description: Ithaca : Cornell University Press, 2017. |
    Includes bibliographical references and index.
Identifiers: LCCN 2016045668 (print) | LCCN 2016050095 (ebook) |
    ISBN 9781501708558 (cloth : alk. paper) | ISBN 9781501708565
    (pbk. : alk. paper) | ISBN 9781501712661 (ret) |
    ISBN 9781501712678 (pdf)
Subjects: LCSH: Autonomy and independence movements—
    History—20th century—Case studies. | Self-determination,
    National—History—20th century—Case studies. | Political
    violence—History—20th century—Case studies. | Organizational
    behavior—History—20th century—Case studies.
Classification: LCC JC311 .K736 2017 (print) | LCC JC311 (ebook) |
    DDC 320.1/50904—dc23
LC record available at https://lccn.loc.gov/2016045668

For my parents

Contents

Tables and Figures

Tables

Figures

Acknowledgments

The core of this book is the interviews and archival work I conducted over the past eight years. I owe a deep debt of gratitude that I can never fully repay to those who were willing to sit with me, chat over tea, engage in deep discussions into the night, and help me locate valuable sources on sensitive histories to which most had devoted the prime of their lives. I hope that I have faithfully presented their experiences and insights, even as I challenge existing interpretations about the actions and outcomes of their organizations and national movements. I thank the many institutions that assisted along the way, including the American University of Beirut, the Begin-Sadat Center for Strategic Studies, the Hebrew University of Jerusalem, the Institute for Palestine Studies, the Interdisciplinary Center at Herzliya, the University of Jordan, and the Palestinian Center for Policy and Survey Research, as well as the staff at the Archives Nationales D'Outre Mer, the British National Archives, the Central Zionist Archives, the Centre d'Études Maghrébines en Algérie, the Haganah Archives, the Jabotinsky Institute, Linen Hall Library, the National Archives of Algeria, and the Palmach Archives.

This book began in the Massachusetts Institute of Technology (MIT) Department of Political Science and Security Studies Program, where I was incredibly fortunate to learn from giants in the field. Stephen Van Evera's push to ask the big questions and focus on the most relevant, clear evidence is on display in this book. Barry Posen's sharp insights always forced me to rethink my most basic assumptions and emerge with a better product. Roger Petersen's ability to combine systematic theory with rigorous fieldwork on political violence was one of the main inspirations for this book. Martha Crenshaw has generously served as an outstanding external mentor.

As I learn each time I start a new project, Martha has already written every-thing on political violence; we just try to refine it.

Other professors at MIT have been wonderful teachers and professional mentors. I thank in particular Fotini Christia, Owen Coté, Taylor Fravel, Richard Samuels, Jim Walsh, Cindy Williams, and Ken Oye, in whose class the prospectus for this project was first drafted. Thanks also go to the won-derful staff of the MIT Political Science Department, Security Studies Pro-gram, and Center for International Studies, among whom John Tirman de-serves special mention for his considerable support of my research.

I was fortunate to finish the first draft of this manuscript while a research fellow at the Harvard Kennedy School Belfer Center in Science and Interna-tional Affairs, where Sean Lynn-Jones, Susan Lynch, Steve Miller, and Steve Walt impressively led an intellectually vibrant program. Having refined much of the theory for the book at Belfer, I then revised the empirics as a research fellow under the guidance of Shai Feldman, Naghmeh Sohrabi, Eva Bellin, and the rest of the excellent faculty at the Crown Center for Middle East Studies at Brandeis University. I benefitted enormously from feedback by Stathis Kalyvas and Ian Lustick at a book workshop at Yale University with the Project on Middle East Political Science (POMEPS), as well as from participants who attended presentations at Harvard Univer-sity, the University of Chicago, George Washington University, and the New Faces Conference with the Triangle Institute for Security Studies at the University of North Carolina.

The faculty, staff, and students at Boston College helped improve the book tremendously. Robert Ross, David Deese, Tim Crawford, Jennifer Erick-son, and Lindsey O'Rourke have been wonderful colleagues, always will-ing to lend kind ears and powerful insights. My numerous research assis-tants in The Project on National Movements and Political Violence inspire me on a daily basis; I thank especially Jodi Brignola, Eleanor Hilde-brandt, Jonathan Makransky, Leor Sapir, James Sauro, and Tyler Wilkinson. The provost and the Department of Political Science, led by Susan Shell, generously funded a workshop for this book. Fotini Christia, Tim Craw-ford, Stacie Goddard, Adria Lawrence, William Quandt, and Nadav Shelef devoted significant effort to improving the manuscript, which I hope they see in the finished product.

It is no coincidence that the combination of political violence, Middle East politics, and historical analysis in this book reflects what my three under-graduate mentors at Williams College—Marc Lynch, James McAllister, and James Wood—taught me so well. I thank them for inspiring me, teaching me how to think, and showing me what it means to be an outstanding professor.

These early passions were subsequently nurtured by the students and military fellows in the MIT Political Science Department and Security Stud-ies Program, who are top-notch scholars and even better human beings. I especially thank Daniel Altman, Michal Ben-Josef Hirsch, Nathan Black,

Francisco Flores-Macías, Kristin Fabbe, Keren Fraiman, Brendan Green, Phil Haun, Stephanie Kaplan, Sameer Lalwani, Jon Lindsay, Gautam Mukunda, Austin Long, Tara Maller, Will Norris, Jeremy Pressman, Andrew Radin, Joshua Rovner, Joshua Shifrinson, Paul Staniland, Caitlin Talmadge, and David Weinberg. I have also benefitted enormously from the guidance and friendship of scholars at other institutions. Thank you to Max Abrahms, Aisha Ahmad, Eitan Alimi, Victor Asal, Mostafa Atamnia, Mia Bloom, Sarah Bush, Erica Chenoweth, Mohammed Daraghmeh, Jennifer Dixon, Alex Downes, David Edelstein, Ehud Eiran, Jeff Friedman, Boaz Ganor, Jill Goldenpine, Kelly Greenhill, Gregory Gause, Frank Gavin, Nadya Hajj, Ron Hassner, Jacqueline Hazelton, John Horgan, Michael Horowitz, Patrick Johnston, Jenna Jordan, Rosemary Kelanic, Noora Lori, Paul MacDonald, John McCauley, Barak Mendelsohn, Jacob Mundy, Vipin Narang, Rich Nielsen, Robert Parks, David Patel, Wendy Pearlman, Brian Phillips, Costa Pischedda, Jonathan Renshon, Larry Rubin, Chiara Ruffa, Yezid Sayigh, Jonah Schulhofer-Wohl, Khalil Shikaki, Ora Szekely, Younasse Tarbouni, Marc Trachtenberg, Joshua Walker, Joe Young, and Yael Zeira.

Cornell University Press and its Security Affairs Series was always the dream home for this book. I am so grateful for the wonderful editorial assistance of Roger Haydon, whose sharp suggestions and good humor made the process a smooth one. Robert Art and an external reviewer put in significant effort to make the book far clearer and more powerful.

This project has benefitted from financial support from the Kathryn Davis Fellowship for Peace at Middlebury College; the MIT Center for International Studies; the Smith-Richardson Foundation; the University of California, Los Angeles; the University of Maryland; and the Tobin Project. Earlier versions of parts of this book were published in "The Structure of Success: How the Internal Distribution of Power Drives Armed Group Behavior and National Movement Effectiveness," *International Security* 38, no. 3 (2014): 72–116, © 2013 by the President and Fellows of Harvard College and the Massachusetts Institute of Technology, published by the MIT Press. I am grateful to MIT Press for its permission to integrate parts of that article here.

The greatest blessing in life is a supportive, loving family, and I have been lucky enough to have one since the day I was born. Thank you to my wonderful sisters, Rebecca and Katie, who provided my first experiences with the challenge of competition amidst movement fragmentation, along with a great deal of love and support. Most of all, thank you to my amazing parents, Peter and Carol Krause. It is no exaggeration to say that everything good that I am today is because of my parents. I often joke that I am an exact 50/50 reflection of the two of them in disposition, appearance, and aspirations. In truth, if I could be even half the person who either my mother or my father is, I would consider myself happy. This book is dedicated to them, who gave everything and asked for nothing in return.

Rebel Power

Power, Violence, and Victory

Zohra Drif, Leila Khaled, Gerry Adams, and Yoske Nachmias all wanted the same thing—a state for their people to call their own—and they all played a prominent role in the struggle to achieve it. Yet when I was interviewing Zohra Drif a stone's throw from the Milk Bar she had bombed in Algiers, discussing Leila Khaled's hijackings and struggle for Palestinian rights in a refugee camp, walking next to Gerry Adams in one of multiple competing Irish republican marches to Bodenstown, and talking with Yoske Nachmias about facing his own brother in a firefight while aboard the *Altalena* off the Tel Aviv coast, I was struck by how different the outcomes were for their nations and the organizations of which they were a part.

Zohra Drif helped achieve an independent Algeria in 1962, and her Front de Libération Nationale (FLN) rules the country to this day. In contrast, Leila Khaled and her fellow Palestinians still do not have a state, and her Popular Front for the Liberation of Palestine (PFLP) finds itself on the margins of the enduring Palestinian national movement. Gerry Adams and Yoske Nachmias face mixed outcomes. Although Adams finds himself at the head of Sinn Féin, a powerful political party with the potential to become the largest in Ireland, he has been unable to bring Northern Ireland into the Republic. Nachmias celebrated the independence of Israel in 1948, but his Irgun was repressed and disbanded by its Zionist rival, and its affiliated party was excluded from power for three decades.

What explains this variation in outcomes? Why did some national movements achieve states while others did not? And what explains the accompanying variation in behavior, in that all four of these groups differed in their use and support of violent and nonviolent tactics across time and space? These are not simply historical puzzles; they are at the forefront of politics today.

Gaza has experienced a significant crackdown on cross-border violence into Israel and the Egyptian Sinai over the past five years. Members of the PFLP have been detained; members of Jaish al-Islam who took Western journalists hostage were arrested; a leader of Islamic Jihad was killed after his involvement in rocket fire against Israel; the flow of fighters and arms into Sinai has been inhibited; the jihadi group Jund Ansar Allah has been all but destroyed; and negotiations commenced with Israel over a long-term cease-fire.[1] The most surprising fact about this entire effort is that each of these actions was taken not by Israel, or Egypt, or even Fatah—but by Hamas.

Why would Hamas, the Palestinian group most associated with political violence against Israel over the past two decades, now restrain violence by the PFLP and negotiate with its enemy? Hamas has not undergone a change in leadership, its ideology and objectives have not been amended, and Israeli counterinsurgency tactics in Gaza have not been transformed. Existing theories would predict precisely the opposite behavior by these armed groups, arguing that groups become less violent with age but more violent with religious ideology and a higher number of total groups in a movement. It should, therefore, be the PFLP restraining Hamas and negotiating with Israel, but the reality is an Islamist Hamas with maximal territorial demands operating amid an increasing number of factions actually *constraining* the violent actions of the PFLP, a far older group with a secular ideology.

Just before Hamas repressed other Palestinian groups in Gaza, it left its headquarters in Syria in 2012 after a falling out with President Bashar al-Assad amid growing conflict there. The most common refrain heard among supporters of the ongoing insurgency has been that Syrian rebel groups must unite to topple Assad, a strikingly familiar appeal for the Palestinian national movement. In fall 2012, U.S. Secretary of State Hillary Clinton declared, "It is encouraging to see some progress toward greater opposition unity, but we all know there is more work to be done."[2] Nonetheless, subsequent talks in Doha, Madrid, and Istanbul failed to unite a fragmented opposition. Dueling alliances among numerous political and military groups such as the Syrian National Coalition, the Army of Conquest, and the Southern Front have been formed, although they have had little discernable impact on a conflict that continues to be marked by extensive infighting among rebels and a general failure to remove Assad from power.

Why would Syrian rebel groups that share a common enemy fail to unite when they and their supporters all publicly proclaim that unity is the key to victory? And when alliances have occurred, why have they done so little to lessen the violence and promote victory? Moreover, why would notoriously self-interested organizations ever put in significant effort toward a common goal such as the overthrow of Assad in the first place? Such behavior surely defies our expectations for collective action.

The only actors that may perceive the ongoing stalemate in Syria as a bright spot are the Syrian Kurds and the members of the People's Protection Units (YPG), who have maintained Kurdish enclaves in northern

Syria against Assad and the Islamic State of Iraq and Syria (ISIS) alike, with the help of the Kurdistan Workers' Party (Partiya Karkerên Kurdistanê, PKK) from Turkey and the Kurdish Peshmerga from Iraq. These groups are part of one of the most prominent national movements in the region, which, like the Palestinians, is fighting for a state it does not yet have. Why do the Algerians and Zionists have a state, but the Kurds and Palestinians do not? The Palestinians and Kurds today have more foreign support than the Algerians and Zionists did when they gained independence, and international norms of self-determination and decolonization have never been stronger. All national movements have periods of failure, of course, but it is also worth asking why Algeria and Israel achieved independence in 1962 and 1948, respectively, and not a decade earlier or later.

After spending much of the past eight years researching in archives and conducting interviews with members of the Palestinian, Zionist, Algerian, and Irish national movements, I recognize that the puzzles posed by national movements and political violence today have extensive historical precedents. My analysis of these movements in this book and the presentation of a new theory of violence and victory will provide answers for the past, present, and future.

National Movements: Definitions and Scope

National movements go by many names across the fields of political science, sociology, economics, and history: social movements, self-determination movements, insurgencies, and revolutions. All these concepts are sometimes labeled *rebellions* and their members *rebels*.[3] Although the terminology is often different, the entities are similar. All involve organizations and individuals struggling to alter the leadership or policies of a state, and all face the challenges that come with attempts at contentious collective action. As such, they are all types of social movements that possess the four characteristics identified by Sidney Tarrow: collective challenge, common purpose, social solidarity, and sustained interaction (see figure 1.1).[4]

The theory that I present here thus applies to all movements, insurgencies, and revolutions to a significant extent, but there are some key distinctions among them in identity, tactics, and objectives. National movements are distinct in that their social solidarity is based on national identity and their common purpose is political autonomy. In other words, (1) all members of national movements perceive themselves as part of a collective nation that share a common history, language, culture, religion, and/or ethnicity with ties to a particular piece of territory, and (2) national movements launch a sustained effort to achieve political autonomy to protect the nation and its people.[5]

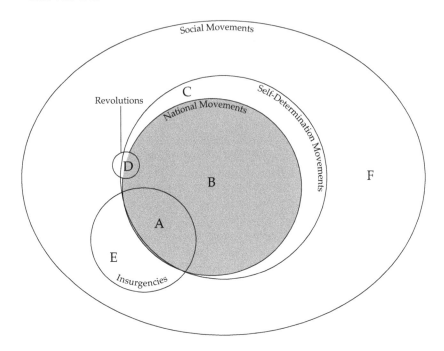

Figure 1.1. Comparing Concepts: Movements, Insurgencies, and Revolutions

The circles and their degree of overlap are constructed to scale using the data sets in the following sources: Bridget Coggins, *Power Politics and State Formation in the Twentieth Century: The Dynamics of Recognition* (New York: Cambridge University Press, 2014); Jason Lyall and Isaiah Wilson, "Rage against the Machines: Explaining Outcomes in Counterinsurgency Wars," *International Organization* 63, no. 1 (January 2009): 67–106; Jeff Goodwin, *No Other Way Out: States and Revolutionary Movements, 1945–1991* (Cambridge: Cambridge University Press, 2001); Kathleen Cunningham, *Inside the Politics of Self-Determination* (Oxford: Oxford University Press, 2014).

Social movements—such as the numerous women's rights movements, labor movements, and environmental movements—exist without nations (figure 1.1, F). There is no reliable count of the untold thousands of social movements in the past century, which include the pursuit of changes in state and class structures and policies along nonnational lines. Nations also exist without movements, as demonstrated by periods when the Gauls, Québécois, and Jews were not represented by an active movement for independence. National movements (figure 1.1, A and B), such as those of the Palestinians, Kurds, and Irish, exist at the nexus of identity and action; Bridget Coggins identifies 259 national movements during 1931–2002—and they are all social movements.[6]

Insurgencies are organized uprisings whose aim is to challenge governmental control of a region or to overthrow the government entirely through the use of force. Insurgencies thus pursue an objective similar to national movements, but they have two key differences. First, insurgencies need not be nationalist (figure 1.1, E). Insurgents can be of the same nation as the ruling regime, as in Cuba in the 1950s or Libya today; or they can hail from multiple nations, as in Ethiopia in the 1980s or Syria today. Second, insurgencies involve the ongoing use of force by definition; national movements do not. Many national movements (figure 1.1, B) are marked by violence at some point, but they also involve civil resistance and periods of peaceful relations with the state, as with the Catalan national movement in Spain today.

Revolutions also need not be violent or nationalist—although they are often one or both (figure 1.1, D)—but their overthrow of the existing political or social order always represents major strategic success by definition and so cannot be identified ex ante (despite the desire of many proponents to do so).[7] Jason Lyall and Isaiah Wilson identify 153 insurgencies during 1931–2002, while Jeff Goodwin identifies 15 revolutions during a shorter period, 1945–1989; 54% and 40% of these were nationalist, respectively.[8]

Self-determination movements (figure 1.1, C) are closest to the concept of national movements that I use in this book, with one small exception. Kathleen Cunningham includes, in her category of self-determination movements, groups that simply want to promote their language and culture—what Eric Hobsbawm would call proto-nationalist movements—whereas the aim of the national movements studied here was to achieve political autonomy and independence.[9] For example, the Berbers in Algeria today would be included in Cunningham's category and study but not in mine because I argue that the dynamics and stakes of pursuing an independent state are significantly different from those of pursuing bilingual education. Still, the claims I make here should largely also apply to self-determination movements, given their significant overlap in cases, and to a lesser but still significant degree they should apply to nonnational insurgencies, revolutions, and social movements.

Why the Use of Violence and the Outcomes of National Movements Matter

Nationalism has arguably been the greatest political force in the world over the past two centuries. As Ernest Gellner and Charles Tilly explain, states existed before nations and helped drive the demand for nationalism by creating a political entity whose profitable, coercive apparatus provided significant private goods to those who captured it.[10] National movements subsequently became the greatest challengers to the massive multiethnic empire states that dominated the globe and ruled by the divine right of kings.

After the American and French revolutions and the Congress of Vienna in 1815, nationalism rose across Europe and then played a leading role in the breakup of the Habsburg Empire and the unifications of Germany and Italy, the end of the Ottoman Empire and the redrawing of borders in the Middle East, two world wars and countless regional conflicts that reshaped the international system, decolonization in Latin America, Africa, and Asia, and the breakup of the Soviet Union. Indeed, the great powers—the United States in Vietnam, France in Algeria, and the United Kingdom in India— and supranationalist revolutionary ideologies—Marxism, pan-Arabism, and Islamism—have broken like once-proud waves on the enduring, sharp rocks of national movements.

The end of the Cold War and the era of globalization ushered in a brief period when some questioned the continued relevance of national identity, but nationalism has come roaring back.[11] This is nowhere more apparent than in the Middle East, where today numerous national movements exist that lack states, attempt to reshape borders, and push to dissolve the post–World War I order. The nation-state remains the fundamental unit of analysis in international relations and comparative politics. Most scholars of international relations conflate "nation" and "state"; in this book, I analyze when and why the former creates and controls the latter.

Although nationalism has been a force on the march for over two hundred years, individual national movements have experienced a mixed record of success and failure across time and space. Most states in the world today are the result of successful national movements—95 out of 154 new states from 1931 to 2002—but, as Gellner notes, the "number (of potential nations) is probably much, *much* larger than that of possible viable states."[12] There are over three hundred nations without states today—although many are without robust movements—and only 37% of national movements gained independence from 1931 to 2002.[13] Furthermore, each of these successful movements had failed campaigns before its ultimate victory; moreover, most failed movements had successful campaigns before their ultimate (or ongoing) defeat.

The variation in the outcomes of national movements is matched only by the variation in the behavior of their constituent groups. Only 23% of national movements involve no violence, meaning that in most movements there are groups employing and restraining violence despite their shared objective, and the same groups vary in their employment of violent and nonviolent tactics over time.[14] In the Zionist movement, the official policy of the Haganah was restraint (*havlagah*), but the Irgun and Lehi attacked British soldiers and Palestinian civilians. In the Algerian national movement, the FLN in 1962 and the Mouvement pour le Triomphe des Libertés Démocratiques (MTLD) in 1954 restrained themselves and other groups from violence, even though less than a decade earlier they had been the groups initiating it.

The ability to explain and predict variation in group behavior and movement outcomes within and across cases is of significant importance to academics and policymakers alike. Despite numerous quality contributions, however, the existing scholarship has not generated a parsimonious and powerful theory that is up to the task.

Why Existing Arguments Are Inadequate

Although a great deal of excellent scholarship exists on group behavior and movement outcomes, three widespread misconceptions prevent adequate answers to the puzzles identified at the outset of this chapter.

First, most scholars who have analyzed the success of movements and the use of political violence have employed a framework of a unitary non-state actor pursuing strategic concessions.[15] On movement success, Tilly, Erica Chenoweth, and Maria Stephan all argue that the more members a movement has in total, the more successful it will be due to increased pressure on the state.[16] Chenoweth and Stephan also suggest that nonviolent movements are more likely to be successful because of their ability to split the opposition. This links to claims by Max Abrahms and Page Fortna that groups and movements that employ terrorism are more likely to fail, a claim countered by William Gamson, Robert Pape, and Andrew Kydd and Barbara Walter, who argue that movements employing violence in general or terrorism in particular are more likely to succeed.[17] Finally, many sociologists and political scientists claim that the success of national movements is driven not by movement resources or actions but, rather, by political opportunity, whether attributable to weak states that cannot effectively repress movements, supporting states that make it more difficult to do so, or shifting norms of decolonization that push states not to try.[18]

Scholars suggest that group behavior is driven by the common economic, political, or social grievances of a movement; its common repression by the state; or its common access to rough terrain, lootable resources, and other conditions that favor insurgency.[19] Others argue that group-level characteristics such as ideology—specifically a certain religious or political belief system, or a radical version of any type—drive a group to use or shun violence, and to negotiate with a state enemy or hold out.[20] Some contend that it is a group leader who drives this decision or that the age of the group is essential. Younger groups are supposedly more likely to innovate and employ violence, whereas older groups are likely to fall victim to the "iron law of oligarchy" and moderate as they ossify internally.[21]

Whether scholars treat movements as unitary entities without multiple autonomous internal groups or analyze a lone group in isolation, the analysis of behavior and success within such frameworks poses numerous problems. The former approach overlooks the organizational objectives of survival and strength that are more important to groups than collective, strategic outcomes; the latter approach misleadingly credits a single group with the actions and effects of many. Both fail to capture the competitive internal dynamics that are at the foundation of the success of groups and the movements of which they are a part. Many of these arguments also deny national movements and their members agency by treating them as undifferentiated masses or explicitly arguing that "movements succeed or fail as the result of forces outside their control."[22]

Second, a growing number of new studies build on the older literature on social movements to make sophisticated arguments concerning how movement structure drives behavior and outcome. One camp contends that united movements with all groups in an alliance are the most successful. As Bard O'Neill notes, "Few, if any, experts on and practitioners of insurgency have not stressed the importance of unity within insurgent ranks."[23] For example, Wendy Pearlman makes a strong theoretical and empirical case that united movements exhibit greater cohesion among groups and less of the infighting and spoiling that prevents strategic progress.[24] In his landmark study of social movements, William Gamson agrees with the relative effectiveness of unity. As for the alternative, he argues, "The sorry reputation of factionalism is a deserved one."[25]

Other scholars have suggested that "internally divided movements are more likely to get concessions from their host states."[26] Cunningham, Herbert Haines, Mark Lichbach, Desirée Nilsson, and Jesse Driscoll claim that fragmented movements with multiple factions can generate beneficial radical flank effects, reduce the principal-agent problem for the base supporters of the movement, and provide flexibility in coalitions that helps to resolve conflict and offers incentives to the target state to make strategic concessions to moderate groups.[27] As Luther Gerlach and Virginia Hine conclude, "When the success of movements is reported as having occurred 'because of' rather than 'in spite of' organizational fission and lack of cohesion, we will have come to understand the nature of movement dynamics much more clearly."[28]

Although these are the best existing studies on movement dynamics and outcomes, the united–fragmented distinction systematically discounts the most important factor that defines the structure of a movement: the balance of power. When we incorporate the balance of power into a typology of movement structure, we find that united and fragmented movements exhibit more similarities than differences because they both contain multiple significant groups and, therefore, internally competitive movement systems.

Third and finally, the aforementioned scholars either fail to systematically operationalize the degree of unity and fragmentation they are discussing, or they do so by simply counting the total number of groups in a movement. The former approach makes it difficult to offer clear predictions of the movement outcome ex ante; the latter treats all groups the same regardless of size and influence. For example, a group of 30 members and a group of 30,000 members do not have the same impact on a movement. The very small group is of little to no consequence; the large group probably changes the behavior of other groups and the outcome of the movement. The most powerful groups play the dominant role in campaign dynamics and outcomes, and typologies of movement structure must capture the strength of groups and the concentration of power to maximize their own explanatory power. Furthermore, although almost all these authors argue that more fragmentation leads to more violence, their failure to differentiate among groups means that few offer a theory that identifies *which* specific groups initiate violence, *which* follow suit, and *which* do not. In this book, I tackle these three challenges to provide clear, powerful explanations for group behavior and movement outcome.

Movement Structure Theory

HIERARCHY AND GROUP BEHAVIOR

Groups in national movements face a dual struggle. They engage in "wars of movement" to achieve common strategic goals characterized by collective-action challenges, such as the founding of a new state, while they simultaneously engage in "wars of position" with rivals in their movement for organizational dominance.[29] Groups seek to ensure their survival and maximize their power above all else, but the structure of a movement drives how a group can best pursue its self-interest and whether the internal or external struggle is paramount.[30] As it is for officials in government or states in the international system, where you stand depends on where you sit.[31] That is, for groups in national movements, where you stand on violence and victory depends on where you sit in the movement hierarchy.

A *hegemon* is a dominant group that is more than three times stronger than any rival in the movement; it is the group most likely to pursue victory because the best way it can gain strength is to cement its top position in a new state and capture the associated spoils of office, wealth, and status.[32] A *leader* is the strongest group in a movement with one or more viable challengers; it will pursue victory for reasons similar to the hegemon, but its more precarious position of power means that it will continue to devote significant resources to internal struggles. Hegemons and leaders are more likely to restrain violence and negotiate with the state, given that their pole position makes them risk-averse and more likely to pay the costs of government repression, which often disproportionately affects the best-known and most powerful group.[33]

A *challenger* is a nonleading group at least one-third as strong as the leader; it will not only *not* pursue victory but will also often work to violently spoil it, thus preserving the private benefits for itself. As one member of the Iraqi Kurdish national movement described the relationship between the challenger Patriotic Union of Kurdistan (PUK) and the leader Kurdistan Democratic Party (KDP), "There are some people within the PUK who are against an independent state of Kurdistan if it is announced at the hands of [KDP leader Masoud] Barzani."[34] Should a challenger rise to become a leader, it will then swiftly shift its strategy to pursue victory (and vice versa for the now dethroned former leader). A *subordinate* is a weak group less than one-third as strong as the leader; it will likely put in little effort toward victory, but the fact that it has almost no chance of becoming the movement leader means that it is less likely to strenuously oppose strategic success than are the challengers (for which independence ensures present losses and destroys potential future gains). As Prospect Theory suggests, challengers and subordinates are more likely to escalate violence, given their desire to "gamble for resurrection" from a risk-acceptant position of weakness, especially because their stronger rivals are likely to pay the costs.[35]

HEGEMONIC MOVEMENTS AND SUCCESS

Just as power determines group position, it also determines movement type. The key distinction between hegemonic movements, which contain one significant group, and fragmented movements and united (allied) movements, which contain two or more, is that both fragmented and united movements contain a challenger and therefore substantial internal competition. In fragmented or united movements, there is less pursuit of victory and more counterproductive violence, making such movements far less successful. These movements include challengers that actively work to prevent victory as well as leaders that have less incentive than hegemons to pursue a victory whose private benefits they are less assured of capturing. Fragmented and united movements experience a version of the security dilemma, in which the actions that groups take to make themselves more secure—such as violent outbids to gain support, infighting to weaken rivals, and spoiling to prevent negotiations—make their movements less secure and less successful.[36]

Such actions result in strategically ineffective movements that expend their resources on internal rather than external struggles, generating mixed messages and little credibility to coerce states or effectively negotiate and uphold agreements. As another observer notes for the Iraqi Kurdish PUK and KDP, "They are obsessed with their party rivalry. . . . They do not work out any common strategy. There is no strategy at all, except to get ahead of the other party."[37] This is "the tragedy of national movements": even foreknowledge of the superiority of hegemonic movements does not help groups because every group wants to be the hegemon, ensuring that counterproductive competition will continue.[38] As Michael Gunter explains, "Although both Barzani [KDP] and Talabani [PUK] have recognized how damaging the fighting is to their cause, they seem unable to end it."[39]

In a hegemonic movement, there is more pursuit of victory and less counterproductive violence, making such movements far more successful. A hegemonic movement—with one dominant group—incentivizes the pursuit of victory and reduces counterproductive violent mechanisms because the hegemon has no challengers to outbid, infight, or spoil. Furthermore, a hegemonic movement has greater coherence in its strategy, clarity in its signaling, and credibility in its threats and assurances. Movements are thus more likely to succeed when there is a significant "imbalance of power" between the hegemon and other groups because a balance of power internally is likely to lead to failure externally.

Therefore, contrary to the spirit of Kenneth Waltz, Movement Structure Theory (MST) suggests that the internal balance of power provides both a theory of national movements *and* a theory of group behavior.[40] MST also provides a prequel of sorts to Waltz, Giovanni Sartori, and Samuel Huntington, in particular, and to international relations, party politics, and democratization, in general. These and other scholars have analyzed competition over power *among* states and *within* states, but MST demonstrates that the struggle never stops—or, more accurately, starts earlier—for those trying to form states.[41] In fact, the competition looks quite familiar in its earliest stages, in that national movements combine the anarchical lack of strong institutions of international relations with the hierarchical positioning of groups based on relative power in party politics. Unfortunately, MST reveals that the movements that are more likely to win are less likely to become stable democracies, given that hegemonic movements are more successful but an effective democracy requires multiple significant parties crafting representative institutions and competing for support. The paradox is that the movement structure that is best for a nation to achieve freedom as a new state may be the worst for subsequent political freedom within it.

To sum up, Movement Structure Theory predicts that a shift in the position of a group in the movement hierarchy is likely to produce an accompanying shift in its behavior. If, however, the hierarchy of the movement shifts over time but the number of *significant* groups in the movement remains the same, the groups are simply exchanging roles in a recurring play that will probably have the same strategic finale.

Research Design and Methodology

The fact that Movement Structure Theory purports to answer more with less marks it as parsimonious; subsequent empirical analysis will determine the extent to which it is powerful. Although MST was not originally designed to be a prequel to Sartori and Waltz, the theory was largely created deductively, based on inspiration from their approach of using the number and relative strength of significant actors in a system to explain behavior and outcome.[42] After I had fleshed out the logic behind the mechanisms of violence and victory, my research design began with the realization that my independent variable—the balance of power among groups in the same national movement over time—was not adequately captured by any previous study. I therefore had to create it myself. In addition to collecting information on my independent variable from scratch, I also had to analyze complex causal mechanisms concerning the relationships among actors in the same movement across time and space. All this required a multimethod approach that combined comparative historical analysis with extensive fieldwork, interviews, and archival research.

As much as I would like to test MST across the universe of cases in the future, getting reliable, yearly, micro-level data on group strength is such a labor-intensive process that I had to start with a small number of cases. For this first test of a new theory with a new typology, I selected movements with diverse values on the dependent variable: the achievement of a new state.[43] As much as the movements I chose contain significant variation across cases—two total successes (the Zionist and Algerian national movements), one limited to moderate success (the Irish national movement), and one movement that has as yet been unsuccessful (the Palestinian national movement)—the within-case variation is even greater. The Zionist and Algerian national movements experienced decades of failure before they achieved ultimate independence, whereas the Irish and Palestinians had successful and unsuccessful campaigns across time and space. These cases were also selected because they represent most-likely cases for competing theories on ground that my competitors have already chosen, thus negating any charges of motivated selection bias.[44] In fact, scholars have implicitly and explicitly claimed that the Palestinian, Zionist, Algerian, and Irish national movements are the paradigmatic examples of how violence works and movements succeed *and also* the paradigmatic examples of how violence does not work and movements fail.[45] Finally, these four movements also vary across time and space, are data rich, and are generally representative of the universe of national movements, which makes it easier to assess competing arguments and identify broad implications for scholarship and policy.[46]

When I selected my cases, I did not have knowledge of their values on the independent variable because data did not exist for when the movements were hegemonic, united, or fragmented and when their member groups were hegemons, leaders, challengers, or subordinates.[47] I still cannot situate the structure of these movements within the universe of cases because adequate information on these aspects of the universe does not yet exist. I was fortunate to discover, however, that there is extensive within- and across-case variation in the movement structures. All four movements experienced periods of hegemony, unity, and fragmentation, and all included groups that moved into and out of the leading position. Even more fortunately, many of these shifts in the movement hierarchy did not correspond with shifts in the movement system, whereas in other periods, the movement hierarchy or movement system changed or remained constant while other key variables did the opposite, allowing for tight within-case comparisons and the isolation of the causal impact of my variables of interest.[48] I therefore carried out a series of longitudinal analyses of forty groups in forty-four total campaigns over 140 years in the Palestinian, Zionist, Algerian, and Irish national movements, which allowed me to increase the number of observations and observable implications of MST and its competitors.[49]

After an extensive analysis of secondary source literature on my cases, I spent a good deal of time conducting fieldwork in the countries related to each national movement, including eight months in Israel focused on the Zionist movement; eight months in the West Bank, Jordan, and Lebanon for the Palestinian national movement; four months in Northern Ireland, Ireland, and London for the Irish national movement; and three months in Algeria and France for the Algerian national movement. First, I sought to analyze the actions and outcomes of the groups within each movement and the regimes they were struggling against using the best archival material available. I analyzed documents in English, Arabic, French, and Hebrew from archives that contained group perspectives, including the Institute for Palestine Studies, the Haganah, Palmach, and Irgun archives, Linen Hall Library, and the National Archives of Algeria, and regime perspectives, including the British National Archives and the Archives Nationales d'Outre Mer.[50] I pored over accounts of group discussions on strategy, intelligence reports, interviews, and other documents that provided a great deal of information on the strength, motivations, and behavior of the groups and regimes alike.

While in the field, I also conducted over 150 interviews with members from multiple political and armed groups in each national movement, government officials, and knowledgeable journalists and academics. I focused on elite interviews in each movement because my unit of analysis is the organization, and leading individuals generally have the most control of organizational policy and are most knowledgeable about group perceptions and deliberations. My knowledge and understanding of the people, organizations, and internal politics of these national movements were immeasurably heightened by these interactions, and I owe my interviewees an enormous debt of gratitude for taking the time to speak with me (often on multiple occasions).[51] This combination of archival analysis and interviews allowed me to triangulate information and develop original data sets and thick historical interpretation to process-trace mechanisms as the groups moved up and down their movement hierarchies while employing a variety of methods to varying degrees of success.[52]

All research designs have weaknesses, and mine is no exception. First, I face the common challenge of conducting causal inference on behavior and outcomes that must be observed amid significant complexity. For logistical and moral reasons, I cannot hold my variables of interest constant or randomly manipulate them. Nevertheless, I was able to identify natural experiment-like conditions in which the movement structure changed while other key factors remained the same, and vice versa. The ability to isolate the causal impact of various factors in these scenarios provided some of my most powerful findings.

Second, I am testing my theory and its competitors on four movements and forty significant groups in forty-four campaigns, which qualifies as a small to medium N by any standard. Some of the excellent studies already noted have the potential to provide more generalizable claims, given that they test their theories on far larger samples. My approach is necessary given the need to create thick data from scratch, however, and it is beneficial given that many of the micro-level behaviors and mechanisms in MST require a deep, longitudinal analysis of movements. Furthermore, I am confident that I have more in-depth, triangulated, reliable, and transparent data on these four movements than other studies.

Finally, like studies with any number of cases, I face the problem of endogeneity. In other words, how can I know that changes in movement outcome are not driving changes in the movement system, instead of vice versa? In a broad sense, my theory builds in some degree of endogeneity because the actions that groups take can affect their position in the hierarchy, which then can affect the expected movement outcome, which then can affect group actions. This is purposeful; actions and outcomes in national movements are endogenous in the long run, and pretending otherwise is intellectually dishonest. That said, my research design of longitudinal analysis of movements with multiple campaigns enables me to analyze the sequencing of these steps because I can identify how actions affect the position of a group at Time 1 and the expected outcome at Time 2, which can affect actions at Time 3. I apply standardized, general questions to each case and trace the entire process, allowing me to identify any feedback that may exist.[53] Ultimately, my findings support MST, and the discovery of a number of unexpected developments that my argument cannot explain (detailed in chapter 7) makes for a richer analysis.

Book Plan

Collectively, the Palestinian, Zionist, Algerian, and Irish national movements provide extensive support for MST: the number of significant groups in each movement drove the success of their campaigns, and the hierarchical positions of the groups in the movement drove their behavior, with strik-ingly similar dynamics emerging again and again. Individually, these cases also highlight different strengths, challenges, and potential extensions of the theory, presented in chapter 2.

Chapter 3, on the Palestinian national movement, provides the best tests of the impact of hierarchy on group behavior. I use a variety of tight within-case comparisons, in which the shifting of variables at different times al-lows for powerful assessments of why groups such as Fatah, the PFLP, and the Jordanian Communist Party used or restrained violence at different pe-riods in their history. In chapter 3, I also provide the best illustrations of "the tragedy of national movements": Palestinian groups knew they needed hegemony to succeed, but their desire for power kept them largely frag-mented. Regardless of changes in time or space, the Palestinian national movement met with strategic failure when the movement was fragmented (1965–1973, 1975–1985, and 2001–2016), limited success when it was united (1974), and its greatest success when the movement was hegemonic (1986–1993 and 1995–2000). Despite numerous shifts in the hierarchy, the fact that the Palestinians were most commonly fragmented meant that most organi-zational shifts resembled rearranging the hierarchical deck chairs on the proverbial *Titanic*.

In chapter 4, I explain how, after decades of fragmentation and the in-ability to secure statehood, a Zionist population that owned 7% of the Pal-estine Mandate and represented 37% of its population was given 55% of the territory by the United Nations and then proceeded to defeat a Pales-tinian national movement that was backed by a population twice as large that controlled more territory, held the high ground, and was supported by significant armies from five neighboring Arab states. The evidence in chapter 4 thus reinforces the virtues of hegemony because the movement achieved victory when it was hegemonic (1942–1949), after failing to achieve independence while fragmented in the previous decades. It also demonstrates that "the balance is greater than the sum of its parts" be-cause the dominant hegemon, Haganah, sunk a massive, much-needed arms shipment rather than allow its content and the associated credit to go to a potential Zionist challenger.

The Palestinians of the 1960s were most inspired by the Algerian national movement, whose history is analyzed in chapter 5. The analysis in chapter 5 best demonstrates the virtues of hegemony and the relative insignificance of unity and total movement strength. Like the Palestinian national move-ment, the Algerian national movement was strategically successful during hegemony (1958–1962) but largely unsuccessful during periods of fragmen-tation (1946–1950 and 1952–1957) and unity (1944–1945 and 1951). In 1944–1945, the Algerians were united and mobilized to a degree not seen before or since, yet that uprising failed while one a decade later, marked by a lack of unity and less total movement strength, succeeded. In chapter 5, I also illuminate the role of external states; the post-1957 FLN position as a credible hegemonic negotiator with limited potential for spoiling or sellout yielded international support and recognition, while the failure of numerous French attempts to refragment the movement forced France to concede full Algerian independence.

In the longitudinal analysis in chapter 6, I describe the most striking feature of the Irish national movement: the clockwork-like actions of republican groups that, while challengers, escalated violence, shunned elections, and denounced negotiated compromise, but that, after they became the leader or hegemon of the movement (or movement wing), shunned violence, participated in elections, and negotiated compromises. Despite their intense criticism of each other, this is the story of Cumann na nGaedheal (later Fine Gael), Fianna Fáil, the Official Irish Republican Army (OIRA)/Official Sinn Féin (OSF), and the Provisional IRA/Sinn Féin over the course of the twentieth century. In *every* case in which abstentionism (the refusal to take seats in the government) was ended, what changed was not what the group ideologically said had to change but, rather, the movement structure and that the group would be guaranteed a leading role in the new order. Historically, the hegemonic campaign of the Irish national movement in 1918–1922 yielded a large-scale British withdrawal and the establishment of the Irish Free State. In contrast, the fragmentation of successive campaigns up to and including The Troubles of 1968–1998 yielded a consistent lack of strategic success, despite the longest sustained period of armed struggle against the British in Irish history. In chapter 6, I also analyze potential expansions of MST by examining the micro-level balance of power inside the republican and nationalist wings of the movement, the use of cross-domain outbidding involving violent and nonviolent strategies alike, and the application of the theory to both secessionist and irredentist national movements.[54]

In chapter 7, I conduct a comparative analysis across all the movements, groups, and campaigns; assess and demonstrate synergies with competing arguments; scrutinize the incorrect predictions of MST; identify remaining questions for future research; and present key policy implications for those whose goal is either to advance or stop national movements and political violence.

CHAPTER 2

Why National Movements Compete, Fight, and Win

The structure of the international system is driven by the number of great powers, the structure of party systems is driven by the number of effective parties, and the structure of movement systems is driven by the number of significant groups.[1] This basic but overlooked fact suggests that the most neglected aspect of movement structure—power—is also the most crucial.[2] In fact, the internal balance of power is the most significant variable driving group behavior and movement outcomes.

The structure of a national movement is first defined by the number of significant groups it contains because the most powerful groups play the dominant role in campaign dynamics and outcomes. The structure of the international system is based on the United States and China, not Belize and Luxembourg; the structure of the U.S. party system is based on the Republican Party and the Democratic Party, not the Modern Whig Party and the Socialist Party; and the structure of a national movement such as that of the Palestinians is based on Fatah and Hamas, not the Palestinian Arab Front and the Palestinian Popular Struggle Front. Even though some movements experience brief periods when the unorganized grassroots or weaker organizations may appear to be taking the lead—as in the Russian Revolution or the First Intifada—strong organizations such as the Bolshevik Party or Fatah soon (re)gain control over the less organized masses and the movement itself.

As Giovanni Sartori notes, "If we resort to counting, we should know how to count."[3] The problem with the current ubiquitous approach to conceptualizing movement fragmentation is that it simply adds up the total number of all groups regardless of size, even though many of them do not "count" for movement dynamics and outcomes. Adding ten groups of ten people each to a national movement is likely to have no impact, whereas adding one group of 10,000 people is likely to significantly alter the behavior of other groups and the outcome of their movement. Furthermore, measuring fragmentation based on the number of significant groups yields far more reliable measurements than attempts to count every single group, regardless of size and strength. It is easy to miss the minnows but nearly impossible to miss the whales.

Any attempt to gauge the relative strength of organizations in a national movement faces challenges of unit homogeneity because we must compare political parties with paramilitaries. Nonetheless, competing groups must constantly do the same thing themselves when they ask how an armed group in their movement might perform in elections—as rivals did with the Irish Republican Army (IRA) and Sinn Féin in Northern Ireland—or how effective a political party might be if it created an armed wing. I therefore measure common denominators that capture the strength of all types of political organizations: members, wealth, and popular support.[4]

For national movements, a *significant group* is either the strongest group in the movement or another strong group that has the capability to realistically challenge the strongest group for leadership in the foreseeable future. Because the strength of nonstate groups is far more volatile than that of states, in this study I consider a group significant if its membership size, economic wealth, *or* popular support (measured via election results and opinion polls) is one-third as large as the strongest group.[5] A group with one-third the strength of another can realistically challenge and overtake it within the foreseeable future, whereas such an outcome is unheard of among states.

A national movement with three or four significant groups may mean more potential rivals, but the key distinction is between movements with one significant group and those with two or more, or, in other words, between movements that contain a competitive and those that contain a noncompetitive internal environment. This distinction has precedents in party systems (hegemony vs. oligarchy) and economics (monopoly vs. oligopoly). A less important distinction in the structure of national movements that weakly mimics some aspects of the number of significant groups involves alliances among these groups, in that alliances create larger power blocs of multiple groups. But alliances between nonstate actors are generally so weak and wracked by commitment problems and struggles over relative power that united movements are often not much different in their actions or outcomes than fragmented movements. In this study, national movements count as united if all the significant groups are in a single alliance.[6] When we use the number of significant groups and their alliances, three types of movement systems emerge, differentiated by their internal distribution of power: hegemonic, united, and fragmented (see figure 2.1).

The typology in figure 2.1 turns the existing debate over movement structure on its head. Existing typologies suggest that the key distinction is between united and fragmented movements, and that there is little to no difference between a hegemonic movement dominated by a single group and a united movement dominated by a single alliance of multiple groups. On the contrary, this typology suggests that the key distinction is between

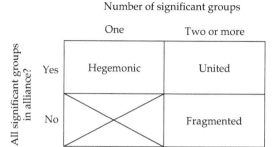

Figure 2.1. A Typology of Movements

Note that the bottom left quadrant is a null set because a movement that has one significant group must, by definition, have all significant groups united.

hegemonic movements (with one significant group) and nonhegemonic movements (with two or more), and that there is little to no difference between united and fragmented movements. For example, existing scholarship holds that an alliance between Hamas and Fatah or the emergence of five new, small Palestinian political parties would significantly change group behavior and the movement outcome, whereas my typology suggests that neither development would have much impact. If Hamas or Fatah becomes the dominant hegemon in the Palestinian national movement, however, then we should expect change.[7]

In MST, the key distinction is the number of significant groups, which determines whether the movement is internally competitive or noncompetitive.[8] This aspect of movement structure drives group incentives and movement dynamics, which together drive group behavior and movement outcome. Alliances have comparatively little impact. In an alliance, individuals are generally loyal to their groups first. Individual group leadership maintains ultimate decision-making power, even if groups agree to try to coordinate certain actions. The power concentrated in a single alliance is therefore far less cohesive in organization, coherent in action, and stable in alignment than a single group, as Fotini Christia expertly demonstrates in her analysis of the countless alliance shifts among warring Afghan factions in 1978–1998.[9] These factors make a movement with a unifying alliance somewhat different from a fragmented movement with no such ties but very different from a hegemonic movement with a single dominant group.

Hierarchy and the Dual Struggle for Autonomy and Survival

Most scholars agree with Charles Tilly that "groups are crucial to social movements, as armies are crucial to wars and parties to electoral campaigns."[10] Unaffiliated individuals rarely influence the dynamics and outcomes of national movements; those who do generally join and direct member organizations. But who are the individuals and organizations that constitute a national movement? To be part of a national movement, an actor must share the national identity and the objective of political autonomy. There are always members of a nation who do not share the goal of national autonomy (e.g., non-Zionist Jews) and some who go so far as to vote against it (e.g., some Québécois) or even violently fight it (e.g., the Harkis in Algeria). There are also individuals and groups that share the goal of autonomy for the nation but are not themselves members of it, such as Norwegians who support a Palestinian state or evangelical Christians who support a Jewish one. They are considered movement supporters rather than members here, because nonnationals cannot serve in the movement in the same way (e.g., as representative leaders) and do not benefit in the same way from its success (e.g., citizenship). In any case, individuals and groups that are *both* members of the nation and support its autonomy are the key drivers of its behavior and success, and only they are considered members of national movements in this book.[11]

To be included in the movement hierarchy, an organization must claim to represent movement members in the struggle for autonomy (so labor unions and environmental groups do not count) and operate or aim to operate in the national territory (so a diaspora group that exists solely to provide financial support does not count). These groups are not seeking to represent the movement politically in the homeland and so are not struggling in the same way. I define *organized groups* as units that have an autonomous leadership that possesses authority over group members, often identified through a general differentiation of roles among internal elements and a duplication of roles compared to other organized groups.[12] For example, Mia Bloom notes that the Liberation Tigers of Tamil Eelam (LTTE) was divided by specialization into the Black Tigers, Sea Tigers, Baby Tigers, Air Tigers, and Women's Military Units and that each possessed a differentiation of roles under a single leadership. To compare, the Tamil Eelam Liberation Organization (TELO) was a different organized group because its units duplicated LTTE roles and had a different, autonomous leadership.[13] In this book, I use the terms *group* and *organization* interchangeably.

Classifying movements by the strength of their constituent groups yields both a typology of movements and of the groups themselves. In the latter case, the key characteristic is the position of a group in the movement hierarchy. *Hierarchy* in this case refers to the ranking of groups by relative power, rather than alliances built on social contracts between actors (see figure 2.2).[14]

Hegemons and leaders are the strongest groups in their respective movements (every movement has a hegemon or a leader, but never both). The difference is that hegemons are the strongest group in their (hegemonic) movements and have no challengers, whereas leaders are the

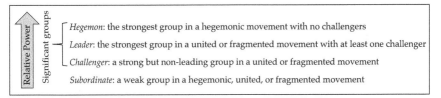

Figure 2.2. Group Types in Movement Hierarchies

strongest group in their (united or fragmented) movements and have at least one challenger. Challengers are groups that possess membership size, economic wealth, *or* popular support that is at least one-third as large as the strongest group in their movement. Hegemons, leaders, and challengers are the three types of significant groups, and these together drive movement dynamics and outcomes. Subordinates are weak groups that do not possess membership size, economic wealth, *or* popular support that is at least one-third as large as the strongest group in their movement. Hegemonic, united, and fragmented movements can have any number of subordinate groups; the key distinction among them is the presence or absence of a single challenger.[15]

Regardless of type, all groups in national movements face a dual struggle of contentious collective action.[16] On the one hand, groups are members of a movement because they support the shared strategic goal of political autonomy. This struggle brings them into direct conflict with one or more states that currently control the territory they desire and rule over the people who constitute their nation. A state first tends to ignore the movement and then to repress it without negotiating, let alone conceding to it.[17] On the other hand, groups must also struggle to survive. Not only do hostile states aim to weaken or destroy them, but so do other groups in their own national movement. As George Pettee tells us, fights over movement leadership mean that "it is competitive, for the unanimous refusal of loyalty to the old is far from implying any unanimous granting of it to anything new."[18] Groups must therefore pursue the sinews of power—recruits, funding, and popular support—to endure in the face of those who wish to marginalize or eliminate them.

In this two-level game, groups in the same movement simultaneously struggle as allies (against the state) and rivals (against each other).[19] This dual struggle is at the heart of the dynamics and outcomes of national movements. How then can we understand and predict the behavior of groups and the outcomes of movements? Similar to role theory in sociology and dominance hierarchies among humans and other animals in psychology and biology—whose alpha, beta, and omega ranks roughly equate to leader, challenger, and subordinate—the relative power position of a group determines its costs and benefits, the extent to which other groups perceive it as a threat, and its own aggressive behavior.[20] Collectively, the success of a national movement depends on the structure in which these groups cooperate and compete.

Structuring Group Incentives and Behavior

THE BENEFITS AND COSTS OF VICTORY

Victory and violence carry costs and benefits. The distribution of these costs and benefits and the uncertainty surrounding them are the key to understanding group behavior and movement outcome. To paraphrase Miles' Law,[21] where you stand on victory and violence depends on where you sit in the movement hierarchy (see figure 2.3).

The benefits of victory accrue disproportionately to the leading group of a national movement. The achievement of a new state includes a mix of public goods (ending a military occupation), club goods (citizenship), and private goods (political office, wealth, and status) for a national movement and its members. These goods are generally "lumpy"; that is, they largely accrue at the successful conclusion of a campaign rather than evenly along the way. The capture of these private goods upon victory has more of a winner-take-all distribution than a proportional one, in part because the independent institutions necessary to help ensure the latter are generally weak or nonexistent in national movements.[22] Furthermore, such institutions are generally (re)built after the achievement of a new state by the strongest group, making them a good to be captured rather

	Costs, benefits, and risk			Group behavior		
Group type	Benefits from victory	Costs from violence	Risk tolerance	Pursue strategic success	Initiate escalatory violence	Join escalatory violence
Hegemon	Very high	Very high	Very low	Very likely	Very unlikely	Very unlikely
Leader	High	High	Low	Likely	Unlikely	Neutral
Challenger	Low	Low	High	Very unlikely	Very likely	Very likely
Subordinate	Very low	Very low	Very high	Unlikely	Likely	Likely

Figure 2.3. How Movement Structure Drives Group Incentives and Behavior

than an independent body to restrain. Finally, any related violent or electoral struggles are likely to be won by this same leading group, which is one of the reasons why the hierarchy of power in a movement generally replicates as the hierarchy of power in a new state. Weaker groups are therefore likely to enjoy the public goods that accrue to all movement members but are unlikely to obtain the private benefits of office, wealth, and status upon victory. This was the case in Mozambique, where the leading nationalist group, the Mozambique Liberation Front (FRELIMO), won independence from Portugal in 1975, set up a one-party state, defeated a weaker challenger in a subsequent civil war, and leads the country to this day. National movements are therefore like a game of musical chairs: groups want to be on top when the music stops.

While the benefits of victory are driven by group position, the costs of victory are driven by group action. Organizations must decide when it is worthwhile to spend their scarce blood and treasure in pursuit of independence. Although group actions drive strategic success, groups are not driven primarily by strategic motivations.[23] Like politicians on the stump, armed groups may openly discuss their struggle to achieve the shared goal of political autonomy, but MST assumes that groups in national movements, like most organizations, are concerned with ensuring their survival and maximizing their strength above all else.[24]

It is not that these groups do not care about strategic goals. They do; otherwise, they would not be part of a movement. It is not that many individuals in the groups are not making enormous sacrifices and taking personal risks for the movement. They are. Zohra Drif, Gerry Adams, Leila Khaled, and Yoske Nachmias (see chapter 1) all spent time in jail as a result of their actions. It is simply that groups generally look after themselves first, often by pursuing organizational goods such as the acquisition of recruits and funding.[25] The prospect of being selected out is not theoretical for groups in a national movement—as it largely is for states—but, rather, an everyday reality due to their relative weakness, extralegal status, and the anarchical environments of civil conflict in which they often exist.[26] Indeed, the history of most national movements is littered with countless acronyms of now defunct militias and political parties. In the late 1980s, the LTTE all but eliminated the Eelam People's Revolutionary Liberation Front (EPRLF), the TELO, and the People's Liberation Organization of Tamil Eelam (PLOT) by killing most of their members.[27] Individuals may strap bombs to their bodies and sacrifice themselves for the greater good, but organizations almost never do.

To borrow phrases from Antonio Gramsci, groups must therefore decide at what point they are best served by a "war of position," in which they struggle against peer groups to improve or maintain their position in the movement hierarchy, or a "war of movement," in which they struggle against the state to win independence.[28] Groups will prosecute a "war of movement" and pursue the common strategic goal when they are more likely to capture its associated private and club goods. This variable is driven by the position of a group in the movement hierarchy, which both determines the distribution of private benefits and the likelihood of groups maintaining their current rank. Hegemons are more likely than leaders, who are more likely than challengers and subordinates to value and capture these goods and, therefore, to pursue independence in the first place.

The dominant group in a hegemonic movement is not any less self-interested than groups in fragmented or united movements, but the different movement structure changes how the hegemon can best pursue its self-interest. The survival of the hegemon and its position at the top of the movement are likely to be secure in the short term because no viable internal rival exists to supplant it. The lack of internal competition in a hegemonic movement means that the biggest threat to the dominant group is the regime itself, which makes the group more likely to focus its attention externally on strategic objectives and the associated state enemy.[29] This was the case for the Vietminh in Vietnam (1946–1954) and the Continental Congress and Continental Army in the American colonies (1775–1783); both focused their efforts on overthrowing the current regime due to a lack of significant challengers in their national movement. The achievement of the ultimate strategic goal of statehood can cement the current movement hierarchy in a nascent government and capture the private benefits of office, wealth, and status for the hegemon—as it did in Vietnam and the United States—because it is most likely to emerge victorious in any civil war or election after independence. It is good to be the head of the movement, but it is far better to be the head of the state, and groups compete fiercely to achieve the former in large part because it is the gateway to the latter. The dominant group in a hegemonic movement is therefore more likely to pursue strategic goals than any other type of group in any other type of movement system.

Like a hegemon, the strongest group in a fragmented or united movement—the leader—will actively pursue the strategic goal of statehood to cement the current movement hierarchy and capture the associated private and club goods. Unlike hegemons, leaders face significant challengers that could supplant them in the short term. Therefore, they are more likely to shift some of their attention and resources to "wars of position" and the pursuit of recruits and funding to protect their standing, although their focus will generally remain on strategic success.

Challengers are unlikely to receive many private goods in a new state because of their weaker position in the hierarchy. Even if they wanted to (and they often do not), leaders can rarely credibly commit to distributing the selective benefits of statehood to challengers due to the fragility of alliances, the anarchical aspects of civil conflict, and the cumulative resources of state power. Challengers therefore have incentives to avoid or actively prevent strategic progress to deny the leader the affiliated private goods of office, wealth, and status and so preserve these goods for themselves in the future. Furthermore, challengers are in a very precarious position and so are likely to focus most of their effort on "wars of position" and obtaining purely organizational goods such as recruits and funding. If challengers are able to later ascend the movement hierarchy and become leaders or hegemons, their pursuit of strategic success will shift accordingly. As Maurice Duverger argues, "extreme parties" that become leaders will "adopt the prudent and moderate attitude that the exercise of power imposes."[30] Groups do not simply want strategic victory; they want strategic victory when they are leading the movement.

Subordinates are the least likely to capture private benefits from strategic success because of their position of extreme weakness. But this does not mean that they will be more obstructionist than challengers. Subordinates will probably put in little effort toward strategic success, but the fact that they have almost no chance of becoming the movement leader means that they are also less likely to strenuously oppose strategic success than challengers (for whom independence would ensure present losses *and* destroy potential future gains). To the small extent that groups can make alliances and promise to split the winnings, subordinates are therefore more likely to bandwagon with the leader or hegemon than are challengers, which have a greater hope of capturing the brass ring themselves and are perceived as a larger threat by the leading group.

THE COSTS AND BENEFITS OF VIOLENCE

The costs and benefits of victory make stronger groups more likely to pursue it, but the costs and benefits of violence make weaker groups more likely to employ it. Movement structure drives the benefits of victory, but it also drives the costs of violence.

Violence by nationalist groups almost always occurs within the borders of an enemy state and targets its citizens or government. Such bombings or shootings are likely to elicit a crackdown from the government. Unfortunately for groups at the top of the movement hierarchy, such crackdowns rarely touch only the perpetrators themselves. The state often does not have good intelligence about weaker challengers and subordinates, but it is more likely to know the identities of individuals in the largest, most prominent organization. Therefore, the state is likely to crack down on the hegemon or leader, regardless of which group launched the attack. For example, proclamations and violence by the challenger Eritrean Liberation Front (ELF) in 1961 generated a crackdown by the Ethiopian government that fell hard on the Eritrean Liberation Movement (ELM), weakening the group and its hold on movement leadership.[31]

The government may think that the strongest group committed the attack because it associates that group with the movement in general. Even if the government knows that a weaker group committed the attack or has no idea who did so, the government will want to "do something" in response, and so it often represses the strong group that it knows better and perceives as a greater threat.[32] Sometimes, governments can even intentionally crack down on the strongest group in the hope that its greater knowledge of the movement will lead the strongest group to crack down on the true perpetrator itself, in a form of trilateral coercion. In any case, the costs of violence emanating from the movement are likely to be disproportionately paid by the strongest groups in the hierarchy, regardless of which group employs it.

The benefits of violence are more difficult to predict ex ante, because they are driven by a combination of factors that are either unknowable or unknown to the attackers at the time.[33] These include public approval of the use of violence and of the intended target, the nature and scope of the government response, and the specific tactical outcome of an operation: Were people killed, and if so, what was their identity?[34] How well did the group communicate its message? How did the media cover the attack?

The significant variation in the organizational effectiveness of violence leaves groups hoping that violence will bring them praise, donations, and recruits, but it leaves them worrying that it will bring them condemnation, raids, and defections. There are clear cases of both. Violence helped strengthen the LTTE in Sri Lanka, Hezbollah in Lebanon, and the Eritrean People's Liberation Front in Eritrea, but it contributed to the downfall of the Quebec Liberation Front, Sikh separatists in India, and the Italian Red Brigades. This uncertainty, nonetheless, provides the basis for strong predictions. The structure of a movement cannot easily predict the organizational benefits of violence, but it can predict the willingness of groups to accept risk.

Stronger groups operate in a realm of gain and weaker groups operate in a realm of loss because more powerful groups are more likely to survive and receive private benefits upon victory, and weaker groups are not. As Prospect Theory suggests, stronger groups are therefore likely to be more risk-averse, while weaker groups are likely to be more risk-acceptant.[35] Because violence is a risky endeavor whose effects are often difficult to foresee, weaker groups are more likely to violently escalate the situation and "gamble for resurrection" in an attempt to alter their position.[36] For any group thinking of employing violence, it is also worth noting that there is an asymmetry of information at the root of the asymmetry of repression. When a weaker group uses violence, those outside of the movement (who are more likely to condemn an attack) are less likely to know that the weak group did so and those inside of the movement (who are more likely to praise and join the attacker) are more likely to know that it did. Violence is therefore particularly attractive to weaker groups because they are more likely to reap the benefits while stronger groups pay the costs.

Hegemons and leaders are thus more likely to shun escalatory violence and even attempt to restrain it themselves because these risk-averse actors are operating in a realm of gain and are the most likely to bear the brunt of any state response. Because leaders are in a more precarious position of power, they are more likely than hegemons to ultimately join escalatory violence to shore up their revolutionary bona fides after weaker groups initiate it—especially if they remove some of the uncertainty by demonstrating that the attacks attract recruits and support. Leaders thus may lead in strength, but they follow in violence. Challengers and subordinates are the most likely to initiate escalatory violence, given that they are risk-acceptant, less likely to benefit from victory under the current movement hierarchy, and less likely to pay the costs of state repression than their stronger rivals.

Victory and violence often intersect, no more so than with negotiations and spoiling. While hegemons and leaders are the most likely to seek negotiations that further strategic progress and to restrain violence, whose costs they would disproportionately pay, challengers are the most likely to denounce negotiations, whose benefits will pass them by, and launch violent attacks to spoil talks and any subsequent agreements.[37] If you're not in line to get the spoils, you are more likely to become a spoiler.[38]

The distribution of the costs, benefits, and risks of victory and violence ensure that the strategies of leadership are different from the strategies of ascent.[39] With a clear understanding of the impact of movement structure on group behavior in hand, we can now assess variation in movement outcome.

Structuring Movement Dynamics and Outcomes

THE PERILS OF UNITED AND FRAGMENTED MOVEMENTS

United and fragmented movements are less likely to achieve victory because they collectively devote few resources to this end (see figure 2.4). These movements include one or more challengers that not only will not devote their significant resources to the common goal, but will even use these resources to prevent strategic progress. The leader of a united or fragmented movement devotes some of its time and effort to pursuing victory, but its precarious position at the top means that it must devote much of its energy to internal "wars of position" against challengers to its perch. The multiple significant groups in the movement also mean that there is a buyer's market for foreign influence because potential state sponsors have more outlets to insert themselves and can play one group off the others to get the best deal for themselves, but the worst one for the movement.[40] The aim of these foreign sponsors is generally to manipulate groups to their own ends; they rarely prize movement independence. The multiple significant groups competing with each other and tying themselves to foreign entities makes it unlikely that the movement will have a cohesive strategy.

Figure 2.4. How United and Fragmented Movements Cause Strategic Failure

The Kurdish national movement is a prime example of these dynamics. Not only are the Kurds divided geographically across Turkey, Syria, Iraq, and Iran, but the movement in each state is also often split among significant competing national groups. This creates a scenario in which no host state wants an independent Kurdistan but every state has supported Kurdish groups in neighboring states for its own ends. For example, Syria and Iran have both supported the PKK in Turkey to pressure Ankara to make concessions on non-Kurdish issues, and Iraq actually sought to sponsor the PKK to get it to fight other Kurdish groups in Iraq. Needless to say, these foreign sponsors did not have the best interests of the Kurdish national movement at heart, nor did their support lead to a Kurdish state.[41]

The most important external actor for a national movement is the enemy state, which will ask itself three key questions: What does the movement want, how realistic is the threat, and can or will the movement uphold any deal? Fragmented and united movements send more mixed signals about the objective, threats, and guarantees of a campaign. This is crucial because the state and its citizens often perceive the movement as a unitary entity, whether that is the case or not. One example of this phenomenon comes from Palestinian groups over forty years ago: "Beirut correspondents, who apparently have easy access to all these organizations, can no longer make heads or tails in this jungle. In fact, one Lebanese paper stopped publishing the names of the organizations and instead used the general title 'Fedayeen.'"[42] The threats and guarantees of united and fragmented movements are far less credible than hegemonic movements because their leader and challenger(s) have opposing incentives to restrain or escalate violence and to negotiate or spoil agreements, respectively. All this adds up to the fact that united and fragmented movements are likely to have far fewer movement resources devoted to strategic success and so are less likely than hegemonic movements to emerge victorious.

The second problem with united and fragmented movements is that, in addition to the fact that leaders and challengers often lack incentive to pursue strategic goals, the dynamics of violence among multiple strong groups in a competitive movement frequently produces strategic failure, regardless of intent. Anarchical movements and their constituent groups therefore face a version of the security dilemma for nonstate actors: actions taken to make a group more secure often make the movement—and at times the group itself—less secure and less strategically effective. Four counterproductive violent mechanisms are likely to emerge and make strategic failure more likely: outbidding, chain-ganging, spoiling, and infighting.

Outbidding occurs when groups use violence in larger quantities or more extreme qualities to set themselves apart from their rivals in ways that relatively costless fiery speeches and unobservable backroom dealings cannot.[43] For example, the Revolutionary Armed Forces of Columbia (FARC) and its rival the National Liberation Army (ELN) regularly engaged in attacks on government installations, economic targets, and progovernment paramilitaries to demonstrate their credibility and attract support.[44]

Chain-ganging occurs when one group launches attacks against the state that start a conflict that envelops other groups in the movement. As the name implies, one or more of these groups would prefer that no conflict exist, but because one group is involved, others in the movement get pulled in.[45] As previously mentioned, spoiling is the use of violence to prevent negotiations or agreements, as the Basque group Euskadi Ta Askatasuna (ETA) has done during negotiations with the Spanish government on numerous occasions.[46] Infighting occurs when one group directly attacks another in the movement, such as when the KDP and the PUK fought each other for control of the Kurdish national movement in Iraq in the mid-1990s.

In a fragmented or united movement, groups can shift hierarchical positions quickly, making potential challenges via outbidding, chain-ganging, spoiling, or infighting both serious and common. Challengers dissatisfied with their position in the hierarchy are most likely to initiate escalatory outbidding violence against the state or infighting with other groups in attempts to improve their position. Fratricidal infighting is "one of the inevitable overhead expenses of a revolution," according to Leon Trotsky,[47] but fragmented and united movements experience more than their share. Attacks by a challenger may chain-gang the unprepared movement into an uncoordinated conflict with the state, which is likely to yield strategic failure. Unlike pluralistic democracies, the pluralism of movements makes them worse at selecting wars that they are likely to win, as well as worse at prosecuting them once they begin.[48] Spoiling is also more likely to occur and succeed amid a competitive movement system, given the presence of challengers with the incentive and capability to scuttle a deal.[49]

Risk-averse leaders and even stronger challengers are likely to initially attempt to restrain such violence, but their position in a competitive movement means that (1) they will often lack the capability to do so and (2) once escalatory outbidding or chain-ganging spirals get going, first stronger challengers and then leaders will often employ violence themselves to avoid losing their tenuous hold on their top positions. Repressing groups in one's movement can also be costly in terms of resources and popular support, which is why leaders are more likely to shy away from doing so than are hegemons. Although a leader is far less likely to initiate escalatory violence, if it ultimately joins in the violent spiral, it is likely to employ the most violence due to its greater capabilities. Collectively, united and fragmented movements are therefore more likely to experience strategically counterproductive violent mechanisms and less likely to achieve victory.

THE SUCCESS OF HEGEMONIC MOVEMENTS

Hegemonic movements are more likely to achieve victory because they have more resources working toward it—and fewer working against it—than united or fragmented movements (see figure 2.5). The lack of challengers means that "wars of position" are neither realistic for weak subordinates nor necessary for the hegemon, leaving "wars of movement" against the state as the best option for the hegemon to increase its power. Their lone significant group also means that hegemonic movements are more likely to have coherent strategies that allow for clearer signaling to external audiences.[50] The considerable power held by the dominant group increases the credibility of a hegemonic movement in its ability to deliver on its commitments to start or stop violence.[51] States understand that spoilers are less likely to emerge or succeed in hegemonic movements, which reduces the

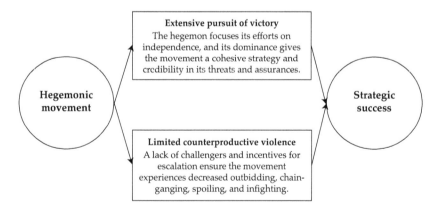

Figure 2.5. How Hegemonic Movements Cause Strategic Success

commitment problem that can emerge with fragmented or united movements. Weak groups in hegemonic movements can even help provide effective good cop–bad cop dynamics that make the hegemon seem more moderate by comparison, without generating significant concern that the radical subordinate will assume the leadership of the movement (as would be the case with a challenger).[52]

In a noncompetitive hegemonic movement, subordinates are also less likely to initiate outbidding, chain-ganging, spoiling, or infighting—and the hegemon has less need to respond—because such actions are unlikely to bring about any significant shifts in the movement hierarchy, pull the hegemon into a conflict, prevent an agreement with the state, or pose a serious threat via direct infighting. Hegemony in the sense of overwhelming power thus leads to hegemony in the Gramscian sense of opposition becoming pointless.[53] These claims are supported by Stathis Kalyvas, who demonstrates that less civil war violence occurs in areas with a dominant actor.[54] Duverger, Huntington, and Sartori agree that extremist party strength (i.e., challengers) makes for a weaker system, more violence, and less stable regimes.[55]

To be clear, it is not that hegemons never employ violence but, rather, that their use of it more generally aligns with external, strategic imperatives rather than internal competition. They are thus more likely to calibrate the ideal amount of violence against the regime to win. Furthermore, the ability of hegemons to restrict violence to certain targets or stop it when necessary during negotiations allows them to consolidate success.

Hegemonic movements further provide potential state sponsors with only a single viable outlet for influence. In such a seller's market, state sponsorship is more likely to further strategic progress and less likely to yield strategically counterproductive mechanisms. A striking example of this mechanism is from the Eritrean national movement: "A visitor is standing in front of an Eritrean exhibition at an international festival. He examines the photos, which show some of the achievements of the revolution, in health, in education, in political participation by the people. He then asks one of the militants standing by: 'Did you get help from the Soviet Union?' 'No,' replies the militant. 'Then you must get it from China?' The answer is 'No' again. 'I see. That means you must be supported by the United States?' Yet again the reply is in the negative. The visitor is quite baffled and concludes: 'you can't possibly win your war then.'" On the contrary, the Eritreans won independence with a hegemonic movement that not only lacked significant foreign support but was also fighting against a regime that was backed at times by both the United States and the Soviet Union.[56]

Hegemonic movements are more likely to get the type of international support they want the most: recognition of their new state. As Coggins has demonstrated, if the enemy state agrees to secession, the international community will probably recognize the new state.[57] Enemy states will generally try to avoid negotiations with and concessions to the movement, but this is harder to do when there is a single clear national voice for diplomacy that leaves the state with no viable alternatives. To the extent that the movement must gain international recognition first to pressure the enemy state to follow suit, Mikulas Fabry demonstrates that recognition follows de facto statehood, which is when a movement demonstrates that it has a single provisional government that controls its military, holds territory, and is responsible to uphold agreements.[58] Furthermore, Coggins shows that movements are more likely to gain recognition if they have lower overall levels of violence and if they win the wars they fight—87% that win wars gain recognition compared to 25% that lose them—which are the exact dynamics of hegemonic movements because they lack internal competition and have better coordination on the battlefield.[59]

In sum, hegemonic movements are more likely than united or fragmented movements to be clear, credible coercers that pursue strategic goals and avoid counterproductive violence, and they are therefore more likely to achieve victory.

THE ORIGINS OF MOVEMENT STRUCTURE

In this book, I focus on the effects of movement structure, but what are its causes? There is no clear, parsimonious answer to this question; the most comprehensive study on the topic identifies no fewer than *nine* significant factors that cause fragmentation under various conditions—including state capacity, regime type, civil war, the size of the movement base, and the presence of foreign fighters—not to mention others such as geographical dispersion and ethnic heterogeneity, which the authors suggest may be influential.[60] External factors such as state collapse or regional wars can lead to the decline of groups, such as communist factions after the fall of the USSR and the General Zionists after World War II. State repression or support can cause change in movement structure as well, although not always as the states themselves intend.[61] For example, French efforts to fragment the Algerian national movement in 1958–1962 were entirely unsuccessful, as were U.S. attempts in 2011–2016 to unify the opposition in the Syrian civil war and create a viable "moderate" organization from scratch.

In a potential flip of the causal arrows in this book, one logical cause of movement structure is success itself. After all, if hegemonic movements are more likely to succeed, surely groups would simply arrange themselves into such a structure in anticipation of victory. Unfortunately for these groups—and for observers seeking clear explanations of movement structure—"the tragedy of national movements" prevents just such an outcome. All groups may well agree that their movement should be hegemonic, but they disagree on which group should be the hegemon (hint: each group chooses itself). Because groups will not weaken themselves for the greater good, they compete to be the hegemon with others doing the same, making it all but impossible for movements to "choose" hegemony and hasten victory.

Some of the internal dynamics that emerge from these competitions can potentially shift movement structure because infighting might lead to the splitting or destruction of a rival group, while outbidding could generate recruits for a new movement leader. Although it is clear that these actions are generally counterproductive for the movement—because they expend scarce resources and rarely result in a new hegemonic movement—it is unclear when they will be productive for a given organization. The tactical skills of the organization, the public opinion of the movement base, and the ability to provoke the state into indiscriminate repression appear to play key roles in organizational success; however, this remains an open question for future research.[62]

As for this book, the fact that the internal struggle can both affect and be affected by the external struggle means that it is problematic to analyze the behavior and success of a movement as single data points. In the next sections, I present the specific predictions of MST and its competitors across the lifespan of a movement, including the methods that will be used to test their explanatory power across time and space.

Predictions of Movement Structure Theory

Movement Structure Theory makes two significant, unique predictions that challenge and advance existing scholarship. First, the hierarchy hypothesis predicts that hegemons and leaders are more likely to pursue national independence, restrain violence, and negotiate, while challengers are more likely to avoid the pursuit of independence, escalate violence, and spoil negotiations. Second, the hegemony hypothesis predicts that hegemonic national movements, with one significant group, are more likely to be strategically successful than united or fragmented national movements, with two or more significant groups. Table 2.1 combines these hypotheses to illustrate the predictions of MST over the course of a national movement.

In the first five years, the movement is fragmented, as Leader A competes with Challengers B and C, who each has a realistic chance at becoming the new leader.[63] These challengers are more likely to take risks and escalate violence to garner attention and to spoil any deal pursued by Leader A. The position of Leader A pushes it to partially pursue independence to capture leadership of a new state, but it must also keep one eye on the challengers, meaning that initial attempts to restrain their violence can quickly turn into attempts to outbid them to avoid appearing weak or hesitant by comparison. Groups A, B, and C may also fight each other directly, all of which

Table 2.1 Predictions of Movement Structure Theory

Time period	Movement system	Movement hierarchy ➡	Predicted group behavior	Predicted movement outcome
Years 1–5	Fragmented	1. Leader A 2. Challenger B 3. Challenger C	Challengers C and B escalate violence and pursue purely organizational goals; Leader A initially attempts to restrain violence and partially pursues victory	Failure
Years 6–8	Fragmented	1. Leader C 2. Challenger A 3. Challenger B	Challengers B and A escalate violence and pursue purely organizational goals; Leader C initially attempts to restrain violence and partially pursues victory	Failure
Years 9–10	United	1. Leader C 2. Challenger A 3. Challenger B	Challengers B and A escalate violence and pursue purely organizational goals; Leader C initially attempts to restrain violence and partially pursues victory	Failure or limited success
Years 11–18	Fragmented	1. Leader C 2. Challenger A	Challenger A escalates violence and pursues purely organizational goals; Leader C initially attempts to restrain violence and partially pursues victory	Failure
Years 19–23	Hegemonic	1. Hegemon C	Hegemon C pursues victory and resists any attempts at violent escalation	Moderate or total success

Notes: Predictions of Movement Structure Theory concerning group behavior, represented by the small arrow, and movement outcome, represented by the large arrow. Note that this table and the movement summary tables in chapters 3–6 present the hierarchy among significant groups—hegemons, leaders, and challengers—for simplicity; each movement had many less powerful subordinates ranked below these groups as well.

leads to a squandering of resources and a noncohesive movement strategy that makes strategic failure likely.

By Year 6, Group C has supplanted A to become the new movement leader. In this campaign period, roles change but the dynamics and outcomes are predicted to stay the same as in Years 1–5. Challengers A and B now are more likely to escalate violence and spoil, while new Leader C is more likely to restrain violence, pursue independence, and negotiate. An alliance among the groups in Year 9 may lead to a slight increase in cooperation, a slight decrease in violence, and a slight increase in the probability of strategic success, but the competition for power continues, meaning that the alliance is likely to soon end with little to show for it.

In Year 11, the alliance has collapsed and Group B has weakened to become a subordinate group. Nonetheless, Group A remains as a challenger, yielding similar competitive dynamics and failed outcomes as in the fragmented movements of Years 1–8. Finally, Group C becomes the dominant hegemon by Year 19, which means that internal competition all but ends. C focuses the majority of movement resources on the goal of independence, and more progress is likely to be made toward this goal than during any other period in the history of the movement.

To sum up these predictions, the position of a group as a hegemon, leader, challenger, or subordinate drives its actions; the type of movement system as hegemonic, united, or fragmented drives its outcome. MST suggests that a hierarchical shift will change group actions but not the movement outcome; a systemic shift will change both actions and the outcome; and a shift in the balance of power that does not alter the movement hierarchy or movement system is unlikely to lead to changes in either actions or outcome.

Research Methods

DEPENDENT VARIABLES

In the remaining five chapters of this book, I focus on testing the hegemony and hierarchy hypotheses against their competitors. As I detail in chapter 1, these competing theories include that a movement is more likely to be successful when it is fragmented, when it is united, the more members it has, the more nonviolent or violent it is, the more state support it has, the weaker its enemy state is, and the longer it exists after the rise of decolonization. These competing theoretical claims also carry competing methodological claims, in that existing scholarship suggests that the unity and fragmentation of a movement should be determined by the total number of groups, whereas MST claims the key is whether there is one or more *significant* groups. I thus analyze whether hegemonic, united, or fragmented movements are more successful using both my typology of the number of significant groups and existing typologies of the number of all groups. Competing arguments for the hierarchy hypothesis suggest that the use of violence by groups and their pursuit of victory are driven by group ideology, leadership, or age.

One missing variable that explains variation in outcomes across all movements is objective type. This is purposeful, because it is clearly more likely that a movement will gain recognition of its existence than its new state, which is why I differentiate here among social movements, insurgencies, and national movements and why I have previously written about the widely varying success rates one obtains with different measuring sticks.[64] Furthermore, although they may have different ideologies and additional goals, groups and individuals in the same national movement are bound together by the desire to achieve a shared strategic objective: political autonomy and the creation of a new state.[65]

For national movements, a dichotomous measure of victory or defeat fails to capture the substantial, accessible variation in movement progress. The achievement of a new state does not easily lend itself to continuous measurement either, however. Therefore, the dependent variable—campaign outcome—is assessed along a four-tiered ordinal scale, which has a significant precedent in the literature on the effectiveness of nonstate violence and social movements (see table 2.1).[66] The achievement of a new state whose territory is controlled by the movement and recognized as such by the United Nations or League of Nations is coded as "total success." Gaining semi-sovereign control of territory for the future state with proto-state institutions that are recognized by the enemy state that previously controlled the territory is coded as "moderate success." Recognition as a legitimate national movement by the United Nations or League of Nations, or agreeing to increased power-sharing in joint institutions is coded as "limited success."[67] A lack of such gains in territory, institutions, or recognition is coded as "failure."

I begin collecting data on a national movement once a majority of its groups support political autonomy, so as to only assess the ability of a movement to achieve a goal it actually seeks. This means that most national movements will have a proto-nationalist period before organizations and their pursuit of autonomy crystallizes—as with the Jews in Europe in the nineteenth century and the Algerians and Palestinians in the first half of the twentieth century—and what was a cultural movement becomes a national one with a supreme political goal of independence.[68] I collect data on a national movement until independence is achieved, or until the present day if the struggle continues.[69]

I assess strategic success and failure at the end of each campaign. Because movement structure varies significantly over time and its impact is most directly felt and easily measured in the short term, I mark any change in movement structure as the beginning of a new campaign (see table 2.1). In other words, any time a movement shifts from being hegemonic to fragmented or fragmented to united, or any time a single significant group moves up or down in the hierarchy, I mark a new campaign period. My breakdown of campaigns is thus distinct from, and a challenge to, existing periodizations, which are generally determined by some vague, post hoc sense of historical "turning points." My contribution here is to identify more systematic, transparent, and powerful turning points that can be recognized ex ante. To the extent the ebbs and flows of violence and strategic success match up with my periodization rather than those of others, MST will have contributed a powerful, predictive theory as well as a new historiography of the movements under study.

Each of the variables of group behavior is measured dichotomously. Groups are considered to be restraining violence when they verbally denounce the violent actions of other groups in the movement or physically try to prevent or stop them. Groups are considered to be escalating violence when they launch an attack when other movement groups are not attacking or strike a more extreme target that other movement groups are not striking.

Groups are considered to be negotiating when they have formal discussions with the enemy state over the political autonomy of their nation and its people. Groups are considered to be spoiling when they launch violence during such negotiations with clear evidence that the violence is intended to scuttle the talks and any subsequent agreement.

INDEPENDENT VARIABLES

Data on the strength of groups by year is very difficult to find, which is probably why the vast majority of previous studies ignore the variable altogether and the remaining few use rough estimates of "fighting capacity" or dependent variables such as territorial control as proxies for strength.[70] Nonetheless, the data are out there, with pieces in state archives, in group pamphlets and private letters, in biographies and secondary sources, in newspapers, and in the memories of group members, enemies, and observers. I painstakingly assembled data on the strength of every significant group in the Palestinian, Zionist, Algerian, and Irish national movements by year with data from 11 archives, over 150 interviews, and hundreds of sources per movement. The key data by year are presented in online appendices A–D.[71]

Given that these are clandestine groups that do not have massive swings in membership, funding, or popular support every year, there are some group-years for which I could not locate data. For those, I used the last reliable group-year data I have, and I have numerous reliable data points for every group in the study. It is more likely that intelligence officers in their reports, journalists in their newspaper articles, group members in their biographies and interviews, and scholars in their books felt it unnecessary to mention group strength in stasis, whereas it is incredibly unlikely that they would miss or fail to report significant growth or decline. For that reason, I am confident that my data set is not missing any major hierarchical changes, and in any case, I am confident that this is the most detailed and accurate data set on group strength in the public realm. It is also the best sourced because most data sets simply publish their numbers with no individual citations and then provide a basic bibliography without clear linkages for any specific number. I present my appendices with citations for every data point with the hope that this will invite confidence in and scrutiny of the data, as well as improvements in the future.

EMPIRICAL ANALYSIS

I test these claims with longitudinal analyses of forty-four total campaigns by forty significant groups across 140 years of the Palestinian, Algerian, Zionist, and Irish national movements. The strongest tests of MST and its competitors occur when natural experiments emerge to allow for tight comparisons among most-similar and most-different campaigns for the same group over time, such as when a group changes hierarchical position but its ideology, leader, and age remain unchanged, or when movement structure stays the same but movement strength and tactics change. The number of campaigns and group-years across this diverse, representative set of cases allows for some initial generalizable conclusions on the behavior and outcomes of national movements. Although I can weigh in conclusively on core claims and provide insight into whether movement structure or other factors are more significant in certain campaigns, the smaller number of cases makes it difficult to provide precise measures of the explanatory power of movement structure compared to other factors.

In any case, a general guide to assessing the explanatory power of MST comes from Robert Jervis, who argues that the importance of leaders can be assessed by reading history without names and then determining if one can guess when a leadership change occurred and whether it seemed to matter.[72] For the next five chapters, MST will succeed to the extent that the history can be read without group names (for behavior) and without movement names (for outcomes), and that, instead, the names of hegemon, leader, challenger, subordinate and hegemonic, united, and fragmented do a better job clarifying and explaining the actions and outcomes. Looking back, if major turning points in violence and victory follow soon after changes in movement structure, then the theory holds significant explanatory power.

CHAPTER 3

The Palestinian National Movement

The Sisyphean Tragedy of Fragmentation

> Better a thousand enemies outside the tent than one within.
> —Arab proverb

In addition to puzzles of group behavior involving Hamas, Fatah, and the PFLP noted in chapter 1, there are recurring patterns in dynamics and outcome.[1] In Gaza in 2012 and 2014, rockets were launched toward neighboring Israeli towns amid increasing Israeli airstrikes, leading to more conflict in the territory. In Ramallah, Palestinian youths camped out in Manara Square on hunger strike, claiming that they would not leave until Fatah and Hamas held unity talks because their continued infighting had held back the Palestinian cause. And across the West Bank, Gaza, and the diaspora, debates raged among Palestinian organizations and civilians over the wisdom of negotiating with the Israelis or of using violence or civil resistance against them, as groups differed over whether to actively support, defer, or attempt to spoil the next round of talks.

The remarkable thing about these stories is not how unique they are but, rather, how seamlessly all of them would fit into a description of the Palestinian national movement at almost any time in the past fifty years. The rockets launched by small groups in Gaza to increase their domestic support or spark a larger conflict—while Hamas dithered over whether to restrain the violence or escalate it—evoke memories of the conflict in southern Lebanon in the 1980s. During the "artillery war," weaker Palestinian groups sent rockets into northern Israel as Fatah, then the leader in the region, debated whether to enforce a cease-fire or take the lead in strikes on the central adversary of the national movement. The calls for unity on the lips of youths today were once spoken by Mufti Haj Amin al-Husseini, Yasser

Arafat, and George Habash, and were enshrined in the Palestinian National Charter in 1964:

> Article 8: The phase in their history, through which the Palestinian people are now living, is that of national struggle for the liberation of Palestine. Thus the conflicts among the Palestinian national forces are secondary, and should be ended for the sake of the basic conflict that exists between the forces of Zionism and of imperialism on the one hand, and the Palestinian Arab people on the other. On this basis the Palestinian masses, regardless of whether they are residing in the national homeland or in diaspora, constitute—both their organizations and the individuals—one national front working for the retrieval of Palestine and its liberation through armed struggle.[2]

The split over potential peace negotiations has literally hundreds of precedents, including the attempts of Fatah and the Democratic Front for the Liberation of Palestine (DFLP)—the key supporters of negotiations since the mid-1990s—to derail peace talks between Israeli and Arab leaders over the fate of the Palestinians in the 1960s and 1970s. The challenge of Salafi jihadist groups to Hamas in Gaza was preceded by the challenge of Hamas to Fatah, which was preceded by the challenge of Fatah to the Palestine Liberation Organization (PLO). This is not mere coincidence. Rather, it is evidence of systematic explanations for the actions and outcomes of the Palestinian national movement that are generalizable across time and space.

In this chapter, I provide answers to these puzzles and explanations for these patterns by demonstrating that movement hierarchy—not ideology, age, or individuals—drove the behavior of Palestinian groups and that hegemony—not unity or fragmentation—drove success.[3] In particular, I provide the best tests of the hierarchy hypothesis using a variety of tight within-case comparisons, as well as the best illustrations of the tragedy of national movements: Palestinian groups that know they need hegemony to succeed but whose desire for power keeps them largely fragmented.

Palestinian Nationalism

Most historians date the origins of Palestinian nationalism to the 1920s, even though a general resistance to Ottoman, British, and Zionist rule emerged in the previous decades.[4] It is unclear whether a Palestinian national movement with a majority pushing for independence existed before 1946–1947, however, because the 1930s and 1940s saw numerous appeals to autonomy and control based on clan, place of origin, and broader Arab and Muslim identities.[5] Indeed, the idea of Palestinian patriotism as part of Arab and Syrian nationalism played a major role until the late 1960s, complicating earlier assessments of campaigns for a Palestinian state.

Nonetheless, the Palestinians certainly had an active proto-nationalist movement from 1920–1948, and its dynamics align with Movement Structure Theory. As Issa Khalaf argues, "If there is one characteristic feature of Palestinian politics and society during the [British] Mandate, it is the pervasiveness of factionalism."[6] Significant Palestinian families such as the Husseinis, Nashashibis, and Khalidis pursued their struggles for power through political parties such as the Independence Party, the National Defence Party, the Palestinian Arab Party, and the Reform Party. None was able to extinguish the others. Haj Amin al-Husseini was appointed Grand Mufti of Jerusalem in 1921 after the Nashashibi-backed candidate had won the election. The Nashashibis won the majority of seats in 1927 municipal elections, but the Husseinis then created and led the Arab High Committee, the central political institution for the Palestinian community in the British Mandate. "Power, position, and privilege took precedence over the nation," before, during, and after the Palestinians rose up in the Revolt of 1936–1939 to protest Jewish immigration driven by the Zionist movement.[7] "Factional fighting grew to unprecedented levels" between rival Palestinian groups; twice as many Arabs were killed by other Arabs—1,000—as the number of Jews killed, in part because the Mufti's forces offered more reward money for killing Palestinian "traitors" than Zionist Jews.[8] The feeling was mutual; "Jerusalem's mayor Raghib al-Nashashibi commented privately that his opposition to Haj Amin al-Husseini was ten times stronger than the aversion of the Jews to the Mufti."[9] The Arab Revolt left the movement without functioning nationalist political parties for decades, contributing to the Arab defeat by Zionist forces in the 1948 War and the loss of a potential Palestinian state (detailed in chapter 4).

In addition to the excellent existing scholarship on the Palestinian national movement, in this chapter I rely on archival work I conducted at the Institute for Palestine Studies and on interviews with key members of the Palestinian national movement across the Middle East. Space limitations prevent an extensive analysis of each subsequent campaign period, but I examine four in depth: 1965–June 1967, July 1967–1968, 1969–1970, and 1986–1993 (see table 3.1).[10] These four campaigns present ideal variation for analysis in that the first two represent most-different cases in which the movement hierarchy and the movement system remained the same but many other relevant variables changed. The third campaign represents a significant change in movement hierarchy but no change in the movement system, and the fourth represents a change in the movement system. MST predicts no change in group actions or outcomes for the first and second campaigns, a change in group actions but not outcome in the third campaign, and a change in both action and outcome in the fourth campaign.[11]

Table 3.1 Summary of Campaigns in the Palestinian National Movement, 1965–2016

Time period	Movement system structure	Hierarchy of groups at start of campaign[a]	Summary of group actions	Strategic outcome of campaign
1965–June 1967	Fragmented	L1. PLO C2. ANM C3. JCP C4. Fatah	Fatah initiated violence; PLO and ANM initially restrained; ANM and PLO later used violence; this helped spark the disastrous Six-Day War	Failure
July 1967–1968	Fragmented	L1. PLO C2. ANM/ PFLP C3. JCP C4. Fatah	Fatah initiated violence; PLO and ANM initially restrained; ANM/PFLP and PLO later used violence; attempted uprising in the West Bank failed	Failure
1969–1970	Fragmented	L1. Fatah C2. PLF/PLA C3. Saiqa C4. PFLP C5. DFLP	Fatah took over the PLO and continued violence in Israel but restrained the PFLP in Jordan; PFLP launched hijackings and sparked Black September defeat	Failure
1971–1973	Fragmented	L1. Fatah C2. Saiqa C3. PFLP	Fatah launched the Black September Organization; groups fought a losing insurgency in Gaza against Israel; relocated to Lebanon and Syria	Failure
1974	United	L1. Fatah C2. Saiqa C3. PFLP	Groups agreed to PLO Ten-Point Program; PFLP then launched spoiling attacks; Fatah followed suit	Limited success
1975–1985	Fragmented	L1. Fatah C2. Saiqa C3. PFLP	PFLP used violence in Lebanon; Fatah and Saiqa tried to restrain but were pulled into civil war with extensive infighting	Failure
1986–1993	Hegemonic	H1. Fatah	Fatah able to control First Intifada, limit violence, and gain recognition of Palestinian state, as well as control of territory and proto-state institutions	Moderate success
1994	Fragmented	L1. Fatah C2. Hamas	Hamas launched first suicide bombings in Israel; Fatah restrained and continued with negotiations	Moderate success
1995–2000	Hegemonic	H1. Fatah	Hamas attempted to spoil talks, while Fatah arrested thousands of its members and continued to pursue negotiations with Israel, which stalled	Moderate success
2001–2016	Fragmented	L1. Fatah C2. Hamas	Fatah initially pursued negotiations and restrained violence; Hamas successfully spoiled; Fatah responded with violence amid Second Intifada; Fatah later repressed violence and pursued unsuccessful negotiations	Failure

Notes: The four periods analyzed in greater depth are shaded. To save space, a few campaigns with the same movement system in consecutive time periods are combined in this table. For example, the DFLP went back and forth between being a challenger and a subordinate from 1975 to 1985, but in this table, 1975–1985 is listed as a single fragmented period instead of six different fragmented campaigns. ANM, Arab Nationalists Movement; DFLP, Democratic Front for the Liberation of Palestine; JCP, Jordanian Communist Party; PFLP, Popular Front for the Liberation of Palestine; PLF/ PLA, Popular Liberation Forces/Palestine Liberation Army; PLO, Palestine Liberation Organization.

[a] In tables 3.1, 4.1, 5.1, and 6.1, group labels are C, challenger; H, hegemon; L, leader.

"Detonating the Revolution," 1965–1967

The mid-1960s to early 1970s was the most dynamic period for the Palestinian national movement.[12] During this time, Palestinian nationalism (re)awakened, almost all the key players for the next half century emerged, and there was a great deal of shifting among groups within the movement hierarchy. The movement remained fragmented and competitive, however, leading to ineffective violence and strategic failure across time and space.

In 1960, the Palestinian national movement was structurally weak. 1948 had truly been the *Nakba* for the movement, because the war with the new Israeli state left the Palestinian population dispersed, dispossessed, and disheartened.[13] The war saw the Palestinians facing a hegemonic adversary while they themselves were fragmented, which led to the uncoordinated and ultimately ineffective use of violence by a variety of armed groups, detailed in the next chapter. The aftermath of the 1948 War left the Palestinians at the mercy of the Israeli and Arab governments that now controlled all of historic Palestine, as well as of those neighboring countries in which hundreds of thousands of Palestinian refugees now resided. Jordan, Egypt, and others in the League of Arab States wasted little time forcibly disbanding the few Palestinian armed groups that remained in existence at the end of the war—the Arab Salvation Army and the Army of Holy War—in part to avoid renewed entanglements with Israel.

Most of these Palestinian soldiers joined the armies of Arab states, which was quite fitting, considering that the Palestinian national movement would find itself deeply embedded in the broader movement of Arab nationalism for the next two decades. To the extent that there was a de facto leader of the Palestinians by 1960, it was either Gamal Abdel Nasser of Egypt or King Hussein of Jordan.[14] Not a Palestinian himself, Nasser's overthrow of King Farouk, nationalization of the Suez Canal, and creation of the United Arab Republic (with Syria) gave significant momentum to his anti-Western platform that had the aim of empowering and unifying Arabs. Many looked to him as a savior for the Palestinian cause, in no small part due to his numerous fiery speeches about Palestine and the challenge of Zionism, including his suggestion for creating a Palestinian "entity" (*kiyan*) in 1959 and a Palestinian army in 1960.

By 1965, there were four significant groups in the Palestinian national movement: the Arab Nationalists Movement (ANM), the Jordanian Communist Party (JCP), the Palestinian National Liberation Movement (Fatah), and the PLO. The ANM had been founded by George Habash, a Palestinian, and Hani al-Hindi, a Syrian, both students at the American University of Beirut (AUB) in the 1950s who had served with the Arab Salvation Army during the 1948 War. By 1965, ANM and its Palestinian branch had grown from a few AUB students to a few thousand members dispersed across the Middle East.[15] The JCP was founded in 1951 in Jordan and the West Bank, which Jordan had annexed the previous year. The majority of JCP members were Palestinians, and the party sought a Palestinian state, although the desired shape of that state shifted over time.[16] Despite sporadic crackdowns by King Hussein, the JCP was "arguably the most organized and experienced party in the occupied territories, they also regarded themselves as the largest," with over two thousand members.[17]

The weakest of these Palestinian organizations in 1960 was the Palestinian National Liberation Movement, known by its reverse acronym in Arabic: Fatah. Fatah had been founded in 1958 by Khalil al-Wazir, Yasser Arafat, and a small number of other Palestinian activists from Syria and Gaza. It soon grew to include Salah Khalaf, Khalid al-Hassan, and Mahmoud Abbas, among others, and Fatah represented a few hundred people in 1959, although those numbers would ebb and flow over the coming years.[18]

Contrary to popular notions, Fatah was both the weakest of the four groups and a rival of the PLO in 1965, rather than its near synonymous ally of more recent years (see table 3.1). The PLO became the movement leader soon after it was founded in mid-1964 with the help of Egypt and other Arab states. It included the foundations of tangible legislative, economic, and military institutions in the form of the Palestinian National Council (PNC), the Palestinian National Fund (PNF), and the Palestine Liberation Army (PLA). Led by Ahmad Shuqeiri, the Palestinian representative to the Arab League, the PLO had hundreds of official representatives, funding from Arab governments and taxes on Palestinian citizens, a growing military force (albeit under de facto Arab state control), and, most important, the sense that, as the strongest group, it was the Palestinian entity in waiting that would form the new government of Palestine once the homeland was reclaimed.

These four groups all shared the strategic objective of a Palestinian state, despite somewhat different visions for what it would ultimately look like. The common desire to unite was apparent from the National Charter adopted by the PLO: "The Palestinians will have three mottoes: national (*wataniyya*) unity, national (*qawmiyya*) mobilization, and liberation."[19] Early strategic Fatah documents carried a similar message: "The armed revolution is required to work to unite the powers of the people and create a coalition, even one particular to this stage, between the different movements or national factions because the stage of fighting against direct colonialism dictates national unity to increase the effectiveness of the revolution and its ability to achieve the desired successes."[20] The PLO, the ANM, and Fatah each sought to unite the movement under its own organization. These efforts all failed, however, because every group wanted unity on its own terms and no significant group wanted to lock itself into a subordinate position. Internal competition soon yielded counterproductive outbidding and chain-ganging.

With attempts by Fatah at favorable unity unrealized, the weakest challenger in the movement looked for options to turn the tide in the fortunes
of its organization. As MST predicts, Fatah opted to launch attacks against
Israel and in the process distinguish itself from competitors as a group of
action, in contrast to those groups whose tactic of choice was simply revolutionary rhetoric.[21] As Fatah noted in its early strategic documents, "There
must be a period in which the armed revolutionary vanguard tries to em-
body its real struggle in front of the public so that it can attract them in the
end."[22] The attacks themselves would "detonate the revolutionary capabilities of the Palestinian people," and the subsequent killing or capturing of
Fatah members would only serve as a further costly signal to the base of
Fatah's commitment to the cause.[23] Indeed, the name used for Palestinian
fighters, *fedayeen*, means "those who sacrifice."

In addition to the desire to employ outbidding, Fatah sought to chain-gang
the rest of the movement and linked Arab states into war with Israel. As co-
founder Khaled al-Hassan reiterated in two separate interviews, Fatah wanted
to liberate Palestine "through action and reaction, action and reaction," as
"our military action provokes an Israeli reaction against our people, who then
become involved [in the struggle] and are supported by the Arab masses."[24]

Fatah had not originally planned to use violence so soon, but after the
emergence of the PLO, its leadership was concerned about the survival of
the group and argued that "intensifying the military bases [*sic*] and starting
operations may limit the crumbling [of membership]."[25] Therefore, the challenger Fatah decided to launch the armed struggle on January 1, 1965.[26] Despite its relatively meager beginnings, which included a raid thwarted by
the Lebanese and faulty explosive charges placed in the Israeli National Water Carrier, Fatah claimed more than eighty attacks against Israel in the first
nine months of the campaign, which involved laying mines on roads, canals,
and rail lines, as well as strikes against power stations and security out-
posts.[27] The attacks began to increase the organizational strength of Fatah, as
Hassan explained, "The real increase, the real support that comes from the
people, and permanently, started in '65 when we started our military action.
Then the people realized that we were not just another movement, talking
like the others."[28] As John Amos suggests, "As far as the younger militants
among the Palestinians were concerned, Fatah was doing the fighting while
the older 'notables' in the PLO were doing the talking."[29]

Leading Palestinian organizations immediately took notice and tried to
restrain the use of violence by Fatah, as MST predicts. The ANM claimed
that the Fatah attacks were counterproductive and that it "aims to entangle
[Egyptian President Gamal Abdel] Nasser in a battle for which he is not prepared."[30] Indeed, the few Fatah members in attendance at the second PNC
openly told the press that they wanted "to entangle the Arab nations in a
war with Israel."[31] The PLO denounced the raids by specifically referencing its
own organizational leadership. Shuqeiri said, "Only the Palestinian Liberation

Army can authorize any Palestinian military operation," and he resolved with the PLO Executive Committee to stop the Fatah attacks "whether through gentle words and promises or with threats."[32] Both methods failed.

The most interesting aspect of the initial responses is not the prescience of Fatah rivals but, rather, that despite their foresight the ANM and PLO found themselves violently outbidding with Fatah in short order and chain-ganged into the very conflict they claimed should be avoided just two years later. This outcome demonstrates the power of movement structure for group behavior—the tragedy of national movements—because even fore-knowledge of the pitfalls of fragmentation could not prevent the groups from succumbing to its deleterious effects.

Despite their public denouncements, privately the ANM and others could not help but recognize the increased support given to Fatah and the stark contrast of the attacks with their own inaction. The impact was palpable. Potential ANM recruits were joining Fatah, and current ANM members were defecting; as Abd al-Karim Hamad, a former ANM leader, explained, "From 1965 onwards, Fatah embarked on armed actions, whereas we were explaining to our militants that we must wait, that we must train, and so on. Then we saw that our militants were joining Fatah. Because of the rightist leadership of the ANM [i.e., George Habash], we lost a historic opportunity."[33] Not just fighters but also funding followed the violence. Donations were often explicitly tied to evidence of attacks, as was the case with Kuwaiti and Algerian donors before the first Fatah attack.

The ANM was certainly not morally opposed to violence. During a meeting of its executive committee in 1960, members had discussed launching attacks against Israel. They warranted classification as an armed group by 1962–1963, when over one hundred of their members received weapons and underwent military training with the Egyptians.[34] The ANM came closer to initiating violence with the emergence of the PLO in 1964, which threatened its position just as it threatened Fatah. A combination of its position as the stronger challenger at the time and its ties to Nasser, however, led the ANM to hold off, although an increasing number of its members called for attacks.[35] Once Fatah started using violence and peeling away ANM recruits, however, the group could no longer remain on the sidelines.

In mid-1966, the ANM decided to form a commando group, Abtal al-Awda (Heroes of Return), in cooperation with a few anti-Shuqeiri members of the PLO, although the ANM largely controlled the group. Abtal al-Awda launched its first attack on October 19, 1966, followed by seven more from December 1966 to June 1967. Although still dwarfed by the attacks by Fatah, the ANM and PLO actions contributed to the ramping up of attacks by multiple organizations that preceded the Six-Day War of 1967. The JCP did not get involved this round, but subordinate groups such as the Palestinian Liberation Front (PLF) and Palestinian National Liberation Front did, contributing to the upsurge in violent competition and revealing the lack of any dominant group to direct the action. The increase in violence even spurred Shuqeiri in mid-1967 to start claiming (falsely) that the PLO had been funding the Fatah attacks and to note the PLO support for such violence, despite the concerns by the group about entanglement with Israel.

The increasing tempo of attacks brought harsh Israeli reprisals, which increased tensions between Israel and its Syrian, Jordanian, and Egyptian neighbors, especially when Nasser and the Syrians started to more openly support various Palestinian armed groups by 1967. Most important, the Palestinian attacks helped to spark the crisis that led to the Six-Day War, the April 1967 Israeli air raid against Syria that included 171 sorties and the downing of 6 Syrian MiGs inside Syrian and Jordanian territory.[36] The Six-Day War was a well-documented disaster for the Palestinians. The Israelis took control of the West Bank, Gaza, and the Golan Heights (see figure 3.1);

Figure 3.1. Israel, the West Bank, Gaza, and Neighboring Countries, since 1967

hundreds of thousands of Palestinians became refugees (some for the second time); the Arab armies were routed; and the Palestinian armed groups fared little better. The outcome cannot be understood as anything but a strategic failure—one to which the use of violence by Palestinian armed groups directly contributed.

The competitive, fragmented national movement had played a clear, dominant role in the use and effectiveness of violence by Palestinian armed groups. As a weaker challenger in the movement hierarchy, Fatah used violence in response to the emergence of the PLO, at a time when it was not prepared or planning to do so, in an attempt to outbid its rival. As predicted, the ANM and the PLO first tried to restrain the Fatah attacks and, when those efforts failed, later launched some of their own attacks with the ANM leading the way. These contradictory actions make little sense from a strategic perspective, but they are directly in line with MST predictions concerning the impact of movement hierarchy on group actions. The fragmented Palestinian national movement further allowed competing Arab states entry to play out their own rivalries within the movement, as the Syrian-backed Fatah faced off against the Egyptian-backed PLO and ANM in another layer of competition that had anything but the Palestinians' collective strategic interests at its heart.[37] A textbook case of outbidding and chain-ganging resulted, against the wishes of the vast majority of the actors, which led to a failed campaign.

The most prominent competing argument, namely that ideology drove the variation in the use of violence, performs poorly. Fatah had supported the concept of armed struggle since its founding, but it did not use violence until the threat to its organizational survival emerged in 1964. A similar argument can be made for the ANM and PLO, which used violence when they felt threatened by Fatah, not due to some ideological change. In each case, we cannot explain a variable with a constant. Even the JCP, whose ideology did not favor violence, eventually joined the armed struggle due to the competition within the fragmented movement, as we see in the next section.

Armed Struggle in a Post-1967 World

Skeptics might suggest that the 1965–June 1967 campaign was a unique case in which the specific time or space played the key role; however, the structure of the Palestinian national movement ironically remained the same as the dust settled after the Six-Day War, even though pretty much everything else—territory held, enemy and supporting state strength, base population geographical distribution, and campaign location—changed dramatically. The post-1967 campaign thus represents a most-different comparison with the pre-1967 war campaign in that so much of the political landscape had changed but the movement system and group positions in the hierarchy of the Palestinian national movement stayed the same.[38] As predicted by MST, the same groups initiated violence, the same groups attempted to restrain it, and the campaign resulted in strategic failure—all in strikingly similar fashion.

Having experienced the problems that result from the uncoordinated use of violence in a fragmented movement, the ANM met with Fatah in mid-July 1967 to ensure that the postwar period would not be a repeat of the prewar period. The two groups came to an agreement on this issue, supported by the PLO, with all consenting to hold off on attacks so the groups could rebuild their organizations.[39] In a shining example of the tragedy of national movements, the best of intentions were thwarted by the inherently competitive movement system. As before, Fatah jumped the gun, in part to get an organizational upper hand. As before, the ANM and PLO were forced to revise their plans and employ violence earlier than desired to prevent the loss of their positions in the hierarchy. As before, strategic concerns did not drive the use of violence, nor did it produce strategic success.

Yasser Arafat infiltrated the West Bank with a number of Fatah cadres in mid-June, and the organization launched its first attacks at the end of August, followed by fifty more over the next four months.[40] The early launch by Fatah was driven in part by its organizational desire to prevent a deal to establish a Palestinian state on part of the territory that would have been struck with Arab regimes, the PLO, or West Bank Palestinians in the aftermath of the war. Fatah did this not simply because it did not like the deal but also because it would have been cut out of it.[41] Fatah thus desired to simultaneously outbid other Palestinian armed groups and spoil initiatives by local Palestinians to benefit its own organizational ends.

Fatah's position as a challenger meant that other groups could not easily stop or ignore its use of violence. Soon after the first Fatah attack, ANM leaders came to the realization that they were losing out to their rival on both recruits and funding. In November 1967, Ahmad Khalifa, a member of the ANM central command, summed it up by saying, "The battle might start without us. . . . Fatah and [Palestinian Liberation Front leader Ahmad] Jibril will be the only ones to reap the credit . . . and that will finish us."[42] The ANM leadership instructed its cadres to initiate attacks despite their lack of adequate preparation.[43] The first attack, a failed operation against Ben-Gurion Airport on December 11, came the same day that the ANM announced the formation of a new organization that was to serve as the main Fatah rival for the next two decades: the PFLP. The ANM, which made up the bulk of the new organization, had joined with the PLF and Heroes of Return in part because of their demonstrated readiness and skill in launching attacks, which they had started again following the second Fatah launch.[44]

Unfortunately for the ANM/PFLP, Fatah, and other Palestinian groups, the lack of preparation and coordination doomed the attempt to launch a popular struggle in the West Bank to a swift, costly end. Fighters' cursory training, inadequate weapons, and lack of experience with proper operational security allowed the Israelis to quickly roll up Palestinian networks. The groups were forced to admit that the campaign was a strategic failure by the beginning of 1968 and to move their headquarters across the border to Jordan.

KARAMEH AND THE RISE OF FATAH

Fatah again led the way with cross-border attacks against the Israelis. Nasser Youssef, the Fatah commander in the area, recalled, "The PLO tried to restrain us, but they were not strong enough to do so."[45] The PLO proceeded to announce the creation of its own guerrilla branch in early March 1968: the Popular Liberation Forces (PLF/PLA). The PLF/PLA was created "as a counter to the growing popularity of commando organizations" because "recruits who might otherwise have joined the PLA were volunteering for Fatah and other groups instead."[46] After the Palestinian armed groups launched thirty-six attacks in March, Israel decided to launch a massive reprisal raid on March 21, 1968, to knock out the guerrillas' headquarters in the village of Karameh and send a message to King Hussein, whose country was serving as a wary but ultimately willing host.[47] While the PFLP followed classic guerrilla strategy of withdrawing in the face of a superior, massed foe, Fatah decided to stand and fight. Although the Israelis won a clear military victory—destroying the village and returning to Israel hours later after killing one hundred guerrillas and capturing more than one hundred more—the defenders had exacted a significant price. The Israeli press reported that the Israel Defense Forces (IDF) suffered twenty killed and ninety wounded, as well as the loss of four tanks, two armored cars, and one airplane.

Although the Israelis achieved their tactical objectives, their significant losses and withdrawal under fire created an image of determined, powerful Palestinian *fedayeen* that were willing to stand up and bloody the noses of the supposedly invincible IDF, in contrast to Arab state armies less than one year earlier. Youssef explained, "We [Fatah] lost a quarter of our fighters in the area, but thousands joined afterwards, so many that we could not train, equip, and pay all of them."[48] One Palestinian teenager described his reaction as follows: "When the news of Karameh came over the radio, all of the students and teachers ran out and celebrated in the streets for the rest of the afternoon. We were all proud to be Palestinians that day, and we were proud of the *fedayeen* who had done what the Arab armies could not do less than a year earlier against the Israelis." Soon after, this teenager, Jibril Rajoub, joined Fatah, and would decades later become Arafat's head of security in the West Bank.[49] Financial contributions "poured in from Palestinian circles," and 5,000 Palestinians attempted to join Fatah within forty-eight hours after Karameh. By May, Fatah claimed it had been approached by 20,000 would-be recruits in Egypt and 1,500 per week in Iraq. Although Fatah could not accommodate even close to these numbers, the group nonetheless tripled in size by June, with the surge further revealing the extensive popular support for the now-public organization.

Fatah became the most powerful group in the movement, and its position as leader was clear from shifts within the PLO itself. Although the representatives to the PNC were originally intended to be elected, obstacles thrown up by Arab regimes and the groups themselves prevented that from happening for decades. Nonetheless, competing groups had the best knowledge of their own membership totals, funding, and popular support (as well as those of their rivals), and they used this information to haggle over their seat distribution. After having been turned down in attempts to bargain for the largest number of PNC seats in previous years, Fatah was able to negotiate for the largest number of PNC seats in the weeks after Karameh and then have Arafat elected PLO chairman in February 1969.[50]

Although the ascendance of Fatah brought hierarchical change, the movement remained fragmented as a result of the continued presence of the PFLP and the emergence of new challengers—the Syrian-sponsored Saiqa organization and the DFLP, which split from the PFLP in 1969.[51] Even the JCP, the last nonviolent holdout, decided to form a guerrilla group the year after Karameh in response to its fading organizational fortunes.[52] Thus, the group that had argued most vociferously that violence was futile and counterproductive introduced Quwwat al-Ansar (Partisan Forces) in early 1970 after seeing its size and influence shrink relative to other groups. Therefore, although Palestinian groups' roles changed in the years after Karameh, the strategic outcome would remain the same yet again.

NEW ROLES, SAME OUTCOME, 1967–1970

As MST predicts, the changed positions of Fatah and the PFLP in the hierarchy led the two to swap approaches to escalatory violence, even though their ideology, leadership, and strategic goals remained the same. Although it was still clearly a significant group, the PFLP leadership recognized by 1968–1969 that its organization was trending downward relative to its rivals and was now third or fourth in the movement hierarchy. Recognizing that it could not paint a quantitative contrast the way Fatah had with its first cross-border attacks because of the ongoing violence, the PFLP opted for a qualitative outbid in tactics that it hoped would allow it to retain its current supporters and gain new ones in its drive for influence.

In the months after the fighting at Karameh, the PFLP decided to embark on what it labeled "external operations." The opening salvo was the hijacking of an El Al flight from Rome to Tel Aviv on July 23, 1968, which caught the Israelis off guard, generated massive press coverage, and resulted in both the release of PFLP prisoners and an increase in recruits.[53] The PFLP went on to launch numerous other international attacks, including bombings of Jewish stores in London, grenade attacks on Israeli embassies and the El Al office in Brussels, and many more hijackings of U.S. and European airlines.[54] The PFLP attempted to justify its actions by noting the link between the Israelis and their Western supporters, arguing, "We will be kidding ourselves if we try to differentiate between hitting Israeli targets and imperial targets, as they are the same."[55] As with the Fatah launch of the armed struggle in 1965, the PFLP launch of "external operations" also inspired competitors: the recent splinter group PFLP-General Command blew up a Swissair aircraft in midflight, and the Palestinian Popular Struggle Front (PPSF) hijacked an Olympic Airways plane en route to Cairo.[56]

The aim of the PFLP was not only to outbid Fatah but also to chain-gang the Palestinian national movement into a direct conflict with King Hussein of Jordan.[57] The PFLP and later the DFLP launched provocative verbal and violent attacks against the monarch, including the public claim of "no authority over the authority of the [Palestinian] resistance" in mid-1970, which was a direct challenge to Hussein's rule.[58]

In striking evidence of MST at work, William Quandt describes the earlier strategy of the DFLP: "The DFLP during 1969 and early 1970 seemed to believe that direct clashes with the Jordanian army might lead to Hussein's overthrow, but that Fatah, not the DFLP, would come to power as a non-revolutionary movement. Fatah would then be likely to turn against the PFLP and DFLP to maintain its dominant position. Thus, until the revolutionary forces held the balance of power, the DFLP favored the avoidance of a showdown with any Arab regime."[59] The PFLP decision to carry out "external operations" inside Jordan subsequently put the movement on the verge of war with its hosts and, soon after, plunged it into one.

The most surprising role reversal—especially for theories that point to the role of ideology, age, or individual leaders to explain group action—may not have been the PFLP attempts to violently outbid and chain-gang but, rather, the efforts by Fatah to restrain them. The formerly weaker group, which just a few years earlier had been launching and relaunching the armed struggle in campaigns to outbid and chain-gang, was now the leader in the movement, looking to prevent conflict that could threaten its position and associated benefits. Fatah proceeded to set up a number of umbrella institutions designed to control and restrain weaker groups, such as the Palestine Armed Struggle Command (PASC), the Unified Command of the Palestinian Resistance (UCPR), and Central Committee of the Palestinian Resistance (CCPR). These were "specifically designed to restrain the proliferation of new organizations and curb the inclination toward carrying out armed attacks in an unauthorized fashion," as well as fulfill "Fatah's wish to regulate activities, and thus prevent the seemingly imminent confrontation from erupting."[60] As MST suggests, and as J. Gaspard noted at the time, "The small groups have nothing to lose and much to gain from revolutionary chaos in the host countries. Fatah has much to lose: the subsidies from the 'moderate' Arab states; its pool of heavy arms and more or less trained military formations that might get broken up in a revolutionary free for all; an established diplomatic and political position in the Arab world and in certain international circles; offices in many Arab countries which are small centers of local government; and a fairly well-oiled propaganda machine."[61]

Fatah understood what the PFLP was trying to do, having done the same in previous campaigns. As Salah Khalaf, a Fatah leader, noted, "Other small organizations are engaged in leftist overbids which are altogether unrealistic."[62] In June 1970, the PFLP took sixty Westerners hostage in two hotels in Amman in a challenge to King Hussein. Fatah stepped in and negotiated a cease-fire that brought the crisis to an end, yet another example of its newfound role.[63] In early September 1970, Fatah and the movement were not so lucky. The PFLP hijacked three airplanes full of more than three hundred largely Western civilians and held them hostage on a desert airstrip a few miles from Amman.[64] As Leila Khaled, a captured hijacker, later noted, "We had a number of objectives in that operation, including not only raising the issue of the Palestinian people to the world, but also challenging the Jordanian regime." She explained that the PFLP had wanted to "ring a bell, supported by a hand grenade" and that "the tactics depended on the situation and the balance of forces."[65]

Outraged at the PFLP attempts to chain-gang the movement to war, Fatah pushed the PFLP to return the airplanes. The PFLP blew them up instead. Fatah pushed the PFLP to return the hostages. The PFLP kept many of them and scattered them to avoid rescue. Fatah forced the expulsion of the PFLP from the PLO Central Committee and then brokered a cease-fire. The PFLP rejected it. The leading position of Fatah in the hierarchy gave it an interest in maintaining the status quo, but the group was not powerful enough to stop the actions of the PFLP, just as the PLO and ANM had been unable to restrain Fatah a few years earlier.

King Hussein was thus convinced of the inevitability of a struggle, and he formed a military government days later. Even though Fatah had noted its desire to avoid a war for months, the Jordanian army's shelling of Palestinian guerrilla positions and refugee camps around Amman helped to convince Fatah that it could no longer hold back. Unfortunately for the PFLP, Fatah, and the rest of the Palestinian national movement, the campaign was a total failure. The Jordanian army routed the divided guerrillas in what became known as Black September, killing thousands and beginning the process of expelling all the Palestinian armed groups from the country, which was completed the following year.[66] This strategic setback would haunt the Palestinians for decades, because they would not find as favorable a political and geographical situation again.[67]

A hegemonic movement would have been more likely to avoid the competitive outbidding and provocative tactics that sparked the ill-advised war, cut a better deal with King Hussein short of expulsion, or previously have avoided alienating the local populace and some of their Arab allies, thus making military victory either unnecessary or far more likely.[68] Khaled al-Hassan of Fatah argued as much: "Had the resistance movement not been divided and full of contradictions, it would have been able, with the support of the masses, to overcome the conspiracies of the [Jordanian] government." As Abu Iyad of Fatah noted, however, "Even in historic and critical decisions, the leadership of the various groups used to put hierarchical gain before the general good."[69] The solution, however, was not a new spirit of altruism or fresh alliances among Palestinian groups, but rather a change in the movement system structure. After subsequent united and fragmented campaigns in Lebanon and beyond over the next fifteen years ended in failure, the movement finally reached its lone hegemonic moment.[70]

THE HEGEMONIC MOMENT, FATAH FROM 1986–2000

For most observers, the conditions in 1987 could not have been worse for the Palestinian national movement. The Palestinians were pushed to the bottom of the Arab League summit agenda, they had been fighting costly conflicts in Lebanon for more than a decade, their leadership was languishing in faraway Tunis, and millions of their people were marking twenty years or more in squalid refugee camps or under Israeli military control. These factors pointed to likely strategic failure, yet structurally the Palestinian national movement had never been in a better position for success according to MST. By the previous year, a confluence of factors had made the movement hegemonic for the first and only time in its history.

First, the Lebanese civil war decimated the rivals of Fatah. Leftist groups such as the PFLP and DFLP were significantly weakened in the struggle they had helped pull the movement into. Saiqa, formerly the second strongest group, suffered from mass Palestinian defections when its leadership forced the group to fight PLO factions in support of the Syrians. By the mid-1980s, not one of these represented a significant group that could seriously challenge Fatah.[71]

Second, just as the old rivals faded away, new ones emerged. Fatah dissidents led by Colonel Said al-Muragha (Abu Musa), who had led the PLO defense of Beirut, split from the group in the aftermath of Arafat's exit from Lebanon in 1982.[72] The dissidents formed a new faction called Fatah-Intifada and proclaimed that Fatah and Arafat's leadership of the movement were at an end. The dissidents represented over 4,000 fighters in Lebanon and Syria, who proceeded to launch attacks on Fatah units that had remained in Lebanon as well as on supportive Palestinian refugee camps. By 1985, however, Fatah-Intifada was down to fewer than 1,000 fighters due largely to defections, and the group soon had no significant support outside of Syria or Syria-controlled Lebanon. A 1986 al-Fajr poll found that 93.5% of Palestinians said that the PLO represented them, and 78.6% picked Arafat as their preferred leader compared to 5.6% for Habash of the PFLP and 1.2% for Abu Musa of Fatah-Intifada.[73]

Finally, the economic and diplomatic clout of Fatah was unmatched. Fatah received two-thirds of the Arab state funding offered in the wake of the Camp David Accords, leaving the remaining third for all the other groups combined.[74] The main financial body of the PLO, the PNF, had cash reserves of at least $1.5 billion (with estimates up to $14 billion). Not only did Fatah control the PNF, but research suggests that the group may have had even more money itself, with an estimated $7–8 billion on hand.[75] The funds of the other groups were paltry by comparison, just enough for a basic military and staff but little else. Many of the smaller groups were now directly financed by Fatah and the PLO leadership, raising the issue of whether they were even independent entities. Fatah's dominance of the movement spread to all corners of its activity; Habash (PFLP) complained that 95% of the over one hundred PLO missions abroad belonged to Fatah.

In short, "[Fatah had] more fighters, more money, and a broader range of support among Palestinians, Arab states, and the international community than all the other PLO groups combined."[76] Internal dissent remained, but Fatah became so powerful politically, militarily, and economically that no other group could realistically unseat it for the foreseeable future. The first taste of hegemony for the movement led to its most significant strategic gains.

Fatah did not start the First Intifada in December 1987, but the overwhelming power of the group soon allowed it to gain considerable control of what began as a grassroots uprising in response to the two-decade-old Israeli military occupation of the West Bank and Gaza. By January 1988, Fatah and the PLO had set up a Unified National Command (UNC), which gave Palestinian civilians in the West Bank and Gaza guidelines for resistance and coordinated action. The UNC helped to organize many of the activities of civil resistance that defined the First Intifada, including strikes by Palestinian workers, refusal to pay taxes, boycotts on Israeli goods, and mass protest marches.[77] The symbol of the First Intifada—the Palestinian youth (shabab) throwing rocks at Israeli soldiers—was not entirely unorganized either. Fatah had previously developed youth organizations such as the Shabiba, which claimed tens of thousands of members and led many of these demonstrations.[78] As one former DFLP member described, "Arafat succeeded in propagating the idea that the whole Palestinian people is Fatah."[79] The dominance of Fatah thus helped to ensure a cohesive strategy that was lacking in previous (and future) campaigns amid fragmentation.

The tactics of the movement were largely nonlethal, if not nonviolent. From the start of the Intifada until 1993, fewer than one hundred Israelis were killed in the territories and fewer than one hundred were killed in Israel as a result of the uprising, numbers that would later be dwarfed by the fragmented Second Intifada. Conversely, Israeli security forces killed more than 1,000 Palestinians during this period; these lopsided casualty figures and contrasting tactics helped to boost popular support for the Palestinian national movement across the globe.[80] Even when the Intifada became more militarized in 1989, partly in response to the Israelis relaxing their rules of fire and increasing the use of plastic bullets, the movement did not devolve into major spirals of violent outbidding. Weaker groups did not have the power to threaten Fatah's leadership, and the dominance by Fatah meant that it did not need to outbid violently to maintain its position. Instead, Fatah saw that the best way to increase its strength was through strategic gains, by pressuring the Israelis and negotiating with Israel and the United States over the future of Palestine, thus cementing the position of the group in a new state. As Yezid Sayigh artfully explained, "If Fatah wanted a big slice of the cake, there had to be a cake."[81]

Over the course of the Intifada, two potential threats to Fatah did arise, although neither became a significant challenger by the time of the Oslo negotiations in 1993. The first was the local leadership in the West Bank, which the Israelis had tried for so long to prop up as an alternative to Fatah and the PLO. The Israelis were thwarted, however, when 85% of seats in the 1976 municipal elections in the West Bank went to PLO supporters, leading Israeli Prime Minister Menachem Begin to cancel and postpone the 1980 and 1982 elections, respectively, because there was no viable alternative to the PLO.[82] Nonetheless, the middle class and intelligentsia in the territories were not entirely beholden to the PLO, even if they refused to act as the Israelis desired. Although many were allied to Fatah through the Shabiba or the UNCs, Arafat feared that, given the right opportunity, individuals such as Faisal al-Husseini could form an alternative leadership and cut a deal with the Israelis.[83] Nonetheless, the cooptation by Fatah of many local elites, in part through its previous distribution of *sumud* funds, largely headed off this challenge. The comparative strength of the refugee-dominated Fatah was confirmed at the 1988 PNC, at which only a few extra seats were added for representatives in the territories.

The second potential threat, Hamas, would ultimately prove more difficult to coopt or defeat, although the group was not strong enough to truly challenge Fatah until the mid-1990s. The Islamist Muslim Brotherhood had long had a foothold in Gaza. Ironically, in fact, many of the original members of Fatah came from the Brotherhood, which was often persecuted by Arab governments in the Levant. The Israelis allowed the weaker Muslim Brotherhood to develop its religious and social networks in Gaza while repressing the larger PLO-affiliated organizations. By the mid-1980s, the

Muslim Brotherhood had a considerable following in Gaza, but some of its members decided that the group should no longer foreswear violent jihad to retake Palestine. The first group left to form Palestinian Islamic Jihad (PIJ) before the Intifada; the larger Hamas formed at its outbreak. Hamas got involved in the Intifada early on, but its membership, funding, and public support were dwarfed by Fatah, and its first attacks against the Israelis in 1989 led to the imprisonment of its leader, Sheik Ahmed Yassin, and the deportation of hundreds of the members it did have.[84] In addition to these early blows, Hamas had little support outside the territories and did not even form an armed wing until the early 1990s. Therefore, it could do little to affect the direction of the movement initially, and it was not a significant challenger in the early years of its existence.

With no internal challengers, the momentum of the Intifada at his back, and the realization that his group was in position to dominate any new government, Arafat announced the founding of the Palestinian state at the nineteenth PNC in November 1988. In a speech at the United Nations the same year, Arafat announced that the PLO accepted UN Resolution 242 and condemned terrorism in all its forms, which led to the United States removing it from its list of terrorist organizations.[85] The timing of these moves was driven in part by a recent announcement by Jordan that it was giving up its claim to the West Bank (a small organizational and strategic success in and of itself) because Fatah feared Israeli annexation. Eighty-four countries offered full recognition of the Palestinian state and twenty offered qualified recognition within two months of the declaration.[86] This was a diplomatic coup for Arafat and Fatah, which also secured PNC acceptance of UN Resolutions 242 and 338, clearing the way for Palestinian negotiations with the United States and Israel over the final status of Israel and Palestine.

The importance of the strength of Fatah in accepting UN Resolution 242 was clear from private discussions with U.S. representatives a decade earlier, when Fatah was simply the movement leader facing challengers backed by Syria. In September 1977, Arafat had said that he would accept UN Resolution 242 *if* the United States promised the creation of a Palestinian state with him at the head. Otherwise, he could not resist the significant pressure he faced from the Syrians and the challengers they backed in the movement.[87] Without such guarantees amid a fragmented movement, the discussions failed and Fatah did not accept the resolution until its hierarchical position had improved a decade later.

In 1988, some subordinate groups still disagreed with these steps, including the PFLP, which did not engage in spoiling attacks, and the PFLP-General Command and Islamic Jihad, which launched a few attacks against Israeli and U.S. targets. Rather than chain-gang the movement or drive Fatah to outbid, the strength and position of Fatah allowed it stay the strategic course, even though, predictably, it did so largely for organizational reasons.

Some scholars suggest that Fatah's support of the 1991 Madrid negotiations was due to its weakness after it lost funding from the Gulf because of its support for Saddam in the Iraq war. Although Fatah and the PLO did take a financial hit, its yearly revenue dropped to $140 million—not counting the billions in reserves—which was still far above any other group. The hit forced Fatah to cut funding for 5,000 people in Lebanon, but this was only a cut of funding for 25% of its members in one foreign country, which still represented a larger figure than the *total* membership of almost any other Palestinian organization. As MST predicts, the rising subordinate, Hamas, directly told Fatah at the Tunis Talks in 1992 that it should abandon negotiations and escalate the Intifada, but hegemonic Arafat and Fatah disagreed. Unlike the Second Intifada of 2000–2006, when Qaddoura Fares, a Fatah member, explained that "Hamas led us by the nose to violence," the continued dominance of Fatah lessened any desire to violently outbid.[88] Its hegemonic position also prevented subsequent violent spoiling attempts by Hamas from derailing strategic progress in the early 1990s, which began in earnest with the signing of the Declaration of Principles on the White House lawn in September 1993.

In the years after the first Oslo agreement, Fatah continued to act like a hegemon, in that it "suppressed Hamas and Islamic Jihad, arrested over 2,000 operatives, and killed twenty of their leaders."[89] Hamas launched its first suicide bombing inside Israel in 1994, just as it became a challenger for the first time. Hamas no doubt gained strength during the First Intifada due to its Islamist appeals and its use of violence, but it remained a strong subordinate until November 1993 and early 1994, when it polled within one-third of Fatah for the first time (albeit barely), 14% (Hamas) to 41% (Fatah).[90] Nonetheless, most of the 1994 polls were taken right after the Hebron massacre by Baruch Goldstein, an Israeli settler, and so represented as much a temporary loss of faith in Fatah as a surge of support for Hamas—as confirmed by the fact that support for Fatah in polls snapped back to more than tripling Hamas until 2001.[91] Some of the best evidence for the explanatory power of the one-third threshold comes from the groups themselves. During negotiations over Hamas's joining the PLO, Hamas demanded 40% of the seats—large enough to make them a strong challenger—but Fatah countered with 20%—small enough to keep Hamas as a subordinate.[92]

The parties could not reach an agreement on the number of PLO seats, although in terms of wealth and membership, it was no contest.[93] The armed wing of Hamas had only one hundred members in 1994, while its annual budget was only $30–50 million, as "its resources in no way [compared] with the financial potential of the PLO, restricting its ability to engage in comparable patronage activities."[94] Therefore, Hamas may in fact have been the perfect size for effective good cop–bad cop dynamics in the early 1990s: a strong subordinate that was large enough to be noticed but weak enough so that its action would not prevent negotiations.[95] This is confirmed by the shared concern of Israeli leaders such as prime ministers Yitzhak Rabin and Shimon Peres that Hamas was rising, as well as their shared belief that Fatah could repress Hamas and that a deal with Fatah was the best way to head off the rise of its rival.[96] Ultimately, the Oslo process yielded the Israelis' greatest concessions when the movement was hegemonic but fell apart as the movement fragmented once more with the rise of Hamas in 2000–2001.

MST does not attempt to explain all of the ins and outs of the Madrid and Oslo negotiations, about which numerous valuable works already exist.[97] More broadly, however, the theory helps to reveal that the increased focus on victory, the decrease in strategically counterproductive violence, the cohesiveness of the First Intifada, the increased credibility of the movement, the crackdown on violent subordinates, and the acceptance of a political program that made these negotiations possible were a direct result of the hegemony of the Palestinian national movement. The Oslo Accords are far less popular today than they were at the time, but they nonetheless represent the most significant strategic success of the Palestinian national movement either before or since. They led to the withdrawal of Israeli forces from Gaza and major cities in the West Bank, the creation of a Palestinian Authority with varying degrees of control in these areas, the return of thousands of refugees into the territories, and the indication of a resolution to the conflict ending in a Palestinian state in a significant part of the West Bank and all of Gaza.

Ultimately, the Oslo negotiations and their critics highlight some of the great strengths and weaknesses of MST. The theory is correct that the movement was more strategically effective during periods of hegemony than in periods of unity or fragmentation. *More* does not necessarily define precisely *how much*, however.[98] To the extent that it does, the mechanisms of the theory suggest that groups will pursue strategic gains as far as these gains are likely to benefit the groups themselves. In this case, the gains of Oslo definitely benefited Fatah, and in the process, they did secure some strategic progress that benefited the larger movement.

Was Fatah self-interested in this? Absolutely. Mustafa al-Barghouti, a former leader of the Palestinian Communist Party (descendant of the JCP), argued that Arafat and Fatah focused more on securing the predominance of their party in the new Palestinian Authority than achieving a state.[99] Indeed, organizational objectives were the reason that Fatah had initiated the secret Oslo negotiations in the first place. Arafat was concerned that the ongoing negotiations in Madrid under the auspices of the United States, which Fatah was controlling but not directly participating in, could revive the elite in the territories to challenge for leadership.[100] Haidar Abdel-Shafi, the head of the Palestinian negotiating team at Madrid, claimed in regards to a question concerning the actions of Fatah, "This is a question you should pose to Chairman Arafat. . . . Surely there was no *national* gain."[101]

Fatah was no less self-interested than other groups that took positions in the newly formed Palestinian Authority, however, or those such as Hamas that launched attacks in part because it had been excluded from the deal. In fact, the actions of Fatah in this regard confirm the predictions of the MST because Fatah accepted strategic gains that it had castigated and killed others for even suggesting two decades earlier, in no small part because its new position in the hierarchy allowed it to enjoy the selective benefits of the formation of the Palestinian Authority. Could further strategic gains have been achieved? Perhaps, but any answer must acknowledge the three previous decades and two subsequent decades that experienced fragmented and united movements with much less to show for their actions.[102] The strategic gains at Oslo were not everything the Palestinians desired, but they were far more than previous or subsequent campaigns achieved.

Fragmentation and Tragedy

More than any observer, the Palestinians themselves have recognized the problems posed by a lack of coherence in strategy and signaling stemming from a movement with so many factions. As Saeb Erekat argued in internal meetings with his Negotiations Support Unit in 2009, "Palestinians are speaking with 2,000 voices just when we need to be speaking with one."[103] The common path to achieving that one voice, suggested by almost every scholar and participant, has been an alliance among the various factions. Indeed, it is hard to find a book on the Palestinian national movement that does *not* lament the lack of unity—the major works by Sayigh, Rashid Khalidi, Walid Khalidi, Wendy Pearlman, Helena Cobban, and Khalaf, among others, all emphasize this theme.[104]

Unfortunately, such an arrangement is not easily attained, stable, or even the best solution to the problem. Such unity has been attempted countless times, most (in)famously with the Politburo of Unified Action for Palestinian Revolutionary Forces, the Permanent Bureau of the Palestinian Guerrilla Organizations, the Palestinian Armed Struggle Command, and various branches of the PLO itself. These attempts, which include some of the most successful of the bunch, brought a unity among the strongest factions that was fleeting at best and illusory at worst due to the contradictory incentives facing the constituent groups, not to mention their state sponsors. The existence of multiple rivals consistently provided entrées for Middle Eastern states that sought to control the Palestinian national movement for their own ends, whether Egypt with the PLO and ANM, Syria with Saiqa and the PFLP-General Command, Iraq with the Arab Liberation Front, Libya with Abu Nidal, or Iran with the Islamic Jihad and Hamas. Numerous Palestinian leaders explained that this hindered independent Palestinian decision making and potential progress, because Fatah had to accommodate dissenting groups to avoid issues with its Arab state supporters (although they claimed that Fatah could more easily disregard state-sponsored groups when they were only weak subordinates).[105]

Even when the PLO became a stronger institutional structure, groups came and went—and thus united or did not—based on power concerns, with significant actors such as Hamas always outside the fold.[106] The movement thus achieved limited success during its one period of unity (1974) and failure during its periods of fragmentation (1965–June 1967, July 1967–1968, 1969–1970, 1971–1973, 1975–1985, and 2001–2016), contrary to competing arguments (see table 3.1).[107] As MST suggests, the movement achieved its greatest success when it was hegemonic (1986–1993 and 1995–2000). The success during the fragmentation of 1994 represents an exception that proves the rule, because Hamas *barely* registered as a challenger—it had less than one-third the members of Fatah, less than one-third the funding of Fatah, and 34% of the popular support of Fatah—and the gains that year are best viewed as part of the broader Oslo process that began before, continued after, and was conducted almost entirely during hegemony.

The position of groups in the hierarchy of the Palestinian national movement also played the dominant role in when, how, and why they employed or restrained violence, and negotiated or spoiled. In addition to the tight within-case comparisons highlighted earlier, competing arguments cannot explain a number of key actions. For example, if the initial use of violence by Fatah was driven by ideology, leadership, or age, then why did it not attack in the previous seven years, when the first two factors were the same and the group was younger? The answer cannot be that the group simply needed to prepare because it was not well prepared when it did launch; its existence was simply threatened by the rise of the PLO. Arguments that the arrows actually go the other way—that Fatah's leadership comes from the positions it took rather than the other way around—fail on an analysis of sequencing. Fatah had become the leader *before* it announced the Ten-Point Program in 1974—which adjusted its earlier aim of a state on all of historic Palestine—and it had become the hegemon *before* it declared a Palestinian state and accepted UN Resolution 242 in 1988, not afterward.

Ultimately, a national movement that involves the actions of more than ten key states and even more groups over the course of a century is incredibly complex, and all its parts are not going to fit perfectly into a parsimonious theory and framework. This is precisely why MST is useful. It helps us to organize and simplify the complexity and focus on certain key aspects of the case while, at the same time, recognizing how many questions are left unanswered.[108]

Without the emergence of a dominant organization, the faces of the leaders and funders may change, as they have for more than fifty years, but unfortunately for the Palestinians, the ending will probably remain the same. An upgrade in status at the United Nations, the lack of progress in talks with the Israelis, and the recent Arab uprisings may help spur these changes, but they are not a substitute for them. Without hegemony, in which power serves to create coherence in ways intentions rarely do, the Palestinian movement will most likely continue to resemble the story of Sisyphus, struggling mightily to achieve a state while the structure of the movement ensures an eerily familiar lack of success.

The Zionist Movement

Victory Hanging in the Balance

> Why was the Second Temple destroyed? Because of sinat chinam,
> senseless hatred of one Jew for another.
>
> —Talmud, Yoma 9b

In June 1948, the *Altalena* arrived off the coast of Tel Aviv carrying a massive Zionist arms shipment of 5,000 rifles, 250 machine guns, and 5 million bullets, the exact items that David Ben-Gurion, Zionist leader, had noted one month earlier would be essential to defeating the Palestinians and their Arab allies. Instead of offloading the sorely needed weapons and using them in the ongoing war for the future of the state of Israel, the newly formed Israel Defense Forces (IDF) sunk the *Altalena* on Ben-Gurion's orders.[1] Why did the nascent Israeli army use its only heavy gun battery not to bombard enemy Arab forces but, rather, to sink the Zionist ship while most of the arms were still on it? Were not those weapons the exact thing that Ben-Gurion claimed the Zionists needed to win the war for their state?[2]

And how exactly did the Zionists win that war anyway, given that they lacked certain advantages that existing theories suggest are essential to victory? In the period just before and after the sinking of the *Altalena*, how was it that a Zionist population that owned 7% of the Palestine Mandate and represented 37% of its population was given 55% of the territory by the United Nations and then proceeded to defeat a Palestinian national movement that was backed by a population twice that size that also controlled more territory, held the high ground, and was supported by significant armies from five neighboring Arab states?

The answer to these puzzles demonstrates the explanatory power of Movement Structure Theory. From the perspective of Ben-Gurion and Mapai (his political party), the most important consideration was not the total strength of the Zionist movement and the Israeli state but, rather, the balance of power within it. As such, the key determination was not whether the arms on the *Altalena* would significantly improve the arsenal of the Zionist forces—they indisputably would—but, rather, which armed groups would receive the weapons and which political groups would receive the credit. Because the *Altalena* was an operation of the rival Irgun, Ben-Gurion was concerned—and Menachem Begin, Irgun leader, was hopeful—that the Irgun would receive both the arms and the credit, and so become a viable military and political challenger to the IDF and Mapai in the nascent Israeli state.

As for the international arena and the ongoing war against the Palestinians and the Arab states, the hegemonic Mapai was able to present United Nations delegations with a clear message of the need for a Jewish state and the willingness to accept less than maximal boundaries, while the fragmented Palestinians viewed the United Nations with distrust and rejected the plan for a smaller-than-envisioned Palestinian state. The story was similar on the battlefield: the hegemonic Zionist forces defeated fragmented Palestinian armed groups and Arab armies with a cohesive effort that minimized infighting and delivered an Israeli state.

The Zionist movement differed from the Palestinian, Algerian, and Irish national movements in a few key ways. It was organized entirely around an ethnoreligious identity, and the members of its nation were scattered across the globe in the early years of the movement. This created early challenges of coordination, but it also helped ensure that competition would be verbal rather than violent, at least in the diaspora. Nonetheless, the patterns of costs and benefits for violence and victory were quite familiar, as was the variation in actions and outcome.

In addition to the analysis of the secondary source literature, in this chapter I rely on research conducted at the Haganah Archives, the Palmach Archives, the Jabotinsky Institute Archives, the Central Zionist Archives, and the British National Archives, as well as on interviews with numerous members of each of the armed groups that were part of the Zionist movement.

The Emergence of the Zionist Movement, 1897–1920

No population in this book better represents an Andersonian "imagined community" than the Jews in the late nineteenth century. A Jewish farmer in the Ukraine was unlikely to ever encounter a Jewish shopkeeper in Amsterdam, let alone an Algerian Jewish soldier.[3] Although they shared a common language in theory, almost no Jews regularly spoke Hebrew in practice. Some European Jews spoke Yiddish, and Theodore Herzl, the founder of the modern Zionist movement, wanted German to be declared the official language of the movement. Jewish populations had lived for so many generations in their countries of residence that the ethnic and cultural differences between them were immense, notwithstanding the more similar (if still quite diverse) religious practices.

When Herzl, a Hungarian Jew living in Paris, published *The Jewish State* in 1896, there was no Zionist movement to speak of. Very few of the millions of Jews around the world conceived of or desired the creation of a Jewish state. Most Jews, instead, sought equal rights and better education in their current countries through organizations such as the Board of Deputies of British Jews or the Alliance Israélite Universelle in France. The individuals seeking to protect the Jewish nation were largely proto-nationalists such as Ahad Ha'am, who did not prioritize or believe in the viability of a Jewish state but, instead, sought to promote Jewish language and culture. Even the group Hovevei Zion (Lovers of Zion), which had organized the establishment of the first settlement in Palestine—Rishon LeZion—was largely apolitical.[4]

Herzl's establishment of the Zionist Organization (ZO) in 1897 was the first step toward a robust national movement in that it brought together individual Jewish leaders (including non-Zionists) from all over the world at the Zionist Congress—held annually starting in 1897 and then biannually after 1901—to elect a president and executive council.[5] Nevertheless, it would be decades before the movement developed functioning political parties with a majority that agreed on the goal of establishing a new state in Eretz Israel, let alone a significant Zionist community actually living in the desired territory. Instead, the early years of the ZO involved individuals debating the nature and objectives of the Zionist movement. For example, most ultra-Orthodox Jews were not Zionists and instead believed that the idea of a Jewish state was blasphemous, especially when led by the often-secular leaders of the ZO. The Mizrahi were the exception, but this religious Zionist party nearly left the ZO on multiple occasions over disagreements on ends and means. The ZO also considered multiple proposals concerning the location of a future Jewish state. The majority of delegates preferred Palestine, given the Jews' historic and religious ties to Jerusalem and the surrounding area. Multiple Zionist congresses debated the possibility of settling in Uganda or the Sinai Peninsula, both of which were offered by the British in 1903 (and ultimately rejected) as possible territories for a Jewish homeland.[6]

Even though ZO delegates had settled on Palestine as the location for the future state by 1905, debates raged over the best means to achieve it. Political Zionists pushed for engagement with great powers such as Germany, the Ottoman Empire, Great Britain, and France to secure a charter for the Jewish state—which generally failed. Practical Zionists chafed at diplomacy and delays, preferring instead to take the immediate small but tangible steps of acquiring and settling land, by which they hoped to build the foundations of a state that could be recognized later. The debate was embodied by the first three presidents of the ZO—Herzl, David Wolffsohn, and Otto Warburg—the first two of whom were political Zionists and the third a practical Zionist. Chaim Weizmann and the General Zionists won the debate by 1911 by pushing Synthetic Zionism, which pursued both strategies on parallel, simultaneous, and, for a time, complementary tracks.

The greatest triumphs of the early days of the ZO were the Balfour Declaration and the building of Zionist institutions. In 1917, British Foreign Secretary Arthur Balfour stated, "His Majesty's Government view with favour the establishment in Palestine of a national home for the Jewish people, and will use their best endeavours to facilitate the achievement of this object." Although Weizmann himself was correct to note that the Declaration was "no more than a framework, which had to be filled in by our own efforts," the subsequent defeat of the Ottoman Empire (which had previously controlled Palestine) in World War I and the establishment of the British Mandate in Palestine by the League of Nations suddenly gave Zionists the political backing necessary to significantly increase their efforts at building the foundations of what they hoped would be their future state.[7]

The ZO had previously created the Jewish National Fund (JNF) to raise money from the Jewish diaspora for the purchase of land in Palestine. By purchasing land and then selling only long-term leases to Jews, the JNF helped build ZO control of the territory for a potential Jewish state. From the 1920s to 1940s, the JNF acquired *one-third* of all Jewish-owned lands, making it by far the dominant landholder in all of Palestine.[8] The Mandate itself called for the establishment of perhaps the most important institution in 1921, the Jewish Agency (originally called the Palestine Zionist Executive). Until the founding of Israel in 1948, the Jewish Agency served as the governing institution of the Jewish population in Palestine.[9]

Following his election to the presidency at the tenth Zionist Congress in 1911, Otto Warburg had presciently proclaimed that, after the geographical center of the Zionist movement had moved around Austria and Germany, "It might in the future, which is as yet unknown to us, move to London, Paris, or to Russia, however, there is one thing we are quite sure about and that is that its final destination will be Jerusalem."[10] In the 1920s, the center of gravity increasingly shifted to Palestine—starting in 1921, ZO members in the Mandate elected twice as many delegates as those in the diaspora (the "double Shekel")—where the emergence of new political challengers on the left and right further fragmented the movement politically and militarily.[11] The ZO and Jewish Agency provided umbrella institutions for the movement to develop and pursue a state, but the division among the parties that developed within them posed familiar challenges in terms of competition and strategy.

In the remainder of the chapter, I analyze the actions and outcomes of the Zionist movement from 1921 to 1949 (see table 4.1). I calculate the relative strength of the groups using membership, funding, and elections to the Zionist

Table 4.1 Summary of Campaigns in the Zionist Movement, 1921–1949

Time period	Movement system structure	Hierarchy of groups at start of campaign	Summary of group actions	Strategic outcome of campaign
1921–1924	Fragmented	L1. General Zionists C2. Ahdut HaAvoda C3. Mizrahi C4: Histadrut HaSephardim C5. Hapoel Hatzair	After receipt of the Balfour Declaration and the establishment of the Palestine Mandate, the GZ continued to lead the movement, but new political parties emerged to challenge	Failure
1925–1926	Fragmented	L1. General Zionists C2. Ahdut HaAvoda C3. Mizrahi C4. Hapoel Hatzair C5. Yemenite Party	The movement acquired more land and brought in more immigrants, but competition increased in the ZO in the diaspora and in the National Assembly in the Mandate	Failure
1927–1930	Fragmented	L1. General Zionists C2. Ahdut HaAvoda C3. Hapoel Hatzair C4. Mizrahi C5. Yemenite Party	The GZ hold on power began to slip as Labor consolidated into Mapai; British issued the detrimental Passfield White Paper, which revealed how far the movement still had to go to achieve a Jewish state	Failure
1931–1932	Fragmented	L1. Mapai/Haganah C2. Alliance (GZ) C3. Revisionists/Irgun C4. Mizrahi C5: Unity (GZ)	Mapai became the new movement leader, but fragmentation continued with the rise of the Revisionists, who came to blows with Mapai over labor organizations and immigration	Failure
1933–1941	Fragmented	L1. Mapai/Haganah C2. General Zionists C3. Revisionists/Irgun	Movement messaging and strategy were mixed as Revisionists split from the ZO, the Irgun responded to the Arab Revolt with attacks on Palestinians and British, while the Haganah practiced *havlagah* (restraint); British responded with a White Paper limiting Jewish immigration and calling for a binational state	Failure
1942–1949	Hegemonic	H1. Mapai/Haganah	Mapai/Haganah became the hegemon; the Irgun split with Lehi and the Revisionist Party and launched a revolt in 1944; Mapai/Haganah restrained them, later accepted the UN partition plan, and defeated Palestinians and Arabs in the 1948 War; Israel gained UN recognition	Total success

Notes: GZ, General Zionists; ZO, Zionist Organization

Congresses and those in Mandate through 1935, after which the Zionist Executive was based in Jerusalem. From 1935 onward, I assess group strength using election results, membership, and funding in the Mandate. Not only does this more accurately reflect the balance of power among groups (which was not seriously affected by how many youth members each had in Poland and Germany) but it also allows for clearer comparisons in like areas where each group was competing for votes, members, and funds.

New Challengers and Fragmentation, 1920–1939

THE DECLINE OF THE GENERAL ZIONISTS

Although the originally loose collection of individuals called General Zionists had led the ZO in its second decade, their hold on power began to slip, largely due to the rise of competing groups that increasingly found their strength in the growing Jewish community of Palestine, the Yishuv. Although the General Zionists held the moderate center, they were outflanked on the left by emerging Labor parties, which were affiliated with unionized workers and the communal agricultural living of the growing kibbutzim (collective agricultural communities), and on the right by the Revisionist Party, which pushed for greater private enterprise and more robust immigration to Palestine.

The elections to the Zionist Congress provide excellent insights into the shifting strength of the three factions. At the twelfth Zionist Congress in 1921, the General Zionists were still near the height of their power, taking in 73% of the vote. At the thirteenth Congress in 1923, the General Zionists won only 50% of the vote, while the Mizrahi and Labor parties won 23% and 21%, respectively. The leading Labor party, Ahdut HaAvoda, won the largest percentage of votes (22.4%) in the first Yishuv National Assembly (Asefat Hanivharim) in 1920, followed by the ethnic party Histadrut HaSephardim (17.3%) and Labor party Hapoel Hatzair (13%). At the seventeenth Zionist Congress in 1931, the General Zionists split into two groups that received 23% and 10% of the vote and "forfeited its traditional hegemony in the Zionist movement," and the newly formed Mapai became the new movement leader with 30%.[12]

THE RISE OF MAPAI

The strongest challenger to (and eventual usurper of) the General Zionists emerged from the Labor wing, which had existed nearly since the dawn of the movement but had multiple competing groups itself until 1930. It was then that the two major Labor parties (Ahdut HaAvoda and Hapoel Hatzair) coalesced into the Palestine Worker's Party (Mifleget Poalei Eretz

Israel, Mapai). As David Ben-Gurion, its leader, proclaimed in August 1932, "I presented the conquest of Zionism as the central objective of our movement [Mapai] at that time."[13] The new party won 44% of the vote in 1933 to the General Zionists 23%, as well as 43% in Third Assembly of Representatives in the Mandate to 16% for the Revisionists, confirming Mapai as the new leader of the Zionist movement.[14] The 1935 Zionist Congress cemented the geographical shift in the center of gravity of the movement, recognizing the Zionist Executive in Jerusalem (The Jewish Agency) over that in London. Not coincidentally, Ben-Gurion had just become the chairman of the Jewish Agency, a position he held until Israeli independence.[15]

Mapai won the leadership of the Zionist movement not through the violent destruction of its foes but, rather, through the creation and capture of institutions that controlled the two most important assets in the Yishuv: land and labor. As Baruch Kimmerling effectively argues, "From the end of the first decade of the century, the settlement activity, one of the central collective tasks, was undertaken by the left wing of the Zionist organization, which in exchange received the lion's share of the land and capital for the development of settlements which flowed from outside the system. As a result, the left succeeded in creating power foci which enabled it to achieve the predominant position within the Yishuv's structure—as the bearer of the power controlling the allocation of resources (national capital, immigration certificates, etc.) and political decisions and, as a result, recognition as the symbolic bearer of the central collective goals."[16] The Mapai control of settlement is reflected in the data. The Jewish National Fund established a large majority of the settlements, and Mapai and its supporters controlled a large majority of those settlements: 152 of 181 JNF settlements were affiliated with Labor.[17]

The capture of the Jewish Agency by Mapai in the early 1930s further enhanced its control of settlements and the immigrants who populated them. The Jewish Agency had been founded as part of the Palestine Mandate in concert with British officials, and as such, it was given control of the visas dispensed to Jews across the globe who wanted to immigrate to Palestine. As predicted by MST, Mapai did not administer land and immigration for purely selfless reasons, as demonstrated by its acceptance of lower immigration quotas as long as the group could control the distribution of visas.[18]

In other words, Mapai had an incentive to build up the Yishuv by building up Mapai in that every new Labor-affiliated settlement and immigrant further entrenched the control of the movement by the party. Not surprisingly, Mapai used its power to distribute many visas to its members and would-be members whom it then settled in cities and on kibbutzim, the collective agricultural communities that were the backbone of Mapai and the Yishuv in general. Many of the young workers would become part of the Histadrut, a massive labor union that was perhaps the most powerful

Jewish institution in the early Mandate. The Histadrut was the largest Yishuv employer; its membership rolls contained over two-thirds of all Jewish workers. Ben-Gurion became its secretary in 1921, and the Histadrut was synonymous with Mapai and its predecessors. Mapai recognized the power it held in controlling *aliyah* (immigration), as confirmed by Ben-Gurion: "They (the Jews of Europe) are coming to us because it seems to them that we are the pipeline for aliyah. If we are not—they will turn elsewhere. Our ideology has attracted the youth in the past. Now there is a different decisive factor—aliyah; and they will go to the place that has control of aliyah."[19] Or, in short: "Control immigration and funds, and you control the Zionist movement."[20]

The influence of Mapai extended beyond the economic realm into military affairs when the Histadrut created and controlled the armed group Haganah in the 1920s to protect the kibbutzim and the rest of the population in the Yishuv. Due to the organizational structure of the kibbutzim, their youthful populations, and their physical construction that often resembled military forts in hostile territory, the kibbutzim provided sanctuaries where military training could be conducted in relative secrecy from the British authorities. This aided the rise of the Haganah; the rival Revisionist forces generally lacked such a sanctuary.[21]

Control of the Haganah shifted from the Histadrut to the Jewish Agency in the early 1930s, with Mapai controlling the armed organization throughout. The Haganah can thus be treated as a single significant group along with Mapai because "The Haganah was a disciplined underground. Its members obeyed their military commanders and the Yishuv's elected political leadership."[22] Unfortunately for the movement, splits in the Haganah and the creation of rival Revisionist institutions meant that the leadership of Mapai would not go unchallenged.

THE RISE OF THE REVISIONISTS

It was actually the Revisionists and their founder, Vladimir Jabotinsky, who first targeted and moved to replace Weizmann and the General Zionists as the leaders of the Zionist movement.[23] Jabotinsky and the Revisionists had a decent relationship with Labor into the early 1920s, but things soured after they became rivals for movement leadership.[24] The Revisionist Party (Berit Ha-Zohar) captured 7% of the vote at the 1929 Zionist Congress but 21% in 1931, putting it within striking distance of the General Zionists and Mapai. After finishing with over one-third of the vote of Mapai in the 1931 National Assembly and nearly one-third of the vote of Mapai at the 1933 Zionist Congress, the Revisionists cemented their position as an autonomous challenger by withdrawing from the ZO and forming the competing National Zionist Organization (NZO) in 1935. Revisionist-minded leaders had previously formed the National Labor Federation as an alternative to the Histadrut in 1934, the Irgun Zvai Leumi as an alternative to the Haganah in 1931, and the Betar youth organization in 1923.

Although these institutions were developed separately, they were soon all under the control of a centralized Revisionist leadership.[25] The Revisionists unsuccessfully made requests to the British Mandate government to give them visa certificates directly because the Jewish Agency discriminated against them and favored Mapai supporters and workers.[26] Ben-Gurion ultimately agreed to a pact with Jabotinsky that gave the Revisionists 25% of the certificates, which was clearly less than—although just within a third of—Mapai.[27] This ratio did not hold up after the creation of the NZO in 1935, and the Revisionists turned to illegal immigration to grow the Yishuv and, just as important, their own strength in the region. The group brought in 40% of the illegal immigrants arriving by sea in the late 1930s.[28] Although the Revisionist and Irgun leadership often claimed that their actions were not political or designed to increase the strength of their group, they focused on immigration from their strongholds in Poland and from Betar, the Revisionist youth organization that provided many recruits for the Irgun. Whether this was simply in response to the similarly discriminatory Mapai policies or not, it was clear that both sides used immigration and settlement in attempts to increase their strength in the movement.

Mapai and the General Zionists had reason to see the Revisionists as a rising challenger. During the Fourth and Fifth Aliyahs of the late 1920s and 1930s, hundreds of thousands of Jewish immigrants arrived from Central Europe, in part due to increased U.S. restrictions on immigration and the rise of Nazism. These new immigrants, many of whom were from Poland and Germany, included merchants and members of the middle class who settled in the cities and were more amenable to the Revisionists than the socialism of Mapai.[29] This growth of the Revisionist base and the uncertainty of the origin and size of future waves of aliyah inspired many Revisionists to dream of taking over the Zionist leadership in the near future.

While the power shifts of the 1930s may have heartened supporters on the left and right, the associated fragmentation set the stage for problems predicted by MST: violence employed by challengers met with attempted restraint by leaders, all while mixed signaling contributed to some of the greatest strategic setbacks of the movement.

THE FRAGMENTED ZIONIST RESPONSE TO THE ARAB REVOLT

A war of words between Revisionists and Mapai escalated in the 1930s with the Mapai platform for the seventeenth Zionist Congress calling to avoid "any coalition that includes circles of a Hitlerist outlook" (meaning the Revisionists) and Jabotinsky publishing articles such as "Red Swastikas" that castigated Mapai. The Mapai dominance of Yishuv labor led to violence and direct clashes between the groups. One Revisionist faction,

Berit ha-Biryonim (Covenant of Thugs), focused its anger on Mapai rather than on the Arabs or British and openly sanctioned attacks against political enemies to attract youths to the Revisionist banner.[30] This culminated in the 1933 murder of Chaim Arlosoroff, a Mapai member and the political director of the Jewish Agency, while he has walking on a Tel Aviv beach. Mapai and its supporters claimed his assassins were Revisionists, although this remains in dispute to this day. In a clear example of "where you stand depends on where you sit" for individuals, Ben-Gurion pushed for a violent response to the Revisionists while he was simply the head of a party challenger, but then reversed course and pushed for restraint almost immediately after Mapai ascended to the head of the Zionist movement.[31]

Amid increased Zionist infighting, the Palestinian resistance to increasing Jewish immigration and British control of the Mandate coalesced into a significant uprising in 1936. In the early period, the Arab High Committee launched a general strike and numerous protests, which were followed by a violent campaign against British authorities and, to a lesser degree, Jewish citizens when initial efforts failed to achieve Palestinian objectives.

Both Mapai/Haganah and the Revisionists/Irgun recognized the desirability of a unified response to the uprising, but attempts to unify failed due to organizational concerns: "Jabotinsky agreed to Haganah-Irgun merger negotiations, but opposed anything but full parity in the command of a united military organization."[32] On the other side, Ben-Gurion cabled, "I agree to negotiations with the Revisionists on only one basis: their acceptance of political obedience to the Zionist Organization. Without this prior condition, I will not discuss with them any joint political action."[33] In other words, Mapai and the Haganah sought hegemony, whereas the Revisionist Party and the Irgun sought parity, meaning that in reality the balance of power was somewhere in between. The British head of the Criminal Investigation Department (CID)—by far the best security and intelligence organization in Palestine—issued a report in December 1935 that estimated Revisionist Party strength as one-third that of Mapai.[34] The Revisionist NZO conference had 750,000 voters for its first convention in 1935 (450,000 of them Revisionists), which was within one-third of the ZO Congress the same year (1.2 million), no matter how you slice it.[35] The Irgun had 1,500–2,000 active members, but the organization was built around its soon having 11,000-strong due to the expectation of continued high levels of immigration.[36] The Haganah was far larger than the Irgun in terms of membership, but it remained a reserve force that lacked adequate equipment and mobilized units. Mapai and the Haganah were thus the clear movement leader—as confirmed again in the 1939 Zionist Congress elections—while the Revisionists and Irgun were a weak challenger that was nonetheless strong enough to represent an internal threat.[37]

MST predicts restraint by the Mapai/Haganah leader, and the Hebrew word for "restraint" was actually the exact name of its policy: *havlagah.*

Havlagah called for no attacks on British forces and no offensive attacks against Palestinians. Mapai and the Haganah, instead, worked hand in hand with the British, providing police forces while attempting to restrain large attacks on Palestinians. This policy complemented the attempts of Mapai and the Haganah to curry favor with the British via the Jewish Agency, which had facilitated Jewish land purchases and immigration. Of course, such cooperation had also yielded the organizational leadership of Mapai in the Yishuv, which the leftists celebrated and the Revisionists detested.

There is no doubt that members of both the Haganah and Irgun were angered by the Palestinian attacks and wanted to strike back. The difference was that, while the Haganah was reluctant to destabilize the status quo and risk its beneficial relationship with the British, the Irgun did not have many settlements, certificates, or a strong relationship with the British to lose and so was willing to engage in riskier, more violent behavior.

In a direct counter to the Haganah policy of *havlagah*, Jabotinsky, the Revisionist leader, sent out a directive in April 1937 saying, "If there is a tendency to attack Jews as well, don't restrain yourselves."[38] The first Irgun attacks came in September 1937, when the Irgun killed a number of Arab civilians. The Irgun attacked in part due to desires to demonstrate its strength after some of its members (re)joined the Haganah and to prevent the potential partition of the Mandate.[39] More attacks followed on November 11, 1937, when the group killed two Palestinians and wounded five near a bus station in Jerusalem. Numerous simultaneous attacks on Palestinian targets three days later confirmed the commitment of Irgun to the use of violence, often against civilian targets.[40] On July 6, 1938, Irgun members dressed as Palestinians placed bombs in the Palestinian market of Haifa, killing twenty-one and wounding fifty-two. Another bomb in the same market on July 25 killed at least thirty-nine Palestinians and wounded at least seventy. On August 26, a bomb in the Jaffa marketplace killed twenty-four Palestinians and wounded thirty-nine.[41] As Yitshaq Ben-Ami, an Irgun member, describes, "When Arabs threw a bomb from the Jaffa-Lydda train passing through Tel Aviv, several unit commanders sprayed the train with automatic gunfire the following day."[42]

In response to the Irgun attacks, the Mapai-led Jewish Agency issued proclamations signed by hundreds of Zionist leaders, that stated, "Let the Yishuv unite to defend the national homeland from the terrorists from within, as from the enemies from without." These proclamations also claimed that the Irgun aimed "not to fight the Mandatory power but to weaken the Yishuv . . . to take over its control."[43] Weizmann wrote from London that he supported *havlagah* and that the Irgun terror tactics were severely undermining the moral legitimacy of Yishuv, and with it, its prospects for support, legal rights, and defense.[44]

Lest we think that such claims were designed only for public or British consumption, Eliyahu Golomb, a Haganah leader, told Irgun leaders in private discussions, "We are interested primarily that you cease those actions that increase the power of gangs in the country and that diminish the power of our actions and the force of our political and real demands against the government of this land and the world."[45] Denunciations and verbal attempts at restraint were not enough to stop the Irgun or the increasing flow of Haganah members to its banner, however. Without taking clear action, the Haganah would have weakened further and perhaps have been surpassed by the Irgun. Instead, the Haganah took three key steps that built its strength while fending off the Irgun challenge.

First, as the man who led the Irgun split in 1931 explains, the Haganah changed "from being a passive defense organization to an actual military organization" with the creation of active, elite commando units in 1937–1938. This signal helped convince half of the former members who had split in 1931 to return to the Haganah, including Avraham Tehomi himself.[46]

Second, these commando units, which had 1,500 members by 1938, launched raids on Palestinian armed groups and their bases of operation under the command of Orde Wingate, a British officer.[47] These strikes were perfectly designed to achieve all of the Haganah goals simultaneously. First, they not only maintained but also strengthened its relationship with the British. Second, they strengthened the organization because the British funded, trained, and armed the units—as well as thousands of Jewish Settlement Police—which also happened to largely be Haganah members. Third, they demonstrated the ability of the Haganah to provide security for the Yishuv. Fourth, they did all this while maintaining the policy of *havlagah*. *Havlagah* is sometimes misrepresented as "nonviolence," but for the Haganah it meant pursuing what its base and the British recognized as acceptable, defensive violence. Unlike the Irgun, the Haganah was not attacking the British, and when it attacked the Palestinians, it did not put bombs in movie theaters and marketplaces to escalate the situation. This strategy yielded comparative legitimacy and support for the group in the Yishuv and internationally.

Furthermore, the Haganah continued to outbid the Irgun the best way it could: not with increasingly extreme violence but with increased settlement construction into more and more remote areas dominated by Arabs. When asked by Shimon Yunitzman, an Irgun leader, what the answer of Haganah to the Arab Revolt was, Golomb responded "Hanita," a new settlement in northern Galilee that pioneered the tower and stockade model. That Hanita was designed more as an outbid was clear from its poor soil and the fact that it was staffed entirely by Haganah members for the first six months, after which time the actual settlers started to arrive.[48] This type of fortified settlement continued to provide land to Jewish civilians while also expanding military control of the territory. Mapai and the Haganah proceeded to build fifty-seven such settlements during the Arab Revolt, which exploited a loophole the British had created by severely constraining new settlement construction except for "defensive" purposes.[49]

Fragmentation of the movement meant that, although the Haganah and Mapai acted as the movement leader, they were not the dominant hegemon they would be in future years that was confident enough to crack down broadly on the Irgun without concerns for public backlash.[50] Indeed, Raziel wrote to Jabotinsky in March 1939, "Gone are the days when we should negotiate with [Haganah]. We will not agree to fifty percent. . . . We will only agree to 'swallow' [Haganah] . . . and today such swallowing is not far from reality; that's what scares Mr. Ben Zvi and his friends and that's why they come with offers to preempt and swallow us, with the assumption that the Etzel [Irgun] is dumb enough in order to agree to this."[51] By 1939, the Irgun not only continued to attack Palestinians in movie theaters and coffee shops, but they also began to target and kill policemen and British intelligence members, which inspired greater crackdowns by the British on all Zionist armed groups.[52]

The fragmentation of the Zionist movement and its subsequent divided strategy contributed to the British issuing a damaging White Paper in 1939 that limited Jewish immigration to 75,000 over five years to maintain a Jewish population that was only one-third of the total in the Mandate. Furthermore, the White Paper proposed a binational state of Jews and (more populous) Arabs in Palestine, with political power proportional to population, rather than a partitioned Jewish state. This was to be the basis for British policy until 1948, and it was the biggest diplomatic disaster to befall the Zionist movement to that point. The specter of World War II and the British desire to placate the Palestinians also played a key role in the content of the White Paper—although Germany did not invade Poland until many months later—but the fragmented Zionist response had helped spur the unrest that inspired it and weakened diplomatic efforts to shape it.

Ironically, the White Paper proved to be less of a catastrophe for the Zionist movement than it might have been due to the similarly fragmented state of the Palestinian national movement. The Nashashibis supported the paper, but the Arab High Committee, led by their rival, the Husseinis, rejected it, in part because—as MST suggests—the paper did not place Mufti Haj Amin al-Husseini at the helm of a new Palestinian state.[53] This divided response and ultimate rejection by the main Palestinian political body gave the British little incentive to work with the Palestinians to implement many of the changes suggested by the White Paper. As a result, the Palestinian national movement squandered a potential major strategic gain, which softened the blow of the White Paper to the Zionists, who subsequently shifted to internal hegemony during one of the most difficult periods in their history.

The Rise of a Hegemon, 1940–1945

World War II and the Holocaust represented the darkest times for the Zionist movement—and perhaps even the vast history of the Jewish people. Six million Jews, one-third of the total Jewish population in the world, were killed in the largest genocide of the twentieth century. The scale of such death can make assessments of political success and failure seem inconsequential by comparison. Nonetheless, the pioneers of the Zionist movement felt that their project now had more of a purpose than ever as they sought both to take in the hundreds of thousands of Jewish refugees from the conflict and found a state to ensure that the Jewish population would never be so vulnerable again.

For his part, Ben-Gurion argued the counterfactual that "Had partition [referring to the 1937 Peel Commission partition plan] been carried out, the history of our people would have been different and six million Jews in Europe would not have been killed—most of them would be in Israel."[54] Fragmentation during the Arab Revolt had prevented the Zionists from accepting the plan and pushing for its implementation, despite Ben-Gurion's best efforts to do so. Soon after, during the darkest hour of the movement, came a promising development that would pay major dividends for the rest of the decade: the structure of the Zionist movement shifted to hegemony, putting it in the best position possible to cope with the tragedy and push on to successfully found a Jewish state.

In the 1940s, Mapai dominated the Jewish Agency—now the central institution in the movement—and its continued rise paralleled the decline of its international rival.[55] "By 1940, Dr. Weizmann had practically lost all influence on actual events in Palestine and was not even informed of what was going on," and the Holocaust subsequently destroyed Weizmann's constituency, as well as that of the Revisionists, which were concentrated in Eastern Europe.[56] Mapai's dominance of the Yishuv government-in-waiting meant that the group could be reasonably certain it would lead an independent Israeli state, and it gave Mapai the strategic incentive and considerable wherewithal to acquire, settle, and defend territory to strengthen itself. In a way, what was good for Mapai was good for the Yishuv—at least one vision of it—and the leadership of Mapai generated strategic progress for the movement.

The Haganah had been the largest armed group in the Yishuv for decades, but until the early 1940s, it was largely an underground reserve force with little fighting experience, whose active strength did not dwarf that of the Irgun.[57] The vast majority of its members were untrained and inactive reserve forces, and most of those who were active served in units commanded by the British.[58] World War II helped to change this. First, the British formed the Palmach in May 1941, a crack group of Haganah members that the British trained, armed, and equipped to help them repel a potential Nazi offensive in the region. As the Nazi threat receded, the British tried to disband the Palmach in fall 1942, but the Mapai leadership recognized that the group could be deployed against its enemies in and around the Mandate—the Palestinians, the Arab states, and the Irgun—

and could prevent the defection of Haganah members to the more active Irgun or Lehi.[59] By 1945, the Palmach had 2,000 fully mobilized troops who lived, worked, and trained on the kibbutzim and represented the strongest non-British force in the Mandate.[60] Meanwhile, more than 30,000 men from the Yishuv gained training and experience serving in the British Army and the Jewish Settlement Police, the majority of whom returned to the ranks of the Haganah by the early to mid-1940s.[61]

The hegemony of Mapai/Haganah was cemented not just through its increase in strength but also through the weakening of its only significant challenger in the Yishuv: the Revisionists/Irgun.[62] From 1940 to 1944, the challenger was hit with one body blow after another. First, the Irgun split in 1940 over the decision to stop attacking the British while they fought Nazi Germany. Over one hundred of its members left to form the Lehi—including many of its leaders—a new group that continued to target the British while fighting former Irgun comrades and competing for new members.[63] Some Irgun members joined the British Army, but the group found itself stagnating and then shrinking in the Yishuv once it lost the ability to recruit via violent outbidding.[64]

The role of hierarchical position created eerily familiar dynamics in which the weaker Lehi rival played the role otherwise held by the Irgun, whose position of relative strength in this dyad meant its actions now mimicked those of the Haganah.[65] The Lehi launched a campaign of brutal violence against the British, which included bombings and assassinations.[66] The Lehi members were not shy about defending their methods, explicitly claiming that "terror" was necessary to "bring the Yishuv out of its complacency" and "start the freedom fight."[67] Former members revealed the chainganging strategy of the group when they claimed that "the horse that pulled the chariot of the fight for freedom was Lehi," and "it was the strategy of Lehi to get the other Zionists to fight."[68]

The weaker Lehi perpetrated more assassinations and more numerous and extreme thefts, which included robbing both unexpecting civilians and bank messengers. The Irgun, which was concerned about risking its more positive public image given its stronger position, generally stuck to limited thefts from major financial institutions.[69]

The Lehi may have been a subordinate group compared to the Haganah, but it was initially perceived as a threat by the Irgun, from which it had taken members, weapons, and, soon after, the banner of being the most violent Zionist group. From its stronger position, the Irgun called for and maintained a cease-fire against the British while it denounced the actions of Lehi, which the group also worried would draw away recruits from the newly restrained Irgun.[70]

When words failed, the Irgun demonstrated yet again that organizational strength trumps ideology and past commitments—the group tracked and directly informed on Lehi members to the British.[71] In a shocking turn,

Irgun intelligence even successfully impersonated representatives from Mussolini's Italy and negotiated a pact with Lehi—which were seeking to be installed at the head of a new state—to further turn the British against the group.[72] When the Lehi members later discovered that they had been tricked, they killed the head of Irgun intelligence, Israel Pritzker.[73]

In addition to the harmful split between Irgun and Lehi, the Revisionists were weakened by the deaths of three of their most prominent leaders in quick succession: Vladimir Jabotinsky in 1940; David Raziel, Irgun leader, in 1941; and Avraham Stern, Lehi leader (and former Irgun leader), in 1942. Finally, by 1944, the Irgun itself formally split from the Revisionist Party, meaning that each group was left without a political or military wing, respectively. Not only did the weakening of the Irgun help the Haganah cement its hegemony, but it also spurred a major change in tactics for a group now fighting to survive.

Playing Your Position

THE IRGUN REVOLT

Publicly, the Irgun claimed that it resumed hostilities in February 1944 because the British were winning World War II, but the more important reason was that the Irgun was losing: losing members, losing prestige, and losing any chance it had of leading the Zionist movement. The Irgun had fewer than 1,000 members by 1944; prospective recruits had increasingly opted either for legal, paid positions as police within the Haganah or as illegal but nonetheless active positions as fighters within the Lehi.[74] For years, the main activities of the Irgun had been propaganda and fundraising through the *Mas Chazit Yisrael* ("Israel Front Tax"), by which Irgun acquired half of its decreasing budget by soliciting donations from wealthy Jews and "psychologically pressuring" reluctant donors.[75] The Irgun focused its initial attacks on government department offices, and on British police stations and military installations, while the Lehi responded with outbids in the form of assassination attempts.[76]

Menachem Begin, the new Irgun leader, thus announced the Revolt to stave off extinction for the Irgun and return the group to its former place as a viable challenger to Mapai/Haganah. Members of the former political party of Irgun agreed that the resumption of violence was driven by the desire of the group to outbid the Lehi: "A prominent Revisionist expressed the opinion that recent events were a competition between the Irgun and the Stern Gang [Lehi], the former being forced to keep its members 'amused' in order to prevent them from joining the latter. He thought that if the authorities took strong action and exterminated the Stern Group [Lehi] the task of the Revisionists in bringing the Irgun under control would be a lot easier."[77] Eliminating the Lehi would indeed have lessened the need to out-bid and perhaps would have forestalled a permanent split between the Ir-gun and the Revisionist Party. But it also would have aided the strongest potential challenger to the Haganah, which was far more concerned with maintaining its hegemony, especially given that Begin made his intentions clear later that year: "Although I have notified the Left that we have no plans to take over control of governance in the Yishuv, they nevertheless understand that objective development might lead to this result."[78]

THE HAGANAH HUNTING SEASON

The spiraling violence of the Lehi and Irgun crescendoed when the Lehi assassinated the top British diplomat in the Middle East, Lord Moyne (Wal-ter Edward Guinness), in Cairo on November 6, 1944. Days later, British Prime Minister Winston Churchill, a long-time Zionist supporter, said to the House of Commons, "If our dreams for Zionism are to end in the smoke of assassins' pistols and our labours for its future to produce only a new set of gangsters worthy of Nazi Germany, many like myself will have to recon-sider the position we have maintained so consistently, and so long in the past."[79] In light of such ominous words from the most important interna-tional figure for the Zionist movement, Mapai and the Haganah knew they had to act because they considered Moyne's assassination more of a danger to them than the British.[80] For its part, the Irgun condemned the assassina-tion of Moyne and objected to the idea that the Lehi would drag it into compulsory actions.[81] Therefore, nothing was "more puzzling" to many ob-servers than "the Haganah's decision to direct all its hostility towards the Irgun and not the Stern group [Lehi], which was more militant and was re-sponsible for the assassination of Lord Moyne."[82]

Such behavior—when the strongest group in a movement cracks down on its strongest rival rather than a weaker subordinate, regardless of culpa-bility for an undesirable action—may be puzzling for other theories and participants, but it is precisely the behavior predicted by MST. Targeting the Irgun was the perfect way for the Haganah to weaken its former and potential challenger while still sating the British demand for action.[83]

Mapai and the Haganah thus launched what became known as the "Hunting Season" or just the "Season," in which they fired Revisionists from their jobs, tipped off British authorities to the whereabouts of Irgun fighters, and even went as far as arresting many of the Irgun themselves. By March 1, 1945, the Mapai-controlled Jewish Agency had provided in-formation on 830 suspects to the British—357 of whom were arrested—while the Haganah itself imprisoned 20 Irgun members and interrogated 91 more.[84] The British recognized that the Season was politically moti-vated: "Unfortunately [the Jewish] Agency's lists of alleged terrorists con-tinue to include many persons unconnected with terrorism but politically objectionable to the Agency. This adds to police difficulty in separating sheep from goats."[85]

In contrast, British intelligence summaries make clear that Mapai and the Haganah did not provide information on Lehi members, which the latter (falsely) claimed was due to "the ultra-secret nature of the group."[86] Another intelligence report notes that "It is strange indeed that while the Agency have been prolific with their information concerning the Irgun they have been unable, with the exception mentioned, to produce even one member of the Stern Group [Lehi] of note."[87] Of course, MST argues that such behavior is not strange at all but rather predictable. The Irgun was a larger organization with previous ties to a significant political party, but the Lehi had fewer than two hundred members and no political wing to speak of.[88] Mapai and the Haganah therefore had a keen interest in the continued existence of the Lehi because the group did not threaten them but did siphon recruits from the Irgun, the true potential challenger of the Haganah.[89] This reality became apparent when the Haganah not only failed to repress the Lehi but even met with its leaders, smuggled them through the British lines, and tried to ally with the Lehi to keep the group intact while preventing its extreme attacks.[90]

Even if cracking down on the Irgun and not the Lehi was in the interests of the Haganah, why would the British go along with such an approach in the aftermath of the Moyne assassination? In short, they had no choice. Another assumption of MST rang true: the quality of intelligence possessed by the ruling regime on each group was inversely proportional to its strength. The British had mediocre intelligence on the personalities and operations of Mapai and the Haganah, but they had very little on the Irgun and Lehi.[91] In the first War Cabinet meeting on the evening of Moyne's death, the British prime minister and secretary of state for the colonies described Moyne's assassins as "consistent with their being members of the Irgun" and did not mention the Lehi.[92] The British learned the identities of the assassins days later when they admitted their Lehi affiliation. Even when the British knew which organization had carried out which operations, they still relied nearly entirely on Mapai and the Haganah for information on the subordinate groups. As one intelligence summary noted in February 1945, "How far the terrorist organizations have been disrupted by the measures taken against them since the Moyne assassination can only be assessed in the light of the information which the Agency themselves are prepared to report since, as already pointed out, our own Authorities are without any substantial amount of information on the subject."[93]

Nonetheless, the British were generally satisfied with the level of cooperation provided by Mapai and the Haganah. The dominance of the hegemon helped the movement avoid strategic setbacks in three ways. First, any fears of mixed messaging emanating from the movement were drowned out by the consistent statements and actions of the hegemon. Second, the power and utility of the hegemon prevented the British from fully cutting off Jewish immigration in the aftermath of the Moyne attack because they had to rely on Mapai and the Haganah to engage the attacking armed groups. Finally, the Season did not degenerate into a civil war because it was an unequal fight. The Irgun leadership told its members to hide rather than fight the Haganah, but a failure to do so would have resulted in the swift destruction of the weaker organization.

As it was, a subsequent head of Irgun intelligence suggested that the Season cut the active membership of the group from over a thousand to fewer than four hundred.[94] The Haganah had knocked down a potential rising challenger just as it had started to regain momentum and so prevented a new era of fragmentation in the movement. As World War II wound down and the gravity of the Holocaust became apparent, the hegemony of the movement helped to see it through its greatest internal and external challenges to date.

Unity and Failure, 1945–1946

Due in part to the fact that the Irgun did not have the strength to potentially defeat the Haganah, the Hunting Season did not degenerate into a civil war. Instead, it was followed by the period of the greatest organizational unity in the Zionist movement. As predicted by MST, however, the alliance among the Haganah, Irgun, and Lehi was joined due to organizational concerns, fell apart due to organizational concerns, and achieved no more than hegemony without unity had before and far less than hegemony without unity did after.

Because of the longtime loyalty of Mapai to the British and the massive desire for Jewish immigration as a result of World War II and the Holocaust, the group expected the British to remove the 1939 White Paper and work swiftly toward the founding of a Jewish state. British foot-dragging and continued restrictions on immigration pushed Mapai to temporarily adjust its perceptions of how best to found a state and ensure that it would rule it. With immigration being pulled from their control and potentially shut down entirely—the last of the 75,000 certificates from the White Paper was used in November 1945—Mapai and the Haganah faced the prospect of losing the tried and true benefit they could deliver to the movement and use to respond to Irgun and Lehi violence. Although neither group was currently a significant challenger to Mapai and the Haganah, the hegemon recognized that its inability to deliver aliyah and settlement could lead to a search for new leadership while changing the game to one in which fighting the British was the best way for a group to demonstrate its commitment and contribution to the cause.

Once the Haganah had decided to employ violence against the British, it immediately sought to control its Zionist competitors. First, the Haganah knew that it would face increased blame and repression for the actions of the Irgun and Lehi once it had crossed the violence threshold, so it wanted to restrain those groups as much as possible.[95] Second, the group wanted to avoid any chance of the Irgun and Lehi initiating an outbidding spiral that could draw away recruits and put pressure on the Haganah to respond in kind or be delegitimized.

The Haganah knew that the best way to achieve these goals and strengthen itself organizationally was to push for a merger into their single group rather than an alliance among multiple autonomous groups. Unfortunately, as British intelligence summarized at the time, "Haganah had been trying hard to get Irgun to break up, and to influence Irgunites to join Haganah as individuals. The same applied to [the Lehi] Sternists. . . . Neither of the terrorist bodies was willing to lose its identity nor to fit in with the Haganah proposals."[96] The Haganah was not alone in its desire to maximize its power and control; the Irgun also tried to have the Lehi merge into its organization, but the Lehi rejected the requests of both groups.[97]

With no mergers forthcoming, Ben-Gurion ordered the Haganah to "Invite the two rival factions [Irgun and Lehi] to join us in full cooperation, on the conditions of unified authority and absolute obedience."[98] The groups agreed to form the Hebrew Resistance Movement (HRM), the leadership of which contained two Haganah members and one member each from the Irgun and Lehi. As Ben-Gurion desired, the structure of the HRM meant that the Haganah would not be obliged to follow any commands from its rivals, whereas the Irgun and Lehi could be ordered to employ or refrain from violence, at least in theory. Furthermore, any operation had to be approved by a political committee, which was initially run by Ben-Gurion and Moshe Sneh, the head of the Haganah. The political committee was later reorganized and renamed "Committee X," but it remained strongly under Mapai control. Three of the six committee members were representatives of Mapai or its affiliates, another was the head of the Haganah (Sneh), and yet another Mapai representative was added to the committee as a "consultant."[99] The Irgun and Lehi had no members on the committee, and Sneh's position as the only individual serving in both the HRM leadership and Committee X was designed to give the Haganah tremendous power.

In practice, however, the HRM largely placed a veneer of unity over factions that still valued their independence and would have acted in a similar fashion with or without the HRM structure. In fact, the parties agreed that the Irgun and Lehi had to get approval from Committee X for all operations *except* those necessary to maintain the strength of their organizations—such as freeing prisoners, stealing arms, and fund-raising—which also happened to make up a majority of their activities.[100] This demonstrates yet again the value of the MST assumption that groups prioritize organizational goals, and it was ultimately the undoing of the alliance.

Unity did nothing to change the fact that the position of a group in the hierarchy still drove its behavior. Haganah was the most risk-averse group seeking the most restrained action—such as sabotage attacks against the British infrastructure—while the weak subordinate Lehi was the most risk-acceptant and least restrained in its use of violence, which included assassinating British officials and killing civilians. For its part, the Irgun attempted to restrain the Lehi and overtake the Haganah; as British intelligence claimed during the HRM, "The declared ultimate objective of the IZL [Irgun] is to bring the entire Jewish Community over to its side."[101]

Mapai and the Haganah were angry with the British, but they still saw them as "bad allies" who held the keys to a Jewish state under their control.[102] As such, they sought to send clear signals that the problem was not the British per se—hence their avoidance of attacks on British civilians or soldiers—but rather their behavior. After freeing over two hundred illegal immigrants from a detention camp, Yoav Harpaz, a Palmach member, recounted, "When radar stations were attacked and the Palmach tried to defuse some of their equipment, the British realized the attacks were only in places where they tried to stop immigration."[103]

As for the Irgun, British intelligence noted that "[The Irgun] are trying to discourage the Stern Group [Lehi] from their new policy of action against individuals, with the object of obtaining support for further [Irgun] actions."[104] The Irgun stole hundreds of rifles and machine guns from the British and then later kidnapped six British officers from a military club in Tel Aviv to prevent death sentences on their own men.[105] This represented a qualitative escalation from the type of violence employed by the Haganah. Ben-Gurion was caught by surprise and denounced the operation, which had not been approved by the HRM and Committee X, although the Irgun believed it fell under the exception of freeing prisoners. Mapai and the Haganah pressured the Irgun to secure the release of the British officers, but it initially resisted, with Begin claiming that the Haganah simply wanted to prevent the Irgun from overshadowing the near simultaneous destruction by the Haganah the previous night of eleven bridges connecting the Palestine Mandate to its neighbors.[106] In any case, this was the last straw for the British, who responded to the kidnapping of their officers with what the Yishuv called Black Sabbath.[107]

The British also saw Mapai and the Haganah as "bad allies" because, despite the strained relationship, these Zionist groups had helped to govern and secure the Mandate and the British Empire during World War II. Their previous cooperation helped create a blind spot for the British, who initially believed that the HRM campaign involved only the Irgun, Lehi, and extreme factions of the Palmach.[108] Committee X was entirely secret and left no records, while the Haganah largely lived and trained in semisovereign kibbutzim. Nonetheless, the British slowly but surely received indications that Mapai and the Haganah had a hand in the HRM, although they lacked evidence of a smoking gun. In the aftermath of the "Night of the Bridges" and the officers' kidnapping, they decided to send a message to the Zionist leadership and acquire hard proof of their complicity. On June 29, 1946, they initiated Operation Agatha, a surprise operation that raided the officers of the Jewish Agency; cordoned and searched 27 Jewish settlements; found and seized Haganah arms; and arrested 2,700 individuals, including Moshe Shertok (Sharett), head of the Jewish Agency political department, and David Remez, chairman of the Vaad Leumi (the National Council selected by the National Assembly), both Mapai members.[109]

Never before had Mapai and the Haganah faced such repression, which largely left the Irgun and Lehi untouched (in part due to a lack of British intelligence now that the Zionist hegemon was not feeding them information on these smaller organizations).[110] The British now had in their possession ironclad evidence linking Mapai and the Haganah to the actions of the HRM.[111] As the British High Commissioner for Palestine wrote, "Just as proof that [Irish Parliamentary Party leader Charles] Parnell had approved political crime, or that his party had been implicated, would have ruined the Irish Party, so the Jewish leaders may well fear the ruin of the Agency in its present form and the discrediting of Zionism by the disclosure of the documents discovered in the recent operation [Agatha]."[112] Agatha did not destroy Mapai and the Haganah by a long shot, but the arrest of many of its members, the capture of sensitive documents, and the prospect of losing its position as the leader of the movement shocked the leadership and forced it to change its behavior to salvage its organizational position.[113]

Committee X subsequently failed to issue final approval for the next round of attacks after the HRM had previously approved them: the bombing of the King David Hotel by the Irgun, along with simultaneous bombings and raids carried out by the Lehi and Haganah, respectively. Sneh called off the Haganah attacks but told the Irgun and Lehi only that their operations were to be postponed. It is unclear whether Sneh was really trying to kill these operations, set a trap for the Irgun and Lehi, or secretly wanted the attacks to proceed.[114] From an organizational standpoint, the final possibility would make some sense, given that the British had taken many of the documents seized in Agatha to the King David Hotel, the central offices for the Mandate authorities. Although the documents included evidence of the guilt of Mapai and the Haganah and the identities of their members, the lack of Hebrew translators among British intelligence meant that two weeks after Agatha, a top secret telegram noted that "scarcely one twentieth of the papers has been examined."[115] This meant that, if the documents could be destroyed soon, the British might not gather enough evidence to arrest the rest of the Mapai and Haganah leadership.[116]

In any case, the Irgun proceeded with the operation, which collapsed an entire wing of the King David Hotel, killing ninety-one people—forty-one Arabs, twenty-eight British, seventeen Jews, two Armenians, one Russian, one Greek, and one Egyptian—and injuring many more, the majority of them civilians. Not one senior British official was killed. The local and international outcry was immense, and in the immediate aftermath of the attack, the British crackdown discovered and seized three more Haganah ammunition dumps. The hegemon realized that, although it could not lose a conflict to the Irgun or Lehi, it was vulnerable to concerted British action and that a slight change in behavior could secure its continued dominance. As one British intelligence summary made clear, if the Haganah and Palmach had suppressed the Irgun and Lehi, or even if they had been simply held in reserve, "it would not have been necessary for any steps to have been taken."[117]

Mapai and the Haganah got the message, and although they did not turn over a large number of names to the British, as during the Season, they did kidnap some Irgun members, take them to the kibbutzim, and rough them up, thus earning the post–King David period the name "Little Season."[118] The British understood precisely the motivations behind the actions of the hegemon: "Attitude of Jewish leaders in Palestine will be determined solely by calculation of what is best for their own position and cause. They are afraid of extremists gaining control and their political claims being prejudiced. They have every reason for wishing to be rid of extremists but preferably of course in circumstances which would strengthen their own position while weakening ours. Hence their desire to establish for themselves, as a condition or collaboration with Government, special position which would place them upon a level with the Government itself."[119]

Despite their involvement in the early planning stages of the King David attack, Mapai and the Haganah blamed the attack entirely on the Irgun. Even though the British recognized that the renewed Haganah campaign against its rivals was a "largely political" attempt to improve the likelihood of joining negotiations with the British toward governing a Jewish state, this led to the British backing off further repression and allowing the release of hundreds of Palmach members who had been detained during Agatha.[120] The British did execute Operation Shark against the Irgun and Lehi days after the King David attack, netting at least eleven Irgun members and six Lehi members, including Yitzhak Shamir, the leader.[121] The Lehi put it less favorably than the British in their newspaper *HaMa'as*, claiming in December 1946 that "Mapai today wants only to govern. . . . All else is lies and babble."[122] MST generally agrees, but it was the hegemony of Mapai that made the prospect of a Jewish state more likely and pushed the group to secure it soon after.

Hegemonic Success and the Founding of Israel

For the Zionist movement to succeed required major victories at the local, national, and international levels. The Zionists had to remove the existing British regime, defeat competing Arab movements and states that themselves wanted to control the territory of the Mandate, and gain recognition of their new state of Israel from the United Nations amid significant international controversy. The hegemony of the Zionist movement played the decisive role in all three of these victories, leading to a total success for the movement and the Mapai/Haganah hegemon.

With the return of thousands of Jewish fighters at the end of World War II, the Haganah had become the only major Zionist armed group. By late 1947 and early 1948, the Irgun had 2,000 fighters and the Lehi had 800 under its control, but the Haganah had 12,000 active duty troops plus 37,000 reservists.[123] The Mapai/Haganah was able to continue to control and dominate immigration and settlement, both legal and illegal. The Haganah controlled eleven of the twelve boats used for illegal Jewish immigration, and 70,700 illegal immigrants made it past the British nets between August 1945 and the founding of the Jewish state on May 14, 1948.[124] From January to October 1947 alone, Mapai and the Haganah helped establish thirty-two new settlements to define the contours of the future Jewish state and protect its borders. The Irgun and Lehi released public statements saying such actions were not as valuable as attacks against the British, but the majority of the Yishuv clearly thought otherwise.[125] On the international front, Chaim Weizmann was replaced as the president of the ZO in 1946 by none other than Ben-Gurion. The ZO had long since been overtaken by the Jewish Agency in Palestine as the epicenter of movement power, however, and the final election of the Assembly of Representatives in late 1944 saw Mapai win three times as many seats as any other party.

THE WITHDRAWAL OF THE BRITISH
AND THE PARTITION OF THE MANDATE

As for the British, their reliance on the United States in the aftermath of World War II forced the creation of the jointly staffed Anglo-American Committee of Inquiry (AAC) to help determine the future of the Palestine Mandate and the hundreds of thousands of Jewish refugees from the war. At the time, the British were not aiming for a Jewish state; Foreign Secretary Ernest Bevin said that the British would give up the Mandate to a trusteeship and ultimately a Palestinian state, not a Jewish one. Benny Morris, a historian, relates how important it was to have hegemonic Zionist leadership during the AAC deliberations in 1946: "Of particular effect was the month the committee spent touring DP [displaced person] centers, especially in Poland. Haganah and Jewish Agency representatives coached the DPs and made sure the AAC met only Jews propounding the Zionist solution."[126] When the time came for Zionist representatives to meet with the AAC, "Ben-Gurion banned all but mainstream spokesmen from appearing."[127] The committee recommended the immediate acceptance of 100,000

Jewish immigrants in Palestine and the removal of the post–Arab Revolt restrictions on Jewish purchases of Arab land.

Mapai welcomed the immigration section of the unanimous AAC report, even though the British government demurred. Nonetheless, after failing to get the Zionists, Arabs, or United States to agree to any of its preferred compromise solutions, the British announced their intention to leave the Palestine Mandate on February 14, 1947, and the United Nations was left to determine the future of the territory and its people. Later that year, the United Nations Special Committee on Palestine (UNSCOP) was created to investigate the issue and recommend a solution. Again, the dominance of Mapai ensured a unified, credible message, and most opposition parties—including the ultra-Orthodox, who were ambivalent or hostile to a Jewish state—were not permitted to present their case. The UN Commission delegates were pleasantly surprised by the accomplishments of the Yishuv. During their three-day tour in the north of the land, three new settlements were established with the support of the Haganah.[128] UNSCOP ultimately proposed the partition of the Mandate into separate Jewish and Palestinian states.

The Palestinians rejected the UN plan, citing their claim to the entire territory. The Irgun and Lehi also opposed the plan, in part due to bald organizational interests. As Nathan Yellin-Mor, a Lehi leader, explained, "In the meeting with Begin I mentioned British evacuation as the plausible scenario. . . . I suggested that we deliberate on the question whether, from our perspective, such an evacuation would be premature, as the underground organizations had not come to the point where they could fill the governmental gap that would be created with the British evacuation. Would it not be worth our while, in light of this, to slow down the pace of [our] war, and acquire more time to consolidate power?"[129] In other words, the key determination was not simply British withdrawal but which Zionist group(s) would be able to take power in the aftermath. For their part, the Irgun and Lehi accused Mapai/Haganah of the same priorities, with the Irgun claiming in its radio broadcast that "The Jewish Agency does, indeed, speak of (Western) Palestine as a Jewish state, but everybody knows that this is a phrase for internal consumption behind which hides the desire to throw off the burden of the 'struggle' and to accept in its place 'the burden of ministerial office' even if only in a small portion of a portion of our homeland."[130]

Had the Irgun and Lehi represented a stronger internal challenge, then Mapai/Haganah would have been less able or willing to accept the imperfect deal for fear of losing its leading position.[131] As it was, the Irgun, Lehi, and small leftist parties that also opposed the plan were too weak to muddle the movement message or garner divisive foreign backers. The Lehi tried to court the USSR, which was shocked by the Holocaust and impressed by their attacks, but the Soviets recognized that there was only one

Zionist actor with real power.[132] A Zionist rejection of the plan would have meant a continued British presence and a lack of cohesive international support because U.S. President Harry Truman had backed a competing plan for federalization under British control. It was the moderation and acceptance of the UN plan from Mapai, the Jewish Agency, and the Zionist Congress that changed his mind and pushed him to support a pro-Mapai, pro-Zionist position.[133]

Amid these debates, the Irgun and Lehi continued to launch attacks against the British and the Palestinians, for example, blowing up the oil refineries at Haifa; assassinating British soldiers; sending letter bombs to British officials overseas; planting bombs in British targets in England, Germany, and Italy; and killing Arab civilians with bombs in movie theaters, in cafés, and at the gates of the Old City in Jerusalem.[134] Just as the Irgun sought to pull the Haganah into the conflict, so too did the Lehi hope to keep the Irgun in it. Israel Eldad, a Lehi leader, told his group that "as long as we exist as a separate entity, they [Irgun] have to fight. They cannot retreat, because their men will come over to us."[135] Although the Lehi challenged the Irgun, the Irgun was not a legitimate challenger to the Haganah, meaning that the Haganah felt no need to respond with violent outbids. Instead, the hegemon gained further credibility by disrupting seventeen Irgun and nine Lehi operations from May to July 1947, including a bombing of the British military regional headquarters in Tel Aviv and the assassination of British General Gordon MacMillan during the UNSCOP visit.[136] Mapai/Haganah continued to deliver settlements and immigration while applying diplomatic pressure to encourage British withdrawal.

The hegemonic, tireless efforts of the diplomats of Mapai-led Jewish Agency were crucial to the outcome.[137] After the United States was won over, U.S. government and business leaders subsequently made threats and concessions to twelve wavering states that swayed many of them to vote for partition at the United Nations; for example, Liberia switched its vote to "aye" after it was threatened with a rubber embargo.[138] Therefore, a vote on November 29, 1947, that initially had looked like it would fail passed 33 to 13, just three votes clear of defeat (UN resolutions required a two-thirds majority vote for passage). Not only did the Zionists win international approval for their state, but their 37% of the Mandate population was given 55% of the land, even though they owned only 7% of it at the time. This represented a strategic triumph that would not have occurred under the incoherent violent strategies and mixed messaging of fragmentation. Nonetheless, the vote existed on paper, and the British moved up their departure date to May 15 and said they would not enforce the UN resolution, leaving the Zionists and Arabs to decide the outcome for themselves. The Zionists still had to establish and defend their new state, as well as receive formal recognition of their state from the United Nations. Hegemony was even more essential to these struggles than it had been for the British withdrawal.

THE 1948 WAR

In the First Jewish-Roman War of 66–73 CE, the Jewish Sicarii, Zealots, and moderates killed each other even as the Roman Army was on their doorstep, leading to the fall of Jerusalem and Jewish power in Judea. Reflecting on this period, Yitshaq Ben-Ami, an Irgun leader, made a counterfactual argument shared by many Zionists: "Had the Galileans and Judeans not fought each other and, instead, engaged in proper preparations for the war [with the Romans], history would have followed a different course."[139] During the 1948 Arab-Israeli War, history did not repeat itself, at least on the Jewish side. This was not, however, because the various armed groups did not come to blows and instead formed an alliance amid renewed proclamations of unity and brotherhood; rather, it was because one powerful group cohesively directed the vast majority of the resources of the movement to win its external struggle and cement the dominant position of the hegemon in the new state.

Ben-Gurion recognized early on that the coming war with neighboring Arab states was, as Meir Pa'il explains, "the only real existential threat to the Zionist project," and that the internal dominance of his group meant it could focus its efforts on preparing for this external fight.[140] Ben-Gurion began reorganizing the Haganah into a professional force in December 1946; the local militia units of the group were reformed into twelve brigades, three of them Palmach and two armored. The best-trained Palmach units themselves increased from 2,000 to 6,000 members by early 1948. Nonetheless, at the end of November 1947, the Haganah had only about 18,000 light arms (rifles, pistols, and machine guns) while the Irgun and Lehi combined possessed 1,000 more.[141]

After the UN approval of partition in November 1947, the Zionists fought the first phase of a war for their independence: a local fight against Palestinian and Arab armed groups that continued until the proclamation of the state of Israel on May 14, 1948. The Palestinians outnumbered the Jews in the Yishuv two to one, they were initially better armed, they controlled more territory, and they held the high ground.[142] The Palestinians used these advantages to control key roads and supply lines, and they maintained the initiative against the Zionists for the first few months of the conflict.

Despite these advantages, the Palestinians were internally fragmented: there was no dominant national armed group. Instead, the Palestinians were loosely organized in numerous armed organizations that largely operated close to their own cities and villages. The two largest forces were Army of the Holy War, led by Abd-al Qadir al-Husseini, and the Arab Liberation Army (ALA), led by Fawzi al-Qawuqji. The ALA, which was composed largely of Arab volunteers from surrounding countries, had been formed by the Arab League to counter the Army of the Holy War, which had been set up by the Arab High Committee and was composed largely of Palestinians.

Both groups had approximately 5,000 fighters, but they rarely coordinated their actions with each other or other Palestinian armed groups, and there was rampant mistrust and infighting between them.[143] The fragmentation of the Palestinians and the hegemony of the Haganah were the most important factors in the latter's ultimate success in this phase of the war.

After defending its cities and far flung settlements for the first few months, the Haganah shifted over to the offensive after receiving two major shipments of arms from Czechoslovakia in early 1948, which included 4,700 rifles, 240 machine guns, and 5 million bullets.[144] The Haganah reestablished supply lines to Jerusalem and then conquered Palestinian populations in Haifa, Tiberias, and numerous villages in the Galilee. For its part, the Irgun led the conquest of Jaffa—in part to respond to the Haganah victories—but the vast majority of Zionist action was planned and executed by the Haganah.[145]

The Haganah knew that the Yishuv and the international community would be more forgiving concerning acts of violence when war was raging, and the members themselves felt more threatened than in any earlier period. Amid engagements with Arab armies far larger than the Irgun, the group mortared civilian populations in Haifa, killed numerous Arab prisoners, expelled Palestinian civilians from their homes, and destroyed entire villages after they had been emptied of inhabitants.[146] Nonetheless, the Irgun and Lehi committed acts that were just as or more brutal; for example, their conquest of Deir Yassin and killing of over one hundred civilians in what had generally been a peaceful Palestinian village received widespread condemnation.

In any case, the Haganah victories on the battlefield were crucial not just to gaining military control of territory but also to maintaining and increasing international support for partition and a Jewish state. The United States and Britain had given strong consideration to a British trusteeship over an undivided territory when the Palestinians held the initiative in early 1948, but after the Haganah turned the tide, the Americans and British recognized that partition was a *fait accompli* and adjusted their policy accordingly.[147] Further political success came in the form of the People's Administration, which took over for the Jewish Agency Executive in mid-April as the key Zionist governing body. This organization, which became the Provisional Government of Israel on May 14, was dominated by Mapai. Mapai held the four most important portfolios in the government—chairman, defense, foreign affairs, and finance—and it could easily get a majority vote on pretty much anything it wanted, in part because the Revisionist Party and the Irgun were comparatively weak and had no seats in the ruling organization.[148]

On May 14, 1948, the British Mandate ended and David Ben-Gurion declared the independence of Israel. The Haganah had triumphed militarily, and Mapai had triumphed politically. Still, the greatest challenge facing the Zionist movement and nascent state was yet to come because it would now have to face off against all of its neighbors—Egypt, Syria, Jordan, Iraq, and Lebanon—which were opposed to the founding of Israel on what they considered to be Arab and Muslim lands.

The main problem for these states, as for the Palestinians, was their fragmentation. They had a common Zionist enemy, but they viewed each other (and the Palestinians also) as rivals for control of the Mandate territory. Egypt sent the largest force, but the Jordanian Arab Legion was the best equipped, and the forces of the Jordanians, the Iraqis, and the Syrians were all within half the size of the Egyptians, leaving the Arab states with no dominant leader and, therefore, a severe lack of coordinated action.[149] Attempts to develop a unified plan at meetings of the Arab League failed because Jordan changed its strategy at the last minute—believing the Arab League plan was pro-Syrian—and Lebanon decided not to invade at all. Foreign volunteers could join local armed groups, auxiliaries to one of four national armies, or the Arab Liberation Army. In contrast, nearly all Zionist recruits—which included 20,000 foreign volunteers and conscripts—joined a single group and then were strategically deployed and coordinated.[150]

The fragmentation of the Arab states had direct effects in predictable ways. Not only did divided forces and a lack of coordination blunt the initial Arab offensives in the north (Syria), east (Jordan and Iraq), and south (Egypt), but ill-advised chain-ganging by smaller factions also gave the Israeli forces the pretext to conquer even more territory. For example, when the ALA attacked Israeli positions on October 22 during a UN-ordered cease-fire, it gave the Israelis—who were otherwise hesitant to break the calm and risk losing international support—the pretext they needed to take Beersheba, the key to the Negev that had previously been in Arab hands.[151] By late 1948, the Israelis controlled not only all the territory marked for a Jewish state in UN Resolution 181 but also the Galilee in the north, the Negev in the south, and far more territory in the east, all the way to West Jerusalem.

The single factor that had the greatest potential to change the game (and the outcome) in 1948 was the return of a significant internal Zionist challenger, which could have prompted Israeli infighting, a failure to respect cease-fires and sign armistice agreements, and a shift in the international sphere from support to condemnation and hostile intervention. Such a possibility arrived in the form of the *Altalena*, an Irgun arms ship that brought the Zionist movement to the brink of civil war. The *Altalena* (Jabotinsky's pen name) was originally a U.S. landing ship that had participated in D-Day. It was ironic that it would play the central role on D-Day for Zionist organizational feuds.

THE *ALTALENA* AND THE RECOGNITION OF ISRAEL

The Zionists' reaction to the arrival of a massive arms shipment in June 1948 poses a puzzle: Given that Ben-Gurion himself had noted one month earlier that the delivery of arms purchased from abroad would be essential to defeating the Arab armies, why did the nascent Israeli army use its only heavy gun battery not to bombard said Arab armies but, rather, to sink the *Altalena* while most of the arms destined for the Israelis were still on it? Surely those weapons were the exact thing Ben-Gurion had claimed the Israelis needed to win.[152]

As noted at the outset of this chapter, the most important consideration was not the total strength of the Zionist movement and the Israeli state but, rather, the balance of power within it. The arms on the *Altalena* would significantly improve the collective arsenal of the Zionist forces, but Ben-Gurion was more concerned with the possibility that the Irgun and the Revisionists would receive both the arms and the credit, and so become a viable military and political challenger to the Haganah and Mapai in the nascent Israeli state.

On June 1, the day the Haganah was officially renamed Tzva HaHagana Le Yisrael (Israel Defense Forces, IDF), Begin signed an agreement that the Irgun would join the IDF in its own battalions within the Alexandroni and Givati Brigades, except in Jerusalem where the group would continue to operate independently because it was outside the jurisdiction of the new Israeli state. From the outset, there was significant distrust. As Yoske Nachmias, an Irgun member, recalls, "In the agreement that we had with the temporary government, it said that the Irgun would come to the IDF with their own arms. And when we came there with our own arms, they said 'No, those will go to the stores and will be distributed as we feel they should be.' Five of our guys had one rifle; they gave them one rifle. We did not even have bullets at the beginning, they went to the Haganah members."[153] Irgun units in Jerusalem continued to fight against Arab forces while openly cursing the reticence of the Israeli leadership to take the holy city and the rest of the West Bank.[154]

After months of planning and delays, the *Altalena* was launched from France on June 11, the day the first UN-sponsored cease-fire of the 1948 War began.[155] Not only did the cease-fire outlaw foreign arms shipments, but so did the Irgun agreement with the Israeli leadership.[156] Ben-Gurion was not so worried about violating the UN truce—the IDF was itself bringing in clandestine arms shipments at the time—which is why he did not protest when he was initially informed by Begin of the voyage of the ship on June 16. Instead, the major concern stemmed from a disagreement over the destination of the cargo of the *Altalena* upon its arrival. Begin initially requested (and believed he had received approval) that 20% of the arms would go the Irgun units fighting in Jerusalem and the other 80% would go to the new Irgun battalions in the IDF.[157] But Ben-Gurion—fearing the return of a strengthened rival—ultimately rejected this proposal and demanded that the arms be placed under the full control of the IDF.

Begin pled his case to Yisrael Galili, IDF leader and former Haganah chief of staff, arguing, "Had the boat come several weeks ago, as we had planned, we of the Irgun would have had all the arms. Wouldn't you agree that our boys ought to come into the Army at least fully-armed and equipped? You yourself demanded that in view of the gravity of the situation all arms and equipment in the possession of the Irgun should be issued to the Irgun boys who were going into the army. What, then, is the difference?"[158] The difference, of course, was that the hegemon did not want the Irgun to get the weapons and the credit for delivering them. Begin, of course, understood this; otherwise, he would have not cared about the "difference" himself and would have agreed to the IDF controlling and distributing the arms as it saw fit.[159]

Of course, despite proclamations that he aimed "to fight for our nation, not to control it," Begin was preparing to do just that.[160] On the same day that he told the Israeli leadership about the arrival of the *Altalena*, he formed his own political party—Herut—with himself at the head.[161] One of the Irgun members on the *Altalena*, in fact, wrote hopefully of how "A successful landing of the *Altalena* might give a great push to the ambitions of Menachem Begin and his newly announced Herut Party, offering a serious threat to Ben-Gurion's political dominance over the Yishuv."[162]

The Irgun and Herut were not yet real threats to Mapai and the IDF, but Ben-Gurion worried that with the arms from the *Altalena*, they would be. In an emergency meeting, he explained, "We have ships with arms but Etzel's [Irgun's] ship has more arms. I see the danger of the existence of 5,000 rifles in Etzel's [Irgun's] ship because I know the nature of [its] people and I know how they will use them. We have to remember that this is not war against Arabs but against Jews, and this ship is armed more than any other. Therefore I will not engage it with our warships."[163] He went on to explain what a difference these arms would make: "For if it is true that they have 5,000 rifles and 250 machine guns, then what [the Irgun] do now is child's play compared to what they will do tomorrow. And then there will be two states and two armies."[164] There is good evidence to suggest that this perception was correct, at least in terms of raw power. The weapons on the *Altalena* were nearly identical to the combined size of the two Czech shipments that had so dramatically changed the position of the Haganah just two months earlier: 5,000 compared to 4,700 rifles, 250 compared to 240 machine guns, and 3–5 million compared to 5 million bullets.[165] The ship also contained 930 immigrants—many of them Irgun recruits who drilled on the decks during the voyage—and its cargo could arm 6,000 soldiers.[166] These numbers would certainly not have allowed the Irgun to overtake the IDF, but they would have potentially made it a viable challenger, and who knows what the political fallout could have been if the Irgun had taken Jerusalem, as its leaders intended and as would have been far more likely with the new arsenal?

Mapai and the Haganah had no intention of finding out; they ordered the *Altalena* to land at a settlement full of their supporters, Kfar Vitkin. As the locals and the Irgun began to offload the arms, the Provisional Government issued an order for the Irgun to relinquish control of the ship and its cargo or suffer the consequences. Begin tried to buy time, but negotiations broke down and fighting broke out between the Irgun—including Irgun members that deserted the IDF and streamed to Kfar Vitkin—and IDF land and naval units that now surrounded the *Altalena*. Two IDF members and one Irgun member died in the initial fighting, during which Begin made it onto the *Altalena* from a rowboat.[167] The *Altalena* then steamed off to Tel Aviv, where the Irgun purposely beached the vessel so it could not be ordered to move and would, instead, be visible to the more supportive urban population.

Concerned about troop loyalty, Ben-Gurion pulled multiple Palmach units and one Haganah unit from their positions facing Arab forces to confront the *Altalena*, and the IDF launched an operation to take control of the vessel that was, ironically, named "Operation Unity."[168] The Irgun battled the IDF on the beaches for hours before giving in. Nineteen men died in the clashes in Kfar Vitkin and Tel Aviv, sixteen of them Irgun and three IDF. It was truly a fight between brothers—both in religion and in blood—because Nachmias's brother was in the Palmach units surrounding the *Altalena* (although he did not fire, knowing his brother was on the ship).[169] The height of this seemingly counterproductive behavior was when Hillel Dalesky, an IDF soldier, was ordered to shell the *Altalena*, which he did after Yosef Aksen refused and Dalesky himself initially protested that "I had not come to Israel to fight Jews." His shot struck the *Altalena* and set it on fire with much of the weaponry still on it.[170]

Although the Irgun initially proclaimed that the "unelected and temporary" Israeli government should resign and that it was no longer an official part of the IDF, a cease-fire was agreed to and further fighting did not occur.[171] In his "crying speech" broadcast on the still independent Irgun radio the night of the destruction of the *Altalena*, Begin cited the ancient destruction of the two Jewish temples as he proclaimed, "Never must there be a civil war."[172] Although Begin and other Zionists certainly felt a strong aversion to killing other Jews, it was also crucial that, without the weapons of the *Altalena* and the new recruits they could have armed, the Irgun simply could not defeat the IDF nor even resist its demands. Instead, although some refused, many Irgun members were absorbed into the IDF, now as dispersed individuals instead of full battalions. Irgun units in Jerusalem continued to operate until September, when they were forcibly disbanded by the government—in a replay of Season dynamics—after the Lehi assassinated Count Folke Bernadotte, the UN mediator.

The IDF conquered more territory in the aftermath of the removal of its former Zionist rival from the field, but significantly, they did not attempt to push deeper into Jerusalem or the West Bank as the Irgun would have done (and would have encouraged the IDF to do; in its own pamphlets, the Irgun claimed to be "the Army of Liberation. It has no function of defense, but the function of conquest").[173] With no viable challenger to outbid or chain-gang it, the IDF was able to exercise restraint at its moment of greatest internal and external superiority because both the Irgun and the Arab armies had collapsed.

This restraint helped make UN recognition possible. Two earlier Israeli applications for recognition by the United Nations during the 1948 War had been rejected, but the third was approved on May 11, 1949. In addition to its control of significant pieces of territory, UN members noted that Israel was recognized because, first, it was able to present a single government authority. This was reinforced by the first Israeli elections in January 1949, which yielded a smashing victory for Mapai, which received more than three times the votes of Herut. The second reason the United Nations granted recognition was that this authority had accepted prior UN cease-fires and resolutions, especially UN Resolution 181.[174] The third reason was that the authority had stopped fighting and signed armistice agreements by May 1949 with all of its Arab neighbors, except Syria (which would be completed in July).[175] The presence of a viable Irgun would have threatened each of these elements because the group rejected UN Resolution 181 and would have prolonged the conflict, possibly instigating British intervention on the side of their Jordanian and Egyptian clients. Yet again hegemony helped to head off potentially destructive infighting, chain-ganging, and foreign backlash.

For his part, Ben-Gurion never regretted the actions concerning the *Altalena*. He stressed the importance of *mamlachtiut* (roughly meaning "state before party") and "a single army, a single government, a single leadership."[176] In 1948, he told the Provisional Government, "What would have been our situation if [the Irgun] had 5000 guns and 250 Bren guns? In what tone of voice would they then be talking to the state?" and "Never did the burning of a ship serve the welfare of the Yishuv so well as the burning of this Irgun ship. . . . The Irgun ship could have blown up our military power and this had to be prevented. . . . Blessed is the gun which exploded this ship. . . . When we build the Temple, that gun should be placed near the main gate."[177] His approval of sending a massive arsenal to the bottom of the ocean to prevent the rise of a competitor reveals that the key was not movement strength but movement structure. Critics were right that Ben-Gurion made a self-interested decision that helped his party, but he also made a decision that helped his movement. The alignment of selfish organizational goals with collective strategic ones under hegemony is the essence of MST.

Fragmentation, Hegemony, and Victory

The Zionist movement was most effective during hegemonic campaigns, winning UN support, conquering territory, defeating multiple Arab armies, declaring independence for the new state of Israel, and gaining international recognition (see table 4.1). How do competing arguments concerning group behavior and movement outcomes hold up to scrutiny? The claim that fragmented movements perform better simply fails. Fierce organizational competition in the 1920s and 1930s led to mixed messages and disjointed strategy during the Arab Revolt of 1936–1939, yielding a strategic failure for the Zionist movement. The British White Paper of 1939 severely curtailed Jewish immigration and called for a binational state in Palestine that would have prevented the ultimate Zionist objective of a Jewish state. Had the Zionist movement been fragmented during later periods, the movement would have fared far worse than it did. A more powerful Irgun would have made the crackdown in the Season less likely to occur, less effective if it did occur, and more likely to spark a civil war. A more powerful Revisionist Party would have led to mixed signals concerning Zionist intentions, less condemnation of what would likely have been a higher number of assassinations and terrorist attacks by Zionist groups, and perhaps a rejection of UN Resolution 181 (either through a contested vote or through the need by Mapai to outbid the Revisionists as a tough Zionist negotiator). Begin himself stated that he aimed "to erase the lines of partition," argued that the Irgun should plan to use force to liberate the rest of Israel, and claimed that the Arab rejection of partition should release the Zionists from having to support it.[178] In fact, it was precisely the Zionist acceptance of partition in the face of the Arab rejection that won the Zionist movement the necessary international support for independence.

Had the Zionists had multiple significant armed groups during the 1948 War, they would have had a less cohesive battle plan and less coordination among fighting units, the exact problems that helped doom their Arab enemies.[179] The British were not going to stay in Palestine forever, but there was no guarantee they would willingly leave a partitioned territory containing a strong, independent Jewish state backed by a large majority of the international community. Hegemony made that possible; fragmentation would most likely have ensured a different outcome.

Unity among the factions had no significant impact on the outcome. The HRM may have led to a slight uptick in coordination and a slight dropoff in infighting, but the decision by the Haganah to employ violence drove the desire for unity, not the other way around. The HRM was formed due to organizational concerns, it fell apart due to organizational concerns, and it utterly failed to change British policy on immigration or withdrawal while it was in existence. All the greatest successes of the Zionist movement came when there was a total lack of unity among the armed groups. The key to victory was the dominance of one faction, not the alliance of many.

Even though hegemony was preferable to fragmentation and unity, did the self-interested actions of Mapai and the Haganah not hurt the movement? For example, in May 1948 the Irgun tried to mobilize fighters to protect

Mishmar HaYarden, a settlement aligned with the Revisionists that the Irgun claimed the Haganah "neglected due to factional hatred." En route to Mishmar HaYarden, Haganah fighters said they would help the Irgun, but then instead took their weapons and beat them.[180] This happened in addition to the Season and the burning of the *Altalena*, which continue to anger many on the Israeli right to this day.[181]

Although it is true that the Mapai and Haganah actions that hurt members of the movement without changing the relative strength of the parties were not helpful, the general impact of the pursuit of self-interest by Mapai/Haganah was positive—just as the pursuit by Irgun would have been had it been the hegemon. When forced to choose between pursuing selfish organizational goals and collective movement goals, individuals may sometimes choose movement objectives, but groups will inevitably prioritize organizational goals. Given that political and military organizations are inevitably self-interested, the best movements can hope for is a power structure that will make that self-interest serve the collective cause. The dominance of Mapai and the Haganah meant that when it was pursuing its own interests—such as establishing and protecting its settlements—it was establishing and protecting the majority of the community and the state. When the IDF destroyed the *Altalena,* it served the broader cause, even if the group was doing so for its own organizational ends. Fragmentation was literally on board the *Altalena*, and the IDF sank it.

Even though hegemony drove Zionist success, does that mean that the actions of the Irgun and Lehi made no contribution to the outcome? Far from it.[182] The attacks of the weaker groups helped raise the costs of occupation for the British, and because the movement was often hegemonic, they did not spark much infighting or outbidding. In particular, the brutal hanging of two British sergeants by the Irgun in 1947 shocked British public opinion and helped increase the momentum for withdrawal.[183] For decades, the Irgun and Lehi provided the "bad cop" to the Haganah "good cop," which denounced them and generally refrained from attacks itself.

Although the balance of power inside of the movement may drive its strategic outcome, the full story of the Zionists certainly cannot be told without key international developments. The existence, timing, and nature of the Balfour Declaration and UN Resolution 181 would have been very different without World War I, World War II, and the Holocaust. These events drove massive amounts of immigrants to the Yishuv and fundamentally changed many people's perspectives on the Zionist movement. Nonetheless, the movement was able to successfully push for the diplomatic gains because of its cohesive and consistent organizational leadership, while its victory on the battlefield in 1948 actually came against British-backed forces. Even though the timing may have changed, the success on the ground from Mapai/Haganah's building of a strong political and military entity made it very likely that the movement would have triumphed whenever conflict came.

Moving beyond the movement outcome to the group behavior that drove it, some scholars claim that communist and socialist groups are more radical and violent, but that was not the case in the Zionist movement. The Mapai/Haganah, the socialist hegemon, was the most restrained group, whereas the Irgun, the free-market challenger and subordinate, escalated violence more often. Ideology may help to explain the Irgun cease-fire in 1940 while it was still a challenger; however, a better explanation might be the balance of power involving an external actor. Jabotinksy had initially planned the initiation of a major revolt against the White Paper, but then he changed course once World War II started and the threat of the Nazis momentarily trumped the British. Regardless, the group returned to violence against the British even as the Nazis were continuing the genocide of the Jewish people because the organization was on the verge of collapse.

One might suggest that Judaism led to restraints on Zionist violence. As Anita Shapira notes, however, "Weizmann was the only leader who, without any sense of shame, could announce that he was disgusted by violence"; all the others "claimed that their motives were pragmatic, based on considerations of profit and loss."[184] Meir Chazan claims that "the Haganah's military actions stemmed mainly from security needs," and Ben-Gurion wrote just before the Mapai decision on *havlagah* that "the moral aspect should not determine whether or not to continue the policy of restraint."[185]

It is more plausible that the general prohibition of killing other Jews contributed to a decrease in infighting among Zionist organizations. There is clear evidence of this from the *Altalena* episode, in which a number of individuals failed to follow orders to attack their fellow Jews. But for every Yosef Aksen who refused to fire the cannon, there was a Hillel Dalesky who did. In fact, there were far more individuals who disobeyed orders and left their units to *join* the fight around the *Altalena* than who did so to avoid it. Elad Peled, Palmach member, recalled that his battalion commander told his unit, "'We are going to fight the Irgun in Tel Aviv. Those who feel that they don't want to do it are free,'" but "nobody moved."[186] Pa'il estimates that only 15% of the IDF would have refused orders to fire on the Irgun and Lehi.[187]

When threatened, the Haganah arrested, beat, fired on, and informed on the Irgun.[188] When threatened, the Irgun informed on the Lehi and killed some of those Jews who informed on them, and the Lehi killed Irgun members who betrayed them.[189] Begin himself may have represented a slight individual exception given his insistence on "no civil war," but even Irgun members admit that he was naïve about how his actions were (and would be seen as) competitive.[190] Judaism certainly helped create strong communal bonds for the Zionist movement, but, with some clear individual exceptions, the competition among groups tracked shifts in the balance of power, not constant Jewish norms.

The Haganah practiced a policy of restraint for nearly the entire two decades it was the leader or hegemon of the movement. The Irgun, a challenger or strong subordinate during this entire period, was more aggressive and employed violence against British troops and Palestinian fighters and civilians. The Lehi, a weak subordinate group, was the most aggressive and extreme of all. Diplomatically, the leading Mapai/Haganah conducted negotiations for a Jewish state that the weaker groups sought to spoil, while these same weak groups accused Mapai/Haganah of accepting restrictions on Jewish immigration and territory as long as the leader or hegemon was able to control both. The hegemon, challenger, and subordinates thus played their predicted roles pretty much to a T, and when they dipped their toes in tactics that MST suggests would be irrational, the groups soon reverted back to tactics that made more sense for their organizational livelihood.

The Algerian National Movement

The Long, Bloody March to Hegemony

> The FLN is your front; its victory is your victory.
> — Proclamation of the Front de Libération Nationale,
> November 1, 1954

The Palestinians in the 1960s were perhaps most inspired by the Algerian national movement,[1] which also had ties to the broader Arab national movement and found success just a few years before the founding of the PLO and the launch of the armed struggle by Fatah. Like the Palestinian movement, the Algerian national movement presents puzzles that confound existing scholarship. First, why did the Algerian People's Party–Mouvement pour le Triomphe des Libertés Démocratiques (PPA/MTLD) initiate a nationalist uprising in 1945, only to condemn the initiation of another uprising in 1954, despite the fact that the group had the same leader and the same ideology during both periods? Second, why did the former uprising fail but the latter one succeed, despite the fact that the former occurred when the movement was more united, had fewer groups, and experienced greater total movement strength? Third, if the post–World War II norm of decolonization drove Algerian independence, why was the United Nations unable to pass a resolution supporting self-determination for Algeria—let alone independence—in 1956? And why did French leaders maintain that "L'Algerie c'est la France" and try numerous times to fragment the Algerian national movement and thwart its independence, only to give in by 1962?

These central developments in the Algerian national movement run directly against the predictions of existing theories, and in this chapter, I demonstrate that they can be distinctly explained by MST. What changed for the PPA/MTLD from 1945 to 1954 was the position of the group in the movement hierarchy as it rose from challenger to leader. This shifted the PPA/MTLD from a risk-acceptant group seeking to initiate attacks against the

French to a risk-averse group that actively denounced the outbreak of violence in 1954. The Front de Libération Nationale (FLN), which launched the uprising in 1954, underwent a similar transformation. As a challenger, the group initiated and escalated the war, but as a hegemon—in line to inherit a dominant position in the new state—it ended the war by negotiating and enforcing a cease-fire agreement with its sworn enemy.

Movement hegemony also explains the second and third puzzles because the internal dominance of the FLN achieved the victory that a smaller total number of united groups backed by a more mobilized movement operating within the same norm of decolonization had failed to secure a decade earlier. The French did all that they could to prevent movement hegemony: they unsuccessfully tried to repress the initiators of the 1954 uprising, to prop up the FLN rival group Mouvement National Algérien (MNA), and to create new rival groups via local elections and splits fostered in the FLN and MNA. Despite these efforts, the FLN achieved hegemony in 1958, and as a result, less effort was devoted to internal feuds, the movement received greater international support, and the FLN thwarted French attempts to concede anything short of independence.

Given the shorter time frame of the Algerian national movement, in this chapter I analyze all of its campaigns, from the first time the majority of the movement supported independence in 1944 to when independence was achieved in 1962 (see table 5.1). My analysis in this chapter is based on research conducted in the Archives Nationales D'Outre Mer, the Algerian National Archives, the Centre d'Études Maghrébines en Algérie (CEMA); interviews with movement members; and an assessment of the secondary source literature.[2]

Table 5.1 Summary of Campaigns in the Algerian National Movement, 1944–1962

Time period	Movement system structure	Hierarchy of groups at start of campaign	Summary of group actions	Strategic outcome of campaign
1944–1945	United	L1. AML C2. PPA C3. AAU C4. PCA	Groups united initially, but the PPA launched violence at Sétif and after; AML denounced it and tried to restrain it; the French dissolved both parties	Failure
1946–1947	Fragmented	L1. UDMA (AML) C2. MTLD (PPA)	UDMA and MTLD (re-)formed, ran in elections, and avoided violence	Failure
1947–1950	Fragmented	L1. MTLD C2. UDMA	The MTLD passed the UDMA in elections, but it fell far short of the rout it expected; French electoral fraud dampened any impact	Failure
1951	United	L1. MTLD C2. UDMA	All groups united briefly after major electoral fraud by French, who made no concessions to the movement	Failure

(Continued)

Table 5.1 (continued)

1952–1953	Fragmented	L1. MTLD C2. UDMA	The Centralists squabbled and then split from MTLD; infighting emerged between them while both tried to prevent the FLN uprising	Failure
1954	Fragmented	L1. MTLD/MNA C2. UDMA C3. Centralists C4. PCA C5. FLN	The FLN initiated a violent uprising against France; other groups first denounced and tried to restrain it; MNA later claimed that it started the uprising	Failure
1955	Fragmented	L1. MNA C2. FLN C3. UDMA C4. Centralists	The FLN gained strength during the year and became the second strongest group, while others were repressed; MNA, Centralists, and PCA began using violence in the growing war	Failure
1956–1957	Fragmented	L1. FLN C2. MNA	The FLN became the strongest group, absorbed the Centralists, UDMA, PCA, and AAU; FLN and MNA infighting bogged down the revolt	Failure
1958–1962	Hegemonic	H1. FLN	The FLN destroyed the MNA and refocused its military and diplomatic struggle against France, which failed to find a "third force" and finally negotiated with the FLN for Algerian independence	Total success

Notes: AAU, Algerian Association of Ulama; AML, Amis du Manifeste de la Liberté; FLN, Front de Libération Nationale; MNA, Mouvement National Algérien; MTLD, Mouvement pour le Triomphe des Libertés Démocratiques; PCA, Parti Communiste Algérien; PPA, Parti du Peuple Algérien; UDMA, Union Démocratique du Manifeste Algérien

The Birth of the Algerian National Movement

The Algerians faced internal division from the very first French invasion of their homeland in 1830.[3] The Algerians offered fierce resistance to the French conquest for fifteen years under a number of leaders, most prominently Abdel Kader Ben Muhieddine. Nonetheless, "Though winning remarkably wide support in western and central Algeria, he was never able to unite totally the warlike Algerian tribes which, traditionally, were little more inclined to submit to his authority than they were to the French."[4] The division between Abdel Kader's forces and the eastern Berber tribes in particular helped doom the Algerian resistance, and France had conquered and officially annexed most of Algeria by 1848. Subsequent violent movements that were initiated to dislodge the French, led by Cheikh Mokrani from 1871 to 1872 in the east and Cheikh Bouamama from 1881 to 1883 in the southwest, also failed amid fragmentation among warring tribes. The Algerians thus have a long history of resisting foreign occupation, but a robust concept of Algerian nationalism did not develop until a century after the French invasion.[5]

Even Ferhat Abbas, one of the most prominent Algerian nationalists, did not support Algerian independence during his early years in politics. Instead, Abbas and his liberal supporters pushed for equal rights for Algerians under French rule in the 1920s and 1930s.[6] At the time, the Muslims, who made up over 95% of the native Algerians, were subjects of France, not citizens. They enjoyed few of the political, economic, or social rights of either the French in France or the French *colons* in Algeria.[7] Abbas and the liberals helped found the Fédération des Elus Indigènes (Federation of Elected Natives, FEI), whose members pushed for equal pay and electoral reform within the government to which many of them were elected. Unlike the Social Democratic and Labour Party (SDLP) in Northern Ireland, however, the liberals initially pushed for these reforms as part of a plan to further integrate Algeria into France, not vice versa. Even after Abbas pushed for independence in the national movement in the 1940s, the trend of Algerian nationals loyal to France continued with politicians whom nationalists derisively called "béni-oui-ouis" ("tribe of the yes-men") and the Harkis, who fought on the side of the French against the nationalists.

In the meantime, two other factions were developing additional aspects of the concept of Algerian nationalism. Muslim religious scholars, led by Abdel Hamid Ben Badis, began encouraging Algerians to return to true Islam and speak Arabic along with a larger push for a renewed Algerian identity. As part of this effort, they also began advocating increased Algerian autonomy and schooling because they saw French influence as corrupting. To these ends, Ben Badis founded the Algerian Association of Ulama (AAU) in 1931. The third article of the AAU constitution forbade it from being involved in political affairs, but the AAU did so nonetheless. Often the group tried to organize alliances among Algerian parties, of which it perceived itself to be "above and ahead."[8]

The first organization within the Algerian national movement to support independence was led by Messali Hadj, an anti-imperialist who hailed from the city of Tlemcen in northwest Algeria. While living in Paris, Messali became president of Étoile Nord-Africaine (North African Star, ENA) in 1927. The ENA, which initially had strong connections to the Algerian Communist Party (PCA), sought independence for Algeria, Tunisia, and Morocco, all then under French control. Although the group was nonviolent and had no armed wing, its ideas alone were enough for the French to dissolve the group and imprison Messali. Undaunted, Messali's Algerian nationalists formed the Parti du Peuple Algérien (Algerian People's Party, PPA) on March 11, 1937, only two months after the dissolution of the ENA. The PPA was similar in outlook to the ENA, but it focused solely on Algerian independence.[9] The emergence of a broad-based Algerian national movement was just around the corner, but the fragmented foundations from the proto-nationalist period led to similar setbacks early on.

The Failure of Unity, 1944–1954

After unity among these fledging proto-nationalist groups failed to deliver any progress in Algerian rights in 1936, the movement was united again in the first year that a majority of its groups sought independence: 1944.[10] Disillusioned by continued French foot-dragging on even moderate political reforms, Abbas issued the Manifesto of the Algerian People in February 1943, in which he finally called for Algerian independence. Abbas's newly formed group, Amis du Manifeste de la Liberté (AML), joined in an alliance with the Ulama, the PCA, and Messali's PPA to push for the realization of the Manifesto. The united movement garnered half a million followers as, "other than the [members of the FEI] who betrayed the Manifest and the communists, the entire population found itself in the AML."[11] Algerians argue that this period represented the greatest unity and mobilization among the political factions and the people, more so than during the later hegemony of the FLN.[12] Despite these developments, power in the movement remained divided among multiple significant groups, even though they were united. As such, the autonomous factions continued to compete for power internally, which led to strategically counterproductive dynamics.

Although he had agreed to unite with the AML, Messali had maintained the PPA as a separate entity, in part because he believed his group should lead the movement. In 1945, Messali took two steps that reflected this desire for organizational power and spelled trouble for the alliance. First, at the AML Congress in March 1945, which was designed to strengthen movement unity, Messali's followers attempted to wrest control of movement policy. They then passed a motion naming Messali "the incontestable leader of the Algerian people," a clear challenge to Abbas and his organization.[13] Groups played their positions to a T: the leading AML sought to moderate and restrain the attempts of the PPA to mount protests, but the PPA managed to organize sabotages and strikes, as well as massive processions calling for the liberation of Messali and complete separation from France. These protests sparked violent clashes with the French around Chellala, Messali's area of confinement, and elsewhere.[14] Although these steps did not bring about the collapse of the alliance, the subsequent escalation by the PPA did.

With the Allied triumph over Germany in World War II—in which over 250,000 Algerians served and thousands gave their lives—many Algerians believed that significant political reforms were (or should be) in the offing—if not complete independence. On May 8, 1945 (VE-Day), Algerians turned out for marches across the country, including in Sétif, a major town in the northeast (see figure 5.1). Some of the marchers displayed

Figure 5.1. Algeria

banners in support of Messali and Algerian independence, including one that would later become the Algerian national flag.[15] When police stepped in, shots were fired; it was unclear by which side. What is clear is that, soon after, the marchers—some of whom were armed and prepared for a fight—overwhelmed the mere twenty policemen in Sétif. The Algerians then began attacking the *colons* in the town and the surrounding areas.[16] Over the next four days, 103 *colons* were killed and another 100 were wounded, with many victims mutilated or raped. The French military responded by killing five hundred to six hundred Algerian civilians, and the *colons* organized vigilante groups that killed many thousands more. The police ultimately arrested thousands of nationalists of all stripes, and the short-lived uprising was put down.[17]

As Alistair Horne relates, "To this day, Abbas believes that Messali, in collusion with the colonial police, instigated [Sétif] with the aim of destroying the unity achieved by his Amis du Manifeste de la Liberté created the previous year."[18] Messali and the PPA had partially organized the massacre and publicly called for insurrection thereafter, while Abbas and the AML had not been involved and denounced the attacks.

Nonetheless, the French crackdown targeted the other significant groups as well. "Out of a list of 40 people involved in the Scout Movement who were arrested in the Sétif and Guelma Massacre, there were 8 Abbas supporters (including Abbas himself), 15 PPA party members and supporters, and 6 Association of Ulama supporters."[19] The AML and PPA were both dissolved and their members were arrested—"For them [the gendarmes, police, and the military], PPA, AML, Ulema supporters, and Muslim scouts are equivalent"—and any hope of strategic success for the movement fizzled.[20] Each of these aspects of Sétif—the risk-acceptant challenger launching attacks to change campaign dynamics and rise to the top, the risk-averse leader attempting to restrain violence, the state repressing groups regardless of their responsibility, and competition yielding strategic failure—is predicted by MST.

Had the movement been hegemonic, the counterproductive violence at Sétif would have been less likely to occur. But if conflict had occurred, it would have been based on better planning and support for a widespread revolt in an attempt to coerce French concessions and benefit from any overreaction. As it was, Sétif presented the worst of both worlds—extreme violence in small amounts amid mixed messages of support and condemnation between competing groups—inspiring the French and *colons* to brutal responses against an adversary lacking both the credibility and organizational cohesion to continue the struggle or cut a deal. Worse still, the violence destroyed the unity that had been achieved in 1944 without leading to the predominance of any one faction. Fragmentation only increased in the next decade, to the detriment of the Algerian national movement.

THE RISE OF MESSALI AND THE MTLD

After the dissolution of the AML, Abbas founded the Union Démocratique du Manifeste Algérien (UDMA), named in direct reference to his 1943 Manifesto. The group aimed to consolidate its top position and pursue independence in part through electoral means.[21] Jail did not prevent Messali from reorganizing either; he remained president of his new group, the Mouvement pour le Triomphe des Libertés Démocratiques (MTLD), which emerged from the ashes of the PPA.[22]

In mid-1946, the UDMA won eleven of thirteen seats for nationalist parties in the French Constituent Assembly elections, but the margin was due to the absence of Messali and many of his followers, who were in prison. When the MTLD ran in the 1947 municipal elections, they triumphed over the UDMA, garnering 31% of the vote compared to 27% for the UDMA among Muslim electors.[23] Mirroring the path of Fatah in 1965, the early move to violence had been strategically ineffective but organizationally effective in that it increased popular support for the PPA/MTLD. While still rising, the MTLD had formed a secret paramilitary branch in 1947, the Organisation Spéciale (OS), whose 4,500 members helped the MTLD cement its position as the movement leader.[24] The MTLD hoped its armed wing could assist in the election campaign as well; one member was captured during the Algerian Assembly elections in 1948 with the following note from his superiors: "If our defeat becomes certain, the ballot boxes must be broken at all costs, by force if necessary. . . . A ballot box must never be broken in a district where we are certain to win, but only in places where the outlook is hopeless."[25]

As MST predicts, however, the MTLD became more risk-averse in its new position of power. Messali now resisted initiating an uprising despite the fact that "the masses were ready for action," according to Abderrazack Chentouf, a MTLD member.[26] After the OS was dismantled in a French crackdown, the MTLD, the UDMA, the Ulama, and the PCA united in the Common Front for the Defense and Respect of Liberty in 1951. This was the second time the movement had fully united in six years (see table 5.1). Like the first campaign under the AML, this second united campaign with the MTLD in the lead did not garner any strategic progress.[27]

On the international front, Messali embarked on a tour of Arab Islamic countries, most notably Egypt, in which he made his case for Arab League support of the Algerian movement and for the MTLD, specifically. Not only did he not receive any significant recognition or support, but he also angered many in the Central Committee of his own organization.[28] Some might suggest that Algerian nationalist participation in elections represented a significant success for the movement, but the commission by the French of major electoral fraud in every single contest undermined any supposed concessions to the Algerians.[29] These elections, like those that had involved "béni-oui-ouis" for generations, were designed to provide the appearance of inclusion without any actual political influence. Abbas—the supposed ideological moderate who sought only gradual progress—called the electoral laws a "regression," and continued fraud pushed a weakening and frustrated Abbas to state "there is nothing more for the Algerian but exile, the bush, and the machine gun."[30]

Just as they had in 1945, internal struggles over power led to the breakup of the Common Front and renewed counterproductive fragmentation by 1953 and 1954. The main cleavage was between Messali and the MTLD Central Committee, with each seeking to assert its control within the organization. Messali and his supporters organized a conference in Belgium in July 1954, which ultimately dissolved the Central Committee and elected Messali president for life.[31] The Centralists, who were purposely absent from the July conference, organized their own conference in Algiers the following month and expelled Messali and his followers.[32] The two groups proceeded to engage in reciprocal rhetorical and violent attacks that exasperated the movement and its supporters.

The organization that both was most angered by the fragmentation and put the most initial effort into reconciliation was the newly created Comité Révolutionnaire d'Unité et d'Action (Revolutionary Committee for Unity and Action, CRUA). Formed in March 1954 in part by former members of the OS and MTLD, CRUA attempted to act as a mediator in negotiations between the Messalists and Centralist factions.[33] It quickly became clear that a renewed merger or even a loose alliance was unlikely, however, because each group saw the other as a competitor for leadership. As Zohra Drif, a future FLN member, explained, "The FLN was fed up with the Centralists and Messalists who it thought were simply fighting for power. The FLN would fight for revolution."[34]

Thus, in late 1954 the MTLD and UDMA remained the strongest groups in the movement, now followed by the Centralists, the PCA, and CRUA. Even though only three out of thirty members from the Central Committee remained with the MTLD, the latter remained a much larger organization.[35] The Centralists succeeded in recruiting individuals from the student movement, the scout movement, and the labor movement, but in many areas of Algeria the "vast majority of grassroots activists vowed loyalty to the charismatic Messali."[36]

The growing fragmentation of the movement created incentives for weak challengers to strike out with more violent tactics, while the movement leader resisted such risky forays against the powerful French, before being pulled into the conflict itself. It did not take long for groups to play to their positions in a revolution that was to change the shape of the Algerian national movement and, subsequently, the future of its homeland.

The FLN and the Pitfalls of Infighting, 1954–1956

AN UPRISING BY THE (MST) BOOK

CRUA—the weakest challenger at the time—met in July 1954 and voted unanimously to initiate a revolt against France until it withdrew from Algeria. In a public statement released to coincide with the first attacks on November 1, 1954, the group—which renamed itself the Front de Libération Nationale (FLN)—explained that its main strategic aim was national independence. In addition, the FLN also noted that it aimed to "rescue our nationalist movement from its impasse—an impasse into which it has been dragged by clashing interests and personal rivalry." Furthermore, "We wish to make it quite clear that we are completely independent of either of the two factions which are struggling for power [the MTLD and the Centralists]. According to true revolutionary principles, we place the interests of our nation above petty and misguided personal disputes or considerations of prestige. Our only enemy is the hostile and blind colonialism which has always rejected our demands for freedom, when presented by peaceful means."[37] Of course, it was a bit rich for the FLN to denounce factionalism and preach unity, given that the group fragmented the movement further by splitting from the MTLD. The aspiration of the group to become the leader of the movement was clear when it described itself as "the guide of the Nation and the motor of the Revolution."[38]

Why did the FLN (and its military wing, the Armée de Libération Nationale, ALN) decide to launch attacks on November 1, 1954? As a challenger, the FLN had the incentive to take risks and shake things up in the movement, which it noted explicitly. As Belkacem Krim, an FLN leader, recounted in spring 1954, "I saw Lahouel [a Centralist commander], I contacted Messali. And on both sides it was only protestations of friendship. 'We are also for action,' they told me. 'But we must still wait.' [Amar] Ouamrane [fellow FLN leader] and I returned disgusted."[39] Lahouel and the Centralists went so far as to try and postpone the uprising, potentially until April 1955.[40] Just before the launch, Lahouel even warned his members and others against being drawn into the CRUA "slaughterhouse." Lahouel was "considerably successful" at the time; so successful, in fact, that Rabah Bitat, the FLN commander of Wilaya 4 (province 4) around Algiers, had so few men that he had to rely on Krim to send him two hundred men from Kabylia to bolster his meager local membership.[41] In total, Ouamrane estimated that "there were perhaps 3000 men ready to act . . . armed with a few pistols, poignards, duk-duks" across all of Algeria.[42] The requests for a delay may have disgusted the FLN, but when the group began to lose members to the Centralists, the FLN decided it could wait no longer.[43]

One FLN member subsequently claimed that the FLN "miscalculation and hasty declaration of war on 'French Algeria' unleashed a war within a war between two rival groups," while another observer suggested that the FLN was less concerned with thorough planning and preparation than with the danger of being detected and further delay. This prioritization of goals led to most of the attacks being bungled or aborted, leaving six dead and a dozen wounded from the thirty attacks, which included the sabotage of communications systems, the burning of stores, and attacks on police barracks on November 1, 1954.[44] By winter 1954, the FLN was down to 350 rebels in the eastern region of the Aurès Mountains, which was the hub of the revolt.[45]

MST does not explain just the desire of the FLN to initiate escalatory violence, but also the attempts by stronger Algerian groups to first restrain it and then use it themselves to compete. As previously noted, the Centralists had tried to prevent the FLN uprising and warned potential participants away. Ali Kafi, a nationalist who joined the FLN in 1955, claimed that the Centralists "considered the revolt premature only because they had not participated and they were not the initiators."[46] Of course, the Centralists were themselves a challenger to the MTLD, so their planning of their own insurrection for the following spring is no surprise.[47] The Ulama did not praise the revolt, which they thought would be short-lived, and they resisted calls from the FLN to fight or join the group.[48] The PCA denounced the revolt and "first gave an order not to support the revolution"; then, it later formed its own armed wing after it became clear the actions were not being committed by scattered individuals but a rival organization.[49] The UDMA was not supportive, and Abbas wrote, "we continue to be persuaded that violence will solve nothing."[50]

The leading MTLD, which had 60,000 supporters in Paris at the time in addition to tens of thousands more in Algeria, had previously assaulted members of the FLN leadership. Messali was outraged at the outbreak of violence and denounced it as ill advised, although—like Shuqeiri and the PLO with the early attacks by Fatah—he allowed rumors to percolate that it was his group that had launched the attacks to reap popular support. Ironically, if predictably according to MST, the leading MTLD was now playing the role of its old rival from Sétif, the UDMA, while the FLN had assumed the historic role of MTLD as a weaker challenger looking to shift campaign dynamics using violence.

Not only were the Algerian groups playing to MST roles, but so were the French. The French "ignored the founding of the FLN, instead decapitating the moderate nationalist movement by arresting its leadership and 2,000 militants."[51] On November 6, 1954, Operation Bitter Orange dissolved the MTLD, banned its publications, and arrested its leader and its members (as well as those of the Centralists and UDMA) on the mistaken assumption that Messali's group was behind the rebellion.[52] Upon release from prison the following year, many of the MTLD and Centralist cadres rallied to the FLN, including Benyoucef Benkhedda, a future FLN leader.[53] The French actions demonstrate perfectly the incentive structure for leaders and challengers: both know that the leader is likely to be held accountable for violent action, thus providing the challenger the incentive to initiate it and the leader to restrain it.[54]

Lest someone suggest that the FLN did not anticipate such a result ex ante, Ahmed Ben Bella, FLN leader, recounted, "We knew that, if the situation became really serious, the French government would not fail to dissolve the MTLD and to imprison its leaders. To our unspeakable relief, this was exactly what happened. The government thereby relieved us of the presence of a lot of political meddlers who were assumed to be our accomplices but who, in fact, were a terrible hindrance to our movement because of the confusion which they created in the mind of the public. Thanks to the enemy, [the FLN] became the only political force in Algeria."[55] The FLN would eventually become the only significant group in the national movement years later; however, the initial French crackdown on the MTLD was helpful but far from sufficient for such a smashing organizational success. Nonetheless, the indiscriminate repression by the

French—and the anticipation and welcoming of it by the FLN—confirm key aspects of MST.

Although all groups spoke openly about the strategic objective of independence that they shared, their actions were driven as much or more by organizational concerns—survival and power—even though each group explained this by saying that the movement would, of course, be best served with it on top. Indeed, the FLN explicitly argued that it had separated from the MTLD and Centralists, and had attacked on November 1 to *unify* the movement, not to tear it asunder. In its public and private statements, the FLN made clear that it wanted other groups to join in the struggle.[56] The problem was that, although other organizations professed their desire for unity as well, every group wanted unity under its own leadership. As such, the actions of the FLN looked more like a challenge than an invitation to its peers (as did their actions to the FLN), and the violence against the French that was supposed to unify the movement instead tore it further apart.

As the head of a leading but nonhegemonic group, Messali was not immune to pressure to initiate action, especially if failing to do so meant a loss of organizational strength. French intelligence claimed that this was exactly what was happening in October 1954 and that Messali "decided to orient the party toward clandestinity and put in place a 'plan of direct action' with the formation of 'combat groups' oriented toward terrorist action. This organization was responding not only to the desire of the 'Committee of Liberation of North Africa' in Cairo, but also to the wish of numerous militants who threatened to withdraw if the party did not enter this path, in coordination with the Moroccan and Tunisian separatists."[57] When the MTLD dissolved in November 1954, the Messalists reorganized into a group called the Mouvement National Algérien (MNA) that was reoriented toward militant action in order to rival the FLN.

The MNA invoked Islamic law and prohibited gambling, tobacco, and alcohol; these measures were designed to outbid the puritanical regulations of the FLN on the Algerian population. At the same time, the MNA constructed a network of Messalist maquis and began to launch scattered attacks, trying to convince Algerians both in Algeria and France that the MNA was leading the uprising as the group displayed its "peacock feathers."[58] Messali initially resisted supporting attacks on civilians, but he first accepted the December 1954 FLN assassination of a police sympathizer due to fear that more of his followers would join the FLN if he did not.[59] Indeed, Ali Boudjadja, an MNA leader, said, "I decided to organize military groups to satisfy our activists who criticized our previous methods."[60] By fall 1955, the French noted that the MNA "appears to have adopted the methods of its rivals" and that Messali, "in order to maintain his superiority, applied 'in turn, terrorism in the cities.'"[61] Not to be outdone, the PCA formed autonomous militant groups in autumn 1955 in a number of northern Algerian villages "in a clear attempt to pass the ALN." Called the Combattants de la Libération, the group committed a few acts of sabotage to signal its existence in the struggle.[62]

Despite the previously expressed desire of the FLN to get the MTLD and other groups to join the struggle, when they finally did so the FLN saw their actions as a potential threat. In 1955, French forces documented the FLN strategy of intensifying violent actions to outbid and appear dominant relative to the MNA. This was an attempt "to make known to the Muslim masses the most recent refusal of the MNA to participate in the armed struggle, that only the FLN and the ALN lead in Algeria against French colonialism."[63]

Even though the Algerian groups competed over attacks on the French, they still hoped to unite. The FLN felt that, with the rebellion begun, others would flock to its banner. It soon found, however, that attempts to unite with the MTLD/MNA after the uprising was initiated were just as difficult, if not more, as before. Just ten days after the first attacks, Messali sent an envoy to Belkacem Krim, the FLN commander in Kabylia. The envoy, Hadj Ali, assured Krim that "Messali has decided to rejoin your movement." Krim immediately saw this message for what it was: "That the Kabyles of Krim rejoin the MTLD, that Messali control them and patronize them. The leader [Messali] had not renounced remaining 'The One' despite the unfolding of the insurrection. He had never compromised." Messali expected that Krim, "the little one," "would be too happy to rejoin his ranks." Messali had calculated poorly, and Krim swiftly refused the envoy.[64] In 1955, the MNA tried again to suggest an accord with the FLN, but Abane Ramdane, an FLN commander, demanded not an alliance but a merger, more specifically the complete dissolution of the MNA into the FLN. The overture came to nothing.[65]

It was not just the MNA doing the offering and the FLN doing the rejecting, however. Abane, in the name of the FLN, asked the MNA to join in a series of spectacular attacks on August 20, 1955, to avenge reprisals from the French Army in North Constantine. Messali and the MNA refused to coordinate.[66] Abane proceeded to express his frustrations regarding both the MNA and the Centralists in a letter to the FLN exterior delegation in Cairo on September 20, 1955. The letter urged decisive action against Messali "and his clique" because he "has become enemy no.1 of Algeria. His friends in Algiers have become auxiliaries of the DST [a directorate of the French National Police] and make chase to our elements." According to Abane, "The Centralists do not budge. They are for us but they are afraid to launch."[67] For its part, the UDMA met with the MNA on May 30, 1955, to discuss a merger, but the UDMA ultimately refused, even though it recognized that this decision opened it to attack from both the MNA and the FLN.[68]

FROM CHAIN-GANGING TO OUTBIDDING TO INFIGHTING

The early years of the uprising did not go as the FLN had planned. Instead of the other groups quickly rallying to its banner and the FLN leading a cohesive struggle against the French, the movement remained fragmented and the FLN operations inspired internal condemnation and competition, which inhibited strategic progress. Indeed, the pitfalls of fragmentation were on full display on the very first day of the uprising when a French ethnologist thwarted an FLN attack on the town of Arris by playing one pro-FLN Auresian tribe off another non-FLN tribe.[69] The inability to create a cohesive movement by allying with rivals or outcompeting them via outbidding left but a third and final option: eliminating them directly via infighting and forced mergers. As Abane's letter suggested, by late 1955 the mood in the FLN had shifted to supporting direct strikes against its Algerian rivals.

Because of movement fragmentation and the internal competition for power, the FLN, the MNA, and other Algerian groups expended far greater efforts killing fellow Algerians than they did the French Army or the *colons* in the early years of the revolt. Even when they targeted the latter groups, it was often to capture arms and ammunition, which the FLN especially lacked.[70] Although the FLN ordered its members to avoid civilians in their initial attacks, by mid-1955 they had shifted their target set to include local Muslim leaders and some French civilians.[71] Abane's previously noted request for MNA assistance included an assault on Philippeville, a city in northeastern Algeria, where the FLN proceeded to massacre 123 people on August 20, 1955.[72] Most of the victims were civilians, including Ferhat Abbas's nephew, who was also a UDMA supporter and had criticized the FLN.

Local and international coverage of the massacre hurt domestic and international support for the movement, and the French and *colons* responded by killing over a thousand Algerians in retaliatory strikes reminiscent of Sétif.[73] Unlike the MTLD during Sétif, however, the FLN had fully planned and prepared to bring in recruits inspired by the French attacks, and Philippeville turned into an organizational success for the group, raising the FLN numbers to 1,400 fighters in the North Constantine area alone.[74] Philippeville was therefore a strategic setback for the movement but an organizational success for the FLN.

As Martha Crenshaw describes, after the FLN had killed off rival Algerian leaders in Philippeville or elsewhere the local Algerian population "was then expected to turn to the FLN for guidance," having been deprived of other sources of leadership. The FLN was so sensitive to challenges to its authority that, although "these acts seem to have had little strategic significance[,] they accompanied any FLN policy. . . . The consistency of this type of violence in time and over geographical regions meant that it became a permanent and almost commonplace feature of the revolution. Almost any random account of FLN violence in Algeria listed among the victims a caid, a garde-champêtre, a mayor, or a municipal councilor." The frequency of these attacks increased when the FLN first entered an area to organize it and when rival groups gained influence.[75]

The FLN focused much of its striking power on the MNA, given that it was still the strongest group in the movement in 1955–1956. The focus was mutual; the MNA "made the fight against the FLN its primary objective."[76] The armed wing of the MNA included a contingent of five hundred fighters in Kabylia, which the FLN destroyed in summer 1955. In September 1955, Messali authorized individual acts of terrorism on the part of MNA fighters after the FLN began menacing and liquidating MNA cells in western Algeria.[77]

As Mohammed Harbi explains, "In the conflict between the MNA and the FLN, the desire for hegemony played a significant role."[78] By winter 1955, Abane asserted that there was no legitimate liberation organization other than the FLN and that it would never be a federation; other groups would have to dissolve themselves within it. Many FLN maquis chiefs were hostile to the idea of integration with the "old classes" on an equal basis. As a result, the FLN resorted to a campaign of violence against its rivals. On December 15, 1955, the FLN attacked Ahmed Riani, a leader of the MNA, marking what the principal commissioner of general intelligence referred to as "a ruthless struggle" between the FLN and MNA. This marked a new phase of armed hostilities between the FLN and MNA; from this point forward, "The FLN . . . did not tolerate intrusion into what it considered its exclusive domain—that of the armed struggle."[79] By the beginning of 1956, Abane declared, "Every conscious Messalist should be shot without trial."[80]

In the first two years of the revolt, the FLN killed 6,352 Muslim civilians compared to only 1,035 Europeans civilians and far fewer French soldiers.[81] In subsequent years, French Interior Ministry statistics note that attacks in France killed 3,889 Algerians as a result of FLN-MNA violence, compared to only 219 non-Algerian French.[82] In addition to the nearly 4,000 killed in France, Benjamin Stora claims 5,000–10,000 Algerians were killed in Algeria due to FLN-MNA infighting, compared to 2,788 French civilians killed in terrorist attacks during entire war.[83]

The discrepancy was not just quantitative. Many of the worst FLN atrocities were against its internal enemies, which often hurt domestic and international support while destroying potential movement resources. From 1954 to 1956, attempts to rectify this image problem on the diplomatic front largely failed because movement fragmentation made it impossible to deliver a clear, cohesive message. While the FLN was trying to garner international support for the Algerian cause among African and Asian nations,

Ferhat Abbas and the UDMA continued to interact with the French; leaders of the Centralists sent their own members abroad as visiting delegations; and MNA representatives visited numerous foreign capitals to smear the FLN and seek support for *their* organization, including Cairo, Tunis, Madrid, and the United Nations itself, not to mention in France, where the MNA was dominant at the time.[84]

Ultimately, violent and diplomatic internal competition helped to bog down the revolt in the first few years. By 1956, the FLN (and the movement) had not achieved the desired popular insurrection against France, a negotiated end to the conflict was not on the horizon, and most conventional accounts argue that the French had reclaimed the initiative militarily. Despite these seemingly dark signs, by late 1956 and early 1957 the FLN strategy finally began to bear fruit internally. The structure of the national movement began to shift significantly toward hegemony for the first time, putting it—and the FLN—in position for victory.

Fighting to Hegemony, 1956–1958

In addition to outbidding and infighting with other Algerian groups, the FLN faced increasingly harsh French repression in 1954–1956 as it transitioned from unknown challenger to movement leader. Nonetheless, the FLN was able to survive and began to tip the balance of power in its favor, both by inspiring new recruits and by augmenting its forces with those of its competitors. Mohammed Ali Haroun, a lawyer in Algiers in 1954, joined the FLN in 1955 after being inspired by its attacks and claimed that the FLN was the only group that could negotiate independence.[85] Zohra Drif, one of the few Algerian students attending the Law School at the University of Algiers, believed that the FLN was clearly leading the charge for independence, which made her choice to select the group an easy one once she decided to get involved.[86] Its increased popularity by summer 1955 meant that the FLN expanded, with recruitment from the Algerian underground led by Saadi Yacef, who was responsible for armed groups in the Casbah.[87] In general, the FLN struck a wise balance, working to integrate Algerians of all ethnicities, religions, and ideologies—as long as they were nationalist— who agreed to be absorbed into the FLN as individuals, not as allied groups. By mid-1956, the FLN had absorbed and removed from the field four of the five other significant Algerian groups that had been in existence since the 1930s: the Centralists, the UDMA, the AAU, and the PCA.

Despite working to prevent the uprising on November 1, 1954, many Centralists were arrested by the French in the following months. Although some of the Centralists who were not imprisoned joined the FLN immediately—such as Mohammed Yazid—the majority did not do so until after the release of most from prison in summer 1955.[88] Saad Dahlab was representative of this group: a Centralist who was arrested in December 1954, joined the FLN after his release the following year, and eventually became its minister for foreign affairs.[89] The Centralists' rivalry with the MNA endured, however; the fact that the MNA continued to label the Centralists "administratifs" meant that the French later released some members who had actually joined the FLN and were fighting in the revolt.[90] Relations between the groups were so bad that the FLN had a Centralist in France, Mohamed Terbouche, observing the Messalists for the FLN. Terbouche even proposed assassinating Messali in May 1955.[91] By the second half of 1955, the Central Committee dissolved itself and "recommended that its members join the [war]."[92] By 1956, most of the Centralists had rallied to the FLN, where they took posts with the governing committees and exterior FLN delegations.[93]

Next came the UDMA and the Ulama. Abbas initially suggested that the FLN ally with or work within the UDMA, but the FLN held the line. On April 22, 1956, Abbas dissolved the UDMA and brought its members into the FLN, of which he himself became a leader.[94] After initially denouncing the uprising and warning Algerians away from it, Tawfik Al-Madani, the secretary general of the AAU, began to preach support for it by late 1955; he entered the FLN along with many of the members of his organization on February 12, 1956.[95] The remaining Ulama members found their funds handed over to the FLN in response to threats, or simply taken, and the group all but ceased to exist by 1957–1958.[96]

The ruthless but shrewd push by the FLN for hegemony was clearly demonstrated in its dealings with the PCA. Despite its initial aversion to violence, the PCA had set up its own armed group in fall 1955, the Combattants de la Libération, partly because the FLN had not responded to PCA overtures for an alliance and partly to manifest force in the face of the FLN. But the FLN did not take kindly to the challenge, and many of the Combattants were soon decimated by pro-French forces, probably due to a tip-off from the FLN. In a letter on July 1, 1956, the PCA agreed to dissolve the Combattants into the FLN. Even though the PCA claimed it was maintaining itself as an autonomous body, it proclaimed that the former Combattants would have no political connection to the PCA during the war, and even more important, the group asserted by 1957 that the French must negotiate with the FLN only.[97]

On August 20, 1956, the FLN held a twenty-day conference in the Soummam Valley, at which they reorganized the group internally, consolidated the integration of former rivals, and established conditions for a cease-fire with the French: full independence, full sovereignty, and the liberation of prisoners.[98] The more cohesive leadership included a few previous members of the Centralists, UDMA, and Ulama, marking the clear dominance of the FLN.[99] The conference helped legitimize the FLN in the eyes of the population and led to increases in fund-raising and popular support.[100] Nonetheless, the FLN had not yet achieved hegemony.

REMOVING THE FINAL OBSTACLE TO HEGEMONY

After the influx of recruits and the absorption of numerous competitors had been consolidated at Soummam, the Algerian national movement was nearly hegemonic. The only significant remaining rival to FLN dominance was a weakening but defiant MNA. The inability of the MNA to defend its members from assassination (e.g., Riani) and always respond in kind during 1955–1956 first revealed that "the balance of power is no longer in its favor."[101] In March 1956, although recognizing that the FLN had become the movement leader, French intelligence wrote a report saying, "The leadership of the MNA would strongly overcome the FLN if we allow them free hands." Furthermore, it seemed the MNA had requested just such an arrangement based on mutual interest: "According to [the Messalists], our interest would be to agree with them because they want to solve the problem by direct agreement, without the intervention of Cairo or of foreigners."[102] In any case, the enduring rivalry between the groups continued to prevent a concerted effort against the French and victory for the movement. These dynamics can be seen in figure 5.2, which clearly demonstrates a rise in violence amid fragmentation, followed by a decline in violence as the movement became hegemonic. Furthermore, to the extent that civilian targets can be perceived as more extreme and counterproductive than security forces, figure 5.3 demonstrates that the former were more prominent during the internal competition of fragmentation and the latter more prominent after the FLN had all but eliminated its internal competition.

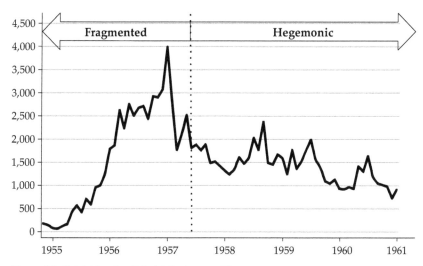

Figure 5.2. Total Algerian Rebel Attacks over Time

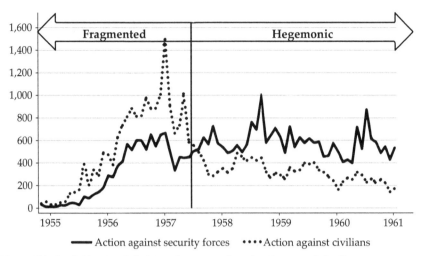

Figure 5.3. Total Algerian Rebel Attacks against Security Forces and Civilians

In 1956, the renewed presence of MNA forces alongside those of the FLN meant that "the Aurès lapsed back substantially into fratricidal warfare, contributing little to the common cause."[103] After the destruction of MNA Commander Bellounis's five-hundred-man unit by the FLN in Kabylia in 1955, he went to Melouza to regroup. The French began to arm Bellounis's 2,000 men in the area as a counterweight to the FLN, an arrangement that Bellounis was increasingly open to after his problems the previous year.[104] Melouza was a town in the mountains about 100 miles southeast of Algiers, whose residents backed the MNA. After the MNA killed a few FLN members in the area, the FLN commander ordered the men of the town "exterminated." On May 28, 1957, "the FLN had rounded up every male above the age of fifteen from the surrounding area, herded them into houses and into the mosque and slaughtered them with rifles, pick-axes and knives: a total of 301 in all, with another fourteen severely wounded survivors."[105] For his part, Bellounis survived and continued to try to rally Algerians to him and the MNA.[106] He increasingly accepted arms and funding from the French, whose security forces received instructions from their command "to make [Bellounis] realize that France is always ready to recognize the services that he could render."[107]

The FLN accused the French Army of being responsible for the massacre, but to no avail. The local FLN leadership had issued a statement glorifying the killings in an apparent bid for support: "These executions rid our region of traitors and provide relief to all the Algerians worthy of this name. They also clearly demonstrate our will to finish with those who do not wish to march with the glorious ALN."[108] In some parts of Algeria the popularity of the FLN decreased dramatically, and local populations sought vengeance against it.[109] Press coverage of the massacre led to more popular backlash against the FLN, both domestically and internationally. The rivalry had reached the point that even when the French killed fifty-three Algerians in a bombing, the European public assumed it was a result of the FLN-MNA feud.[110]

Mohammed Maroc, an imprisoned MNA leader, submitted a protocol of accord between the MNA and the FLN to Ben Bella on June 17, 1957, to "put an end to the fratricidal conflicts that can only benefit the enemy, and to concentrate all efforts against the occupation forces in Algeria (and establish) proper committees to ensure the satisfaction of the Algerian people's aspirations."[111] Although Maroc correctly identified the drawbacks of infighting, the FLN was not prepared to reconcile with a group it now perceived as treasonous.[112] Indeed, on the day of the Melouza massacre, local FLN Commander Mohammed Saïd said, "The number one enemy was the traitor [MNA], the French soldier came after."[113]

By this time, the French were well versed in Algerian fragmentation and the benefits it had for their counterinsurgency efforts. Both the MNA and FLN accused the other of providing information on its rival to the French. When the French knew about FLN-MNA infighting—as in the Kabylia region in winter 1956—they generally chose not to intervene. Instead, the French allowed the violence to continue to better determine which group was stronger and, therefore, which group they should target. A report from the Deuxième French Bureau stated, "This hatred that the FLN leadership has toward that of the MNA merits our attention and it seems that we would have the greatest interest in throwing oil on the fire."[114]

This use of extreme violence against other Algerians as opposed to the French was certainly strategically counterproductive, and had it continued in a similar pattern, this could have led to the downfall of the revolt. But anger at the FLN did not translate into a resurgent MNA or the appearance of a new Algerian challenger. Unlike the Palestinians, who had relied on outbidding and limited feuds, the FLN was able to escape this cycle of infighting by destroying its rival through continued direct assaults. FLN leaders such as Amirouche Aït Hammouda systematically executed high-level members of MNA and integrated their foot soldiers into the FLN to such an extent that when Hamou Amirouche (no relation) joined his forces in mid-1957, he claims there were almost no MNA groups left in Wilaya 3, freeing up the group to focus on the struggle with the French.[115] The Deuxième French Bureau had already spoken of "the practical elimination of the MNA in the department of Oran" after a failed MNA offensive in late 1955, and the FLN had virtually destroyed or absorbed the MNA cells in South Oran by early 1957.[116] Algeria was now dominated by the FLN, but there remained a last bastion of MNA superiority: France.

In 1957, the FLN expanded its violent operations into the Algerian community in metropolitan France, primarily to win over MNA supporters.[117]

Although the MNA had been dominant among the Algerians there since before 1954, the FLN had won the backing of the vast majority of the 500,000 Algerians working in France (the FLN suggested 90%) by 1957–1958 through a combination of violent intimidation, individual lobbying, and natural shifts in support stemming from the FLN rise. The number of monthly contributors to the FLN in France increased from 30,000 in May 1957 to 90,000 one year later, whereas those of the MNA in the same time and place decreased from 19,000 to 9,000.[118] This diaspora population contributed crucial funds to the FLN, totaling 600 million francs per year by 1958. This constituted the majority of its finances and was more than the donations of any foreign country.[119] By 1958, the FLN thus had eliminated the MNA as a significant threat to its leadership of the national movement—dominating it in size, funds, and support—and so created the hegemony that made strategic success far more likely.[120]

BUILDING DIPLOMATIC MOMENTUM

Internationally, the growing hegemony of the FLN ensured that the movement spoke with one voice and was a seller's market for potential state support. This had not always been the case. For example, an FLN delegation approached the Colombo group of neutral Asian countries (including Burma, Ceylon, India, Indonesia, and Pakistan) in December 1954, asking it to bring up the Algerian movement in its statement. The member states refused, declaring that Arab states had to assume leadership of the issue.[121] Unfortunately for the movement, the Arab League refused to challenge French control over Algeria in response to separate requests by Messali and the FLN.[122] For its part, "the French government declared that it was out of the question 'to grant independence to people who are killing each other in a fratricidal struggle.'"[123]

By late 1956, the situation had begun to change. The FLN created eight different bureaus throughout the world—Cairo, Damascus, Tunis, Beirut, Baghdad, Karachi, Jakarta, and New York—that faced no equivalent foreign contingent of UDMA, Centralist, or MNA emissaries.[124] The group's growing position of dominance in Algeria and abroad enabled it to garner support from Arab states, which helped place the Algerian question on the UN Agenda by October 1956. An Arab summit of Egypt, Saudi Arabia, Syria, and Jordan subsequently declared support for the Algerian cause after the rise of the FLN in 1957.

FLN dominance was essential to maintaining the support of Tunisia and Morocco, the two most important countries because their proximity meant they served as sanctuaries for the majority of FLN fighters. Tunisia agreed to continue to assist the FLN with arms shipments, but only if the group avoided clashes with French troops stationed in Tunisia and respected its sovereignty. The lack of any significant competing groups made it far easier for the FLN to uphold this agreement, which resulted in 70% of all FLN arms shipments arriving through Tunisia.[125]

FLN hegemony was solidified with the formation of the Provisional Government of the Algeria Republic (GPRA) in 1958, and the United Nations came close to passing a resolution that same year recognizing the right of Algeria to self-determination and calling for the French to negotiate with the GPRA (the thirty-two to eighteen vote, with thirty abstentions, was just short of the two-thirds majority required).[126] Arab states provided $34 million per month after the formation of the GPRA, and by October 1958, the GPRA had "offices in West Germany, Spain, Finland, Britain, Italy, Sweden, and Switzerland." "Along with the United States, Japan, India, and Indonesia . . . there were some forty-five Algerian representatives in twenty countries," and the group convinced the United States to abstain rather than veto UN Security Council resolutions concerning French actions in Algeria.[127] Eighteen countries recognized the GPRA as the official Algerian government by 1959, which was significant not simply because that was eighteen against the French but also because there was not even a possibility that any state would recognize any other Algerian organization.[128] When Messali asked Habib Bourguiba for support in 1959, the Tunisian president told Messali to forget the past and join the FLN. When MNA delegates met with Moroccan officials the following year, "the Moroccan authorities refused to allow the MNA to open an office in Morocco and reasserted their close relationship with the GPRA."[129]

In April 1959, the FLN began a campaign against "the colonial barbarism that shut one million Algerians in concentration camps."[130] The campaign both focused internally and included appeals to the UN Secretary General. In 1960, the UN General Assembly voted in favor of Algerian independence (sixty-three to eight, with twenty-seven abstentions), granting significant diplomatic support to the FLN and the movement.[131] FLN military and diplomatic actions made this major shift possible, as did the lack of any alternative Algerian party. The pressure on the French to concede multiplied tenfold as their closest allies now pushed them to withdraw from Algeria.

A SHIFT IN FOCUS AND A COHESIVE CAMPAIGN

The shift of the FLN from challenger to leader to hegemon not only allowed for more effective diplomatic efforts, but also led to a shift in the relative focus of the FLN from Algerian to French enemies. Without a significant Algerian rival to challenge for leadership, the organizational and strategic goals of the group aligned: the best way for the FLN now to increase its power was to gain Algerian independence, which would allow the FLN to cement itself in the leading position of a new state. One of the first operations launched amid the growing dominance of the FLN was the Battle of Algiers from late 1956 to late 1957, in which the FLN took the fight to the heart of French control and the *colon* population. The FLN launched attacks against French soldiers and civilians, which were met by bombings against Algerian civilians by *colon* armed groups as well as raids, mass arrests, and torture by the French military and police. As Zohra Drif—who was part of an operation in which three women planted bombs in the Milk Bar, a cafeteria, and an Air France terminal—explained, "Our bombs mark a decisive turn in our liberation struggle. . . . We had to bring the war into enemy territory, into 'their territory.'"[132]

Although it took a year of painstaking effort led by the 8,000 men of the French Tenth Parachute Division, FLN cells in the city were eventually rooted out. Tactically, this was a clear defeat for the FLN because the group had failed to bring the French to their knees in Algiers. Nevertheless, the extreme tactics the French had employed during the Battle of Algiers helped FLN recruiting and disgusted parts of the population in France and around the world. Saadi Yacef explained that "During that period from 1956 to 1957, the FLN grew from having 50% of the population's support to 95%."[133] A few months later, the UN General Assembly voted for a "pacific, just, and democratic peace" in Algeria, and then-Senator John F. Kennedy gave a speech in which he attacked the French for their tactics of repression and called for negotiations with the FLN.[134]

Rather than being an unintended outcome, this had been the FLN plan all along. The group knew that the UN Political Commission was debating the question of the Algerian national movement in 1956–1957, so the group embarked on this campaign to prove that it was the only representative of the majority of Algerians.[135] Benkhedda explained that the Battle of Algiers was initiated "to support the efforts of the Arab-Asian nations in [the] UN and to destroy the myth of Algérie Française, and to show that only the FLN represented the Algerians." In his opinion, "[The strike] was successful." Saad Dahlab and Zohra Drif agreed, with the former adding that the conflict separated the French from the Algerians and provoked the French to repress harshly in a counterproductive way, ultimately driving many more recruits to the FLN.[136] These were not simply self-serving opinions delivered in retrospect. In September 1958, the French delegation of the United Nations ordered up a chart to show the clear relationship between the General Assembly debates on Algeria and the incidence of FLN attacks.[137]

The internal dominance of the FLN did not ensure that it could not commit tactical mistakes—such as the call for a weeklong general strike that could not be realized—but it did mean that the FLN could survive such setbacks, self-evaluate, and adjust its strategy without fear of losing its position. Had the movement been fragmented or united in late 1957 to early 1958, the fallout from the Battle of Algiers could have been marked by extensive outbidding and infighting as competing significant groups smelled opportunity and the FLN felt the need to demonstrate its continued vitality in strategically counterproductive ways. Instead, despite some squabbling by leadership in the aftermath, Benkhedda noted, "The base of the pyramid held firm."[138] The FLN had the breathing room to learn and implement the right lessons from the Battle of Algiers—that it could not face French forces directly in the cities and should, instead, wear them down in the countryside while ensuring that it retained the only Algerian address for a resolution to the conflict. As diplomatic pressure on the French continued to build, FLN hegemony would prove to be the key factor in achieving independence.

Negotiations with France, 1958–1962

THE SEARCH FOR AN ALGERIAN THIRD FORCE

If the first four years of the conflict were about inflicting rising human, economic, and political costs to make it clear to the French that a change in Algeria was needed, the second four were about the French trying to end the conflict with as little change in Algeria as possible. The most important factor in the dynamics and outcome of numerous negotiations was the structure of the Algerian national movement. The French understood that, if the movement was fragmented, they could play Algerian groups off each other and get one to agree to smaller strategic concessions in exchange for organizational incentives.[139] If, instead, the French had to talk to a single hegemon from the national movement, they would probably have to give in to the FLN demands as stated in its first declaration on November 1, 1954: full French withdrawal, full independence for Algeria, and no dual citizenship for any *colons* who remained. The ability of the FLN to foresee this very development drove its uncompromising destruction and absorption of its internal rivals; it had instructed its units to "liquidate all personalities who want to play the role of *interlocuteur valable*," or legitimate negotiator.[140] As much as there were countless debates over the terms of any agreement, the real drama was over whether a significant Algerian group could be found to sit at the table alongside—or in place of—the FLN.

Despite victories on the battlefield and attempts to escalate and win the war to keep Algeria French, President Charles de Gaulle concluded by 1959 that Algeria "undermines the position of France in the world. . . . As long as we are not relieved of it, we can do nothing in the world. This is a terrible burden. It is necessary to relinquish it."[141] Shifts in French public opinion revealed that his constituents agreed. In 1956, a plurality of French citizens favored maintaining the status quo and only 39% supported negotiations, but by 1958, 56% of the French public favored negotiations with the FLN, with opposition to negotiations decreasing to 18% by 1959.[142] Given the demographics, de Gaulle's speech on September 16, 1959—in which he called for self-determination for Algeria—all but ensured rule by native Algerians, although de Gaulle hoped that meant autonomous rule under French control, not full independence. De Gaulle kept looking for an Algerian "third force" with which to negotiate such an outcome, and where none existed, he tried to create one, leading to four identifiable French efforts to fragment the Algerian national movement.

First, the French tried to revive the longtime FLN rival, the MNA. During Bellounis's downfall in 1957–1958, the MNA had weakened from a challenger to a subordinate group. After Bellounis broke with the French, declared that he was fighting for Algerian independence, and refused to participate in negotiations, French forces launched an operation that culminated in his death and the destruction of his unit.[143] A number of high-level defections to the FLN occurred among members of the MNA leadership in late 1959, particularly among MNA groups in France. Many MNA leaders no longer saw the purpose of the MNA and believed it did not have a significant role to play in the resolution of the conflict, given the overwhelming superiority of the FLN.[144] Nonetheless, French intelligence noted that, at least among the remaining holdouts, "The MNA seeks to constitute a 'third force.' . . . Its aim would be to progressively move Algeria toward an independence analogous to that of Madagascar."[145]

Foudili Brahim, one of Messali's most devoted followers, was given the task of returning from France to Algeria in 1960 to equip and reorganize Algerian MNA cells and revitalize recruitment efforts. As part of this organizational strategy development, Brahim cooperated with the French and obtained permission to move in and out of the country.[146] Brahim told the French that "only a strong and organized MNA could fight effectively against this organization (the FLN) and regain control of the population." Foudili expected "absolutely all of the French authorities (especially civil) to support the MNA and to permit it to 'restart' effectively. He said multiple times that this was also in the interest of the French."[147] Not only did the French not crack down on the MNA armed groups, but French authorities also let several MNA "shock groups" enter Algeria from France in spring 1961. The French knew perfectly well that these groups were "killers in the pay of the MNA," that they "had committed many of their active political crimes in the Métropole (Paris)," and that their mission was "to cut down influential members of the FLN in the Algerian region."[148]

The goal of the French was not for the MNA to take military control of the country but, rather, to regain enough strength to be a viable negotiating partner. Starting in 1960, Messali had envisioned round table–style negotiations without exclusivity or preconditions that included the MNA in discussions alongside the FLN and the French. The purpose of these negotiations would be for the self-determination of Algeria and to ensure that the MNA would be able to participate in the subsequent electoral campaigns in the country alongside the FLN.[149] French Prime Minister Michel Debré insisted that the MNA be present in any subsequent negotiations on the future of Algeria. Jean Morin, the delegate-general of the French government in Algiers, believed he was acting in accordance with de Gaulle's position when he stated that the FLN would be only one among many actors in determining the definition of the future Algerian state.[150]

Unfortunately for the French, they realized by 1961 that plans for resuscitating the MNA were hopeless. Messali's attempts to display "the best Gaullist sentiments" and cooperate with the French undercut the legitimacy of the MNA in the eyes of the movement, making it impossible for the group to increase its minimal popular support.[151] The Deuxième French Bureau reported that "Everyone is certain that the MNA does not practically exist in Algeria and that all manifestations of this movement are only a show of the French administration [. . .]. The fact that the Muslim community judges the party 'inconsistent' and its partisans traitors to the Algerian homeland does not encourage prospective partisans."[152] For its part, the FLN not only rejected negotiations with the MNA at the table, but it was also "not prepared to tolerate . . . parallel negotiations . . . carried on with a body that was quite falsely represented as being as important as themselves."[153] FLN assaults and additional MNA defections in 1961–1962 all but eliminated the remaining fighters in this subordinate group.

Unable to salvage the MNA, the French turned to the next best thing: a splinter group harvested from its ashes. After Khelifa Ben Amar and other leaders left the MNA in 1961, Khelifa launched a "neo-MNA" known as the Algerian Democratic Action Front (FAAD). From the beginning of the existence of FAAD, the French bankrolled it, armed it, and manipulated it to serve French interests. In exchange, the group claimed to support a close association with France and numerous guarantees for the *colons*—including 50% of the seats reserved for them in a new Algerian Senate—while its raison d'être was to actively struggle against the FLN. Despite an outreach to cultural minorities and groups that could feel threatened by an overwhelming FLN presence in an independent Algeria—such as the Jewish community, the Mozabites (a Berber ethnic group), the Tidjaniya Sufi brotherhood, and former UDMA adherents—FAAD failed to gain much traction and never became a significant challenger to the FLN. The French minister of the interior "abandoned the leaders [of the FAAD and MNA] to their fate," and those who could not or did not rally to the FLN were labeled as collaborators and were jailed or killed.[154]

In addition to their attempts to resuscitate the MNA in whole or in part, the French sought to inspire the rise of new Algerian challengers by holding local elections. The French claimed that there was "deadlock in Algeria because the Government could not negotiate with the FLN unless and until the FLN's claim to represent the whole of Muslim opinion had been proved in free election."[155] The FLN saw the elections as an attempt by the French to divide Algerians and avoid negotiations with the dominant party. The group threatened a boycott via "locally crafted tracts and posters, threatening letters addressed to electoral agents and to candidates, slogans hawked in mosques, bars, cafes, or in markets by singers or teams of propagandists going door to door and leaving posters."[156] Rumors circulated among the population of the Constantine Wilaya that the FLN had designated 2,000 fighters to target candidates in the 1960 cantonal elections to enforce the boycott. While some "spectacular attacks" did take place, French intelligence believed that the FLN tolerated the "least hostile" candidates to its agenda or "those that it believed it could use later against France."[157] In any case, no significant national group arose during the elections, and the FLN was subsequently able to use its control of the movement to call successfully on its supporters to boycott de Gaulle's 1961 referendum on Algerian self-determination. The success of this tactic seems to have convinced de Gaulle that "it was no use trying to run the country without the FLN."[158]

Unable to find or create a challenger from outside the FLN, the French pursued their fourth and final option: splintering the FLN itself. In any organization that was so large and spread across multiple countries, there were bound to be internal tensions, which Ouamrane described as "normal."[159] There was "wilayism"—the tendency for commanders in different areas of Algeria to squabble with the central leadership—although this decreased significantly after the Soummam conference in 1956.[160] The collective leadership of the FLN constantly debated strategy, while tensions between the GPRA and military commanders threatened to boil over on numerous occasions. After becoming disillusioned with the external FLN leadership in Tunis during the years that his unit had taken heavy losses, the military commander of the Algiers Wilaya (Si Salah) made contact with the French in early 1960 and then met secretly with de Gaulle in June in what became known as Operation Tilsitt. Salah and his lieutenants offered to lay down their weapons and try to convince the other wilaya commanders to do the same in exchange for autonomy and equality within France. Once the GPRA learned of the plan, however, another commander in the wilaya quickly took charge and began executing those involved. Salah was killed the following year, and the split the French had so long desired was quickly snuffed out.[161]

THE EVIAN NEGOTIATIONS

Having failed to prop up the MNA, create a challenger such as FAAD via clandestine support or local elections, or split the FLN, de Gaulle and the French recognized that dealing with the FLN and ceding to its demands for independence was the only option. Hegemony had ensured that the FLN signals were clear: it was the only group with which to negotiate, and the French knew that only the FLN could credibly threaten to continue the war and credibly guarantee an end to violence. When the French finally turned to the FLN to negotiate their departure, the hegemony of the Algerian national movement helped ensure that a deal for independence would be consummated.

After French intentions to grant Algerians significant concessions became clear with the holding of a 1961 referendum in France that approved self-determination for the territory, a number of *colons* formed an armed group of their own to spoil the peace, the Organisation de l'Armée Secrète (OAS). In addition to a failed coup attempt by OAS-affiliated military leaders in April 1961 against de Gaulle, the OAS launched attacks against French soldiers and Muslim civilians alike in attempts to drive the parties apart and prevent a deal. As Benyoucef Benkhedda, an FLN leader, described, "Our greatest danger was that, because of the OAS, anybody treating with the French might be regarded as a traitor by his own side."[162]

Had the movement contained multiple significant groups, the OAS violence would have made it less likely that the FLN could have negotiated with the French because the FLN would have been worried that a loss of legitimacy would lead to the ascendance of a rival. Given that the movement was hegemonic, however, the FLN knew that there was no viable challenger to benefit from any loss of face. They therefore proceeded with the negotiations amid the attacks, just as they had done when the MNA had launched attacks against the FLN in 1961 to force the FLN to violate their cease-fire agreement with the French.[163] The OAS was certainly not a member of the Algerian national movement, and as such, its attempt to spoil does not contradict MST. On the contrary, the lack of significant spoilers from within the movement is testament to the FLN hegemony. Furthermore, the ability of the FLN to resist the temptation to reignite the war and call off negotiations perfectly aligns with the predictions of MST.

The OAS coup attempt and violence drove a larger wedge between the *colons* and the French public, so that, by April 1961, 78% of the French public favored the opening of negotiations with the FLN and, by May 1961, 69% believed that Algeria would soon be independent. Many of the French, particularly those in the Metropole, viewed the OAS as a dangerous fascist organization; by August, as many as 48% believed that it was actively trying to overthrow the French government (this figure rose to 53% by January 1962).[164] By 1962, a full 53% of the French public no longer felt any solidarity with the French population in Algeria, and only 23% felt "some level" of solidarity or "complete solidarity." Just as a lack of fragmentation on the Algerian side helped their cause, the presence of fragmentation among the French helped contribute to their defeat, as Ian Lustick and Hendrik Spruyt expertly detail.[165] The two developments were not unrelated because the breakdown of the hegemonic concept of "Algérie Française" in France was driven by a hegemonic Algerian uprising whose "stubborn reality" toppled multiple French governments by making any outcome that kept Algeria as part of France impossible.[166]

The two sides agreed to the Evian Accords, which called for a cease-fire on March 18, 1962, verified by referenda in France and Algeria in June and July. According to a poll on March 20, 82% of the French public was "satisfied" with the Evian negotiations, 8% was not content and 10% was indifferent. By April 8, a full 91% of the French public approved of the Evian Accords.[167] As for the FLN, Dahlab noted, "all accepted GPRA authority, even the EMG [FLN General Staff] who were the only one to vote against Evian, but even they 'didn't want to jeopardize the ceasefire.'"[168]

Following the cease-fire that was reached during the Evian Accords, the OAS knew that it had its last chance to disrupt the peace process. The OAS leadership created a plan to attack a number of Muslim civilians to provoke Algerian mobs to descend on the European quarter in Algiers. It sought to "overwhelm" the FLN provision of order, which was "desperately trying to contain that powder keg that was the Casbah." Crowds of Algerians were indeed provoked, but FLN forces managed to disperse them before a crisis erupted.[169]

In response to these OAS attempts to violently spoil the deal, the FLN held off from retaliating for months. Employing logic that fits perfectly with MST, Alistair Horne explains why: "Up to this point the FLN in Algiers—secure in the knowledge it was about to inherit the earth—had shown remarkable discipline and restraint."[170] The eventual retaliation by the FLN in May remained limited, even though the OAS had killed three times as many civilians in the Algiers area during the first six months of 1962 as the FLN had from 1956 to 1962 combined, including their Battle of Algiers. Nonetheless, the FLN resisted the *colon* spoiling and even negotiated a truce with the OAS in June. As the FLN had proclaimed to Algerians on November 1, 1954: "The FLN is your front; its victory is your victory." The FLN celebrated its ascendance and the independence of Algeria on July 5, 1962, its organizational and strategic goals achieved after the movement structure had shifted to hegemony for the first time in its history.

Negotiating Hegemony

Today, many of the streets in major cities such as Algiers and Oran are named after individuals who played a significant role in the Algerian national movement. Although it is rarely noted in the commemorative plaques that dot the cities' walls, many of these individuals were killed by other Algerians—an uneasy legacy of the internal divisions, and the brutal struggles to end them, that lingers to this day.

Like the Palestinian national movement, the Algerian national movement was strategically successful during its one period of hegemony (1958–1962) and unsuccessful during periods of fragmentation (1946–1947, 1947–1950, 1952–1953, 1954, 1955, and 1956–1957) and unity (1944–1945 and 1951) (see table 5.1). Whereas the fragmented and united periods were marked by mixed strategies and signals, greater efforts expended on internal fights than on external ones, and failed attempts at side deals, the movement under the dominance of the FLN yielded clear, consistent signals; a massive, concerted strategic effort at expelling the French; and a single, credible negotiator with limited potential for spoiling or sellout given the lack of an internal challenger—which ultimately spelled victory.

Competing theories suggest that the Algerian national movement should have been more successful when fragmented, which was clearly not the case. French actions speak to one of the most valuable implications of Kathleen Cunningham's work, however, namely that the state often seeks to negotiate with a group that is not necessarily the strongest in the opposing movement, as the French did with the MNA and FAAD.[171] Nonetheless, as I demonstrate in this chapter, although the state may be able to successfully negotiate with a number of significant groups, it can rarely pull off a deal with a subordinate group that will be perceived as legitimate and end a campaign of violence. This, again, demonstrates the importance of assessing the relative strength of groups, rather than merely counting them. Cunningham's study suggests a further reason why the dominant group in a hegemonic movement is more secure organizationally and more likely to coerce larger strategic concessions: there is no alternative group with which the state can close a credible deal. Indeed, fragmentation would have made it more likely that de Gaulle's attempted referendum for Algerian autonomy within France would have received support from a significant nationalist group. Because of movement hegemony, the Algerians gained far more significant concessions.

Others see an independent Algeria as the result of a broader norm of decolonization. The preceding longitudinal analysis reveals significant problems with this argument, which reads history backward and cannot explain changes over time. In November 1954, French Interior Minister François Mitterand said that "L'Algerie c'est la France" while only 4% of French citizens believed North Africa was the first issue the government should address.[172] By 1956, the United Nations still could not pass resolutions supporting self-determination for Algeria, let alone independence. Yet just a few years later, the government of France, the majority of its people, and the United Nations all supported Algerian independence. Did the norm of decolonization not exist in 1956 but suddenly appear in 1960? Obviously not. Furthermore, even after the movement had coerced and convinced the French to pull back, de Gaulle did everything he could to avoid granting Algerian independence. He did not ultimately give in because the international pressures of decolonization were too strong; he gave in because the hegemonic FLN gave him no other choice. What changed from 1956 to 1960 was the structure of the national movement. The victory of the Algerian national movement played a large role in the subsequent spread of the concept and norm of decolonization, but its independence in 1962 cannot be predominantly explained by it in timing or outcome.

In terms of explaining variation in group behavior, many scholars of Algerian history look to ideology and label Abbas and his groups "the moderates" and Messali and his groups "the radicals."[173] This certainly explains the actions of their groups in the 1940s, but it fails to do so in the 1950s. MST explains both; Abbas and the AML/UDMA were against the uprising in 1945 while they were the movement leader and then later supported and joined the 1954 uprising while they were a movement challenger.[174] Messali and the PPA/MTLD initiated the 1945 uprising while a challenger, denounced the 1954 uprising while the movement leader, and then sought to spoil the negotiations of the new movement leader and hegemon after being displaced. Thus ideology may help us to explain the rhetoric and other policy platforms, but movement structure does a superior job of explaining Algerian group actions concerning violence and victory.

The Irish National Movement

Where You Stand Depends on Where You Sit

> Any practical statesman will, under duress, swallow a dozen oaths to
> get his hand on the driving wheel.
>
> —George Bernard Shaw, 1921

The Irish national movement has a long history of ideological and geographical division between nationalists and republicans, north and south.[1]
Nationalists generally accepted moderate concessions toward independence via elections and negotiations, whereas republicans generally demanded a more robust version of independence and were more willing to
take up arms to achieve it. As one former member of the republican wing
noted, "The [nationalist] SDLP's national aspirations were the same, but
their tactics and pacing were different."[2] This suggests that ideology drives
action, which poses a puzzle: Why has every significant republican group—
including Fine Gael, Fianna Fáil, and Sinn Féin, the three largest political
parties in Ireland today—negotiated, restrained violence, and agreed to
concessions short of its intended goal? Surely those are the actions of nationalists, not republicans. Second, the greatest success of the Irish national
movement—the creation of the Irish Free State in 1921–1922—led to a geographical division when Northern Ireland remained in the United Kingdom, which set off a struggle for its inclusion in the Irish Republic that
continues to this day. Why would the movement have been more successful
in the 1920s, at the height of colonialism, than in the past four decades of
the post-colonial period?

MST helps us understand the clockwork-like actions of republican
groups that escalated violence, shunned elections, and denounced negotiated compromise while challengers only to then shun violence, participate
in elections, and negotiate compromises after they became the leader or hegemon. Despite their intense criticism of each other, this is the story of the

most important groups in the Irish national movement in the twentieth century: Cumann na nGaedheal (later Fine Gael), Fianna Fáil, the Official IRA/Sinn Féin (OIRA/Sinn Féin), and the Provisional IRA/Sinn Féin (PIRA/Sinn Féin). In *every* case in which abstentionism (the refusal to take seats in government) was ended—with these four groups within Ireland, and with the nationalist Social Democratic and Labour Party (SDLP) with internment in Northern Ireland—what changed was not what the group ideologically said had to change but, rather, the movement structure and the fact that the group would be guaranteed a leading role in the new order. In this sense, *nationalist* and *republican* may be helpful descriptors of current policies, but they are comparatively poor predictors of future action because the "republicans" of today are often the "nationalists" of tomorrow.

In terms of success, the hegemonic Irish national movement of 1918–1922 had a dominant party and military focused on victory, while the fragmented movement of The Troubles in 1968–1998 often degenerated into political competition and counterproductive violence. The use of violence was not entirely ineffective during The Troubles because it drove shifts in the hierarchy that represented organizational success for some groups, such as the PIRA. Nonetheless, the outcome for the movement remained largely the same, so much so that the Good Friday Agreement of 1998 was called "Sunningdale for slow learners," in that it was similar to that deal rejected by the PIRA/Sinn Féin twenty-five years earlier. Because the structure of the movement system changed little in thirty years, neither did strategic progress. The hierarchy of the movement did shift, however; hence, the decision by Sinn Féin to reverse itself and agree to a deal with the British that was similar in content but, more important, different in terms of which groups signed on the dotted line.

MST thus provides powerful explanations for the most prominent actions and outcomes of the Irish national movement in the twentieth century. The Irish national movement also provides an opportunity to expand the horizons of MST. First, it is the only movement analyzed in this book after it had achieved a state. As Ian Lustick and Nadav Shelef demonstrate, the irrendentist struggle over enlarging a state may have similar dynamics to the secessionist struggle in founding one.[3] The analysis of The Troubles tests the extent to which MST applies in both contexts while also providing across-case and within-case comparisons across time and space. Second, this case provides a test of external validity geographically because it is located outside the Middle East.

Finally, the Irish case provides an opportunity to analyze potential expansions of MST that provide a more complete picture. For example, the PIRA/Sinn Féin did gain significant strength from its emergence in 1970 to its signing of the Good Friday Agreement in 1998, but it was a shift from a weak to strong challenger. MST therefore predicts that the group would be more likely to employ violence and spoil. It did this in 1996–1997, but then it signed the agreement the following year despite its not being a leader or hegemon. Why? In this case, the PIRA/Sinn Féin was a slight challenger to the SDLP in the movement, but it had become the hegemon in the republican wing with the expectation of soon becoming the movement leader. As such, it wore two hats. It challenged and outbid the SDLP for movement leadership while it found itself more secure and able to pursue negotiations without the existence of other significant republican challengers. Therefore, although ideology may not drive group behavior, it can help provide context to movement cleavages that allow for the assessment of finer-grained balances of power. In this chapter, I largely analyze the Irish national movement with the original form of MST, but I also add a consideration of additional hierarchies within the movement wings to demonstrate the potential for expansion.

In addition to my analysis of secondary sources, I base the analysis in this chapter on research conducted in the British National Archives at Kew, Linen Hall Library in Belfast, the Public Records Office of Northern Ireland (PRONI), and interviews with current and former members of the PIRA, the OIRA, the Irish National Liberation Army (INLA), Sinn Féin, Republic Sinn Féin, the Irish Republican Socialist Party and the SDLP.

The Origins of the Irish National Movement

Although the Irish resisted foreign invasions and promoted Gaelic culture for centuries, most scholars mark the beginnings of Irish proto-nationalism at the end of the eighteenth century. One of its leaders, Wolfe Tone, believed that a united front was necessary to achieve the main goal of Irish nationalism: independence from Great Britain. The problem was that power was historically fragmented among multiple groups in the movement that supported various combinations of Irish political autonomy and rights for Catholics and Presbyterians. Tone's generation was no exception, in that his attempt to liberate Ireland at the close of the eighteenth century was not supported by many nationalists. Without unity, let alone hegemony, Tone's campaign failed, yielding the establishment of the United Kingdom of Great Britain and Ireland in 1801.

Unfortunately for the Irish, this pattern of fragmented, failed campaigns was to repeat itself numerous times over the next two hundred years. None was more (in)famous than the Easter Rising of 1916, still commemorated to this day. As with its predecessors and many of its successors, the Rising was marked by a short-term burst of violence launched by a faction that did not enjoy a dominant position in the national movement, let alone a leading one. Nonetheless, the aftermath of the Rising contributed to the emergence of the only hegemonic Irish national movement for the next one hundred years. As MST predicts, this campaign yielded major strategic success and the most significant gains for Irish independence before or since (see table 6.1).[4]

Table 6.1 Summary of Campaigns in the Irish National Movement, 1914–1998

Time period	Movement system structure	Hierarchy of groups at start of campaign	Summary of group actions	Strategic outcome of campaign
1914–1917	Fragmented	L1. IPP (NH) C2. SF (RH)	IPP unsuccessfully pushed for home rule and denounced the failed Easter Rising by the Irish Volunteers; Sinn Féin began to challenge the IPP at the polls	Failure
1917–1918	Fragmented	L1. IPP (NH) C2. SF/IRA (RH)	Sinn Féin won four by-elections against the IPP and merged with the IRA	Failure
1918–1922	Hegemonic	H1. SF/IRA (RH)	Sinn Féin won 73 seats in Parliament to 6 for the IPP; the IRA initiated the War of Independence and then agreed to a truce and negotiated for an Irish Free State	Moderate success[a]
1922–1923	Fragmented	L1. Pro-Treaty SF/IRA (RL) C2. Anti-Treaty SF/IRA (RC)	Sinn Féin and the IRA splintered; the pro-treaty forces prevailed in elections and civil war, but the movement and the republicans were fragmented for decades	Failure
1968–1969	Fragmented	L1. Nationalist Party (NL) C2. NDP (NC) C3. PD (NC) C4. SF/IRA (RH)	The Troubles began amid a fragmented civil rights movement that faced violent repression; the Nationalist Party and the SF/IRA fell apart in 1969–1970	Failure
1970–1971	Fragmented	L1. SDLP (NH) C2. OSF/OIRA (RL) C3. PSF/PIRA (RC)	SDLP formed and the SF/IRA splintered; the OIRA and PIRA outbid and infought, while the SDLP tried to restrain violence	Failure
1972–1973	Fragmented	L1. SDLP (NH) C2. PSF/PIRA (RL) C3. OSF/OIRA (RC)	The PIRA surpassed the OIRA as sectarian violence increased; the PIRA failed in its negotiations and spoiled the Sunningdale agreement for the SDLP	Failure
1974–1985	Fragmented	L1. SDLP (NH) C2. PSF/PIRA (RL) C3. OSF/OIRA (RC) C4. IRSP/INLA (RC)	INLA split from the OIRA as the two groups infought, followed by PIRA-OIRA infighting and INLA-PIRA outbidding; SDLP negotiations failed and republican groups began to run in elections	Failure
1986–1998	Fragmented	L1. SDLP (NH) C2. SF/IRA (RH)	SF/IRA became hegemon in the republican wing and ended abstentionism in the Dáil; SDLP and SF began talks; the IRA announced a cease-fire and demonstrated credibility to start/stop violence; SDLP and SF negotiated the Good Friday Agreement	Limited success

Notes: To save space, a few campaigns with the same movement system in consecutive time periods are combined in this table. The hierarchical rank of groups in the republican and nationalist wings are listed to the right in parentheses: NC, nationalist challenger; NL, nationalist leader; NH, nationalist hegemon; RC, republican challenger; RL, republican leader; RH, republican hegemon. I list groups with military and political wings as SF/IRA and IRSP/INLA, fully recognizing that there are individuals who were members of one and not the other, as well as disagreements over tactics and strategy. I think they can be profitably analyzed as single units, and doing otherwise in many periods would be misleading, because the political label was used for what was really a military organization (or vice versa). Sinn Féin is not affiliated with any IRA groups today, and the IRA itself decommissioned its arsenal in 2005. INLA, Irish National Liberation Army; IPP, Irish Parliamentary Party; IRA, Irish Republican Army; IRSP, Irish Republican Socialist Party; NDP, National Democratic Party; OIRA, Official Irish Republican Army; OSF, Official Sinn Féin; PD, People's Democracy; PIRA, Provisional Irish Republican Army; PSF, Provisional Sinn Féin; SDLP, Social Democratic and Labour Party; SF, Sinn Féin.

[a] The Free State became a member of the League of Nations in 1923, but it was not immediately fully sovereign. I thus mark it as a moderate success rather than a total success, although switching the coding would not change the fact that this was the greatest victory for the movement.

For decades before the Rising, the Irish Parliamentary Party (IPP) led the national movement. As a nationalist party and the leading group, it pushed for Home Rule within the United Kingdom while focusing on elections and parliamentary politics. Its separation from, and distaste for, numerous armed revolts by competing republican groups in the 1800s helped doom them to failure.[5] In the years before the Rising, two key groups emerged that would shockingly dethrone the IPP and change the course of Irish history: Sinn Féin and the Irish Republican Army (IRA).

The Easter Rising and the Irish War of Independence, 1916–1923

FRAGMENTATION AND FAILURE

Arthur Griffith founded Sinn Féin in Dublin in 1905 as an explicitly non-factional organization; as he wrote two years later, "The Sinn Féin platform is and is intended to be broad enough to hold all Irishmen who believe in Irish independence, whether they be republicans or whether they be not."[6] Griffith's mission called for self-reliance and separation from Great Britain, hence the name Sinn Féin, which means "We Ourselves." Griffith may have longed for total independence, but his original vision was for a dual monarchy in the model of Austria-Hungary, believing London could not stomach anything bolder.

Despite the growing attractiveness of Griffith's approach, the IPP bested the first Sinn Féin candidate for Parliament in a 1908 by-election, 73% to 27%. Sinn Féin took slight comfort in the fact that nearly all unionists voted for the IPP candidate, demonstrating who the real leader for Irish independence was, at least in their eyes.[7] In any case, the showing by Sinn Féin demonstrated that it represented a new challenger to IPP leadership in the movement.

The nationalist-republican rivalry was clearly displayed in the early years of the Óglaigh na hÉireann, the Irish Volunteers or, as they were later known, the IRA. With semi-autonomous Home Rule a possibility, the largely Protestant unionists in the north formed the paramilitary group Ulster Volunteer Force (UVF) in early 1913 to keep Ireland firmly under British control. In response, Eoin MacNeill founded the paramilitary Irish Volunteers in November of the same year with encouragement from the Irish Republican Brotherhood (IRB), a longtime rival of the IPP and secretive republican organization founded in 1858. Although originally against the creation of an Irish Volunteer force that could serve as a rival to the IPP, John Redmond, an IPP leader, later sought to grow and control it. This led to an Irish Volunteer executive council littered with republicans and nationalists from all relevant organizations: the IPP, Sinn Féin, and the IRB. Although the Volunteers could have served as a vehicle for movement unity, the armed group was initially the forum for power struggles and little coordinated action.

The Volunteers ultimately split over World War I, with Redmond encouraging them to fight alongside the British and the republican groups urging them to secede and stay home. The National Volunteers loyal to Redmond numbered 147,050, as opposed to the 9,700 Irish Volunteers who split with the republicans, a further indication of IPP superiority at the time.[8] In the struggle for control of the Irish national movement, however, Redmond's victory may have been a Pyrrhic one. Over 120,000 of the National Volunteers did not enlist in the British Army, existing largely on paper due to its poor organization and general inaction, whereas the growing 12,000-strong Irish Volunteers trained regularly with a substantial arsenal.[9]

A number of the remaining Irish Volunteers now set their sights on an armed uprising to expel the British, who were thought to be vulnerable with their forces deployed on the European mainland. The already severely diminished Volunteers were weakened by further splits, however, as MacNeill (supported by Griffith) tried to stop the Rising just as it was scheduled to begin on April 23, 1916: Easter Sunday.[10] The IRB-led conspirators decided to push on without MacNeill, Griffith, and their supporters, leaving them with approximately 1,000 men to occupy key positions in Dublin and a few other cities and towns such as Galway and Wexford. Despite being caught entirely by surprise, the British crushed the Rising, which resembled more of a Dublin-based coup due to its lack of significant mass or elite support, in less than a week.

As J. Bowyer Bell notes, "The IRB accepted that the Rising would probably be a military failure," and indeed it was.[11] As MST predicts, the weaker challenger tried to chain-gang the movement into a conflict for which it was not prepared, and the fragmented structure of the movement helped ensure the defeat of the campaign. Notwithstanding media reports to the contrary, it was not a "Sinn Féin Rising" because Sinn Féin had worked to stop the revolt. As the theory predicts, the leading IPP was even less supportive, and some units in Redmond's National Volunteers volunteered to help the British constabulary put down the Rising.[12] Redmond himself argued that the Rising was "even more an attempt to hit us than to hit England."[13]

Also as predicted, these larger, better-known parties paid significant costs despite their lack of involvement. The British imposed martial law on all of Ireland. General John Maxwell, the newly installed military governor, issued orders to dispatch soldiers "throughout Ireland with a view to arresting dangerous Sinn Féiners who have actually supported the movement throughout the country even though they have not taken part in the rising," leading to 3,500 arrests in the following days.[14] The British arrested and threatened to execute Eoin MacNeill to get him to implicate the IPP.[15]

The outcome, at least, supports Redmond's claim in that the Rising was at best an organizational success for the Volunteers and the IRB. Although it generated no concessions from the British, their reaction to the uprising helped turn the tide of popular support in favor of these republican factions. In a story that was to repeat itself time and again in the twentieth century, the majority of the Irish people did not approve of the use of violence against the British, but they hated the British use of violence against Irishmen even more. As Eamon De Valera, a Rising conspirator, had suggested, "England pretends it is not by the naked sword, but by the good will of the people of the country that she is here. We will draw the naked sword to make her bare her own naked sword."[16] In the aftermath of the Rising, the British miscalculated. They believed that, as Maxwell explained, a harsh line would "ensure that there will be no treason whispered, even whispered, in Ireland for a hundred years."[17] Instead, their decision to execute the leaders of the Rising (including the tying of a crippled James Connolly to a chair before a firing squad) and to intern thousands of Irish without a trial sparked a wave of anger against the British that translated into support for the harder-line republican groups.[18] As Liam Deasy, a subsequent IRA member describes, "In consequence of the events that occurred in the decisive week of the Easter Rising of 1916, and more particularly of the events that followed it, thousands of young men all over Ireland, indeed thousands of men of all ages in the country, turned irrevocably against the English government and became uncompromisingly dedicated to the cause of obliterating the last vestiges of British rule in Ireland. I was one of them."[19]

HEGEMON RISING

The increase in popular support and recruits more than outweighed any losses from the Rising, but the problem for the Irish national movement was not its size but its structure. The Rising had failed in large part because the movement had been split among competing groups for years. A subsequent campaign was far more likely to succeed if, first, a hegemon rose internally to dominate the movement for the greater strategic good.

The process started on the republican side of the ledger, whose own internal squabbles would have doomed the Rising even without the presence of the nationalists. The decisive moment was the conventions of Sinn Féin and the Irish Volunteers in October 1917. Going in, these were two separate organizations, each with significant disagreements over leadership and objectives. Coming out, they approached a single unit, with the same leader, governing elite, and strategic purpose.

After significant debate at the Ard Fheis (convention) among its 2,000 delegates, Arthur Griffith agreed to yield the presidency of Sinn Féin to Eamon De Valera, a former IRB member and a leader of the Rising. In the process, the two reconciled the supporters of their competing visions for Ireland of a dual monarchy and a republic. De Valera claimed that "We are not doctrinaire republicans," and the leadership agreed to focus on achieving Irish independence, after which time the Irish people could vote in a referendum on whether they preferred a monarchy or a republic.[20] After being unanimously elected president of Sinn Féin (with Griffith as vice president), De Valera was then elected president of the Irish Volunteers at its convention the next day, again in unanimous fashion, with Cathal Brugha as the chief of staff and Michael Collins as the director of organization. De Valera was not alone in his dual role: "The dual membership of both Sinn Féin and the Volunteers [IRA], which was normal at the local level, simply reflected what existed throughout the organizations from the top down."[21] At the time, six out of twenty were executives in both organizations, including the president and most key posts.

The outcome of these conventions was unprecedented. The factions could have gone their separate ways. They could have remained disconnected but pledged to work together. Instead, they institutionally bound themselves as one with a single leadership, thus shunning fragmentation or unity while putting themselves on the path to a hegemonic movement for the first time. Whether, as Michael Collins suggested, the Sinn Féin politicians had captured the Volunteers, or "as Sean Ó Faoláin put it years later, the IRB [and the Volunteers] captured Sinn Féin," matters little for MST.[22] The key was that the republicans were now dominated by a single group; only the nationalists stood in their way within the movement, not each other.

The momentum for Sinn Féin/IRA began building with four straight victories over IPP candidates in the by-elections of 1917.[23] The synergy of the political and military wings of Sinn Féin/IRA was on display in these campaigns, as candidates were often dual members and IRA Volunteers made up most of the canvassers. In the first by-election in Roscommon, "The worst snowfall anyone could remember made electioneering extremely unpleasant. There was a big freeze; people and animals died. In the midst of all of this the young Volunteers, icicles hanging from their hair, struggled along highways and byways, carrying shovels to dig themselves out of snowdrifts. By contrast, Redmond's teams of MPs and paid organizers sat in warm hotels. They were snowed in, unable to canvass, they said."[24] Setting a precedent for an even more famous act during The Troubles, one of the elections saw a Sinn Féin/IRA candidate win while in prison.[25] The motto? "Put him in to get him out."[26]

These victories were only a preview of what was to come in the December 1918 elections. Driven by the reaction to the Rising, the unification of the republicans, and the unpopular threat of British conscription in World War I that had further driven support from the nationalists, Sinn Féin won 73 of 105 seats in Ireland, including a clean sweep in 24 of the 32 counties. The IPP won only six seats, despite the fact that Sinn Féin candidates campaigned to varying degrees on an abstentionist platform, meaning they would refuse to take their seats in Parliament. The unionists won twenty-six seats, all but three in Ulster, meaning that they represented a challenge to independence, but not one internal to the movement. The 1918 elections cemented Sinn Féin/IRA as the hegemon in the Irish national movement.[27] It really almost was "Ourselves Alone," as Sinn Féin is sometimes (mis) translated. As David Fitzpatrick of Trinity College noted, 'There was a wonderful oneness about Irish politics.'[28]

THE IRISH WAR OF INDEPENDENCE, 1919-1923

Refusing to legitimize the British hold on Ireland, Sinn Féin set up its own parliament in Dublin (the Dáil Éireann) on January 21, 1919, with those members who were not in prison or otherwise impaired. The coalescing between Sinn Féin and the Volunteers was repeated with the Dáil and the IRA, now the official name of the Volunteers. De Valera was again president of both the Dáil and the IRA, Michael Collins was the finance minister of the former and the director of intelligence for the latter, and Cathal Brugha (and later Richard Mulcahy) was minister of defense in the Dáil and IRA chief of staff. The day of the first meeting of the Dáil also marked the beginning of the Irish War of Independence (also known as the Anglo-Irish War or the Tan War) when the IRA killed two Royal Irish Constabulary (RIC) policemen in Soloheadbeg of County Tipperary.

Unlike its predecessor from the days of the Rising, the IRA of 1919–1921 was neither conventional nor split between competing nationalist and republican groups. Collins had rebuilt the IRA to conduct guerrilla warfare and counterintelligence operations, rather than large-scale engagements. The initial attack on the RIC was thus emblematic of a larger strategy. By late 1920, the IRA had destroyed 513 RIC barracks, killed 117 RIC men, and helped coerce 2,000 resignations as well as a significant drop in new RIC recruitment.[29] Negating this force destroyed the eyes and ears of Britain in Ireland, weakening British control and helping spur them to further indiscriminate, counterproductive tactics. Coupled with the killing of British intelligence agents and the launching of strikes and boycotts, the IRA and Sinn Féin ensured that "the pacification of Ireland would require a commitment of Boer War proportions: a raising of troop levels to 100,000 men, the establishment of security zones . . . at a probable cost of around £100 million per annum."[30] Ultimately, the British public and government were not ready to pay that price, either in blood, treasure, or reputation as a colonial oppressor over their own United Kingdom.

The hegemony of the movement was the key factor in the success of the campaign. The IRA and Sinn Féin were able to carry out the boycotts and killings of the RIC men due to significant, nearly undivided support from the populace. The lack of internal competition—Sinn Féin won 1,079 seats to 288 by the IPP in 1920 local elections and 124 of 128 seats in the southern

Irish elections of 1921—allowed movement leaders to focus their energy on the strategic goal of independence rather than internal competition with other groups.[31] There was no outbidding among factions and no initial spoiling when the truce came. When escalations by individuals and smaller groups did spring up, as with land seizures in western Ireland, Sinn Féin responded by setting up land courts to regulate redistribution while the IRA condemned the seizures and pledged to enforce the Dáil court rulings.[32]

From the perspective of Britain, the movement had significant credibility to continue a long war because there was no significant nationalist challenger to turn to and split its adversary. Finally, it was not just a numbers game because the IRA had far fewer than the 160,000 members it had had in 1914. In fact, Michael L. R. Smith claims that the focus of the war involved 80,000 British police, soldiers, and auxiliaries against 3,000 Irish irregulars (the British counted 14,842 in 1918).[33] The difference was not the number of armed men in the movement but, rather, the number of significant groups leading it: one.

With a hegemonic movement, Sinn Féin and the IRA successfully coerced the British to sue for peace in July 1921. Subsequent negotiations in London did not yield the republic, but the proposed Free State did achieve far more than Home Rule. As Arthur Griffith explains, "We have come back from London with that Treaty—Saorstat na hÉireann recognized—the Free State of Ireland. We have brought back the flag; we have brought back the evacuation of Ireland after 700 years by British troops and the formation of the Irish army. We have brought back to Ireland her full rights and powers of fiscal control. We have brought back to Ireland equality with England."[34]

As MST predicts, and as would recur with the successors of the IRA, the leading group cut a deal and so did what they claimed they would never do when they had been a challenger to Redmond's nationalists. To be fair, however, Sinn Féin did get much more than Home Rule, which the nationalists never achieved in any case. Although subsequent debates would rage over whether the rebellion could achieve more, this outcome can only be considered a major strategic success.

CIVIL WAR, PARTITION, AND A RETURN TO FRAGMENTATION

Although Sinn Féin and the IRA held together throughout the war, the Treaty ultimately led both groups to split down the middle. Pro-Treaty members such as Collins and Griffith argued that, although imperfect, the Treaty represented the best possible deal at the time and was a significant step toward an independent republic. Anti-Treaty foes such as De Valera and Brugha argued that the Treaty did not go far enough and that a (symbolic) oath to England and the partition of the North was not what they and their comrades in the Easter Rising and the recent war had sacrificed to achieve.

The pro-Treaty side won the day in the Dáil (sixty-four ministers voting in favor to fifty-seven against), with the Irish people (fifty-eight pro-Treaty Sinn Féin candidates winning seats to thirty-five anti-Treaty Sinn Féin candidates in the 1922 elections), and, ultimately, on the battlefield. Having refused to honor the majority vote of the Dáil, the anti-Treaty forces had by April 1922 occupied much of western Ireland as well as key points in Dublin. In scenes reminiscent of the Easter Rising, civil war began in earnest on June 28, 1922, as Collins's Free State army began shelling his old comrades holed up in the major judicial building in Dublin, the Four Courts. Brugha, Collins, and others were among the casualties in a conflict that was bloodier than the war just concluded with England, but the Free State army crushed the rebellion within a year.

In the 1923 Free State General Election, the pro-Treaty Cumann na nGaedheal (Society of the Gaels) cemented its victory over the anti-Treaty Republicans, although the latter's capture of 44 of 153 seats meant that hegemony was finished. These two groups would soon evolve into the two leading political parties in Ireland to this day: Fine Gael (pro-Treaty) and Fianna Fáil (anti-Treaty). The latter, headed by Eamon De Valera, would ultimately sign the oath of allegiance to Britain and join the Dáil after electoral gains in 1927, proving yet again that power often trumps ideology. As the opening quotation from George Bernard Shaw suggests, "Any practical statesman will, under duress, swallow a dozen oaths to get his hand on the driving wheel."[35] In any case, the Treaty laid the groundwork for Ireland to become a republic, as it did officially in 1949. Nonetheless, the Irish national movement lived on with its focus shifting to the North, the only part of the nation still within the United Kingdom. In the future, however, the movement would remain split not only between North and South but also between republican and nationalist groups that would never again establish movement hegemony.

Variations on a Theme: The Troubles

Given the success of the Irish War of Independence, many theories would predict a similar result from the national movement after 1968. The Troubles, as they became known, represented the longest sustained campaign of violence in Irish history. The number of attacks, casualties, and paramilitary recruits were equal to or larger than those of the war fifty years earlier. As with the previous conflict, Irish strategy shunned conventional battles in favor of guerrilla warfare, bombings, and hunger strikes while the British countered with internment, curfews, and a sizable local constabulary force backed by the regular army. The ideology of the main participants was the same: movement members sought an independent, united Ireland, and the British sought to prevent such an outcome.

There was one key difference, however. During The Troubles, the national movement was always fragmented internally, both within and between nationalists and republicans, North and South. Groups wanted to pull the movement in different directions, but unlike in 1918, none was able to coopt, rub out, outcompete, or otherwise sweep the competition from the field. A lack of hegemony thus doomed each campaign of The Troubles to strategic failure or, at best, limited success. As predicted by MST, internal competition led to violent outbidding, chain-ganging, and spoiling that yielded counterproductive sectarian attacks, powerful loyalist militias, and fruitless negotiations.[36] The infighting and lack of coordination among groups produced unclear signals and gave the movement little credibility in the eyes of the British and their allies. Violence and elections did help groups move up and down the movement hierarchy, but their inability to change the fragmented movement structure meant that groups simply changed roles, not the strategic outcome. As predicted, the group whose position in the hierarchy did not change—the nationalist hegemon and movement leader, the SDLP—exhibited the least change in behavior, while the group that experienced the biggest change in hierarchal position—the PIRA/Sinn Féin, going from challenger to leader to hegemon within the republican wing of the movement—showed the biggest change in behavior, following the well-trodden path from violent challenger rejecting deals to restrained, status quo leader settling for less.

BEFORE THE TROUBLES: A MOVEMENT ADRIFT

As if the human divisions emerging from internal political and military conflicts were not enough, the 1921 Treaty divided the movement geographically as well (see figure 6.1). Although the North always had a different socioethnic composition from the rest of the island, it never before had been part of a separate state. What had been a 32-County National Movement evolved into more of a six-county one, as those who sought a unified Ireland turned to the last bastion of British rule. The geographic shift made the fight harder, not easier, because the physical division helped split the groups in the movement as well (perhaps as the British had intended). Now there were not only nationalists and republicans but also northern and southern IRAs, northern and southern Sinn Féins, and northern and southern nationalist parties, all of which often disagreed over tactics and failed to coordinate their efforts.

In this section, I consider the balance of power of the movement for groups focused in Northern Ireland. Although some parties in the Republic would have preferred a thirty-two-county movement in the abstract, many were satisfied with their twenty-six-county state and paid the North scant attention, considering it more trouble than it was worth. Individuals and groups in the Republic were more external supporters of the Irish national

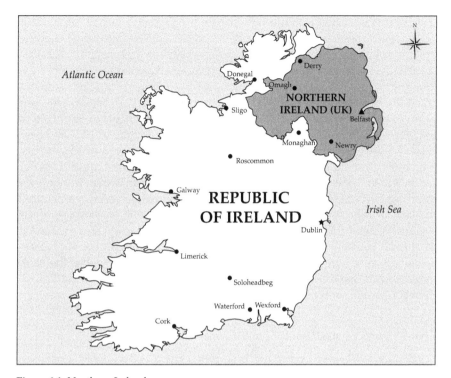

Figure 6.1. Northern Ireland

movement in the North than internal, integral parts of it. If we were, none-theless, to include groups such as Fianna Fáil or Fine Gael in the movement hierarchy, this would only further support MST. The movement would then be coded as even more fragmented when unsuccessful. Fianna Fáil, which would be coded as the leading group for most of The Troubles if in-cluded in the movement hierarchy, acted even more like a typical move-ment leader than the SDLP, accepting partition and the status quo, impris-oning IRA members, denouncing violence, and generally doing what it could to maintain its hold on power in the Republic. Regardless, the stron-gest northern groups did not compete in the Republic and vice versa until after 1998, creating two separate balances of power.

Divisions in the Irish national movement were on display in every armed campaign leading up to The Troubles, including the British Campaign of 1939, the Northern Campaign of 1942–1944, and the Border Campaign of 1956–1962. The IRA was the strongest group in the republican wing, but it remained a challenger in the movement to the Nationalist Party (the IPP successor), which itself was a weak party at best.[37] In dynamics that would be repeated step by step during The Troubles, the leading republican group (the IRA) was drawn into the Border Campaign after a weaker challenger (Saor Uladh) launched more attacks in the mid-1950s. Concerned that the upstart splinter group was drawing away recruits and support, the IRA launched its own campaign while continuing to denounce the more extreme attacks of its challenger, which the IRA blamed for a government crackdown in which it suffered disproportionately due to the size and prominence of its membership.[38] Despite the electoral gains of Sinn Féin in the North in 1955, Fianna Fáil took power in the Republic in 1957 and proceeded to institute the internment without trial of suspected IRA members, which was the final nail in the coffin for a campaign based around border raids between the Republic and the North. The fact that the strongest republican party in the South actively worked against the IRA demonstrated the lack of cohesiveness in the movement. This was to say nothing of the nationalists in the North, who did not support the campaign and proceeded to outpoll Sinn Féin in future elections. With hegemony in the short term seemingly unattainable, unity remained the best alternative, but the challenges of internal rivalry and the allure of organizational gain would prove to be too strong to overcome.

The late 1960s were a unique time when the less-organized grassroots briefly propelled the movement: "The civil rights movement was in part a rejection of both armed struggle [IRA] and constitutionalism [Nationalist Party] which had failed to deliver. The thought was: Forget about the Republic for a moment, let's deal with why Catholics can't get housing, why work places are overwhelmingly unionist and Protestant, and why gerrymandering exists to weaken the Catholic voice."[39] After the failure of the Border Campaign, Cathal Goulding took over as IRA chief of staff from Ruairí Ó Brádaigh and led a reassessment of the strategy of the group. The civil rights movement in the late 1960s appealed to much of the IRA leadership, in part because the demise of Saor Uladh left the IRA without a significant republican challenger. The IRA operated to a degree under the umbrella of the Northern Ireland Civil Rights Association (NICRA), which pushed to reform formal and informal housing, employment, and voting policies that disadvantaged Catholics and the working class. Inspired in part by the civil rights movement in the United States, NICRA and the newly formed People's Democracy began to hold protests, sit-ins, and marches to bring attention to the second-class status of Catholics in the North and put pressure on the governments at Stormont and London to enact reforms.[40]

Although the vast majority of the civil rights marchers were nonviolent, their actions were provocative, often deliberately so. They helped raise the temperature in the North, leading to attacks by Royal Ulster Constabulary

(RUC) members and Protestant civilians on Catholics, and vice versa. After the first civil rights march in August 1968, subsequent acts of civil disobedience centered around Derry, long a nationalist stronghold near the western border with the Republic that held a Catholic majority yet a unionist, Protestant government. When a counter-march by the Protestant Apprentice Boys attempted to pass through the Catholic Bogside area of Derry on August 12, 1969, rioting erupted between Catholics and the RUC for days, leading to a number of deaths. These events became known as The Battle of the Bogside and marked the start of The Troubles.

In response to the RUC crackdown, NICRA called for uprisings in other parts of Northern Ireland to show solidarity and to stretch RUC resources. The greatest violence erupted in Belfast, where six people were killed and forty-two were injured from gunshot wounds alone on the night of August 14.[41] By the end of the riots on August 17, over 750 people in Belfast had been injured and hundreds of homes and businesses had been destroyed (over 80% of them Catholic-owned). Catholic areas in Derry and Belfast put up barricades to protect themselves from the RUC, the B-Specials (a reserve police force infamous for its brutality among Catholics), and Protestant mobs led by paramilitaries such as the small but effective UVF.

Despite growing unity, a focus on nonviolent protest, and greater mobilization of individuals across the movement, the campaign failed to make significant progress. The IRA was literally the radical flank of the civil rights marches, in that its members often served as stewards in smaller numbers to protect marchers.[42] Unfortunately, the good cop–bad cop approach was ineffective because the good cop's credibility and signaling were hurt by the presence of a significant bad cop who many believed could not change its ways. As the leader of the Ulster Unionist Party (UUP) later claimed, "The behavior and tactics of the Civil Rights movement soon clarified the matter. . . . This was really just the republican movement in another guise."[43]

The IRA had known that violence was a possibility from the beginning, as it often assigned members to protect Catholic neighborhoods. But Goulding's desire to shift the focus away from armed struggle left the IRA unprepared for the scope of the riots, which initially surprised all the parties in fall 1969. The IRA had too few men deployed with too few weapons.[44] As a result, many felt that the leading republican group had failed in its historic mission of protecting Catholic civilians, leading them to look for an alternative to stop what many considered a growing pogrom against Catholics by the majority Protestant population.

Despite the riots, the IRA leadership initially decided to double-down on its shift toward nonviolent political action. At the annual convention in December 1969, the leadership and a majority of the party voted to end abstentionism and recognize the Irish government in Dublin, the British government in London, and the Northern Irish government at Stormont. For many, this was the final straw because recognizing the governments of the partitioned states and the responsible colonialist power was the antithesis of achieving a thirty-two-county republic. Abstentionism had split the pro- and anti-Treaty IRA, it had split De Valera's Fianna Fáil from the IRA, and it would now split the IRA once more, and not for the last time.

Close to a quarter of IRA members broke off to form the Provisional Irish Republican Army (PIRA, or Provos), with the majority group now known as the Official IRA (OIRA, or Officials). At the Sinn Féin Ard Fheis in January 1970, the party split in similar fashion, with a new Provisional Sinn Féin set up to support the PIRA.[45] The PIRA saw itself as the true inheritors of the Easter Rising and the War of Independence, and most of its early leaders were of the older generation of the 1940s and 1950s, who had conducted the Border Campaign. Although comparatively smaller initially, the existence of the PIRA ensured that there would be no hegemonic republican wing, let alone a hegemonic national movement. The rivalry between the OIRA and PIRA drove the dynamics of the movement at the outset of The Troubles. Although the infighting and outbidding ultimately helped the PIRA leapfrog the OIRA in the movement hierarchy, it was strategically counterproductive.

THE RISE OF THE PROVOS AND THE VALUE OF "DEFENSIVE" VIOLENCE

The OIRA initially thought that the PIRA would "fizzle out," in part because "At first the Provisionals were dwarfed by the Official IRA and there were sufficient members and new recruits for only one battalion in the [Belfast] Brigade area."[46] Even though the PIRA had its General Headquarters in Dublin, its Belfast Brigade soon became the military and political center of the group, in large part because Belfast was the front line in The Troubles. D Company of that battalion was responsible for the Lower Falls Area, the Catholic heartland of Belfast based precariously near the Protestant stronghold of Shankill Road. D Company later became the largest unit in Belfast, but it started out with only twelve members and a few obsolete guns.

One of those twelve members was Brendan Hughes, who described how he and others were drawn to the PIRA not by ideology but by a desire to defend Catholics and hit back against the unionist enemy. There was no guarantee that the weak PIRA challenger would survive in its first months; the group needed something to distinguish itself and pull its strength up from the depths. Force was the answer, employed initially to defend Catholic areas against loyalist mobs, paramilitaries, and the Protestant-dominated security forces. Hughes provides a picture of the early operations, which were largely defensive in nature: "In 1970–71, a lot of time was spent on standby, which meant that you were armed, you were sent to a particular house and told to wait there for further instructions—either an operation was going to take place or you were to patrol the streets with weapons to let the people of the area know that there was protection."[47] Even when the PIRA resorted to violence in its early days, it was largely in defense of Catholic areas, such as when a few of its volunteers deployed to Short Strand, a small Catholic enclave of 6,000 surrounded by 60,000 Protestants in East Belfast. Although loyalists and republicans disagree over who started the violence, it is clear that after a (unionist) Orange Order march in the area, the groups exchanged fire. The PIRA men were perched atop the local Catholic Church, St. Matthew's, which they claimed the loyalist mobs were aiming to burn down. PIRA Belfast Brigade Commander Billy McKee led the republicans, who, despite their few armaments, gained a significant popular victory in the eyes of many Catholics for their efforts.

Thus in addition to their members' individual desires to protect their neighborhoods, the Provos' use of violence served as costly signals of their commitment to the cause for potential supporters in Northern Ireland and beyond. The group who got and used guns first and most often had a big organizational advantage. Joe Doherty, a new PIRA member, was drawn to the group after he heard that, "Provisionals have all the guns, Officials have all the typewriters."[48] Despite their meager beginnings, the PIRA had several hundred volunteers in the Belfast Brigade by the end of 1970 and over a thousand members in Belfast by early 1971.[49] The use of violence by the group not only attracted new recruits but also some OIRA members who had initially stuck with the organization. By spring 1970, fifteen of the sixteen original OIRA companies in Belfast had shifted to the PIRA, with only the crucial Lower Falls still largely in the OIRA column.[50] This influx of new recruits and OIRA defectors allowed the PIRA to expand to three brigades, as well as four battalions in Belfast alone.

The popular support generated by the PIRA use of defensive force helped secure warm meals, open doors, and helpful information from the local populace. As Hughes noted, "Most people cooperated with the IRA; they left their back doors open, or if they saw you jumping over the yard wall, they'd open the back door if it was closed. So you had that sort of relationship; we were the fish and the water was our local community."[51] The group also needed significant funding to maintain itself, however, and was unlikely to find much among its working-class Northern Ireland base. Luckily for the PIRA, the attacks against Catholic communities and its defensive efforts convinced a number of funders in the Irish Republic and the United States to support the group.

In the South, Fianna Fáil had been outraged by the 1969 riots, and some of its members looked to clandestinely support groups that would prevent a recurrence while also weakening a potential rival (OIRA/Official Sinn Féin [OSF]) that had discussed overthrowing the government in the South.[52] Fianna Fáil began to provide limited funding, armaments, and training in late 1969 and early 1970. Although the subsequent public revelation of these acts led to the sacking of government ministers and an end to the policy, this early boost had helped the PIRA along in the early stages when its survival was in doubt.[53] Far more significant and sustained financial support came from the United States, where massive Irish-American communities harbored significant pockets of wealth and goodwill for the republican cause. Donations from the Irish Northern Aid Committee (Noraid) and shipments of Armalite assault rifles significantly increased the strength of the PIRA.[54]

Defensive violence did not cause the PIRA too many problems because their supporters would not disapprove of RUC men or even loyalist civilians being killed while the PIRA was directly defending Catholic homes. Furthermore, this approach allowed the PIRA to benefit from the heavy-handedness of the government and the security forces, as one PIRA recruit who joined in 1970 noted, "The British Army, the British government, were our best recruiting agents."[55]

Many British problems stemmed from an initial lack of good intelligence, particularly concerning the smaller and newer PIRA. Doherty described how "British intelligence was bad early on. One time they knocked on the door of the Sean South and Fergal O'Hanlon Club and asked to speak to 'Sean South and Fergal O'Hanlon.' The IRA guys there told them that they should look for them at the cemetery. The British asked if the two lived near there, and then were informed that they were buried there. The IRA often named clubs after members who had been martyred."[56] To the extent the British did target an organization initially, it was the less violent OIRA, simply because the British had more information about its membership. OIRA members were often jailed after attacks by weaker, lesser known republican groups such as the PIRA and Saor Éire.[57] One OIRA member claimed that "80% of the people arrested in the first wave of internment were Officials, because the British had intel on us from Operation Harvest [the Border Campaign] and our political activity."[58]

The image of the PIRA as a defensive force sacrificing for the cause was also significantly heightened by the government initiation of internment without trial in August 1971. The widespread arrest and detention of Catholics suspected of involvement with the armed groups generated support from across the movement.[59] Indeed, some of the most forceful protests *against* internment came from a new nationalist rival that felt that the PIRA and OIRA would crumble if the detainees were released: the SDLP.[60]

A NEW LEADER: THE SDLP

The IRA British Campaign, Northern Campaign, and Border Campaign all had one thing in common: the leading group in the Irish national movement in the North was nationalist throughout, not republican. The civil rights period leading up to The Troubles was no different; however, the reinvigoration brought by marches, boycotts, and sit-ins came at the price of splintering the nationalist camp. The Nationalist Party, the descendant of the IPP in the North after partition, had been a weak movement leader for decades. But even as some of its members helped initiate the civil rights protests, the lack of cohesiveness in the party came to the fore.[61] The Nationalist Party had to contend with the rising National Democratic Party and People's Democracy, each of which polled within striking distance in late 1960s elections. Had this trend continued, the PIRA may well have had a chance to repeat the story of 1918, getting its republican house in order and then sweeping the divided nationalist opposition from the field. Unfortunately for the republicans (and perhaps the movement), the rise of the SDLP ensured that the nationalists would retain a significant group in the movement, and one at the top of the hierarchy at that.

Frustrated by the division and direction of the existing nationalist parties, six existing Stormont members of Parliament (MPs)—Ivan Cooper, Austin Currie, Paddy Devlin, Gerry Fitt, John Hume, and Paddy O'Hanlon—agreed in August 1970 to found the SDLP. Indeed, John Hume wrote of the Nationalist Party in 1964, "In forty years of opposition, they have not produced one constructive contribution on either the social or economic plane to the development of Northern Ireland."[62] The aim of the SDLP was to change that by serving as the proactive dominant face of nationalism in the region.

From the outset, the SDLP shared the ultimate objective of all parties in the Irish national movement: a unified, independent Ireland. An internal SDLP policy paper from September 1971 said that the group would "ultimately wish to seek a socialist 32-County Republic enjoying a harmonious relationship with Britain and other countries."[63] Contrary to the PIRA, however, the SDLP believed that the best way to achieve this was through constitutionalism, community building, and consent. The founding document of the SDLP called for "friendship and understanding between North and South with the view to the eventual reunification of Ireland through the consent of the majority of the people in the North and in the South."[64]

The SDLP strategy for Irish unity was thus based on working with unionists in Stormont and building bridges between the Catholic and Protestant communities to, over time, dispel prejudices and fears of a unified Ireland. The civil rights movement was a reflection of this strategy; the goal was to better the lives of the people in the North as an end in and of itself, as well as a stepping stone to unity. The strategy thus depended heavily on Protestants and unionists because the SDLP believed that the goals of the Irish national movement could not be achieved if they remained an implacable enemy.

The SDLP denounced violence and sought to restrain it, not only because many of its members considered the use of force abhorrent but also because it recognized that polarization of the population threatened the position and strategy of the group. SDLP MPs described a 1971 PIRA attack on the Four Step Inn on the Shankill Road as "a criminal outrage and clearly a callous murderous attempt to stir up sectarian strife in Belfast."[65] In response to growing support for PIRA campaigns in the United States, MP John Hume visited U.S. politicians and Irish-American groups in early 1972 to argue that "violence was only exacerbating a bad situation and making it worse."[66] As an organization that worked with the British and unionists more than any other in the national movement, the SDLP knew that its legitimacy and power were diminished the more hatred and distrust existed between the sides it sought to bring together. Even when the SDLP "found it expedient to temper their condemnations of the IRA," it was due to concerns surrounding popular support because many in the nationalist community believed that the paramilitaries still provided a measure of defense, particularly in Belfast.[67]

That SDLP actions were driven by movement competition is clear from MP Gerry Fitt's secret meeting with British Home Secretary Reginald Maudling in December 1971. First, Fitt told the British that a recent OIRA attack on a unionist senator had not been "properly exploited" and that better propaganda that played up the destruction of his body "could have had a considerable effect on Catholic public opinion." Second, in regards to a recent bombing at McGurk's Bar (the deadliest in the entire history of The Troubles), Fitt argued that "every effort should be made to pin responsibility for the explosion on the Provisionals," even though he was not certain they had done it (and it turned out to be a UVF attack). These suggestions were explicitly designed to weaken SDLP challengers and "give [the SDLP] the excuse to join discussions" with the British, thus furthering the organizational and strategic progress of the SDLP.[68]

For their part, republican groups viewed the SDLP as "a pro-British, 'Redmondite' party, located within the tradition of the compromisers of the IPP nearly a century earlier."[69] Republican attacks on the SDLP often went beyond mere words, as Denis Haughey, a founding member, explained, "The Provos and their supporters attacked me and my family in the streets, threw rocks and bottles at my house, made threatening phone calls, and others in the SDLP like John Hume faced far worse. We faced more attacks and threats from the Provos than from the loyalists."[70] The PIRA believed that the British were responsible for creating the sectarianism and division, so British withdrawal was a necessary step to end sectarianism, not vice versa.

As distasteful as the SDLP strategy was to the republicans, it was the strength of the party that made them a real threat. After all, the PIRA was not nearly as concerned with the ideologically similar but now far weaker Nationalist Party. After its founding, the SDLP immediately began to consolidate power. Its initial six MPs (and one senator)—coming from the

National Democrats, the Republican Labour Party, the Nationalist Party, and the Northern Ireland Labour Party—made it the strongest nationalist group on the day of its founding.[71] It then moved to absorb other parties, including the National Democratic Party, which dissolved itself and passed a resolution that all of its members should join the SDLP.[72] The first SDLP conference in October 1971 drew over three hundred delegates representing tens of thousands of supporters.[73] The fact that the SDLP did not form an armed wing and Provisional Sinn Féin did not run for elections at the time makes it difficult to compare the strength of these competing groups directly.[74] Nevertheless, it is safe to say that the SDLP was stronger than the republican groups in Derry and overall in the North, although the PIRA may have held sway in Belfast.

In any case, the rise of the SDLP alongside a fragmented republican wing helped ensure that a hegemonic Irish national movement was unlikely to emerge. Unfortunately for the SDLP and the Irish national movement in general, many unionists and loyalists saw the SDLP as a conspirator at worst or a cat's paw at best for the IRA, despite these internal rivalries. Thus, not only did the SDLP, PIRA, and OIRA compete for power and pursue contradictory strategies, but their presence also sent mixed signals to the unionists and British, undermining the credibility of all parties in the movement. As Haughey explained from the SDLP perspective, "We kept arguing with the Provos and their supporters. They hurt our ability to deliver for the national community; they weakened our case. We could have gotten the British to the table and gotten a lot further if it weren't for the Provos."[75]

RACING TO THE BOTTOM IN A RACE TO THE TOP

As the rivalries with the OIRA and SDLP heated up, it became difficult for the PIRA to continually demonstrate that it was protecting Catholics. After all, it is far easier to prove that one had taken a life than that one had saved one. Being on the front lines facing down British curfews and loyalist mobs certainly helped, as the PIRA did during the Siege of St. Matthew's in Short Strand. Sectarian killings were another matter, however. In discussing such attacks, Anthony McIntyre, a former PIRA-member, notes, "The [P]IRA, who were supposed to be defenders, could never actually defend. There was no way to defend against these things. So the only way to appear to be defending, to appear to be active, was to take out other people."[76] In other words, deterrence via active "defense" was necessary, which quickly spiraled into an offensive campaign against British soldiers, unionist businesses, and, ultimately, Protestant civilians.[77]

Up until the latter part of 1970, the PIRA focused its attacks on RUC barracks. In February 1971, the group killed its first British soldier, after which the prime minister of Ireland, James Chichester-Clark, announced that "Northern Ireland is at war with the Irish Republican Army Provisionals."[78] Soon after, the PIRA began its bombing campaign in earnest, launching fifty such attacks in June 1971. As the PIRA expanded attacks to include the killing of loyalist and unionist politicians, militia members, and civilians, a former commander of a North Belfast PIRA unit said, "Those sectarian killings actually benefitted the [P]IRA. They led to greater support for us in those areas. We could respond eventually by taking out leading loyalists, which proved to the people that the [P]IRA was there protecting them."[79]

The actions of the PIRA were closely watched not only by its supporters and enemies but also by its competitors. The closest competitor was the OIRA, the leader of the republican wing at the outset of The Troubles that saw its relative power decrease as recruits flocked to the PIRA.[80] The desire by OIRA for hegemony is clear from its own internal documents, which state that "no tactical objective should be such as to divide the people or any group 50/50, it should be 90/10."[81] But the OIRA also made it clear before the PIRA campaign began that it wished to avoid violence if possible. In part because of its position of relative strength within the republican wing, it sought to work toward strategic objectives through political means. Furthermore, like the leading nationalist group, the OIRA claimed to recognize the importance of the Protestants to their ultimate success: "We want to try to get through to the Protestant working classes. We realize our success there depends on the amount of understanding. If these people understand, I believe they would support us."[82] Unfortunately for the OIRA and the broader movement, its desire to compete for the top spot in the hierarchy pulled it into strategically counterproductive infighting and outbidding with its PIRA challenger.

The OIRA engaged in violence to regain support that was now given to the PIRA, even though such actions violated the nonviolent, nonsectarian proclamations of the OIRA. As with the PIRA, violence provided the costly signals the group needed to prove its legitimacy, as Harry Donaghy, an Official member, explained, "As the violence increased, people would say 'What are you doing for the struggle?' At some points, your revolutionary bona fides were the bodies you had."[83] The OIRA explicitly used those bodies in appeals for support, in one case claiming it had killed British soldiers and inflicted at least "six fatalities" on the loyalist UVF in a 1971 appeal for financial support in the United States.[84] The OIRA continued to condemn certain types of (PIRA) violence—such as "irresponsible bombing of public buildings during working hours"—but carried out numerous bombings, shootings, robberies, and kidnappings of its own.[85]

Furthermore, the OIRA was not above attacking its rivals directly. As Danny Morrison, a former Sinn Féin leader, noted, "For all of the Officials' statements about pacifism and reform, they killed a member of the Provisionals first and they killed a member of the INLA first [a subsequent challenger that had also split from the OIRA]."[86] The OIRA killing of Charles Hughes, member of PIRA and Brendan's cousin, in March 1971 was one of the reasons Brendan noted that, "Every night we had to have people on standby to protect ourselves from the Official IRA, not from the RUC, not from the British Army, but from the Official IRA. . . . The Official IRA made an attempt to kill the Provisional IRA at birth."[87] Doherty—a former PIRA member who went to prison for getting into a fight with an Official—said that the rivalry ran so deep that "We had more engagement with the loyalists than with the Officials in prison."[88]

The OIRA had recognized the potential for violence to spiral out of control early on: "In mid-1971 [OIRA Adjutant-General Sean] Garland warned the movement against allowing itself to be swept up by the gathering momentum of PIRA's violence: 'Unfortunately, because of our history as a movement committed to force, we are liable to be brought down along with these elements.'"[89] Another OIRA member claimed, "We felt we were going to be dragged into a sectarian war we didn't want."[90] Despite this note of caution, the OIRA desire to keep pace with the PIRA overtook its dream of a nonsectarian workers' struggle for a united Ireland, leading to many more extreme attacks than the OIRA and the movement would otherwise desire.[91] In addition to the detonation by the PIRA of twenty-three bombs in one day in April 1972, the OIRA set off a car bomb in England at the Aldershot Army barracks that killed five female kitchen staff, a gardener, and a priest (but no soldiers) in February and murdered a nineteen-year old Catholic British soldier on leave in Derry in May.[92] In the days after the Aldershot bombing—which the OIRA initially claimed had killed at least twelve officers, rather than seven noncombatants—the OIRA launched "prestige" attacks against government ministers to demonstrate its position as a viable community defender in the aftermath of Bloody Sunday.[93] The PIRA challenger carried out more attacks using more extreme methods (e.g., car bombs), but the OIRA still held its own, and both were more violent because of the presence of the other.[94]

The OIRA actions were even more surprising given its assessment of the PIRA as apolitical gangsters of minimal intelligence that "were in it just to fight Prods [Protestants]."[95] Indeed, the fact that the OIRA thought little of the PIRA and its actions, had a strategy to largely stay out of the violence, recognized the dangers of outbidding ahead of time, and *still* succumbed to large-scale, counterproductive violence demonstrates the power of movement hierarchy and the problems of violence amid fragmentation.

Although the OIRA and PIRA were involved in a race to the top of the movement, their infighting and outbidding resembled a race to the bottom that expended scarce resources on increasingly extreme operations, muddled the movement message, and helped create new and dangerous enemies. Despite their marches and the rioting that often resulted, the unionist community was relatively subdued during the early period of The Troubles,

so much so that PIRA Chief of Staff MacStiofain said, "I can't see these people [the unionists] preparing themselves for a protracted guerrilla war. It's
just not in them."[96] Tommy Herron of the Ulster Defense Association
(UDA), the other major loyalist armed group, noted, "Remember, we
waited three and a half years. All that time we just didn't believe the security forces would let us down—would leave us so exposed."[97] When they
did feel exposed to the mass bombings of the OIRA in April 1972 and the
PIRA three months later, loyalists began to hit back in force, mostly against
Catholic civilians. Loyalists killed 102 people in 1972 and 531 by 1977, led
by the UVF and UDA.

Outbidding and the subsequent rise in sectarian violence created five
major problems for the Irish national movement. First, it led to a decrease
in support from the Catholic base as its feeling of invulnerability slipped
away with each sectarian attack and retaliation. Second, the PIRA strategy
was based on facing off solely against a colonial power. The rise of the
UVF and UDA meant that it had to cope with a new enemy, which introduced a newly committed and violent veto player. Third, increased sectarian violence played into the hands of the British, who claimed that they
had to remain in Northern Ireland to keep loyalists and republicans from
killing each other, making withdrawal less likely. Fourth, the PIRA Bloody
Friday attack led to the British launch of Operation Motorman, which involved the forcible dismantling of the barricades in Catholic areas of Derry
and Belfast, ending the no-go zones that were the best sanctuaries of the
movement.

Finally, when considered along with the SDLP, the nonviolent movement leader, fragmentation yielded competing groups within the movement
working at cross-purposes, which stymied strategic progress. On the one
hand, the PIRA aimed to coerce a British withdrawal to yield a united
Ireland. As spokesman Morrison later explained, "It isn't a question of
driving the British Army into the sea. It's a question of breaking the political will of the British government to remain."[98] However, the strongest
group in the movement, the SDLP, not only refused to join the armed
struggle, but it actively worked to stop it. This prevented the Irish national movement from raising the costs above what the British government was willing to bear. On the other hand, the SDLP aimed to build
bridges with the unionists to eliminate sectarian barriers to the prospect
of a united Ireland. But the spiraling violence of the PIRA and OIRA kept
destroying these bridges and ultimately helped to strengthen the extremist loyalist groups that worked to veto the SDLP platform. These dynamics came to a head in 1972 and 1973, when each wing of the Irish national
movement came the closest they ever would to their version of "victory,"
only to have the actions of internal competitors prevent organizational
and strategic success.

EQUAL BUT OPPOSITE FAILURES

In many ways, 1972 was a high-water mark for the PIRA. Provos, Officials, and SDLP members agree that by 1972 the PIRA had become the leading republican group.[99] Never again would the PIRA kill more people, bring in more recruits, or have greater support. In addition, never again would it come closer to successfully coercing a British withdrawal. Yet the existence of its internal rivals ensured that even its best was far from what was necessary to achieve the strategic success the group envisioned.

In an attempt to secure a cease-fire and take measure of the PIRA, British Secretary of State for Northern Ireland William Whitelaw agreed to meet with the PIRA leadership in late June 1972. The cease-fire and meeting—which was criticized by the sidelined OIRA—occurred in part due to SDLP efforts to bring the two sides together.[100] This was no surprise because the SDLP had a strong organizational interest in ending the violence. It recognized that its more moderate stance lost support as the violence against its base increased, and the group knew that any attempt to work openly with the unionists or the British in such a climate could threaten its leading position.

The cease-fire commenced on June 27 and held until the two sides met in London on July 7, demonstrating yet again the significant internal cohesion of the PIRA. The PIRA delegation included Sean MacStiofain, Martin McGuinness (Officer Commanding in Derry), and Gerry Adams, among others, with Adams having been released from prison for the occasion.[101] The PIRA representatives met directly with Northern Ireland Secretary William Whitelaw in what some of them thought would be the beginning of the end of British rule in Northern Ireland. The PIRA issued three demands, which were subsequently made public: "1) A public declaration by the British Government that it is the right of all the people of Ireland acting as a unit to decide the future of Ireland 2) A declaration of intent to withdraw British forces from Irish soil by January 1, 1975 3) A general amnesty [of prisoners]."[102] This amounted to the maximal strategic objectives of the republicans, and they showed no willingness to negotiate on these conditions.

Although Whitelaw agreed to respond a week later (he never did), it was clear that there was no chance of the British accepting such a deal. This was an attempt by the PIRA to impose an unconditional surrender, yet the strength of its fragmented movement and its subsequent actions were not nearly adequate for such an outcome. For one, although the PIRA (and OIRA) had inflicted significant damage, it had not brought the economy or the people of Northern Ireland or Britain to their knees. British Home Secretary Reginald Maudling famously noted that the British would stay with the violence at "an acceptable level," and Whitelaw's delegates told MacStiofain that "the level of casualties was not especially worrisome."[103]

Had the forces of the PIRA, OIRA, and SDLP joined into a single group, successful coercion may have been possible, but it certainly was not possible in a fragmented movement in which the group leading the violence was only a challenger.[104] Furthermore, the existence of other, nonviolent groups in the movement (and the leading group at that) gave the British hope that the PIRA could be marginalized or simply defeated. Indeed, this was precisely the British strategy coming out of the talks with the Provos. It was ironic, then, if predictable according to MST, that the group that set up the talks for the PIRA (the SDLP) was itself a major reason they were doomed to fail. In any case, the cease-fire ended two days after the negotiations, with the PIRA and the movement no closer to its strategic goals. Just two weeks later, the PIRA initiated the Bloody Friday bombings, helping to drive the rise of the loyalist militias along with their sectarian violence and extremist politics. This significantly hurt the next chance of the Irish national movement for progress, this time led by the SDLP.

Having prorogued Stormont and instituted direct rule in March 1972, Whitelaw and the British looked for a way to return to more local control, while maintaining British sovereignty over Northern Ireland.[105] The British solution came in the form of a White Paper in March 1973, *Northern Ireland Constitutional Proposals*, which envisioned a power-sharing government that represented significant concessions to the Irish national movement on its strategic goals. The new Northern Ireland Assembly would be based on proportional representation and was specifically designed to avoid the tyranny of the (unionist) majority that had been Stormont for over fifty years. Furthermore, the new government would boast a two-chamber Council of Ireland that included representatives of both Northern Ireland and the Dáil Éireann, thus institutionalizing links with the Republic for the first time since independence. Although the powers of the council were vague, it was intended to help coordinate North-South policy on industry, agriculture, tourism, and transport. These were significant concessions that were directly in line with the SDLP platform.

The subsequent bill passed in May brought the SDLP back into the Northern Irish government for the first time in two years as it stood for the 1973 elections for the first Assembly. The SDLP had pledged on numerous occasions that it would never rejoin the government as long as internment without trial continued, yet it was first in line for the elections despite the fact that more prisoners were interned than ever. Criticism of the SDLP move was not limited to republicans; the nationalist Unity group accused the SDLP of "selfishly collaborating with Whitelaw's plans to gain the spoils of office."[106] The SDLP leadership knew that it had broken its oath, but it also knew that with proportional representation the party stood to have its best electoral showing in history. As predicted by MST, the group opted for power over principle.[107]

In its 1973 Assembly Elections Manifesto, the SDLP proclaimed its pursuit of hegemony: "To achieve the necessary political changes requires maximum political strength. The SLDP seeks that maximum strength in this election."[108] The SDLP sought to further shore up its position by having Sinn Féin run as well, which would legitimize the SDLP gambit and—in the estimation of the SDLP—lead to a clear defeat for its republican rival.[109] The SDLP hopes for organizational gains were vindicated, as 82 of the 166 SDLP candidates won in the local elections, giving it 14% of the total vote. This made the SDLP the second strongest party at the local level to the long-dominant UUP, as well as the strongest party in the Irish national movement. Sinn Féin did not participate in the elections, however, and instead encouraged voters to boycott the elections. The high turnout of 72% was further evidence of the relative strength of the SDLP. In the Assembly elections in late June, the SDLP performed even better, winning 22% of the vote and nineteen out of seventy-eight seats in the Assembly. No other nationalist party won a seat, and the SDLP was within five seats of the leading (unionist) party as well as eleven seats clear of its next closest challenger. The SDLP was now the sole significant nationalist group and had a strong claim to the leading position in the movement over all republican challengers.

The problem for the SDLP was consolidating this electoral triumph. The SDLP was able to reach an agreement for a power-sharing executive in November with the dominant UUP, an accomplishment in and of itself. SDLP representatives now headed the housing and local government, health and social services, and commerce ministries of Northern Ireland for the first time, with Gerry Fitt as deputy prime minister. Negotiations concerning the Council of Ireland were held between the Irish and British governments, the UUP, and the SDLP in Sunningdale, England, in December 1973. Although the power of the council was agreed to be far less than the SDLP initially had wanted, the party was happy that precedents had been set for cooperation on the RUC and other matters that it hoped could lead to greater coordination with the Republic over time. With this, the SDLP ministers entered Stormont and began their work, side by side with their new unionist colleagues. The long-standing fragmentation of the Irish national movement would soon come back to haunt them, however.

The need of the SDLP to outbid was apparent in its overselling of Sunningdale as a major step toward a united Ireland, which angered loyalists without convincing republicans, leading both to reject it.[110] Sunningdale brought criticism of the SDLP from all sides, including from Dáil Teachta Dálas (TDs) such as Neil Blaney, who said "I am ashamed of [the SDLP] now as I have never been ashamed of 'Irish' representatives before. They have sold out while they are participating in this sham assembly."[111] Then came massive PIRA bombings in the unionist-dominated towns of Lisburn and Bangor, which had been designed specifically to target Sunningdale. The fatal blow, however, came from the loyalist side. The sectarian violence that the PIRA and OIRA had helped to spiral out of control for years had made many unionists wary of any deal with the nationalists and had led to the burgeoning of the loyalist militias. In the days after Sunningdale, the more extreme unionist groups passed a resolution against the agreement, splitting the party. Then, the Ulster Workers' Council called for a general strike, which was given great heft by the UVF and UDA, the largest loyalist paramilitaries. The UVF detonated car bombs in Dublin and Monaghan, killing thirty-three and wounding close to three hundred people, making May 17 the bloodiest single day of The Troubles. The UDA set up barricades in Protestant areas and led extensive rioting that was crucial to the success of the strike. Within two weeks, the unionist ministers were forced to resign, bringing about the collapse of the power-sharing executive, the Council of Ireland, and everything the SDLP had worked to build since its founding. Unfortunately for the SDLP, PIRA actions helped make the realization of Sunningdale impossible, and the marginalized position of the PIRA outside the negotiations gave it no incentive to try to quell the dragons its violence had unleashed.

With the PIRA on its side (or, better, the SDLP as hegemon), the Sunningdale Agreement would have had a better chance of enduring. Because of the fragmented movement and the actions it inspired amid internal competition, however, the SDLP and, more important, the Irish national movement lost out on strategic progress for the second time in two years. The Sunningdale Agreement may have been "Nationalism's answer to armed struggle," but it could not endure what competition amid fragmentation had sown.

THE LONG WAR AND REPUBLICAN INFIGHTING

After the dual failures of 1972–1973, all significant groups in the Irish national movement endured: the SDLP, PIRA, and OIRA. Despite some shifts in the republican wing, movement fragmentation was to remain firmly in place for the next quarter century. Tactics would change, weaker challengers would come and go, but the Long War would simply resemble variations on a theme: some new musicians, a slightly altered tune, but the same reprise.

After a failed campaign of bombings in England—based on the idea that "one bomb in Britain was worth ten in Belfast"—the PIRA agreed to another cease-fire with the British in February 1975.[112] Like its predecessor from 1939, however, the campaign yielded little more for the PIRA than near-universal popular condemnation and no new British concessions. The OIRA and PIRA had swapped positions in the hierarchy, and the OIRA called its rivals the "Royal Ulster Provisionals" and "the Queen's own Provos" after the PIRA began to police from incident centers granted by the British as part of the cease-fire.[113] Claiming to finally recognize that victory was not around the corner, the PIRA launched a Long War strategy. Despite the new name, however, the plan had most of the same elements as previous campaigns: make Northern Ireland ungovernable via attacks on security forces and keep the pressure on the British via attacks in England.[114]

The biggest change in the armed struggle in the mid-1970s involved a second splitting of the OIRA, which yielded actions and outcomes in line with MST: weaker groups challenging for predominance, increases in in-fighting and outbidding, and a lack of strategic success. The roots of the second major OIRA split lay in the decision by the group to agree to a seem-ingly indefinite cease-fire in May 1972, despite the continued pull of competition with the PIRA. The official OIRA newspaper, the *United Irish-man*, acknowledged the effective chain-ganging of the PIRA in analyzing the cease-fire: "The reason for taking this crucial decision lay in a growing awareness by the leadership of the Republican Movement that we had been drawn into a war that was not of our choosing, and that we were being forced to fight on enemy ground."[115]

Although the group reminded its members that "a row with a Provo is doing nothing to free Ireland," the fact that the OIRA continued to employ violence in the coming years demonstrates yet again the pull of internal competition.[116] After losing members to the PIRA during the cease-fire, the OIRA leadership caved and allowed attacks on army bases to avoid a fur-ther loss of strength and morale. Despite the cease-fire, OIRA violence in Belfast actually increased, in no small part due to its continuing rivalry with the PIRA, which called the OIRA the "rusty guns."[117] Accounts later revealed the extent to which the OIRA was concerned with its republican rival. One former OIRA man claimed, "The Sticks [OIRA] supplied shit to the North, except when the Provos got out of hand."[118] The fact that the OIRA leadership did not send sufficient weapons to field units unless the PIRA threatened led Jack Holland and Henry McDonald to argue that "The Official IRA volunteers who were troubled by the ceasefire began to have even more serious doubts about just who it was their leaders were expect-ing them to oppose—the Provos or the British."[119]

Ultimately, Seamus Costello, an OIRA member, led a split from the group, and was joined by individuals such as Terry Robson, who suggested that "We were opposed to the ceasefire, because we felt we were building up support, competing with the Provos."[120] Costello first founded a political party in December 1974, the Irish Republican Socialist Party (IRSP), and then an armed group, the INLA. Although the IRSP was held publicly to be the main force, the reality was the reverse: the INLA held most of the membership and all of the decision-making capability. As the IRSP name indicated, the main ideology of the group was socialism and republican-ism.[121] It claimed that the PIRA lacked the former and the OIRA the latter. The three groups did not wage ideological battles in debate halls, however; they waged violent fights over power in the streets.

The INLA defined itself by the use of violence, which paid early divi-dends. The new republican challenger took eighty to one hundred members from the OIRA at the outset, which already represented a considerable portion of the Officials' roughly 800–1,000 members at the time.[122] Within two months, the INLA had won many more defectors, peeling off most of the OIRA in Derry, half of its membership in the Belfast Market district, and the entire OIRA unit in Divis Flats in the Lower Falls.[123] By January 1975, Costello claimed that the IRSP (in truth, largely the INLA) had eight hundred members, and the OIRA had lost over a third of its membership.[124]

Costello thought that the INLA and OIRA would not come to blows. Not surprisingly, however, the OIRA decided to put aside its stated desire for nonviolence in an attempt to squash this internal threat. The OIRA did not want to make the same mistakes it had with the PIRA and, instead, undertook an "all-out effort to destroy this group."[125] By February 1975, the two groups were in an open feud that included INLA accusations that the OIRA had given names of their members to the UVF for elimination.[126] Numerous members on each side were attacked, including Sean Garland of the OIRA, who had warned his group back in 1971 that it was "liable to be brought down" by outbidding and infighting.[127]

From the perspective of the Irish national movement, the problem presented by the INLA was twofold. First, its emergence led to increased infighting in the movement. As one OIRA member noted, "The feud with the INLA did more damage to the OIRA than the feud with the Provos. Good quality people who we had fought alongside left; it gutted the party."[128] Second, that infighting did not initially lead to the INLA or any of its rivals being eliminated, ensuring that counterproductive outbidding was likely to continue, if not increase. With now three significant armed groups, sectarian violence rose. By the beginning of 1975, more Protestants were killed by assassination gangs than Catholics for the first time.[129]

Just as the OIRA decided to end the fighting with the INLA "to preserve ourselves" because "nobody was winning," the PIRA launched a campaign to eliminate the OIRA in fall 1975.[130] Danny Morrison, a Provisional Sinn Féin member, explained that infighting had organizational concerns at its core:

> The feuds were driven by competition, especially over guns and money. Sometimes one side or the other would find out where the other side's weapons were and would lift them. Other times the groups would raise money for prisoners or the organization, but the other group would claim that that was a Provo shop or a Stickie pub and tell them to stay away. Sometimes fights would break out between those trying to sell the *Republican News* and *The United Irishman* in the same spot. The rivalries were over building organizations. It was stupid but understandable, because you saw them as competitors and as responsible for the failure of 1969.[131]

Unfortunately for the PIRA and movement hegemony, they "made the mistake of thinking the Officials had nothing left." As one former OIRA member observed, "They were wrong."[132] Two weeks of fighting saw daily arson attacks on OIRA and PIRA pubs in Belfast, over one hundred armed attacks, eleven dead, fifty injured, and both significant groups left standing.[133] The problem of strategic focus was clear from the proclamation of one Provo who said, "If I had a gun with one bullet and I had to choose between a Stick and a Brit, I'd blitz the Stick."[134]

One of the best indications that these feuds hurt the national movement is that the British helped facilitate them. All republicans agree on this score. Danny Morrison noted, "When the British saw feuds between republican groups, they would leave the area and let it happen."[135] An OIRA member explained, "When the Provos tried to wipe us out completely in 1975, there were thirty cars with guns driving through checkpoints, and one where a tied up hostage jumped out of the car, and yet nobody was arrested. The British and police attitude was 'We'll give them so many hours to do their internal housecleaning.'"[136] In addition to allowing the groups to fight it out, the British worked to instigate infighting through General Kitson's Military Reaction Force and other military intelligence units "which used plainclothes people to commit drive-by shootings and assassinations."[137]

These actions could sow significant discord, especially because the competing groups often did not know who was attacking them. Many initially thought that it was the INLA and not the PIRA who attacked the OIRA in October 1975. Later, "In 1977 the Provos and Sticks agreed to have ceremonies at the Milltown cemetery one hour apart. A bomb went off in the area and the Sticks thought it was the Provos and opened fire, and the Provos fought back and killed 1–2 people. It turned out that it was the UVF who planted the bomb, but the OIRA jumped to the conclusion that it was the Provos."[138] Unlike the beginning of The Troubles when the British had little knowledge of groups and members, by the mid-1970s their intelligence had improved significantly: "One time they pulled me and many others into an army barracks and they had laid out in the room all of the positions of the organization on desks, and they started telling people where to sit based on their knowledge of each individual's position. When you were arrested, they would tell you what group you were in."[139]

Although the INLA and PIRA were initially friendly, as the INLA grew in stature the two groups predictably started to compete. "[The INLA's] aim was to outgun the Provos, according to one of its founding members, who said: 'The INLA had to compete with the Provos. We had to out-shoot them.'" These words were not mere bluster, as the group carried out more operations in mid- to late 1975 than did the PIRA, which soon after pulled out of its cease-fire, a move that Gerry Adams believed had weakened the group considerably.[140] Just as the 1972 OIRA cease-fire had led some members to leave for PIRA, the 1975 PIRA cease-fire led a few members to join the INLA.[141] One member who joined the group later noted that "I joined the INLA because it was more active than the Provos. I saw them on the street with guns the most often and so I joined to get the Brits out. If the PIRA had more guns and were more active, I probably would have joined them instead. I just wanted to get the Brits out."[142]

The PIRA condemned most INLA attacks, in no small part because "The Provisional leadership strongly resented any attempt being made by the INLA to present itself as the 'protector' of the Catholics in Derry."[143] After all, the PIRA saw that as its job. One former INLA member noted, "When we hit the loyalists, that got the INLA support and kudos, the PIRA would sometimes feel that they needed to do something in response because of the support the INLA got."[144]

Given the significant advantages that PIRA had in funding, weaponry, and membership, the INLA could not ultimately compete in quantity of attacks. Therefore, it looked to continue to outbid with more visible, extreme targets. Following this strategy, in March 1979 the INLA killed Airey Neave, Northern Irish shadow secretary of state and friend of soon-to-be British prime minister Margaret Thatcher, with a car bomb detonated using a new mercury tilt switch. Assassinating Neave may have "put the INLA on the map," but it did little to bring strategic success.[145] For its part, the PIRA "sought to regain the initiative"—from the INLA, not the British—by killing the queen of England's cousin and last viceroy of India, Earl Louis Mountbatten, along with his grandson and two other civilians, while also ambushing and killing eighteen British soldiers on the same day.[146]

To unionists, loyalists, and British alike, it mattered little which group committed or claimed which act: "For Protestants it appeared as if republican gunmen—no distinction was made between the tiny INLA and the IRA, one Fenian killer much like the next—were striking out at local Protestants as well as the police."[147] Fragmentation posed problems for the signaling and credibility of the movement, however. One IRSP member noted, "Martin McGuinness would have preferred that the IRSP wasn't around. It would have made it easier to give a clear message, so others don't say 'What about these other people?'"[148] It seemed as if any time one group agreed to a cease-fire, another launched attacks, drawing the previous group back in, all making it difficult for the other side to have faith in any deal with the movement. Furthermore, the infighting allowed the British to paint the conflict internationally as civil strife rather than a cohesive national movement.

PRISONERS, HUNGER STRIKES, AND ELECTIONS

The PIRA had been the leading republican group since 1972, but it began to approach hegemon status within its wing by the early 1980s. As this occurred, the PIRA began to shift its focus from internal republican politics to competition with the nationalist hegemon and movement leader, the SDLP. The currency of power in this new competition was not bombs, however, but votes. To engage, the PIRA had to increasingly cede influence to Sinn Féin.[149] Nonetheless, the continued existence of OIRA and INLA rivals meant that the PIRA kept a foot firmly planted in the demands and tactics of republicanism while it dipped a toe in nationalism, which brought new challenges for the group as it sought to straddle the divide.

The shift in strategy by the PIRA had its roots in the prisons of Northern Ireland, which played a central role in the development of armed groups and the course of The Troubles. With the initiation of internment, thousands of PIRA, OIRA, and INLA members (among others) spent time in the infamous Maze prison, called Long Kesh by its inhabitants. The special category status granted paramilitary members—which included freer association among prisoners and the ability to wear their own clothes instead of prison garb—was ended in March 1976 as part of the British desire to criminalize what they perceived as terrorist violence. New prisoners were unhappy to be housed in the recently constructed H-block wings of Long Kesh without special category status. Protests began, which included prisoners going naked and refusing to bathe to avoid wearing the prison uniform. When these protests had little effect, the prisoners, led by Brendan Hughes of the PIRA, upped the ante in October 1980. Seven prisoners began a hunger strike that they claimed would end either in their death or the granting of their demands, which roughly amounted to a return to special category status for political prisoners.

Even in prison, the familiar dynamics of The Troubles emerged. The INLA, which "both inside and outside prison need to be more militant than the Provos," pushed to have multiple members in the first hunger strike.[150] Hughes allowed only one INLA member to participate alongside six PIRA members (including himself), however, thus ensuring the dominance of his group.[151] The Officials, who had few prisoners by this time and did not acknowledge them publicly, supported British Prime Minister Margaret Thatcher during the hunger strikes due to their hatred of the PIRA: "Our thinking on hunger strikes was 'the enemy of my enemy is my friend' in this case with 'my enemy' being the Provos, we called for an end to internment but also denounced the hunger strikes."[152] OIRA members felt that the hunger strikes were a new version of costly signaling for the PIRA: "The Provos manipulated the prisoner issue. First they needed prisoners through internment to then bring in supporters and recruits from their family members and friends. Then they needed coffins from the hunger strikes to galvanize the people and increase their support."[153]

The coercive logic of the strike inside was similar to that of violence outside: raise the costs to the British so that they would comply with the demands. The fact that the hunger strikes risked no casualties beyond the strikers themselves helped the prisoners and their armed groups gain popular support. Indeed, the hunger strike has deep roots in Irish history, with Irishmen in the War of Independence using it as a political weapon. After

Hughes's hunger strike was called off without all the demands being met, Bobby Sands of the PIRA was determined to lead a second hunger strike to compel the British or, at the very least, reestablish that the movement and its members were credible in their threats.

The Sands-led strike involved waves of prisoners refusing food in roughly one-week intervals after Sands began on March 1, 1981. Thatcher and the British held firm: no concessions would be forthcoming. In a move that echoed actions from 1917, the PIRA/Sinn Féin decided to run Sands as a candidate for the April by-election in the Northern Ireland Fermanagh and South Tyrone district for British Parliament.[154] Sands's shocking victory over the unionist candidate put an imprisoned PIRA member on the fortieth day of a hunger strike in Parliament. Despite his new position, the British refused to give in to his demands, and Sands perished on May 5, 1981. His funeral was attended by over 100,000 people and was watched by many supporters and sympathizers across the globe.[155]

The most significant impact of Sands's ordeal was not on the British but, rather, on the future of his own organization. Sands's victory helped republican groups recognize the potential of electoral politics; however, many in the PIRA were wary of throwing their hat in the electoral ring, especially in light of how they had delegitimized the OIRA after it took the same step. As Morrison explains, "We were very concerned about not having what happened to the Sticks happen to us. We didn't want to weaken our group and its psyche; we sought to stand for elections without dismissing the armed struggle."[156] Just as with violent outbidding, a weaker challenger took the risky plunge first. The IRSP ran candidates in the May 1981 Northern Ireland council elections under an "Anti H-block" banner. Two IRSP candidates won seats in Belfast, along with two others from the radical socialist People's Democracy, one of whom displaced Gerry Fitt. As one IRSP member explains, "Publicly Sinn Féin might say that they were not concerned with the IRSP, but privately they were very concerned in the 1970s and 1980s, especially after the 1981 elections of IRSP-affiliated candidates."[157] Sinn Féin had not run candidates in the 1981 council elections, yet they saw their republican rivals score significant victories, including one over the former leader of the SDLP.

The 1981 elections demonstrated that republican groups could win elections, and the actions of the INLA/IRSP made the participation of Sinn Féin in future elections far more likely. First, the INLA/IRSP demonstrated that it represented a viable republican challenger whose actions required a response. Second, the fact that there was now no viable challenger denouncing elections meant that the PIRA/Sinn Féin could participate without worrying about an existing rival delegitimizing it for participating and then swooping in to claim leadership.

Sinn Féin members make it clear that the IRSP actions changed everything. Jim Gibney, the man who first suggested that Sinn Féin stand Bobby Sands for election, noted, "I was previously on record advocating for Sinn Féin to stand for elections, but I lost that debate. The IRSP ran anti-H Block candidates and did well. There is no doubt in my mind that the IRSP's performance convinced Sinn Féin to run in 1982, once they saw there was a base of support for this."[158] Danny Morrison went on to explain that the concern of Sinn Féin was not just with the INLA/IRSP, but also with the SDLP.

> I actually spoke against Sinn Féin running in elections when a proposal was raised for it in 1981. I then saw people out protesting during the hunger strikes—doctors nurses, nuns—that I hadn't seen protesting since the civil rights movement. That helped change my mind about the potential for people to vote for us. Nonetheless, there was risk there: What if the people rejected you? In a way we missed the boat in 1981, when we saw the IRSP and People's Democracy winning seats, it convinced us to run next round. We were quite concerned that the SDLP would be able to go in and mop up after what we had accomplished with Bobby Sands's election.[159]

At the Sinn Féin Ard Fheis in November 1981, Morrison famously proclaimed, "Who here really believes we can win the war through the ballot box? But will anyone here object, if with a ballot paper in this hand and an Armalite in this hand, we take power in Ireland?"[160] Sinn Féin decided to contest the 1982 Northern Ireland Assembly elections on an abstentionist platform.

Although most applications of MST have been to violence, the 1981–1982 elections clearly demonstrate that outbidding between leaders and challengers is perhaps just as likely to occur with nonviolent tactics, from civil resistance to electoral participation. The previous year, the SDLP had decided not to contest Bobby Sands's election because "It became clear that if we contested the election, we would lose a lot of support."[161] Just as the IRSP gave Sinn Féin legitimate cover to run and a viable challenger to pressure them to do so, so did Sinn Féin give and push the SDLP to do the same. But the fact that Sinn Féin ran on an abstentionist platform meant that the SDLP would risk delegitimization and loss of leadership if it chose otherwise, especially if it took its seats and failed to deliver, as with Sunningdale.[162] Sean Farren, an SDLP member, made clear that internal competition played a key role in the SDLP decision making: "There was a very detailed and intense debate over elections; I chaired the discussion in August 1982. The clear motivation was that it was necessary to stand and have democratic nationalism measured. Furthermore, if you abandon the election field, someone would inevitably take your place. To a certain extent there was a fear; it wasn't clear what the impact of the Sinners [Sinn Féin] was going to be in the 1982 elections. Some said we needed to make an impact to prevent those who support violence from becoming ascendant."[163]

The SDLP contested seats in every constituency on an abstentionist platform, wary of being sold out by the unionists and defeated by Sinn Féin.

The party won fourteen seats, which Farren describes as the first serious decline in the electoral fortunes of the party: "Overall, the SDLP's vote showed a significant drop from 159,773 in 1973 to 118,891 in October 1982."[164] Sinn Féin won five seats, 40% of the nationalist vote, and more than half the votes of the SDLP: a clear organizational success for a party that many saw as a rising challenger.

The 1982 election was only the beginning of a more direct rivalry between the SDLP and Sinn Féin. As Denis Haughey, SDLP member, explains, "Once the Provos started competing with us for votes, we had to more directly denounce them, compete with them, and deal directly with their criticisms."[165] Farren concurs, "The Provos very much saw the SDLP as their rival. Their chief target was us. They tore down my SDLP posters and left up unionist posters. Once they finally got more votes than we did in 2003, they began to see themselves as dominant; until then they regularly intimidated voters. They also stole votes via impersonation, and when Austin Currie and his brother tried to stop them from doing so in one polling station by challenging false voters, the Provos attacked them outside the polling station and broke both of their arms by dropping cement blocks on them."[166] Jim Gibney says of the SDLP, "The rivalry is bitter to this day. They dominated the nationalist, Catholic community for so long, now they think, 'How dare you challenge us; it is our rightful place to be the leading group.'"[167]

Although SDLP members claimed, "It was the violence we were trying to sideline," the New Ireland Forum of 1983–1984 and the Anglo-Irish Agreement were attempts by the SDLP and the Irish and British governments to end The Troubles that sidelined Sinn Féin.[168] The PIRA launched spoiling attacks, including the 1984 bombing of the Conservative Party Conference in Brighton—which almost killed British Prime Minister Margaret Thatcher and did kill five others and injure thirty more. Over time, the SDLP recognized that Sinn Féin was a viable challenger that had to be dealt with: "Some said we should have let the IRA weaken to the point that they imploded, but Sinn Féin was a voice that could not be ignored. We were the stronger party, but they were consistently polling 10–11 percent of the vote."[169]

Despite the shifting fortunes of the competing organizations, however, the Provos' new approach did not bear fruit strategically. From the perspective of the movement, "Armalite and ballot box" had been the defining strategy since the start of The Troubles, if not before. The PIRA, OIRA, and INLA provided the Armalites, and the Nationalist Party and SDLP sought gains at the ballot boxes. As with the new strategy of Sinn Féin/PIRA, however, all this produced were coercion campaigns that were not adequately coercive or credible, and power-sharing agreements that were spoiled at the polls and in the streets by powerful armed groups. The main impact of the strategy was that the PIRA was competing with republicans with Armalites while Sinn Féin was competing with nationalists at the ballot box. By engaging in both competitions at once, the group hoped to retain supporters who backed the use of force while gaining new ones who voted in elections, but movement fragmentation continued to prevent strategic success.

SINN FÉIN, REPUBLICAN HEGEMON, MOVEMENT CHALLENGER

By 1986, Sinn Féin/IRA became the hegemon in the republican wing of the Irish national movement due to three significant developments.[170] First, the rising challenger of the early 1980s, the INLA/IRSP, consumed itself in numerous splits, brutal infighting, and cooperative informers via the supergrass system that "decimated us more than any other group."[171] Second, the Officials had lost their position as a viable republican challenger. The longtime republican rival had undergone multiple name changes—from OSF to Sinn Féin, the Workers' Party in 1977 to the Workers' Party in 1982, and from OIRA to Group B by the late 1970s—while shifting its focus to socialist politics. Despite beliefs that the hunger strikes were the "last kick" of the Provos or that the SDLP would splinter and the Workers' Party would become "the largest publicly represented anti-Unionist force in the North," the Officials largely employed violence in racketeering efforts and their political party generally polled between 1 and 2% of the vote in Northern Ireland.[172] Finally, just as the Workers' Party was dropping *Sinn Féin* from its name, (Provisional) Sinn Féin continued to grow by pulling in voters and members from other parties, including People's Democracy, which all but merged into Sinn Féin by 1986.

As MST predicts, a shift in the hierarchy altered how Sinn Féin/IRA could gain organizationally, thus changing the behavior of the group. In 1986, the Sinn Féin/IRA leadership decided to give up abstentionism in the Dáil, meaning its elected candidates would take their seats in the government of the twenty-six-county Republic. This story is familiar because it had played out before in 1969, not to mention 1922. Holding to the script, dissenters led by former President Ruairí Ó Brádaigh walked out of the Ard Fheis and formed Republican Sinn Féin (RSF), believing that abstentionism was a principle of republicanism, not a tactic to be discarded when politically expedient. The key difference this time from 1969 and 1922 was that the new dissenting Sinn Féin faction was significantly weaker and not backed by a strong armed wing at the outset (the affiliated Continuity IRA was formed in 1986 but was not active until 1994).[173] Therefore despite low-level rhetorical and violent outbidding, the republican wing of the movement did not descend into civil war yet again because it remained hegemonic, unlike the fragmented republicans of the 1920s and 1970s. When infighting did occur—such as when the IRA forcibly disbanded the INLA splinter group the Irish People's Liberation Organization (IPLO) in 1992—it was completed quickly and at little cost to the IRA/Sinn Féin due to its relative dominance. As Des Dalton, the current president of the RSF, explains, "Ruairí himself noted that the genius of Adams was following a 70/30 approach and never going back to the 50/50 approach of 1969. Adams would fragment his opponents, who would leave at different times, for different reasons," thus maintaining hegemony for the republican wing of the movement.[174]

The shift to hegemony in the republican wing opened the eyes of Sinn Féin/IRA to understanding and engaging with those outside it. Tom Hartley, a Sinn Féin member and former Belfast mayor, explained, "They think we wake up thinking about loyalists, but we weren't, we were thinking about internal issues. We didn't even consider unionists as part of the issue until the 1980s."[175] Despite the hegemony of the republican and nationalist wings, continued fragmentation in the movement meant that competition, mixed messaging, and concerns about credibility remained to prevent victory. Nonetheless, the long-desired hegemony of the republican wing provided structural incentives and a bit of breathing room to pursue strategic progress that had evaded the movement for so long.

THE GOOD FRIDAY AGREEMENT AND BEYOND

After thirty years of conflict, The Troubles ended with a puzzle: Why could the Good Friday Agreement not have been signed and enacted twenty-five years earlier, when it was called the Sunningdale Agreement? After all, despite some improvements from the Irish perspective, the basics of the deal—power-sharing between unionists/loyalists and nationalist/republicans, Northern Ireland and the Republic, and Irish Republic and Great Britain—were the same.[176] Various parts of the conventional wisdom suggest that the answer lies in ideological shifts, the involvement of the United States, or simply the fact that key parties had learned from their mistakes. After all, Seamus Mallon, the SDLP deputy leader, called the Good Friday Agreement "Sunningdale for slow *learners.*"[177] Contrary to much of the existing analysis, however, the discrepancy is not due to philosophical changes, external actors, or organizational learning. The first is a symptom of the main cause (power shifts), the second is a relevant but secondary element, and the third suggests a development that was not new. The Good Friday Agreement was offered, agreed to, and endured because of changes in the structure of the Irish national movement. In short, Sunningdale hurt significant actors in the Irish national movement, but Good Friday helped them all.

The PIRA had previously been against such a deal because it was weaker than the OIRA, let alone the SDLP. Although it became the strongest republican group in the mid-1970s, there were still other significant challengers.

By the late 1980s and early 1990s, Sinn Féin/IRA was the only strong republican group left standing.[178] Groups such as RSF and the Real IRA splin-
tered off as Sinn Féin/IRA moved toward the Good Friday Agreement, but
they never became significant challengers to their former group and could
not force it to extensively outbid or chain-gang it into unproductive violence.[179] Instead, the IRA was able to effectively start and stop violence on
its own. It called for a cease-fire in 1994, which gave it popular support and
significant public exposure in the United States and beyond. Having been
promised a seat at the negotiating table, repeated British foot-dragging on
this score led the IRA to end the cease-fire and employ limited bombings in
1996 and 1997 to remind the other side of its potential to inflict significant
costs.[180] With its position reassured, Sinn Féin/IRA then called another
cease-fire in July 1997, which held as the group signed the Good Friday
Agreement. The IRA cease-fires helped encourage similar cease-fires by
loyalist militias and a corresponding drop in sectarian violence. Had there
been another significant republican armed group at the time, the potential
for outbidding and spoiling that would have prevented the deal in some
form would have been much higher.

In addition to their ability to control violence within the movement, the
position of Sinn Féin gave it a greater incentive to join with the SDLP and sign
the agreement because its potential organizational gains were much higher
than they would have been at any previous time. Jim Gibney explains Sinn
Féin's perspective: "Sunningdale and Hillsborough [the Anglo-Irish Agree-
ment] were about isolating and defeating the IRA. By the late 1980s, there was
an awareness that the IRA have to be part of the solution, republicans have to
be part of the solution. Sinn Féin and the IRA were also more ready to negotiate in 1994 because we had become the strong leader of the republicans. The
SDLP were very powerful, but we were in control of the republican community, which helped give us the confidence to make the deal."[181]

Even though Sinn Féin/IRA was the second strongest group, it was a
near equal to the SDLP, and within three years of the signing of the deal it
had overtaken the SDLP at the polls.[182] As Denis Haughey of SDLP said,
"Sinn Féin stole our clothes."[183] Of course, Sinn Féin was not the only group
that thought the Good Friday Agreement would bolster its organization. As
Séanna Walsh explained, after the Good Friday Agreement was signed,
"Bríd Rodgers of the SDLP apparently turned around to Sinn Féin members and said, 'We have you where we want you now.' The SDLP thought
that the Good Friday Agreement would lock the Republicans into a process
that would sideline Sinn Féin and lead to its demise. They thought it would
make Sinn Féin peripheral players, but they were wrong."[184] Competition
in the movement did not disappear—indeed the PIRA maintained its arms
for years—but the Good Friday Agreement succeeded because the hegemons of both the republican and nationalist wings thought that it would
benefit their organizations.

We need not marginalize the individuals themselves and the peace process to demonstrate the importance of movement structure. The secret talks between Gerry Adams of Sinn Féin and John Hume of the SDLP, which began in 1985, were an important step toward later cooperation within the movement.[185] The bridges built by Mary McAleese, president of Ireland, and Senator Martin McAleese, her husband (both natives of Northern Ireland), with the republican and unionist communities "cracked up an old way of doing and being and helped create a new way of seeing."[186] The involvement of the United States, which ably fulfilled the role of honest broker, helped bring credibility to the process and the various factions. The tireless work of the leaders of the SDLP, Sinn Féin, the UUP, and the Irish and British governments—which shifted to Labor control under Prime Minister Tony Blair in 1997—involved a great deal of discovery and statesmanship, without which a deal may not have happened exactly when it did.[187] Nonetheless, the key lessons for the Irish had been learned long ago; groups simply needed shifts in the power structure to act on them.

The IRA had clearly understood the importance of a joint effort for some time. OSF created a pamphlet in 1970 answering the exact same question as I do in this book—When do revolutions succeed?—presented a theory, and then analyzed that theory on ten Irish campaigns.[188] Indeed, republican and nationalist groups from Wolfe Tone's United Irishmen to the SDLP were unanimous in their criticism of fragmentation and their calls for hegemony and unity. Nonetheless, if Sinn Féin/IRA were still not a republican hegemon and not at the table, it would have rejected Good Friday just as it did Sunningdale and the deal would likely have failed.

Therefore, if there was any learning going on over the years, it was not that a hegemonic movement could yield strategic success, as is often implied, but rather that, unlike in 1918, movement hegemony was simply not going to happen. Sinn Féin/IRA realized that it could not destroy its nationalist rivals, so its best hope for organizational and strategic success was cooperation. This realization shines new light on the pithy quotation of Cathal Goulding, former chief of staff of the IRA: "We [Official Sinn Féin] were right, but we were right too soon. Adams [Sinn Féin] may be right, but he's right too late. And Ó Brádaigh [Republican Sinn Féin] will never be right."[189]

This realization did not prevent Sinn Féin/IRA from suffering the slings and arrows of new and old rivals alike; Marian Price, a 32-County Sovereignty Movement member, flipped Seamus Mallon's claim by suggesting that the Good Friday Agreement was "Sunningdale for retards," implying that the Good Friday Agreement resulted from a lack of learning, not its presence.[190] As Anthony McIntyre, a former PIRA member, asked, "Why did so many people have to die to bring us back round to accepting what we rejected in 1974, and called everybody else bastards for accepting?"[191] Although no dispassionate justification can be given for so much death and destruction, a single-level strategic analysis makes this a puzzle; a two-level framework that incorporates organizational concerns provides the answer. In short, small but important shifts in the structure of the Irish national movement explain both why the two deals were similar and also why the later deal succeeded but the earlier one did not.

Patterns of Negotiation and Restraint

The clockwork-like shifts of leading republican groups to nationalist positions of negotiation and restraint remain the most striking pattern of the Irish national movement. These shifts inevitably caused splits among individuals who held steadfast to ideological principles and led each group to face its "Four Courts Moment" between fighting old comrades to stay in power and giving up organizational and strategic gains to join the armed struggle once again.[192] In every case—from the original Four Courts shelling of anti-Treaty forces by the pro-Treaty forces in 1922 to the decommissioning of the (P)IRA and the actions of Sinn Féin against the Real IRA—the leader has opted to face down its former friends and preserve its position.[193]

Existing theories of victory that are based on the number of total groups would predict greater success and less infighting at the outset of The Troubles, when the number of total groups was smaller, and more infighting and less success at the conclusion, when the number of groups had increased due to splits. In contrast, as MST predicts, the opposite occurred because the key variable is the number of *significant* groups (which declined to its lowest figure in 1998), not the number of total groups (which increased to its highest number by 1998).[194] Contrary to other arguments on mobilization and nonviolence, the War of Independence was far more successful than the civil rights movement and The Troubles, even though the latter campaign involved far more nonviolent action and mobilized far more members of the movement. The gross size of the movement may matter on the very low end—even a hegemonic movement in Northern Ireland in the 1940s may not have succeeded with so few members mobilized—but for the periods of considerable mobilization, more was not necessarily better, and the movement structure was more important than size.

It is fair to note that before 1922 significant strategic success was possible by gaining independence for the South alone. It is seemingly harder to subsequently gain such independence for the majority unionist North, which the earlier campaign did not achieve in any case. Fair enough. But the largest impact of the Anglo-Irish Treaty was not shifting the geographic focus of the movement but, rather, fragmenting its member groups. As I noted at the outset, the second part of this chapter has focused on the balance of power in the North during The Troubles. The fragmentation of the broader movement was even more severe, however; a united Ireland would have required accommodating Fianna Fáil and Fine Gael, whose presence would have blunted the organizational benefits upon victory for Sinn Féin and the SDLP. This is not simply a speculative scenario. In 2016, Sinn Féin challenged Fianna Fáil and Fine Gael to become the leading party in the Republic, and Fianna Fáil and Fine Gael have considered or announced plans to contest elections in Northern Ireland in the coming years.

Even if comparing the War of Independence to The Troubles is comparing apples to oranges, there are apples-to-apples comparisons to be found in each time period, and those definitively demonstrate that hegemony yielded more success than did fragmentation. Campaigns in the South before 1916 aimed for Irish independence and failed, in no small part due to a lack of a strong, hegemonic movement that wedded violence and politics. In the post-1922 period, variation in effectiveness strongly correlates with the degree of hegemony in the movement. Unfortunately for the purposes of theory testing, full hegemony in the North was never achieved. Nonetheless, the impact of hegemony within the republican wing of the movement suggests that overall hegemony would have performed even better, with no spoiling of a better Sunningdale deal, no infighting or outbidding contributing to sectarian violence, and greater credibility.

Overall, I raise the possibility in this chapter of exciting and fruitful expansions of the MST. First, rather than simply analyzing a single balance of power across the entire human and geographical space of a movement, the Irish national movement reveals that the balance of power within movement wings and geographic regions can provide additional valuable insights into group behavior and movement outcomes. Finer-grained hierarchies in movement wings or regions appear to have similar, if less significant, effects on the behavior of a leading group as those based on hierarchy within the entire movement (as seen with the PIRA/Sinn Féin and the SDLP).[195] Nonetheless, balances of power within wings and regions can complement the broader balances of power to provide more precise predictions about movement actions and outcomes. For example, the most successful War of Independence campaign had hegemony across human and geographic dimensions; both nationalist and republican wings had a hegemon and Sinn Féin/IRA was the hegemon in the movement and across the country. The least successful campaign of the early Troubles saw fragmentation across Ireland and in the republican wing, while the limited success of the late Troubles had fragmentation across Ireland but hegemony in both wings. The significant potential for fresh insights from these expansions necessitates more research to better define and analyze the wings, fronts, groups and the balances of power within them. Finally, the theory should be applied more directly to explain cross-domain outbidding involving civil disobedience and electoral strategies; even groups sworn to nonviolence exhibit similar competitive behavior based on their hierarchical position.[196]

The Politics of National Movements and the Future of Rebel Power

In national movements—as in international relations, democratic politics, and economic markets—the number and strength of the actors explain the greatest variation in behavior and outcome. International systems, party systems, and markets are labeled unipolar or multipolar, one-party or multiparty, and monopoly or oligopoly, respectively. This simple variable drives the level of competition and the strategic outcome, be it war and peace, public policy, or prices and profits. The same is true for national movements, whose actors share a common strategic goal of statehood but whose groups compete with each other over which one will lead the new state and reap the associated private benefits of office, wealth, and status. As with theories of democracy, capitalism, and natural selection—in which actors seeking to maximize private goods such as votes, wealth, and progeny often end up maximizing political, economic, and social public goods—MST offers a parsimonious explanation of how and when selfish actions by nationalist groups can generate collectively beneficial outcomes for national movements.

When a political candidate or a sports team is up by thirty points in the polls or on the scoreboard, it pursues low-risk, low-reward, low-variance strategies to maintain its lead. The candidate and team play various versions of "prevent defense": the candidate avoids debates with other candidates, the team holds the ball and runs the clock, and both stick to a basic message to prevent their opponents from making any large, swift gains to unseat them while they push to end the competition as soon as possible. The candidate or team that is trailing by thirty points does just the opposite, pursuing high-risk, high-reward, high-variance strategies to try and change its position and lengthen the game. They both throw literal and figurative "Hail Mary" passes: the candidate takes extreme positions to outbid and grab headlines while aggressively targeting the leader to spark debate, and the team shoots three-pointers or pulls its goalie to gain an extra attacker. These risk-acceptant strategies are more likely to result in far greater losses for the challenger than the risk-averse strategies, but they are also more likely to result in far greater gains (hence, the high variance), making these strategies attractive to those whose only hope for organizational success is a major game change.

As with MST, challengers will pursue less-risky strategies if they are behind by three points instead of thirty, and leaders up by three points will be more likely to be pulled into a competition to score more rhetorical or actual points than hegemons that are up by thirty, knowing that a failure to outbid may lead to a loss of leadership. Whether it is a political candidate, a sports team, or an armed group, where you stand on strategy and priorities depends on where you sit in the hierarchy of your competition. Of course, hierarchical change may switch the roles of the groups in these struggles from leader to challenger and back again, but if a national movement continues to contain multiple significant groups, organizational successes and failures are likely to resemble a shifting of the deck chairs on a proverbial strategic *Titanic*. Hegemonic movements with one dominant group avoid these problems because the best way for the hegemon to gain organizationally is for the movement to succeed strategically, thus reducing counterproductive, competitive violence to achieve victory.

Explaining Violence and Victory

In this book, I make significant contributions to theory, empirics, and policy. First, I provide a parsimonious and powerful theory that explains a lot with a little. MST starts with a simple, original, and replicable typology of groups and movements built on counting the number of significant groups and placing them in hierarchical order based on their relative strength. Using this typology, the theory develops novel claims concerning the distribution of the costs, benefits, and risks of violence and victory that explain variation in group behavior and movement outcomes. Using the theory, I further demonstrate that movement structure has a significant impact on other key variables in the social sciences, including the conditions of the provision of public goods, the impact of radical flanks on movement dynamics and outcomes, the calculation of credibility, the clarity of signaling, and the dynamics of (nonstate) coercive diplomacy.[1]

Empirically, the combination of fieldwork, interviews, and archival analysis across four national movements in this study allowed the creation of rich longitudinal case studies that provide powerful insights into these key questions. The best tests of MST are the tight comparisons of most-similar and most-different cases for the same groups over time in chapters 3–6. For example, in addition to there being a hegemon in the Mandate such as the Haganah making its official policy "restraint" (*havlagah*), the MTLD escalated violence while a challenger at Sétif in 1945 but then condemned the escalation of violence while a leader in 1954. In addition, the Algerian challenger that escalated violence in 1954—the FLN—itself proceeded to restrain violence in the face of spoiling attacks against Algerian civilians and to negotiate a deal with the French after it became the movement hegemon.

For the Palestinians, the Six Day War of 1967 changed everything—territory held, enemy and supporting state strength, base population geographical distribution, and campaign location—except for the structure of the Palestinian national movement, which remained the same. This most-different comparison sees the same group initiating violence (Fatah) and the same groups attempting to restrain it (the ANM/PFLP and PLO) in strikingly similar fashion. The following year, a most-similar comparison provides further evidence of the power of MST because Fatah and the PFLP changed positions in the hierarchy, which led the two groups to swap approaches to escalatory violence, even though their ideologies, leaderships, and strategic goals remained the same.

The Irish national movement revealed a dynamic in group behavior following hierarchical change that appears as regular as the Irish Sea tides: republican groups that escalated violence, shunned elections, and denounced negotiated compromise while they were challengers, only to shun violence, participate in elections, and negotiate compromises after they become the leader or hegemon of the republican wing or the entire national movement. Despite their intense criticism of each other, this is the story of Fine Gael, Fianna Fáil, the OIRA/OSF, and the PIRA/Sinn Féin over the course of the twentieth century. In each case, moving from challenger to leader to hegemon made a group more risk-averse (and more risk-acceptant when moving in the opposite direction), with striking impacts on its behavior.

In terms of victory, the Algerian national movement failed in 1945 when it had greater unity and total movement strength, but then succeeded in 1962 only after the movement structure had shifted to hegemony during an ongoing war. The victories of the Zionists and Irish occurred a few years after hegemony, surrounded by decades of fragmented failures. The Palestinians have not yet achieved a state, but they nonetheless experienced their greatest success in a period when they had a hegemon but otherwise had been counted out diplomatically and militarily.

In addition to these tight comparisons within the movements, it is worth comparing group behavior and movement outcome across them. Tables 7.1

Table 7.1 Summary of Movement Structure and Victory across Campaigns

	Hegemonic	United	Fragmented
Total success	Algerians: 1958–1962 Zionists: 1942–1949		
Moderate success	Irish: 1918–1921 Palestinians: 1986–1993, 1995–2000		Palestinians: 1994
Limited success		Palestinians: 1974	Irish: 1986–1998
Failure		Algerians: 1944–1945, 1951	Algerians: 1946, 1947–1950, 1952–1953, 1954, 1955, 1956–1957 Irish: 1914–1917, 1922, 1968, 1969, 1970–1971, 1972–1973, 1974–1975, 1976–1977, 1978–1985 Palestinians: 1965–1967, 1968, 1969, 1970, 1971–1973, 1975–1976, 1977–1981, 1982, 1983, 1984, 1985, 1994, 2001–2016 Zionists: 1920, 1921–1924, 1925–1926, 1927–1930, 1931–1932, 1933–1941
Total success rate (%)	40	0	0
Any success rate (%)	100	33	5

Notes: To save space, a few campaigns with the same movement system in consecutive time periods are combined in tables 3.1 and 6.1, but in this table, every campaign that includes any change in movement system or movement hierarchy is listed and analyzed. Also note that for the Palestinians 1965–1967 is treated as a single fragmented campaign here, whereas it is split into two in table 3.1. This adjustment has no significant impact on the findings here; its reversal would simply lead to one more fragmented campaign that ended in failure.

and 7.2 provide a comparative overview of the impact of movement structure on victory and violence, respectively. These summaries do not hold competing variables constant, as do my previous comparisons, but they do provide further evidence of the explanatory power of MST.

The evidence overwhelmingly supports MST. Hegemonic movements were far more likely than united or fragmented movements to achieve any type of success (100, 33, and 5%) and total success (40, 0, and 0%), in particular. These findings hold up across movements; the Algerian, Zionist, Irish, and Palestinian national movements *all* had their greatest gains when their structures were hegemonic, regardless of variation in the strength of the other state, history of violence, institutions, or other factors.

Table 7.2 Summary of Movement Structure and Violence across Campaigns

	Hegemons	*Leaders*	*Challengers*
A. Total	5	34	83
Algerians	FLN: 1958–1962	AML: 1944–1945 UDMA: 1946 MTLD/MNA: 1947–1953, 1954, 1955 FLN: 1956–1957	AAU: 1944–1945 PCA: 1944–1945, 1954 PPA: 1944–1945 MTLD/MNA: 1946, 1956–1957 UDMA: 1947–1953, 1954, 1955 Centralists: 1954, 1955 FLN: 1954, 1955
Irish	Sinn Féin/IRA: 1918–1921	IPP: 1914–1917 Pro-treaty SF/IRA: 1922 Nationalist Party: 1968, 1969 SDLP: 1970–1971, 1972–1973, 1974–1975, 1976–1977, 1978–1985, 1986–1998	Sinn Féin/IRA: 1914–1917 Anti-treaty Sinn Féin/IRA: 1922 Sinn Féin/IRA: 1968 NDP: 1968, 1969 People's Democracy: 1969 OSF/OIRA: 1969, 1970–1971, 1972–1973, 1974–1975, 1976–1977, 1978–1985 PSF/PIRA: 1969, 1970–1971, 1972–1973, 1974–1975, 1976–1977, 1978–1985, 1986–1998 IRSP/INLA: 1974–1975, 1978–1985
Palestinians	Fatah: 1986–1993, 1995–2000	PLO: 1965–1967, 1968 Fatah: 1969, 1970, 1971–1976, 1977–1981, 1982, 1983, 1984, 1985, 1994, 2001–2016	ANM: 1965–1967JCP: 1965–1967 Fatah: 1965–1967, 1968 Saiqa: 1968, 1969, 1970, 1971–1976, 1977–1981 PFLP: 1968, 1969, 1970, 1971–1976, 1977–1981, 1982, 1983, 1984 DFLP: 1969, 1970, 1977–1981, 1983 PLF/PLA: 1969, 1970 Fatah-Intifada: 1983, 1984, 1985 Hamas: 1994, 2001–2016
Zionists	Mapai/Haganah: 1942–1949	General Zionists: 1920, 1921–1924, 1925–1926, 1927–1930 Mapai/Haganah: 1931–1932, 1933–1941	Ahdut HaAvoda: 1920, 1921–1924, 1925–1926, 1927–1930 Histadrut HaSephardim: 1920, 1921–1924 Haopel Hatzair: 1920, 1921–1924, 1925–1926, 1927–1930 Mizrahi: 1921–1924, 1925–1926, 1927–1930, 1931–1932 Yemenite Party: 1925–1926, 1927–1930 Alliance (GZ): 1931–1932 Unity (GZ): 1931–1932, 1933–1941 Revisionists/Irgun: 1931–1932, 1933–1941
B. Restraining violence[a]	100%	91%	45%
Algerians	FLN: 1958–1962	AML: 1944–1945 UDMA: 1946 MTLD/MNA: 1947–1953, 1954	AAU: 1944–1945 PCA: 1944–1945, 1954 UDMA: 1947–1953, 1954, 1955 Centralists: 1954

(Continued)

Table 7.2 (continued)

	Hegemons	Leaders	Challengers
Irish	Sinn Féin/IRA: 1918–1921	IPP: 1914–1917 Pro-Treaty SF/IRA: 1922 Nationalist Party: 1968, 1969 SDLP: 1970–1971, 1972–1973, 1974–1975, 1976–1977, 1978–1985, 1986–1998	Sinn Féin/IRA: 1968 NDP: 1968, 1969 OSF/OIRA: 1972–1973, 1974–1975, 1976–1977, 1978–1985 PSF/PIRA: 1986–1998
Palestinians	Fatah: 1986–1993, 1995–2000	PLO: 1965–1967, 1968 Fatah: 1970, 1971–1976, 1977–1981, 1982, 1983, 1984, 1985, 1994, 2001–2016	ANM: 1965–1967 JCP: 1965–1967 Hamas: 2001–2016
Zionists	Mapai/Haganah: 1942–1949	General Zionists: 1920, 1921–1924, 1925–1926, 1927–1930 Mapai/Haganah: 1931–1932, 1933–1941	Ahdut HaAvoda: 1920, 1921–1924, 1925–1926, 1927–1930 Histadrut HaSephardim: 1920, 1921–1924 Haopel Hatzair: 1920, 1921–1924, 1925–1926, 1927–1930 Mizrahi: 1921–1924, 1925–1926, 1927–1930, 1931–1932 Yemenite Party: 1925–1926, 1927–1930 Alliance (GZ): 1931–1932 Unity (GZ): 1931–1932, 1933–1941
C. Escalating violence[b]	20%	24%	52%
Algerians	—	MTLD/MNA: 1955 FLN: 1956–1957	PPA: 1944–1945 FLN: 1954, 1955
Irish	Sinn Féin/IRA 1918–1921	—	Sinn Féin/IRA: 1914–1917 Anti-Treaty Sinn Féin/IRA: 1922 OSF/OIRA: 1969, 1970–1971, 1972–1973, 1974–1975 PSF/PIRA: 1969, 1970–1971, 1972–1973, 1974–1975, 1976–1977, 1978–1985, 1986–1998 IRSP/INLA: 1974–1975, 1978–1985
Palestinians	—	Fatah: 1969, 1971–1976, 1983, 1984, 1985, 2001–2016	Fatah: 1965–1967, 1968 Saiqa: 1968, 1969, 1970, 1971–1976 PFLP: 1968, 1969, 1970, 1971–1976, 1977–1981, 1982, 1983, 1984 DFLP: 1969, 1970, 1977–1981, 1983 Fatah-Intifada: 1983, 1984, 1985 Hamas: 1994, 2001–2016
Zionists	—	—	Revisionists/Irgun: 1931–1932, 1933–1941

	Hegemons	Leaders	Challengers
D. Negotiating with the government[c]	100%	56%	13%
Algerians	FLN: 1958–1962	AML: 1944–1945	UDMA: 1947–1953
Irish	Sinn Féin/IRA: 1918–1921	IPP: 1914–1917 Pro-Treaty SF/IRA: 1922 Nationalist Party: 1968, 1969 SDLP: 1970–1971, 1972–1973, 1974–1975, 1976–1977, 1978–1985, 1986–1998	NDP: 1968, 1969 People's Democracy: 1969 PSF/PIRA: 1972–1973, 1974–1975, 1986–1998
Palestinians	Fatah: 1986–1993, 1995–2000	Fatah: 1994, 2001–2016	Hamas: 2001–2016
Zionists	Mapai/Haganah: 1942–1949	General Zionists: 1920, 1921–1924, 1925–1926, 1927–1930 Mapai/Haganah: 1931–1932, 1933–1941	Alliance (GZ): 1931–1932 Unity (GZ): 1931–1932, 1933–1941
E. Spoiling[d]	0%	3%	14%
Algerians	—	—	PPA: 1944–1945
Irish	—	—	Anti-Treaty SF/IRA: 1922 PSF/PIRA: 1972–1973, 1978–1985, 1986–1998 IRSP/INLA: 1974–1975
Palestinians	—	Fatah: 1977–1981	Fatah: 1965–1967, 1968 PFLP: 1970 Hamas: 1994, 2001–2016
Zionists	—	—	Revisionists/Irgun: 1933–1941

Notes: To save space, a few campaigns with the same movement system in consecutive time periods are combined in tables 3.1 and 6.1, but in this table, every campaign that includes any change in movement system or movement hierarchy is listed and analyzed. *Algerian groups:* AAU, Algerian Association of Ulama; AML, Amis du Manifeste de la Liberté; FLN, Front de Libération Nationale; MNA, Mouvement National Algérien; MTLD, Mouvement pour le Triomphe des Libertés Démocratiques; PCA, Parti Communiste Algérien; PPA, Parti du Peuple Algérien; UDMA, Union Démocratique du Manifeste Algérien. *Irish groups:* INLA, Irish National Liberation Army; IPP, Irish Parliamentary Party; IRA, Irish Republican Army; IRSP, Irish Republican Socialist Party; NDP, National Democratic Party; OIRA, Official Irish Republican Army; OSF, Official Sinn Féin; PD, People's Democracy; PIRA, Provisional Irish Republican Army; PSF, Provisional Sinn Féin; SDLP, Social Democratic and Labour Party. *Palestinian groups:* ANM, Arab Nationalists Movement; DFLP, Democratic Front for the Liberation of Palestine; JCP, Jordanian Communist Party; PFLP, Popular Front for the Liberation of Palestine; PLF/PLA, Popular Liberation Forces/Palestine Liberation Army; PLO, Palestine Liberation Organization.

[a] Groups are coded as "restraining violence" if they verbally denounce the violent actions of other groups in the movement or physically try to stop or prevent them.
[b] Groups are coded as "escalating violence" if they launch an attack when other movement groups are not attacking or strike a more extreme target that other movement groups are not striking.
[c] Groups are coded as "negotiating" when they have formal discussions with the enemy state over the political autonomy of their nation and its people.
[d] Groups are coded as "spoiling" when they launch violence during such negotiations with clear evidence that the violence is intended to scuttle the talks and any subsequent agreement.

The Algerian and Zionist movements gained statehood during hegemony after years of failed fragmentation and unity. Once the FLN dominated the Algerian movement, the group effectively pressured the French, garnered international recognition, and ensured that there was only one Algerian address for negotiating an end to the conflict. The rise of Mapai/Haganah allowed the Zionist movement to develop a cohesive political and military strategy that won the support of the United Nations, defeated multiple Arab armies, and avoided the infighting that could have spoiled the founding of Israel. The one hegemonic Irish campaign under the dominance of Sinn Fein/IRA saw large-scale British withdrawal, the Anglo-Irish Treaty, and the establishment of the Irish Free State in 1921–1922, only six years after the Easter Rising had failed due to internal divisions caused by fragmentation. After decades of Palestinian movement fragmentation and failure, the hegemony of Fatah just before the First Intifada allowed the group to gain control of the uprising in the West Bank and Gaza and to employ a cohesive strategy of strikes, protests, and largely nonlethal violence that successfully coerced the Israelis and generated significant international sympathy and momentum for the most significant strategic gains to that point in the struggle, even if they fell far short of Palestinian aspirations.

In fact, none of the movements achieved total success—and almost none achieved even moderate success—in a campaign that was either united or fragmented. The lone moderate success of a fragmented movement happened in the Palestinian national movement when Hamas *barely* edged into significance, sandwiched by years of Fatah hegemony on both ends. As such, it is the exception that proves the rule. Instead, united and fragmented movement structures saw the darkest days for the Algerians, Zionists, Irish, and Palestinians. As predicted, united movements achieved more success than fragmented ones, and the difference (0% vs. 0% for total success and 33% vs. 5% for any success) was far smaller than the difference between hegemonic and nonhegemonic movements, confirming that the key distinction in movement structure is the balance of power, not the degree of unity.

Table 7.2 reveals strong support for MST claims about the impact of movement structure on group behavior. On the key predictions of whether groups escalate or restrain violence and negotiate or spoil, the percentages break down largely as predicted. Hegemons restrained violence more often than leaders, who restrained violence more often than challengers (100, 91, and 45%), while challengers escalated violence more often than leaders or hegemons (52, 24, and 20%).[2] Hegemons negotiated more often than leaders, who negotiated more often than challengers (100, 56, and 13%), while challengers spoiled far more often than leaders or hegemons (14, 3, and 0%). It is quite striking that *every* hegemon negotiated and restrained violence, while almost *no* hegemons or leaders spoiled, which aligns perfectly with MST claims about groups acting based on the likely organizational benefits tied to strategic success.[3] Ben-Gurion suggested that "The assumption that a party in power resembles a party in opposition is not proven."[4] This analysis demonstrates that not only is that assumption not proven but that, in fact, the truth is precisely the opposite, as Ben-Gurion implied.

Some exceptions even more strongly prove the rule because groups such as the JCP in the Palestinian case and the MNA in the Algerian case did in fact employ violence and spoil, respectively, but they are not counted as doing so here because their violence and spoiling occurred a year or two after they had weakened from challengers to subordinates. Furthermore, as discussed in chapter 6, the analysis of the wings in the Irish national movement would lead to even fewer challengers restraining violence and negotiating because the Sinn Féin/IRA decision to do so in the late 1990s occurred after the group had become the hegemon of the republican wing, although not yet of the movement.

MST thus provides new periodizations of national movements that anticipate otherwise unexpected changes and stasis in group behavior and movement outcome. The theory helps us recognize that conflicts such as the 1967 War and World War II did less to alter the actions and outcomes of the Palestinian and Algerian national movements than previously assumed and that overlooked changes during what are otherwise assumed to be dark periods in 1986 and 1958 helped spur these movements to success. MST also helps us recognize that leadership changes did not usher in new eras and strategies for Hamas and the IRA; new positions in the movement hierarchy did. MST thus meets Robert Jervis's standard of reading history without group names because replacing the alphabet soup of group acronyms with hegemon, leader, challenger, and subordinate is both conceptually clarifying and analytically powerful.[5] MST provides a powerful new lens through which to view these crucial cases in particular and national movements in general, making possible a reevaluation of previous theoretical assumptions and historical interpretations.

Integrating Subfields and Analyzing Competing Arguments

MST attempts to explain the greatest variation in group behavior and movement success. Scholars in a variety of subfields—social movements, civil war, insurgency, revolution, terrorism, and asymmetric conflict—have analyzed these issues extensively, although rarely together. Most studies of movement success do not offer a theory of group behavior; most studies of group behavior do not offer a theory of movement success. The greatest strengths of MST stem from its integrated framework, which identifies the conditions under which organizational and strategic objectives are complementary or contradictory. In doing so, MST reconciles the two major competing schools of thought for social movements: resource mobilization and political opportunity. MST demonstrates the centrality of organizations in social movements, while arguing that movement dynamics are driven by opportunities *within* a movement, as opposed to simply external opportunities presented by the existing regime.[6]

Nonetheless, by attempting to explain so much with so little, MST also makes a number of incorrect predictions. In this section, I analyze the explanatory power of competing arguments for the campaigns of the Palestinian, Zionist, Algerian, and Irish national movements. I find that, although none explains a greater amount of variation in actions or outcomes than MST, some serve as valuable complements and highlight areas for future research.

CORE COMPETING ARGUMENTS FOR VARIATION IN MOVEMENT VICTORY

First, all scholars who have presented arguments about the impact of movement fragmentation on effectiveness have suggested that either united or fragmented movements are the most successful. On the contrary, in these case studies armed groups and their national movements suffered continuous, costly strategic failures during their united and fragmented campaigns, which were far less likely to be successful than hegemonic campaigns.

Those movements that had the most fragmentation—the Palestinians and the Irish during The Troubles—were the least successful due to a lack of credibility and clear signaling during repeated infighting, outbidding, chain-ganging, spoiling, and foreign meddling. Unity made little difference—for the Algerians in 1944–1945 and 1951, the Zionists in 1945–1946, or the Palestinians in 1974—because groups continued to compete amid alliances that were viewed skeptically by the members themselves and their state enemy alike. For example, Hamas was not a part of unifying institutions during either the First or Second Intifada; the key difference was the increase in the relative strength of the group in the interim and the impact this had on movement dynamics (more counterproductive violence) and outcomes (less strategic success). All four movements studied here received their greatest concessions toward a new state when they were hegemonic (see figures 7.1–7.4).

This analysis further reveals that the MST typology based on the number of significant groups provides more explanatory power than other existing models that rely on a simple count of all groups. First, the MST typology is more reliable given the low likelihood of missing significant groups and the high likelihood of missing small groups, which became a certainty in these cases. For example, the Nonviolent and Violent Campaigns and Outcomes (NAVCO) data set suggests that there were six Zionist political groups in 1948, whereas I identified twenty-two.[7] The Armed Conflict data set from

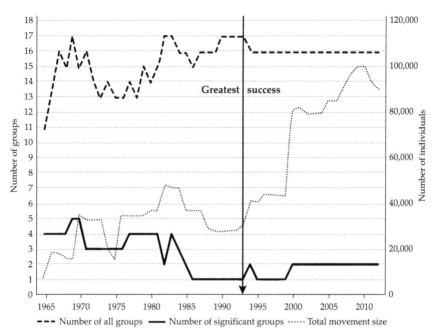

Figure 7.1. Power, Fragmentation, and Mobilization in the Palestinian National Movement

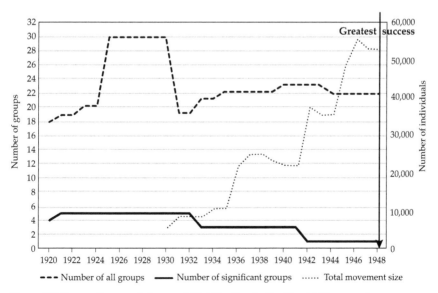

Figure 7.2. Power, Fragmentation, and Mobilization in the Zionist Movement

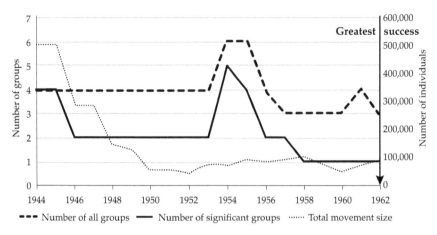

Figure 7.3. Power, Fragmentation, and Mobilization in the Algerian National Movement

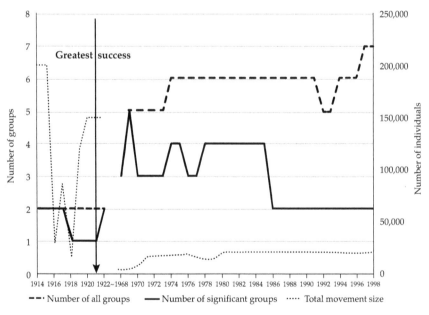

Figure 7.4. Power, Fragmentation, and Mobilization in the Irish National Movement

Uppsala Conflict Data Program/Peace Research Institute Oslo (UCDP/PRIO) seems to change its rules for counting the Palestinian groups over time, claiming one group from 1949–1964 ("Palestinian insurgents"), two from 1965–1989 ("PLO groups" and "Non-PLO groups"), and then a range of groups (up to five) after it starts listing the names of single organizations through 2008.[8] The Minorities at Risk Organizational Behavior (MAROB) data set has the best coding on this variable, although I still find discrepancies with my cases.[9]

Second, to the extent that an observer might suggest that excluding or adding these small groups does not change anything, well, MST could not agree more. Analysis of the Palestinian, Zionist, Algerian, and Irish national movements revealed the inconsequential impact of the vast majority of small groups. I have presented the history of these movements without discussing small groups such as the Palestinian Popular Struggle Front or Ha-Oved HaTzioni, and those subordinates I have briefly highlighted, such as FAAD and the 32-County Sovereignty Movement, had no significant impact on group behavior and movement outcome. When the OIRA and PFLP weakened enough to drop from the ranks of significant challengers, it had a major impact on the degree of violence and success; when subordinates such as the Jewish State Party appeared and disappeared, it did not. An analysis of figures 7.1–7.4 supports this: the greatest success of the Palestinian national movement came when there was a high number of groups as there had been in many other periods; the greatest success of the Algerian national movement came when there was a low number of groups as there had been in other periods. The greatest success of the Zionist movement came at a time when there were the most groups it had had in two decades; the greatest success of the Irish national movement came at a time when there were the fewest groups it had ever had. The number of total groups therefore provides little explanatory power for these four movements and the forty-four campaigns within them.

Nevertheless, MST and other existing arguments about united and fragmented movements are not entirely at odds. MST suggests that one particular type of alliance can change the game: merger. When two groups become one with a single leadership and clear lines of authority, *that* can change group behavior and movement outcomes, especially if it eliminates a significant group, as with the absorption by the FLN of its rivals in the mid-1950s. All other types of unions between groups are far less cohesive and enduring, and therefore are unlikely to significantly impact movement dynamics and outcomes. The theory and analysis here suggest that mergers are unlikely to occur between equals; instead, they occur between strong and weak nonrivals. One way to sum this up is that "challengers balance, subordinates bandwagon, (because) hegemons win."

Furthermore, although fragmented campaigns consistently yielded strategic failures in all four movements, the dynamic identified by Cunningham, whereby states seeking weaker or more "moderate" groups to negotiate with, is a real and powerful one. This is demonstrated by the actions of Charles de Gaulle (who sought a moderate alternative to the FLN) and the Israelis (who made concessions to Fatah when Hamas was weaker but were more hesitant to do so once Hamas had the potential to inherit the leadership of the movement). MST may provide a key scope condition to this mechanism: states will make concessions to more moderate factions but are more likely to do so with hegemonic movements than with fragmented or united movements. States certainly seek to head off extremist groups, but they are also wary of providing concessions to a moderate group that may soon lose its place in the hierarchy, leaving an extremist leader to operate from a newly strengthened position.[10]

SECONDARY COMPETING ARGUMENTS FOR VARIATION IN MOVEMENT VICTORY

MST agrees with competing theories centered on unity and fragmentation that movement structure drives movement outcome, at least in some form. This places all these theories at odds with the broader literature on effectiveness, which treats movements as unitary and movement structure as insignificant, suggesting no variation in strategic success across campaigns as the movement system structure changes, ceteris paribus. Contrary to these arguments, however, the unitary nature of a movement proved to be a powerful explanatory variable—not an assumable constant—that had a greater impact on movement success than did total movement strength, (non)violence, terrorism, regime type, regime strength, decolonization, and state sponsorship.

The first of these secondary competitors suggests that total movement strength—defined as the total number of mobilized individuals in a movement—best explains the variation in outcome. The Zionist and Irish national movements achieved their greatest success during their period of greatest total movement strength, but the greatest victories for the Palestinians and Algerians came either long after or before peaks in mobilization (see figures 7.1–7.4).[11] Nonetheless, total movement strength may help identify a scope condition for MST because no national movement is likely to succeed with ten members, even if they are all organized in a single group. All four movements had nascent periods of proto-nationalism—the mid- to late 1800s for the Zionists, the early 1900s for the Algerians and Palestinians, and the seventeenth and eighteenth centuries for the Irish—in which the number of pro-independence groups (and individuals) was not enough to constitute a robust national movement. Total movement strength is thus a worthwhile complement to MST but not a preferable alternative because the balance is greater than the sum of its parts.

Second, nonviolence was not the key to success for these movements because all four employed extensive violence and the Irish, Algerians, and Zionists employed massive amounts of violence in the years directly coinciding with their greatest victories. As MST suggests, however, less counterproductive violence—which generally translates to less total violence—

is beneficial to movements, and all four movements experienced less outbidding and infighting during their periods of greatest success. In terms of terrorism, groups in all four movements used it, so conventional approaches would suggest that terrorism totally succeeded 50–75% of the time and partially succeeded 100% of the time.[12] Nevertheless, a deep analysis of these movements reveals that terrorism was not the driving factor in movement success or failure; it mainly served as a form of escalation that, like nonviolence, was driven by movement structure. It is worth noting, however, that Erica Chenoweth and Maria Stephan find that nonviolence is more effective than violence *except* in secessionist movements, so the findings of this study are consistent with their argument.[13]

Third, external variables such as regime type and state strength did not predict outcomes nearly as well as movement structure. The three state adversaries for the national movements—Great Britain, Israel, and France—were all democracies, yet their opponents experienced a wide range of successes and failures against them. Indeed, there was even variation across cases for a single state, in that Great Britain withdrew entirely from the Palestinian Mandate but not from Ireland. Moreover, the state strength hypothesis was turned on its head because the movement fighting by far the weakest of the three states (the Palestinians against Israel) was the least successful strategically.

Fourth, there is a significant competing theory for the strategic outcome of these four cases in particular: colonialism. Some suggest that the rise of colonialism explains the failure of national movements and that the era of decolonization explains their success. We certainly cannot ignore the broad shifts in power projection and conquest that marked the colonial enterprise. After all, as William Roger Louis notes, "The number of people under British rule in the two decades after 1945 was reduced from 700 million people to five million," while the French experienced a similarly drastic decline.[14]

Nonetheless, this explanation yields predictions that are entirely wrong for half the cases in this study and partially wrong for the other half. The Irish achieved their greatest strategic success—a free state on the path to a republic—during the height of colonization, and they failed to secure a similar outcome for Northern Ireland at the height of decolonization (hence making them part of Louis's remaining 5 million). The Palestinians have as yet failed to achieve a state, even though their struggle reached its peak during a global period of decolonization. In the Algeria case, the French government made a clear distinction between Morocco and Tunisia—former colonies to which it granted independence in 1956—and Algeria, which it retained and considered part of France.[15] The Zionist case provides some potential support for the colonialism hypothesis,[16] although it does not account for why the British did not remain in Palestine until the 1960s (as they did in southern Africa and Southeast Asia), why they supported a partition plan that was favorable to the Zionists, and, of course, why the Zionists were able to defeat Palestinian armed groups and Arab states on the battle-field (some led by British officers).

These four movements, all of which consider themselves and are considered by many to be anti-colonial, had their greatest successes at very different times—1922, 1948, 1962, and 1993—that do not fit into any clean post-colonial periodization. Unlike MST, the colonialism hypothesis also fails to explain the variation in strategic success during periods of colonialism or decolonization in all four cases, which is as important as cross-case comparison. The costs of continued rule certainly helped drive states out of disputed territory, but the most important costs were those driven by the national movements themselves, not nebulous norms that often rely on reading history backward.[17] As Tony Smith argues, "history ran by other clocks whose timing and mechanisms synchronized only occasionally with the pacing of events in Europe."[18] Nonetheless, combining MST with the excellent insights of Hendrik Spruyt, Ian Lustick, and Bridget Coggins on internal state politics allows a sophisticated analysis of the two-level games of national movements and international recognition. This can provide more comprehensive explanations for puzzles that MST cannot answer by itself (and vice versa), such as why the Palestinians failed to achieve a state despite movement hegemony.[19]

Fifth, state sponsorship via the provision of wealth, guns, and sanctuary certainly helped keep groups such as Saiqa and the Arab Liberation Front afloat, but if anything, greater state sponsorship led to movement failure. The least successful movement—the Palestinians—had the *most* external state support, while the most successful—the Algerians and the Zionists—had the *least*. As MST explains, this is not a coincidence because greater movement fragmentation provides a buyer's market with more outlets for foreign meddling.[20]

Finally, this analysis helps to address another potential concern, namely that strategic success and failure drive movement structure, rather than the other way around.[21] In addition to external state actions—such as that World War I and World War II decimated the base of the General Zionists and Revisionist Zionists—exogenous factors that shape movement structure include the geographical, ethnic, religious, and economic distribution of the popular base; the presence of natural resources; personal clashes; and ideological differences.[22] Sequencing is the key to determining temporal and causal precedence, for which longitudinal analysis is well positioned. Hegemony preceded the greatest strategic successes in the Palestinian, Algerian, Zionist, and Irish national movements, but strategic successes preceded hegemony, fragmentation, and attempts at unity, and strategic failures also preceded hegemony, fragmentation, and unity across the movements. Process tracing reveals that strategic success and failure tell us little about which movement structure would come next, whereas movement hegemony almost always signaled a subsequent victory.

Also, it was not the case that hegemony came about because the movement or its base thought that victory was just around the corner. The hegemony of Fatah was established during some of the darkest days for the Palestinian national movement, and the hegemony of the FLN was achieved while the French were winning militarily and French leaders were still claiming that Algeria was part of France. As MST suggests, the distribution of the benefits of victory may be predictable, but the timing is less so. Even if or when groups recognize that hegemony makes them more likely to succeed, none will willingly put itself out of business to make it happen. Instead, the groups will compete with each other to be the hegemon, making it impossible for the groups or movements to easily "choose" hegemony and hasten victory.

It logically follows that strategic failure might help weaken the top group because it is seen as the leader and so most responsible for any outcome. This would give the top group even more reason to push for victory and the challengers further incentive to prevent progress and credit going to their rival, instead of blame. At least in these movements, however, this did not seem to be the case because the SDLP, Fatah, and Mapai stayed on top through decades of strategic failure.

As Waltz suggests, a structural theory such as MST will be better at explaining the impact of structure on behavior and outcomes than on when and why structure changes.[23] We may know what did not drive movement structure in these cases—strategic success—but more research is necessary to pinpoint what actually did. Thankfully, an excellent new wave of scholarship has begun to take up the challenge.[24]

COMPETING ARGUMENTS FOR VARIATION IN GROUP BEHAVIOR

MST offers better predictions not only for movement outcome but also for group behavior. Most of the competing theories discussed so far do not offer an explanation for the latter. MST agrees with the basic claim of those who do offer an explanation, specifically that more fragmentation leads to more violence. But MST goes further by making predictions about the actions of specific groups based on their position in the hierarchy. As demonstrated in chapters 3–6 and my discussion of table 7.2, the hierarchical position of groups explains the significant variation in their decision to escalate or restrain violence and negotiate or spoil. Alternative explanations for group behavior fare relatively poorly.

First, many scholars argue that ideology—specifically a certain religious or political belief system, or a radical version of any type—drives a group to escalate or shun violence, and to compromise with a state enemy or hold out. In contrast, in the Palestinian and Irish national movements, groups such as Fatah and the PIRA—whose very mission statements foreswore cease-fires, negotiations, and participation in elections *and* which used violence against stronger groups for these very reasons—reneged on these ideological positions like clockwork after they moved up the ladder. Ideology may help to explain the actions of some groups that foreswore violence, such as the SDLP in the Irish national movement. It is fair to note, however, that the SDLP was never a weaker group like the Palestinian or Algerian communists or the UDMA, all three of which similarly foreswore violence for years before forming their own armed wing or joining other violent groups and launching attacks when they felt their survival was at stake. Although they were not selected on this basis, my cases include movements that are predominantly Christian (Irish), Jewish (Zionist), and Muslim (Algerian and Palestinian). What stands out from a comparison across them is not their differences but their similarities, and how power drove group behavior and movement dynamics regardless of which religion dominated the movement.

Second, the impact of leaders on the use of violence was far less important than that of group position. When the hierarchical position changed but the group leadership remained the same, or vice versa, group behavior followed the position. Fatah had the same individual leader for forty years, yet the group varied significantly in its pursuit of victory and use of violence over time due to its rise from challenger to leader, to hegemon, and back to leader. When Mahmoud Abbas took control of the group after Arafat's death, it maintained its pursuit of negotiations with Israel and restraint of Hamas. The assassination of a leader may lead to revenge strikes for a couple of weeks, but behavior is largely driven by position and the incentives it provides.

Third, the age of groups was a less significant factor than group position. The PFLP and Fatah were both close to forty years old at the start of the Second Intifada, yet the PFLP challenger shunned negotiations and escalated suicide bombings earlier, while the Fatah leader initially resisted such attacks and continued to pursue negotiations. Some republican groups in the Irish national movement did move away from violence over time, but the change generally followed a shift to the top, which rarely happened overnight. If a group subsequently fell back to the ranks of the challengers or subordinates, as was the case with the OIRA, earlier pledges of giving up the gun were often reneged on.

In addition to challenging the conventional wisdom that group behavior is driven by ideology, leadership, or age, MST offers two potential new synergies. First, to the extent scholars use group strength to explain behavior, it is in an absolute sense, as in "terrorism is a weapon of the weak (or the strong)."[25] The analysis here reveals that these claims can be bolstered if the measure captures group strength relative to other groups in the same movement. MST therefore argues that terrorism and other attempts to escalate violence is the weapon of the relatively weak (i.e., the challengers) that have both the capability to carry out attacks and the incentive to do so.

Second, although this study held the objectives constant, MST potentially offers a theory of how the position of a group in the hierarchy drives the political positions it takes. This engages well with the foundational works of Stacie Goddard and Nadav Shelef, who effectively argue that group competition can generate incentives for outbidding in rhetoric over territorial claims and an evolutionary dynamic that rewards national visions that help a group gain power.[26] MST agrees, although also contends that groups and their leaders will temper their harsh rhetoric and make concessions they once criticized if or when they come to power as a prelude to the inclusion-moderation thesis.[27] These movements offer initial evidence for these claims, including the willingness of groups such as Sinn Féin, Fatah, and Begin's Likud to make concessions after they came to power.

Hierarchical position certainly cannot explain all variation in group behavior. Sometimes subordinates actively resist chain-ganging for ideological reasons, as did the Palestine Liberation Front for the Palestinians in the 1960s.[28] Still, for hegemons, leaders, and challengers with strong structural pressures for victory and violence, the predictions of MST perform better than any competitor. Similarly, hegemony alone is certainly not sufficient for movement success nor are unity and fragmentation sufficient for movement failure, but we are on solid ground in concluding that hegemonic movements achieved victory significantly more often than united and fragmented movements. Furthermore, although other factors such as regime type and movement strength may help provide a more complete explanation—such as why hegemony yielded greater success for the Algerians, Zionists, and Irish than for the Palestinians—MST does a better job explaining the variation in outcome for these four movements and forty-four campaigns than any other competing theory. Nonetheless, MST generated additional incorrect predictions and loose ends that can help define the next steps.

Implications for Scholarship and Future Research

PURSUING THE LOOSE ENDS OF MST

The analysis in this book provides a number of additional implications for scholarship and a roadmap for future research. First, MST itself contains many assumptions and assertions that would benefit from further examination. For example, the benefits of victory are posited to concentrate at the top of the movement, but is that truly the case? Groups seem to think so, and the initial evidence presented here backs them up. The four groups leading at the moment of greatest victory continued to lead their new states or proto-states for the first twenty-eight years on average—and no less than nine years—revealing that alliances, institutions, post-victory conflict, and simple bad luck were all unable to keep the hegemon out of the top spot for a decade or more. Nonetheless, these are claims that can and should be verified with further empirical evidence because the failure of hegemons to regularly secure leadership in a new state would generate a version of the "hegemon's dilemma," whereby the top group worries about paying the costs of national struggle while other groups free ride and benefit from victory regardless of who was responsible for it.[29]

Given that MST claims that relative power plays the key role in group behavior, it is also worth examining the extent to which group perceptions match up with the systematic, objective measures of strength presented here. As Wohlforth demonstrates for the international balance of power among states, actor perceptions do not always match up with the numbers assembled by observers, and it is these perceptions that drive behavior.[30] Do groups internalize hegemony as Antonio Gramsci suggests? Do groups believe their own rhetoric and act as if they are more powerful than they actually are? Do groups swiftly adjust to drops in their position in the hierarchy, or, like former great powers, do they continue to act like the significant players they once were due to inertia or pride?[31] And does the upward or downward trajectory of group strength create windows of opportunity that change perceptions, such as when Ben-Gurion decided to confront the Irgun on the *Altalena*, before it could become a strong challenger?[32] I undertook significant effort to verify my findings on movement hierarchy with my interviewees, but this issue requires further examination.

In terms of violence, the cases in this book suggest that spoiling is more successful in a fragmented movement and that the costs of repression are disproportionately focused on the strongest groups.[33] Both claims would benefit from a more focused analysis in light of the growing literature on spoiling and state repression. Furthermore, this book does not answer why some groups and movements engage in one type of competitive behavior more than another. Why did Algerian groups often infight, but Palestinian groups largely avoided doing so and instead focused on outbidding? Were the decisions of Zionist groups to build settlements and of Irish groups to run in elections also forms of outbidding, as suggested in chapters 4 and 6, respectively? MST did well to establish the key condition for *when* (and which) groups compete, but further research is needed to establish the conditions for precisely *how* that competition occurs.[34]

One potential approach would be to incorporate Pearlman's argument that robust prestate institutions can restrict violent competition. I find initial support for this claim because 45% of challengers nonetheless restrained violence, the majority of which were Zionist groups that focused their efforts on accumulating power within the ZO, internationally, and within the National Assembly and other governing institutions in the Palestine Mandate. The fact that 100% of Zionist hegemons and leaders restrained violence and some challengers did not demonstrates the continued relevance of MST; however, an analysis of the relative strength of both groups and the institutions in which they operate may provide the most complete picture of the nature of group competition.

Finally, the issue of time within movements deserves further analysis. How are campaigns linked within movements over time? Can some of the short-term counterproductive mechanisms in one campaign actually lay the foundation for victory in future campaigns, either by piling up costs on the adversary, teaching groups the perils of fragmentation, or shifting the movement structure?[35] This represents a potential bridge to competing theories because movements may benefit from periods of both fragmentation and hegemony. Fragmentation could create a competitive environment in which weaker challengers are selected out, followed by an experienced hegemon carrying the movement to victory. Such an evolution would fit with the concept of stages that was central to the thinking of the most prominent practitioners and theorists of nonstate violence, including Mao Zedong, Che Guevara, Carlos Marighella, Vo Ngyuen Giap, and Abu Bakr Naji.

That said, initial evidence suggests that cumulating costs and learning are not the most important links between campaigns. Victory did not happen after a certain number of the enemy were dead or a certain length of the conflict; it occurred after a movement became hegemonic. Groups also seem to grasp the problems of fragmentation from the outset and rarely need new lessons. Indeed, when asked early in the Algerian national movement how they could possibly defeat the better-armed and -trained French, Hamou Amirouche's father, an FLN fighter, replied, "With all the people. Never again in fragmented ranks as with Mokrani in 1871, or the Ouled Sidi Cheikh tribes in 1881."[36] The tragedy of national movements is that, despite this knowledge, all groups struggle to be the hegemon, resulting in behavior that is counterproductive for the movement. For every FLN that fights to the top, there are multiple Irguns and PIRAs that compete violently for decades without becoming dominant. The key breakthrough for future research will therefore be determining under what conditions competition leads to hegemony and other shifts in movement structure.

WIDER APPLICATIONS TO OTHER CONFLICTS

How well does MST explain national movements across time and space? First, the theory can explain what many consider the very first successful national movement from 240 years ago: the American Revolution. The creation of a hegemonic political and military actor with the Continental Congress and its Continental Army in 1776 was not without its problems. Nonetheless, it directed a cohesive struggle that would not have been successful if the thirteen colonies and their respective militias had simply fought independently. This counterfactual claim is best evidenced by the military setbacks before the creation of the Continental Army and the fact that the British plan for victory was based on fragmenting the colonies.

Colonial militias subsequently served as able supplementary forces under command of the Continental Army, but they did not represent or behave as significant challengers. Even the best competing argument explaining the success of the American Revolution—the support of the French—was a direct result of a victory by the Continental Army at Saratoga and a concerted diplomatic effort by Benjamin Franklin under the auspices of the Continental Congress. Without the credibility won on the battlefield and the clarity in messaging concerning treaties and trade deals, France would not have thought the game worth the candle. Finally, like the FLN, the Continental Congress turned down British offers of limited autonomy in 1782 and won full independence the following year, having left the British with no other partners, and so no other options.[37]

Second, the theory can explain the actions and outcomes of movements outside of North America, Europe, and the Middle East. In Southeast Asia, the Vietnamese national movement failed in its struggle against France for decades with a fragmented movement torn by rivalry. After the rise of the dominant Indochinese Communist Party and the Vietminh led by Ho Chi Minh, the Vietnamese defeated the French and gained independence in North Vietnam in 1954. The Vietminh under Ho initially appeared to be forming alliances with nationalist and communist party rivals, but they soon violently eliminated their competitors and dominated the Democratic Republic of Vietnam (North Vietnam)—winning with movement hegemony, not unity.[38] The continued hegemony of Ho's group throughout the subsequent war with the United States led to a cohesive struggle that yielded an independent, unified Vietnam in 1975.

In Africa, the first successful post-colonial national movement on the continent (Eritrea) and most recent success (South Sudan) both fit MST. In Eritrea, a national movement with the same actors, same foreign supporters, same demands, and same strategies failed in the 1960s and 1970s yet succeeded in the 1980s and 1990s because the movement structure shifted from fragmented and united to hegemonic. In earlier campaigns, "The bulk of the fighting in the Eritrean countryside between February 1972 and October 1974 was between rival groups of Eritrean nationalists," the Eritrean Liberation Front (ELF) and the Eritrean People's Liberation Front (EPLF).[39] After the ELF was reduced to a subordinate position by the mid-1980s, the EPLF was able to conduct cohesive diplomacy—the ELF had cast the movement as purely Muslim or Arab, which turned off African and Western states at the United Nations—and won a major battlefield victory against Ethiopia in 1988, "one of the biggest ever scored by any liberation movement anywhere since Dien Bien Phu [by the Vietminh] in 1954."[40] In South Sudan, movement hegemony in the 1960s under the Anya-Nya gained autonomy under the Addis Ababa Agreement in 1972. Fragmentation in the 1980s and 1990s led to infighting between the Anya-Nya II and various splinter groups of the Sudan People's Liberation Army (SPLA), and the movement floundered for two decades. In the early 2000s, the SPLA became the dominant hegemon in the movement and began a series of negotiations that resulted in an independent South Sudan.[41]

Third, MST provides insights into national movements today, including the ongoing Palestinian and Kurdish national movements. I used the foundations of MST to argue in 2012 that a much hyped unity deal between Fatah and Hamas would not be consummated and would not impact the outcome of the Palestinian national movement if it were.[42] Despite extensive international support, optimistic news coverage, and an agreed five-week time limit to form a unity government and six-month time limit to hold elections, no significant steps have been taken and the deal (and movement success) seems as distant as ever.

As the Iraqi Kurds struggle with the dual threats of ISIS and the Iraqi government on their doorstep, they cannot escape the internal competition between the KDP and PUK that has plagued them for decades. In the 1990s, "[KDP leader Masoud] Barzani himself has admitted that in part at least the fighting [with the PUK] 'has to do . . . with the question of hegemony.'"[43] As a nongovernmental organization worker in northern Iraq put it, "Barzani thinks he's the true leader of the Kurds. So does [PUK leader] Talabani and they'll fight each other down to their last peshmerga to prove themselves right."[44] Masoud Barzani's father, Mullah Mustafa Barzani, was the first leader of the KDP and the most prominent politician in the history of the Iraqi Kurdish national movement. In the 1960s, he told Dana Schmidt, "In the lives of nations it is only strength that counts. . . . The Kurds had been beaten over and over again because they were disunited and weak. Because they were weak they had not been able to assert their rights."[45] The basic lessons of MST have thus been known to—and have applied to—the Iraqi Kurdish national movement for half a century, to the extent that one of their leaders aptly titled his book *Fingers That Break Each Other*.[46]

Fourth, how well does MST explain movements and conflicts that are not nationalist? As noted in chapter 1, national movements are distinct in that their social solidarity is based on national identity and their common purpose is political autonomy. But all social movements, insurgencies, and civil wars involve organizations and individuals struggling to alter the leadership or policies of a state, and all face the challenges that come with attempts at contentious collective action. The theory is most applicable to movements, insurgencies, and civil wars that aim for regime change and have a common identity—ethnic, religious, or otherwise—because these lead to similar costs, benefits, and dynamics of violence and victory as national movements. Thus, the Cuban revolution saw a hegemonic group (the 26th of July Movement commanded by Fidel Castro) successfully overthrow the Batista regime in 1959. In Nicaragua, splitting and infighting bogged down an insurgency against the Anastasio Somoza government for years until the competing groups merged into the Sandinista National Liberation Front (FSLN), which proceeded to overthrow the government in 1979 and rule Nicaragua for a decade.[47]

In Syria today, the insurgents agree on the aim of overthrowing the Assad regime, but the different ethnic groups and nationalities of the combatants make aggregated analysis a bit messier. Nonetheless, MST provides insight on a number of fronts. Fragmentation among ISIS, Jabhat al-Nusra, the Free Syrian Army, and countless other factions has indeed led to extensive infighting, foreign meddling, and an unsuccessful hurting stalemate.[48] Were ISIS or another group to rise to become an insurgent hegemon, the Assad regime would be more likely to fall, although the anti–nation-state ideology of ISIS makes it a somewhat unique actor that may not view victory and its aftermath in the same fashion as most other groups.[49] In any case, extensive U.S. and international efforts to unite the opposition or back subordinate groups have been disasters, as predicted by MST.

Finally, MST provides insights into movements that are nonviolent. Many of the key mechanisms of the theory apply, including the pursuit of organizational and strategic objectives, counterproductive competition, and external meddling. The movements in this book suggest as much, in that the Algerians and Palestinians were most strategically successful when hegemonic, but the former was very violent and the latter was more nonviolent than it had generally been at the time of its greatest success. In addition, the dynamics of the labor movement in the United States clearly changed between the early dominance of the Knights of Labor, to fragmentation and competition with American Federation of Labor (AFL) and later the Congress of Industrial Organizations (CIO), before a return to hegemony with the AFL-CIO merger. Competition is key for labor because one of its most effective tactics—strikes—cannot succeed if there are significant challengers waiting in the wings to negotiate with a company and take those jobs.[50]

In any case, the combined study of violent and nonviolent groups in the same movement is the basis of a research program on radical flanks, which debates whether such fringe groups are a boon or a curse to their campaigns. MST offers a key potential scope condition, suggesting that flanks in hegemonic movements (e.g., the Lehi and Irgun in the latter period of the Zionist movement) may allow for beneficial good cop–bad cop dynamics, but that flanks in fragmented or united movements (e.g., Fatah, the PIRA, and the Irgun in their early years) are likely to muddle the messaging and pull others into counterproductive internal competition. In some sense then, hegemonic movements may do better than fragmented or united movements, but hegemonic movements with active subordinate groups may be the most successful of all.

POLITICS OF NATIONAL MOVEMENTS, FUTURE OF REBEL POWER

WHERE YOU STAND DEPENDS ON WHERE YOU SIT

All movements have struggles across three levels of analysis: among individuals within a group, among groups within a movement, and between a movement and a state. So far my use of MST has largely ignored the individual level and has explained that dynamics at the group level are key to explaining the outcomes at the movement level. But the basic claim of MST for group behavior—where you stand depends on where you sit—originated as a theory of individual behavior based on an individual's position in government.[51] As such, it can and should be profitably applied to explain the behavior of individuals in movements, who face a similar tension between the desire to survive and strengthen themselves and the desire to pursue political autonomy for their nation. As one Vietcong prisoner noted, "I do not know which side is winning. . . . I did not think about which side was winning. I take the side which can do the most for me."[52] In contrast, an Algerian fighter asked himself at the time, "We thought the Moroccans and Tunisians were just informers, how can they struggle against the French while we do not? Are they better than us?"[53] Power, hierarchy, and competition all matter to individuals as well as groups.

Similar costs and benefits of victory and violence apply because the well-known leaders of groups are likely to disproportionately enjoy high office and status after the victory, making them more likely to support negotiations. Foot soldiers are likely to enjoy fewer such benefits, and so they should be more likely to spoil deals or switch groups. Initial evidence bears this out, as the Evian negotiations for the independence of Algeria were carried out by FLN politicians who would receive offices in the new state, not by FLN fighters who would receive less and were not as supportive. In the Irish national movement, Fine Gael, Fianna Fáil, and Provisional Sinn Féin were all started by individuals who felt that certain principles were more important than power. When they each had a chance to gain power by holding office, however, they took it and went back on some of their prior principles, while fighters in the field were often less supportive and more likely to break from the group.[54] Indeed, a majority of Sinn Féin were for the 1921 Anglo-Irish Treaty and a majority of the IRA were against it. MST thus helps to explain not just when group splits happen but also *who* splits.[55]

Implications for Policy

The analysis in this book generates a number of powerful policy implications.

HEGEMONIC MOVEMENTS PREVENT VIOLENCE, FRAGMENTED MOVEMENTS PREVENT VICTORY

First, those trying to counter national movements should recognize the tension between preventing violence and preventing strategic progress. If a state wants to prevent escalatory violent attacks, then it should push for a hegemonic movement adversary. If a state wants to prevent the strategic progress of a movement, then it should push for a fragmented movement adversary.[56] Current thinking among scholars and policymakers often addresses counterinsurgency and counterterrorism strategy without appreciating these dual objectives and the inherent trade-off in their achievement. The absence of prioritization is found at the root of many state policies that resulted in costly failures.

UNITY IN MOVEMENTS AND INSURGENCIES IS DIFFICULT TO ACHIEVE AND OFTEN INEFFECTIVE

Second, those policymakers, participants, and supporters seeking to help national movements achieve strategic success should avoid trying to make groups altruistic allies and, instead, should work to change the movement power structure so that it has a single, dominant hegemon. We need to look no further than Libya, where the United States was convinced in 2011 that an alliance among rebel groups would create a new state, only to see the alliance and the country fragment under multiple warring governments in the absence of a dominant group.[57] For the Palestinian and Kurdish national movements and the Syrian insurgency today, the evidence in this book suggests that comprehensive unity deals between Fatah and Hamas; Kurdish groups such as the KDP, PUK, YPG, and PKK; or various Syrian factions will probably not be consummated and that they are far less relevant to the strategic success of the movements than a change in the internal balance of power.

SUPPORT, NEGOTIATE, OR DESTROY: PICKING ENEMIES AND ALLIES BASED ON STRENGTH NOT IDEOLOGY

Third, to the extent that policymakers do plan to work with or combat groups in national movements and insurgencies, understanding the interplay between the internal and external dynamics is essential to cracking their operational code, as well as to predicting (and influencing) their likely actions and effects. The position of a group as a "moderate" or "extremist" on issues of violence and negotiation is often driven more by its place in the movement hierarchy than its ideology, which reveals that the United States may have more potential allies (and enemies) than can be discerned through limited frames that evaluate groups based on religion (Sunni vs. Shia) or ethnicity (Arab vs. African).[58]

Unfortunately, the search for ideological "moderates" often leads to costly setbacks, such as the misguided U.S. search for a "moderate" Syrian faction that trained only 60 fighters in 2015—half of whom were captured or killed—far short of the goal of 5,400, which would itself represent little more than a subordinate group in Syria.[59] In contrast, the British decision to work with Sinn Féin/IRA—as opposed to shutting it out, as in previous negotiations—led to a peace in Northern Ireland that, although imperfect, is far better than those who said the British could never trust those "extremists" ever suggested. Therefore, unless they are willing and able to change a movement structure with a massive commitment of support, policymakers should either not engage in a conflict or should work with the existing significant groups to decrease violence and/or achieve victory.

AFTER VICTORY: THE IMPACT OF MOVEMENT STRUCTURE ON REGIME TYPE AND STABILITY

Of course, policymakers care not only about the cessation of conflict and the victory of national movements, but also what comes next.[60] Fourth, and unfortunately for the United States and believers in the democratic peace, although hegemonic movements may be most likely to succeed, they also appear least likely to democratize. Democracy is built on pluralism in which the control of government changes among competing groups on a regular basis. Hegemonic movements are positioned to become de facto or de jure one-party states in which the hegemon dominates free and fair elections or may use its strong position to ensure that nascent electoral and governing institutions are slanted in its favor.[61]

Thus, the hegemonic FLN was able to win independence from the French, but it has since ruled a nondemocratic Algeria without yielding control in the subsequent six decades.[62] The lack of competition that gave the national movement a cohesive diplomatic and military strategy gave the state few political liberties and a struggling economy that lacks diversity and innovation. Ironically, fragmentation may be the best way to set the stage for post-conflict democracy, although it makes the regime change that is necessary to get there less likely.[63] Furthermore, new nation-states marked by fragmentation may be more unstable and war-prone as the factions fight for control and neighboring states perceive opportunity and uncertainty, as detailed by Stephen Walt, and Edward Mansfield and Jack Snyder.[64]

No single structure or strategy is therefore ideal for ending violence, achieving victory, *and* initiating democracy and stability. Nonetheless, recognizing that these objectives require different approaches, and analyzing the movement that precedes the state will provide policymakers with key insights into how best to match means to ends.

As Tom Hartley, Sinn Féin member and former Belfast mayor, explained, "One thing I found about politics is that we rarely know what's on the other side of the hill."[65] In this book, I have taken the reader to the "other side," deep into the internal politics of national movements, to understand what drives them to competition and cooperation, violence and nonviolence, victory and defeat. Those seeking to understand the past, present, and future of rebel power would do well to heed its lessons.

Group Strength Appendixes

I present and cite the key data on group membership, funding, and popular support for the Palestinian, Zionist, Algerian, and Irish national movements in chapters 3–6. I include the full data and sourcing for every significant group in every year in my online appendices A–D, which can be accessed at http://www.peterjpkrause.com.

The appendices provide all data I used to determine the codings for group hierarchy and movement system structure. To maximize transparency, for each datum I provide a direct citation from primary documents, secondary sources, or interviews. In addition to the information that my research assistants and I collected, I sent the appendices to three experts in each movement, and in every case, they agreed with over 90% of the codings. I welcome all assessments and suggested additions to the data, especially those that rely on additional quality sources I have not included.

Notes

1. Power, Violence, and Victory

1. "PFLP: Hamas Security Force Detain Fighters in Gaza," *Maan News Agency*, August 28, 2013; Ron Ben-Yishai, "Standoff between Hamas, Islamic Jihad behind Rocket Fire on Israel," *Ynet*, June 24, 2013; Adnan Abu Amer, "Hamas, Gaza's Armed Factions Struggle to Avoid Sinai Conflict," *Al-Monitor*, August 15, 2013; "Radical Islam in Gaza," *International Crisis Group*, Middle East Report No. 104, March 2011; Uri Savir, "Israel, Hamas Negotiate, but Truce Still Far Off," *Al-Monitor*, June 30, 2015.

2. Hillary Clinton, remarks at the Ad Hoc Friends of the Syrian People Ministerial, New York, September 28, 2012.

3. Marco Giugni, Doug McAdam, and Charles Tilly, eds., *How Social Movements Matter* (Minneapolis: University of Minnesota Press, 1999); Kathleen Cunningham, *Inside the Politics of Self-Determination* (Oxford: Oxford University Press, 2014); Stathis Kalyvas, *The Logic of Violence in Civil War* (Cambridge, UK: Cambridge University Press, 2006); Theda Skocpol, *States and Social Revolutions: A Comparative Analysis of France, Russia, and China* (Cambridge, UK: Cambridge University Press, 1979); Timothy Wickham-Crowley, *Guerrillas and Revolution in Latin America: A Comparative Study of Insurgents and Regimes since 1956* (Princeton: Princeton University Press, 1991); Ted Robert Gurr, *Why Men Rebel* (Boulder, CO: Paradigm, 2011).

4. Sidney Tarrow, *Power in Movement: Social Movements and Contentious Politics* (Cambridge, UK: Cambridge University Press, 1998), 3–5.

5. Ernest Gellner, *Nations and Nationalism* (Ithaca: Cornell University Press, 1983); Stephen van Evera, "Hypotheses on Nationalism and War," *International Security* 18, no. 4 (April 1994): 5–39.

6. Bridget Coggins, *Power Politics and State Formation in the Twentieth Century: The Dynamics of Recognition* (New York: Cambridge University Press, 2014).

7. Samuel Huntington, *Political Order in Changing Societies* (New Haven: Yale University Press, 1968), 264; Stephen M. Walt, *Revolution and War*, Cornell Studies in Security Affairs (Ithaca: Cornell University Press, 1996).

8. Jason Lyall and Isaiah Wilson, "Rage against the Machines: Explaining Outcomes in Counterinsurgency Wars," *International Organization* 63, no. 1 (January 2009): 67–106; Jeff Goodwin, *No Other Way Out: States and Revolutionary Movements, 1945–1991* (Cambridge, UK: Cambridge University Press, 2001). The more apt comparison would be to revolutionary movements, but they are tough to identify ex ante, and Goodwin does not count them.

9. Cunningham, *Inside the Politics of Self-Determination*; Eric Hobsbawm, *Nations and Nationalism since 1780: Programme, Myth, Reality* (Cambridge, UK: Cambridge University Press, 1992).

10. Gellner, *Nations and Nationalism*, 4; Charles Tilly, "States and Nationalism in Europe 1492–1992," *Theory and Society* 23, no. 1 (1994): 131–46.

11. Francis Fukuyama, *The End of History and the Last Man* (New York: Free Press, 1992).

12. Coggins, *Power Politics and State Formation*; Gellner, *Nations and Nationalism*, 2.

13. James Minahan, ed., *Encyclopedia of the Stateless Nations: Ethnic and National Groups around the World* (Westport, CT: Greenwood Press, 2002). This is strikingly similar to the rates of strategic success for insurgencies (38%) and social movements (33%), although standardizing the definitions of *success* across studies is important. Lyall and Wilson, "Rage against the Machines"; Edwin Amenta, Neal Caren, Elizabeth Chiarello, and Yang Su, "The Political Consequences of Social Movements," *Annual Review of Sociology* 36, no. 1 (2010): 287–307; Peter Krause, "The Political Effectiveness of Non-State Violence: A Two-Level Framework to Transform a Deceptive Debate," *Security Studies* 22, no. 2 (June 2013): 259–94.

14. Coggins, *Power Politics and State Formation*.

15. Ivan Arreguín-Toft, *How the Weak Win Wars: A Theory of Asymmetric Conflict* (Cambridge, UK: Cambridge University Press, 2006); Seth G. Jones and Martin C. Libicki, *How Terrorist Groups End: Lessons for Countering al Qa'ida* (Santa Monica: RAND, 2008); Audrey Kurth Cronin, *How Terrorism Ends: Understanding the Decline and Demise of Terrorist Campaigns* (Princeton: Princeton University Press, 2011).

16. Giugni, McAdam, and Tilly, *How Social Movements Matter*; Erica Chenoweth and Maria J. Stephan, *Why Civil Resistance Works: The Strategic Logic of Nonviolent Conflict* (New York: Columbia University Press, 2011).

17. Max Abrahms, "Why Terrorism Does Not Work," *International Security* 31, no. 2 (Fall 2006): 42–78; Robert Pape, *Dying to Win: The Strategic Logic of Suicide Terrorism* (New York: Random House, 2005); Andrew H. Kydd and Barbara F. Walter, "The Strategies of Terrorism," *International Security* 31, no. 1 (July 2006): 49–80; Virginia Page Fortna, "Do Terrorists Win? Rebels' Use of Terrorism and Civil War Outcomes," *International Organization* 69, No. 3 (June 2015): 1–38.

18. Doug McAdam, *Political Process and the Development of Black Insurgency, 1930–1970* (Chicago: University of Chicago Press, 1999); Skocpol, *States and Social Revolutions*; Wickham-Crowley, *Guerrillas and Revolution in Latin America*; Robert Holland, *European Decolonization, 1918–1981: An Introductory Survey* (Basingstoke, UK: Macmillan, 1985).

19. Gurr, *Why Men Rebel*; Roger Petersen, *Understanding Ethnic Violence: Fear, Hatred, and Resentment in Twentieth-Century Eastern Europe* (Cambridge, UK: Cambridge University Press, 2002); Goodwin, *No Other Way Out*; Paul Collier and Anke Hoeffler, *Greed and Grievance in Civil War* (Oxford: Center for the Study of African Economics, 2002); James Fearon and David Laitin, "Ethnicity, Insurgency, and Civil War," *American Political Science Review* 97, no. 1 (2003): 75–90.

20. Jessica Stern, *Terror in the Name of God: Why Religious Militants Kill* (New York: Harper Perennial, 2004); James Piazza, "Is Islamist Terrorism More Dangerous?: An Empirical Study of Group Ideology, Organization, and Goal Structure," *Terrorism and Political Violence* 21, no. 1 (2009): 62–88.

21. Robert Michels, *Political Parties: A Sociological Study of the Oligarchical Tendencies of Modern Democracy* (New York: Hearst's International Library, 1915): 393–409; Michael Horowitz, "Nonstate Actors and the Diffusion of Innovations: The Case of Suicide Terrorism," *International Organization* 64, no. 1 (2010): 33–64.

22. Tarrow, *Power in Movement*, 24.

23. Bard E O'Neill, *Insurgency & Terrorism: Inside Modern Revolutionary Warfare* (Washington: Brassey's, 1990), 98.

24. Wendy Pearlman, *Violence, Nonviolence, and the Palestinian National Movement* (New York: Cambridge University Press, 2011).

25. William Gamson, *The Strategy of Social Protest* (Belmont: Wadsworth, 1990), 101.

26. Kathleen Gallagher Cunningham, "Divide and Conquer or Divide and Concede: How Do States Respond to Internally Divided Separatists?" *American Political Science Review* 105, no. 2 (2011), 276.

27. Ibid.; Herbert Haines, *Black Radicals and the Civil Rights Mainstream, 1954–1970* (Knoxville: University of Tennessee Press, 1988); Mark Lichbach, *The Cooperator's Dilemma* (Ann Arbor: University of Michigan Press, 1996), 167; Desirée Nilsson, "Turning Weakness into Strength: Military Capabilities, Multiple Rebel Groups and Negotiated Settlements," *Conflict Management and Peace Science* 27, no. 3 (June 2010): 253–71; Jesse Driscoll, "Commitment Problems or Bidding Wars? Rebel Fragmentation as Peace Building," *Journal of Conflict Resolution* 56, no. 1 (February 2012): 1118–49.

28. Luther Gerlach and Virginia Hine, *People, Power, Change; Movements of Social Transformation* (Indianapolis: Bobbs-Merrill, 1970), 64.

29. Antonio Gramsci, *Selections from the Prison Notebooks* (New York: International Publishers, 1971).

30. Bruce Bueno de Mesquita, Alastair Smith, Randolph Siverson, and James Morrow, *The Logic of Political Survival* (Cambridge, MA: MIT Press, 2003), 9.

31. Rufus Miles, "The Origin and Meaning of Miles' Law," *Public Administration Review* 38, no. 5 (October 1978): 399–403.

32. I use a combination of membership size, funding, and popular support to assess group strength.

33. This parallels observations that states can trilaterally coerce enemy armed groups by coercing other states to repress the groups within their borders. Boaz Atzili and Wendy Pearlman, "Triadic Deterrence: Coercing Strength, Beaten by Weakness," *Security Studies* 21, no. 2 (June 2012): 301–35; Keren Fraiman, "Not in Your Backyard: Coercion, Base States and Violent Non-State Actors," PhD diss., Massachusetts Institute of Technology, 2014.

34. Kamal Chomani, "Push for Kurdish Independence Divides Iraqi Kurds," *Al-Monitor*, July 9, 2014.

35. George Downs and David Rocke, "Conflict, Agency, and Gambling for Resurrection: The Principal-Agent Problem Goes to War," *American Journal of Political Science* 38, no. 2 (1994): 362–380. Daniel Kahneman and Amos Tversky, "Prospect Theory: An Analysis of Decision under Risk," *Econometrica* 47, no. 2 (1979): 263–91.

36. Robert Jervis, "Cooperation under the Security Dilemma," *World Politics* 30, no. 2 (1978): 167–214.

37. David McDowall, *A Modern History of the Kurds* (London: I. B. Tauris, 2007).

38. John Mearsheimer, *The Tragedy of Great Power Politics* (New York: W. W. Norton, 2001).

39. Michael Gunter, "The KDP-PUK Conflict in Northern Iraq," *Middle East Journal* 50, no. 2 (Spring 1996), 239.

40. Kenneth Waltz, *Theory of International Politics* (New York: McGraw-Hill, 1979). For an attempt to create a related theory of foreign policy, see Stephen Walt, *The Origins of Alliances* (Ithaca: Cornell University Press, 1990).

41. Waltz, *Theory of International Politics*; Giovanni Sartori, *Parties and Party Systems: A Framework for Analysis* (Cambridge, UK: Cambridge University Press, 1976); Samuel Huntington, *The Third Wave: Democratization in the Late Twentieth Century* (Norman: University of Oklahoma Press, 1993).

42. Additional inductive inspiration came from my exploratory fieldwork trip to the West Bank, which lasted one month. As such, the theory was formed long before I began fieldwork and analysis of the Zionist, Algerian, and Irish cases, as well as before I conducted 95% of the analysis on the Palestinian case.

43. Jason Seawright and John Gerring, "Case Selection Techniques in Case Study Research: A Menu of Qualitative and Quantitative Options," *Political Research Quarterly* 61, no. 2 (2008): 294–308.

44. Alexander George and Andrew Bennett, *Case Studies and Theory Development in the Social Sciences* (Cambridge, MA: MIT Press, 2005).

45. Martha Crenshaw, *Revolutionary Terrorism: The FLN in Algeria, 1954–1962* (Stanford: Hoover Institution Press, Stanford University, 1978); Michael L. R. Smith, *Fighting for Ireland?: The Military Strategy of the Irish Republican Movement* (New York: Routledge, 1997); Pape, *Dying to Win*; Abrahms, "Why Terrorism Does Not Work"; Bruce Hoffman, *Anonymous Soldiers: The Struggle for Israel, 1917–1947* (New York: Knopf, 2015).

46. Stephen Van Evera, *Guide to Methods for Students of Political Science* (Ithaca: Cornell University Press, 1997), 49–88.

47. I also did not know the quantity and type of violence in each movement over time, all the groups in each movement, and which groups carried out which actions at which times.

48. John Gerring and Rose McDermott, "An Experimental Template for Case Study Research," *American Journal of Political Science* 51, no. 3 (2007): 688–701.

49. As detailed in chapter 2, I mark any change in movement structure—from hegemonic to fragmented or from fragmented to united, and any time a single significant group moves up or down in the hierarchy—as the beginning of a new campaign. Gary King, Robert O. Keohane, and Sidney Verba, *Designing Social Inquiry: Scientific Inference in Qualitative Research* (Princeton: Princeton University Press, 1994).

50. Hebrew is the only one of the four languages that I cannot currently read myself. Nonetheless, I worked closely with research assistants to search for and identify the relevant data, interviews, and historical accounts from Hebrew sources.

51. To maximize transparency and replicability, I cite material other than interviews wherever possible, given that some of my interviewees have requested anonymity.

52. Henry Brady and David Collier, *Rethinking Social Inquiry: Diverse Tools, Shared Standards* (Lanham: Rowman & Littlefield, 2010).

53. George and Bennett, *Case Studies and Theory Development*.

54. Stephen M. Saideman and R. William Ayres, "Determining the Causes of Irredentism: Logit Analyses of Minorities at Risk Data from the 1980s and 1990s," *Journal of Politics* 62, no. 4 (2000): 1126–44.

2. Why National Movements Compete, Fight, and Win

1. Kenneth Waltz, *Theory of International Politics* (New York: McGraw-Hill, 1979); Giovanni Sartori, *Parties and Party Systems: A Framework for Analysis* (Cambridge, UK: Cambridge University Press, 1976).

2. Kristin M. Bakke, Kathleen Gallagher Cunningham, and Lee J. M. Seymour, "A Plague of Initials: Fragmentation, Cohesion, and Infighting in Civil Wars," *Perspectives on Politics* 10, no. 2 (June 2012): 267.

3. Sartori, *Parties and Party Systems*, 120–21.

4. For this very reason, I do not use the quality or quantity of weapons as a proxy for strength—not all groups possess arms or try to attain them.

5. Scholars consider a state that is 50–80% as strong as the strongest state in the international system to be a great power: Randall L Schweller, *Deadly Imbalances: Tripolarity and Hitler's Strategy of World Conquest* (New York: Columbia University Press, 1998), 16–17; Abramo F. K. Organski and Jacek Kugler, *The War Ledger* (Chicago: University of Chicago Press, 1981), 44. On effective parties, see Markku Laakso and Rein Taagepera, "'Effective' Number of Parties: A Measure with Application to West Europe," *Comparative Political Studies* 12, no. 1 (April 1979): 3–27.

6. I treat a front as a single organization if its members generally yield to its decision-making authority, for example, the FLN. If a front contains autonomous factions that come and go and that generally make their own decisions, I treat them as multiple groups, for example, the Zionist Organization or PLO. If one group merges into another and its members adhere to a single leadership, then I treat it as one group. If two groups agree to unite or cooperate but maintain their autonomy, I treat this as an alliance between two organizations.

7. Peter Krause, "Many Roads to Palestine? The Potential and Peril of Multiple Strategies within a Divided Palestinian National Movement," *Crown Center for Middle East Studies Brief*, no. 60 (March 2012): 10.

8. Other authors use the term *unitary* to refer to movements with only one group or to treat movements as if they included only one group. This concept is distinct from hegemonic movements that have one significant group and, generally, many other subordinate groups. Every hegemonic movement campaign in this study had multiple groups and so would not be labeled

unitary. Kathleen Gallagher Cunningham, "Actor Fragmentation and Civil War Bargaining: How Internal Divisions Generate Civil Conflict," *American Journal of Political Science* 57, no. 3 (2013): 659–72.

9. Fotini Christia, *Alliance Formation in Civil Wars* (Cambridge, UK: Cambridge University Press, 2012). See also Costantino Pischedda, "Wars within Wars: Understanding Inter-Rebel Fighting" (PhD diss., Columbia University, 2015).

10. Charles Tilly, "Social Movements and National Politics," CRSO Working Paper No. 197 (Ann Arbor: University of Michigan Center of Research on Social Organization, 1979), 13.

11. Individuals and groups in national movements can and do pursue additional strategic objectives and ideologies beyond political autonomy. Although the more important distinction is between those inside and outside a movement, we can use these additional goals to make a distinction among the various wings of a movement. For example, the Irish national movement contained republican and nationalist wings, and the Zionist movement contained Labor and Revisionist wings, which are distinguished by opposing political and economic ideologies beyond the shared national objective.

12. Some groups may include the word *movement* in their name (e.g., Fatah and Hamas are both acronyms that include the Arabic word meaning "movement," *haraka*), but a single organization never includes all of the individuals in a national movement.

13. Mia Bloom, *Dying to Kill: The Allure of Suicide Terror* (New York: Columbia University Press, 2005), 58–62.

14. David Lake, *Hierarchy in International Relations* (Ithaca: Cornell University Press, 2011).

15. Strong alliances and institutions could make subordinate groups more important, but their general absence is yet another reason these weak groups matter even less than in party systems, in which they are already marginal players.

16. Donatella Della Porta, *Social Movements, Political Violence, and the State: A Comparative Analysis of Italy and Germany* (Cambridge, UK: Cambridge University Press, 1995).

17. Victor Asal, Daniel J. Gustafson, and Peter Krause, "How to Get the State to Talk to You: Why Violent Territorial Conquest Is an Organization's Best Hope," unpublished manuscript.

18. George Pettee, *The Process of Revolution* (New York: Howard Fertig, 1971), 106.

19. Wendy Pearlman, "Spoiling Inside and Out: Internal Political Contestation and the Middle East Peace Process," *International Security* 33, no. 3 (2008): 79–109; Kathleen Gallagher Cunningham, Kristin M. Bakke, and Lee J. M. Seymour, "Shirts Today, Skins Tomorrow: Dual Contests and the Effects of Fragmentation in Self-Determination Disputes," *Journal of Conflict Resolution* 56, no. 1 (2012): 67–93.

20. Ritch Savin-Williams, "Dominance Hierarchies in Groups of Early Adolescents," *Child Development* 50, no. 4 (1979): 923–35; Bruce J. Biddle, "Recent Development in Role Theory," *Annual Review of Sociology* 12 (1986): 67–92.

21. Rufus Miles, "The Origin and Meaning of Miles' Law," *Public Administration Review* 38, no. 5 (October 1978): 399–403.

22. This is also true of the costs of failure, in that the strongest and most visible group in a movement is the most likely to be blamed by the movement base for any setbacks, thus giving hegemons and leaders even more incentive to push for victory.

23. Peter Krause, "The Political Effectiveness of Non-State Violence: A Two-Level Framework to Transform a Deceptive Debate," *Security Studies* 22, no. 2 (June 2013): 259–94; David Lake, "Rational Extremism: Understanding Terrorism in the Twenty-First Century," *Dialog-IO* 1 (2002): 15–29.

24. Bruce Bueno de Mesquita, Alastair Smith, Randolph Siverson, and James Morrow, *The Logic of Political Survival* (Cambridge, MA: MIT Press, 2003), 9.

25. Reinhold Niebuhr argues that groups are more selfish than individuals; *Moral Man and Immoral Society: A Study in Ethics and Politics* (Westminster: John Knox Press, 2001). This argument is supported by E. E. Schattschneider: "A political party is first of all an organized attempt to get power," and by Joseph Schumpeter: "A party is not . . . a group of men who intend to promote public welfare 'upon some principle on which they are all agreed. . . .' A party is a group whose members propose to act in concert in the competitive struggle for political power." Quoted in Sartori, *Parties and Party Systems*, 59.

26. In this sense, the common assumption of group extinction in international relations is far more applicable in movement systems than in the international system; Joseph Young and Laura Dugan, "Survival of the Fittest: Why Terrorist Groups Endure," *Perspectives on Terrorism* 8, no. 2 (2014): 2–23; Brian J. Phillips, "Enemies with Benefits? Violent Rivalry and Terrorist Group Longevity," *Journal of Peace Research* 52, no. 1 (2015): 62–75; Tanisha M. Fazal, *State Death: The Politics and Geography of Conquest, Occupation, and Annexation* (Princeton: Princeton University Press, 2011).

27. Paul Staniland, *Networks of Rebellion: Explaining Insurgent Cohesion and Collapse* (Ithaca: Cornell University Press, 2014), 163–65.

28. Antonio Gramsci, *Selections from the Prison Notebooks* (New York: International Publishers, 1971).

29. Steven David, "Explaining Third World Alignment," *World Politics* 43, no. 2 (1991): 233–56.

30. Maurice Duverger, *Political Parties, Their Organization and Activity in the Modern State* (London: Methuen, 1969), 346.

31. John Markakis, *National and Class Conflict in the Horn of Africa* (Cambridge, UK: Cambridge University Press, 1987), 108.

32. Stathis Kalyvas and Matthew Kocher, "How 'Free' Is Free Riding in Civil Wars?: Violence, Insurgency, and the Collective Action Problem," *World Politics* 59, no. 2 (2007): 177–216; Reed Wood, "Rebel Capability and Strategic Violence against Civilians," *Journal of Peace Research* 47, no. 5 (September 1, 2010): 601–14.

33. Adria Lawrence, "Driven to Arms? The Escalation to Violence in Nationalist Conflicts," in *Rethinking Violence: States and Non-State Actors in Conflict*, ed. Erica Chenoweth and Adria Lawrence (Cambridge, MA: MIT Press, 2010), 147–48; Brian C. Rathbun, "Uncertain about Uncertainty: Understanding the Multiple Meanings of a Crucial Concept in International Relations Theory," *International Studies Quarterly* 51, no. 3 (2007): 533–57.

34. Mia Bloom, "Palestinian Suicide Bombing: Public Support, Market Share, and Outbidding," *Political Science Quarterly* 119, no. 1 (2004): 61–88; Peter Krause, "When Terrorism Works: Explaining Success and Failure across Varying Targets and Objectives," in *When Does Terrorism Work?* ed. Diego Muro, forthcoming.

35. Daniel Kahneman and Amos Tversky, "Prospect Theory: An Analysis of Decision under Risk," *Econometrica* 47, no. 2 (1979): 263–91.

36. George Downs and David Rocke, "Conflict, Agency, and Gambling for Resurrection: The Principal-Agent Problem Goes to War," *American Journal of Political Science* 38, no. 2 (1994): 362–80.

37. Negotiations are also when the benefits from victory appear the clearest and most certain, meaning that MST claims about group behavior should be the most accurate at these times.

38. I thank Stacie Goddard for suggesting this wording.

39. This dovetails with Duverger, who breaks down parties into "parties with a majority bent" (hegemons), major parties (leaders and challengers), and minor parties (subordinates) and who also argues that leading parties are more realistic and less extreme than weaker parties; *Political Parties*, 283–84.

40. Jonah B. Schulhofer-Wohl, "Dynamics of Civil Wars: The Causes and Consequences of Subsidies to Armed Groups" (PhD diss., Yale University, 2012); David Cunningham, "Blocking Resolution: How External States Can Prolong Civil Wars," *Journal of Peace Research* 47, no. 2 (2010): 115–27.

41. Aliza Marcus, ed., *Blood and Belief: The PKK and the Kurdish Fight for Independence* (New York: New York University Press, 2007), 99–103.

42. Ehud Yaari, *Strike Terror: The Story of Fatah* (New York: Sabra Books, 1970), 199.

43. Adria Lawrence, "Triggering Nationalist Violence: Competition and Conflict in Uprisings against Colonial Rule," *International Security* 35, no. 2 (2010): 88–122.

44. Phillips, "Enemies with Benefits?" 65–66.

45. Thomas J. Christensen and Jack Snyder, "Chain Gangs and Passed Bucks: Predicting Alliance Patterns in Multipolarity," *International Organization* 44, no. 2 (1990): 137–68.

46. Kelly M. Greenhill and Solomon Major, "The Perils of Profiling Civil War Spoilers and the Collapse of Intrastate Peace Accords," *International Security* 31, no. 3 (2006): 7–40; David E. Cunningham, "Veto Players and Civil War Duration," *American Journal of Political Science* 50, no. 4 (2006): 875–92.

47. Leon Trotsky, *The History of the Russian Revolution* (Ann Arbor: University of Michigan Press, 1967), 2: 36.

48. Michael Desch, *Power and Military Effectiveness: The Fallacy of Democratic Triumphalism* (Baltimore: Johns Hopkins University Press, 2008); Caitlin Talmadge, *The Dictator's Army: Battlefield Effectiveness in Authoritarian Regimes* (Ithaca: Cornell University Press, 2015).

49. Pearlman, "Spoiling Inside and Out."

50. The key comparison, therefore, for a (mis)match in strategy for MST is the groups in the movement with each other, not the movement and the state; Ivan Arreguin-Toft, *How the Weak Win Wars: A Theory of Asymmetric Conflict* (Cambridge, UK: Cambridge University Press, 2006).

51. Daryl Press, *Calculating Credibility: How Leaders Assess Military Threats* (Ithaca: Cornell University Press, 2005).

52. Ian Lustick, *Unsettled States, Disputed Lands: Britain and Ireland, France and Algeria, Israel and the West Bank-Gaza* (Ithaca: Cornell University Press, 1993).

53. Gramsci, *Selections from the Prison Notebooks*.

54. Stathis Kalyvas, *The Logic of Violence in Civil War* (Cambridge, UK: Cambridge University Press, 2006).

55. Duverger, *Political Parties*; Samuel P. Huntington, *Political Order in Changing Societies* (New Haven: Yale University Press, 2006); Sartori, *Parties and Party Systems*.

56. "Editorial," *Eritrea Information* 2, no. 11 (1980), 1.

57. Bridget Coggins, *Power Politics and State Formation in the Twentieth Century: The Dynamics of Recognition* (New York: Cambridge University Press, 2014).

58. Mikulas Fabry, *Recognizing States: International Society and the Establishment of New States since 1776* (Oxford: Oxford University Press, 2010).

59. Bridget Coggins, *Power Politics and State Formation*, 53, 70.

60. Lee Seymour, Kristin Bakke, and Kathleen Cunningham, "E Pluribus Unum, Ex Uno Plures: Competition, Violence, and Fragmentation in Ethnopolitical Movements," *Journal of Peace Research* 53, no. 1 (2016): 3–18; Donald Horowitz, *Ethnic Groups in Conflict* (Berkeley: University of California Press, 1985); Jeremy Weinstein, *Inside Rebellion: The Politics of Insurgent Violence* (Cambridge, UK: Cambridge University Press, 2007); Monica Duffy Toft, *The Geography of Ethnic Violence: Identity, Interests, and the Indivisibility of Territory* (Princeton, Princeton University Press, 2003).

61. Theodore McLauchlin and Wendy Pearlman, "Out-Group Conflict, In-Group Unity? Exploring the Effect of Repression on Intramovement Cooperation," *Journal of Conflict Resolution* 56, no. 1 (2012): 41–66.

62. Martha Crenshaw, "An Organizational Approach to the Analysis of Political Terrorism," *Orbis* 29, no. 3 (1985): 465–89; Bloom, "Palestinian Suicide Bombing"; Lake, "Rational Extremism."

63. In the single hypothetical national movement in table 2.1, the position of a group in the hierarchy is determined by whether it is ahead or behind the others in more of the three categories that make up group strength: membership, funding, and popular support. For example, if Group A has more members and popular support, but less funding than Group B, Group A will be ranked first.

64. Krause, "Political Effectiveness of Non-State Violence." See also numerous chapters in Kelly Greenhill and Peter Krause, eds., *The Power to Hurt: Coercion in Theory and Practice*, forthcoming.

65. I do not attempt to explain why groups and movements push for and achieve certain types of regimes or certain borders for their state. Those interested in these issues should read the excellent works by Lustick, *Unsettled States, Disputed Lands*; Nadav Shelef, *Evolving Nationalism: Homeland, Identity, and Religion in Israel, 1925–2005* (Ithaca: Cornell University Press, 2010).

66. Max Abrahms, "Why Terrorism Does Not Work," *International Security* 31, no. 2 (2006): 42–78; Erica Chenoweth and Maria J Stephan, *Why Civil Resistance Works: The Strategic Logic of Nonviolent Conflict* (New York: Columbia University Press, 2011).

67. Nadav Shelef and Yael Zeira, "Recognition Matters! UN State Status and Attitudes Towards Territorial Compromise," *Journal of Conflict Resolution*, August 2015, doi: 10.1177/0022002715595865.

68. I am not arguing that independence-seeking nationalism is somehow more "developed." I simply do not want to measure the success of a movement at achieving something that it is not aiming to achieve; Eric Hobsbawm, *Nations and Nationalism since 1780: Programme, Myth, Reality* (Cambridge, UK: Cambridge University Press, 1992), 46–79.

69. The one exception is the Irish national movement in chapter 6, in that I analyze the struggle in Northern Ireland after the independence of Ireland to assess potential extensions of MST. Nationalism certainly endures after statehood. For an excellent look at nations with states and their policies for assimilating, accommodating, or excluding other national groups in and around their borders, see Harris Mylonas, *The Politics of Nation-Building: Making Co-Nationals, Refugees and Minorities* (Cambridge, UK: Cambridge University Press, 2013).

70. David Cunningham, Kristian Gleditsch, and Idean Salehyan, "It Takes Two: A Dyadic Analysis of Civil War Duration and Outcome," *Journal of Conflict Resolution* 53, no. 4 (2009): 570–97. Christia measures the relative strength of groups but does so via territorial control—part of my dependent variable—because she claims that data on group strength at regular intervals are unavailable; *Alliance Formation in Civil Wars*, 75–83, 221.

71. For online appendices A–D, see http://www.peterjpkrause.com.

72. Robert Jervis, "Do Leaders Matter and How Would We Know?" *Security Studies* 22, no. 2 (2013): 153–79.

3. The Palestinian National Movement

1. A different version of the proverb at the beginning of the chapter was used by Mustafa Akhmais, Palestinian Liberation Front (PLF) member, to describe his desire to unite the Palestinian national movement. Ehud Yaari, *Strike Terror: The Story of Fatah* (New York: Sabra Books, 1970), 165. Regarding the chapter subtitle, according to Greek mythology King Sisyphus was condemned by the gods to roll a boulder up a hill, only to have to it roll back down to the bottom again every time he neared the peak. Thus, a Sisyphean task is one that is seemingly repetitive and endless, with its successful completion always just out of reach.

2. Leila Kadi, ed., *Basic Political Documents of the Armed Palestinian Resistance Movement* (Beirut: Palestine Liberation Organization Research Center, 1969), 138.

3. Numerous excellent works have been penned on the Palestinian national movement across multiple levels of analysis, including Ian Lustick, "Terrorism in the Arab-Israeli Conflict: Targets and Audiences," in *Terrorism in Context*, ed. Martha Crenshaw (University Park: Pennsylvania State University Press, 1995), 514–52. The relative few that have systematically analyzed movement structure point to the perils of division and the preeminence of unity, however. See Bard O'Neill, *Armed Struggle in Palestine: A Political-Military Analysis* (Boulder: Westview Press, 1978); Issa Khalaf, *Politics in Palestine: Arab Factionalism and Social Disintegration, 1939–1948* (Albany: SUNY Press, 1991); Graham Usher, "Facing Defeat: The Intifada Two Years On," *Journal of Palestine Studies* 32, no. 2 (2003): 21–40; Rashid Khalidi, *The Iron Cage: The Story of the Palestinian Struggle for Statehood* (Boston: Beacon Press, 2007); Wendy Pearlman, *Violence, Nonviolence, and the Palestinian National Movement* (New York: Cambridge University Press, 2011). I agree with these authors that the Palestinian national movement has been continuously marked by numerous groups and alliances across multiple cleavages, but I argue that it is the power on each side of those cleavages that creates structure and drives group behavior and movement outcome.

4. Rashid Khalidi, *Palestinian Identity: The Construction of Modern National Consciousness* (New York: Columbia University Press, 1997); Walid Khalidi, *Before Their Diaspora: A Photographic History of the Palestinians 1876–1948* (Washington, DC: Institute for Palestine Studies, 1984); Pearlman, *Violence, Nonviolence*; Yehoshua Porath, *The Emergence of the Palestinian-Arab National Movement, 1918–1929* (London: Frank Cass, 1974); Muhammad Muslih, *The Origins of Palestinian Nationalism* (New York: Columbia University Press, 1988).

5. Yezid Sayigh, *Armed Struggle and the Search for State: The Palestinian National Movement, 1949–1993* (Oxford: Oxford University Press, 1997), 9–10.

6. Khalaf, *Politics in Palestine*, 1.

7. Ibid., 35. The emphasis of MST on the tension between organizational and strategic objectives is particularly interesting because it runs counter to a central argument in what is unquestionably the best book on the armed struggle within the Palestinian national movement: Sayigh, *Armed Struggle*. Although I agree with Sayigh that the armed struggle did help construct and strengthen a Palestinian identity, a leadership elite, and some basic institutions, the coercive and constitutive aspects of violence were often at odds, as were the strategic and organizational objectives with which they were associated.

8. Baruch Kimmerling and Joel Migdal, *The Palestinian People: A History* (Cambridge, MA: Harvard University Press, 2003), 107; Hillel Cohen, *Army of Shadows: Palestinian Collaboration with Zionism, 1917–1948* (Berkeley: University of California Press, 2008), 121–44.

9. Kimmerling and Migdal, *Palestinian People*, 107.

10. As previously noted, I exclude earlier campaigns from my analysis due to the complexities of assessing structure and relative strength in an Arab national movement that overlapped with, if not subsumed, the Palestinian national movement. Including campaigns from earlier periods in the analysis would only add to the explanatory power of MST, however, due to their fragmented infighting and repeated failures amid struggles to secure movement leadership.

11. Tables 3.1, 4.1, 5.1, and 6.1 provide overviews of the campaigns in each movement, but due to space limitations, some campaigns with the same movement system in consecutive years are combined (e.g., the Palestinians had six fragmented campaigns from 1975 to 1985 that all failed). All campaigns are counted and analyzed in chapter 7.

12. The phrase "detonate the revolution" comes from the early strategic documents of Fatah concerning its use of violence in the mid- to late 1960s. Fatah, "Kayf Tanfajir al-Thawra al-Musallaha, Wa Kayf Fajjarat 'Fatah' al-Thawra al-Filastiniyya [How the Armed Revolution Ignites, and How Fatah Detonated the Palestinian Revolution]," n.d.

13. *Nakba* means "catastrophe" in Arabic and is used to describe the 1948 War and the displacement of the Palestinian refugees.

14. One of the unique challenges for the Palestinians was that not only did they have to struggle with the Israelis for what they saw as their homeland but they also had to contend with Jordan, which had annexed the West Bank in 1950 and wanted it back after the 1967 war, and Syria, which considered parts of Palestine to be "Southern Syria." Moshe Shemesh, *The Palestinian Entity 1959–1974: Arab Politics and the PLO* (London: Frank Cass, 1988), 206.

15. Sayigh, *Armed Struggle*, 108–11.

16. Emile Sahliyeh, *In Search of Leadership: West Bank Politics Since 1967* (Washington, DC: Brookings Institution, 1988), 88–92.

17. Sayigh, *Armed Struggle*, 167.

18. Abu Iyad, *My Home, My Land* (New York: Times Books, 1981), 29.

19. Palestinian National Charter, Article 11.

20. Fatah, "Tahrir al-Aqtar al-Muhtalla Wa Uslub al-Kifah al-Musallah Dud al-Isti'mar al-Mubashir [The Liberation of the Occupied Lands and the Method of Armed Struggle against Direct Colonialism]," n.d., 13–14.

21. Nasser's and Shuqeiri's reputations as fiery speakers certainly did not hurt this charge.

22. Fatah, "Tahrir al-Aqtar al-Muhtalla," 11–12.

23. Fatah, "Kayf Tanfajir al-Thawra al-Musallaha," 22.

24. Quoted in, respectively, Helena Cobban, *The Palestinian Liberation Organization: People, Power and Politics* (Cambridge, UK: Cambridge University Press, 1984), 33; Sayigh, *Armed Struggle*, 120.

25. Sayigh, *Armed Struggle*, 102.

26. Yaari, *Strike Terror*, 73–74.

27. William B. Quandt, Fuad Jabber, and Ann Mosely Lesch, *The Politics of Palestinian Nationalism* (Berkeley: University of California Press, 1973), 172.

28. In Cobban, *Palestinian Liberation Organisation*, 24–25. It is worth noting, however, that despite the upswing in support, the Fatah attacks did not inspire the massive popular uprising Fatah wanted. Yaari, *Strike Terror*, 72–73.

29. John W. Amos, *Palestinian Resistance: Organization of a Nationalist Movement* (New York: Pergamon Press, 1980), 39.

30. Sayigh, *Armed Struggle*, 108.

31. Yaari, *Strike Terror*, 71.

32. In ibid., 63, 71.

33. In Alain Gresh, *The PLO: The Struggle Within: Towards an Independent Palestinian State* (London: Zed Books, 1988), 24.

34. Sayigh, *Armed Struggle*, 78.

35. The ANM did launch some nonviolent reconnaissance missions into Israel late in 1964 to try to assuage their more militant members. They lost their first "martyr" to Jordanian border patrols but did not publish information about the operation until years later. Ibid., 110–11.

36. Quandt, Jabber, and Lesch, *Politics of Palestinian Nationalism*, 157; Charles Yost, "How It Began," *Foreign Affairs* 46, no. 2 (1968): 304–20.

37. Shafiq al-Hout, PLF member, noted, "What hurt me most, however, were the mutual grudges between Arab States, which were more intense than those against the common enemy." Shafiq al-Hout, *My Life in the PLO: The Inside Story of the Palestinian Struggle* (London: Pluto Press, 2011), 59.

38. Although the PLO and ANM took a hit among the base for their ties to the Arab regimes, the role of Fatah in sparking what they (incorrectly) claimed would be a successful war won them few favors with their supporters, state or civilian.

39. Sayigh, *Armed Struggle*, 161.

40. Fatah, *Political and Armed Struggle* (Beirut, 1969), 31–32; Benny Morris, *Righteous Victims: A History of the Zionist-Arab Conflict, 1881–1999* (New York: Knopf, 1999), 366.

41. In this regard, it is also instructive that the Palestinians whom Fatah targeted for death during this period were West Bank leaders who called for a separate Palestinian state. Yaari, *Strike Terror*, 147–148.

42. In Sayigh, *Armed Struggle*, 166.

43. Popular Front for the Liberation of Palestine, "Al-Fikr al-'Askari Li al-Jabha al-Sha'biyya Li-Tahrir Filastin [Military Thinking of the PFLP]," n.d., 7.

44. Yaari, *Strike Terror*, 137–38.

45. Nasser Youssef, interview by author, June 2013.

46. Amos, *Palestinian Resistance*, 181.

47. See Boaz Atzili and Wendy Pearlman, "Triadic Deterrence: Coercing Strength, Beaten by Weakness," *Security Studies* 21, no. 2 (June 2012): 301–35.

48. Nasser Youssef, interview.

49. Jibril Rajoub, interview by author, July 2009. The Jordanians were far from pleased with this perception because they claimed that it had, in fact, been their artillery that knocked out the Israeli tanks, which were then paraded through the streets of Jordanian cities and Palestinian refugee camps as war trophies.

50. Even when a group refused to take its seats, the negotiations provide insight into its relative strength. For example, the PFLP later demanded fifteen seats, the same as the strongest challenger (Saiqa) but no more, which was slightly less than half of Fatah (thirty-three) at the time. Quandt, Jabber, and Lesch, *Politics of Palestinian Nationalism*, 32, 179; Gresh, *PLO*, 27–28; Rashid Hamid, *Resolutions of the Palestine National Assembly, 1964–1974* (Beirut: Research Center, Palestine Liberation Organization, 1975). Unfortunately, the seat totals became ossified due to a lack of elections and renewed negotiations, making the PNC seats a good proxy for the relative strength of groups in the late 1960s and 1970s, but not in subsequent years.

51. Fatah had around 3,500 fighters in Jordan by summer 1969. The PFLP and Saiqa each had about 1,200 fighters in Jordan at that time, although each also had significant concentrations of guerrillas based elsewhere, in Gaza (PFLP) or Syria (Saiqa). The refusal of the PFLP to take its PNC seats due to disagreements over the seat distribution helped ensure the movement remained fragmented rather than united. Sayigh, *Armed Struggle*, 181–82; Qais Abdul Karim and Fahd Suleiman, *The Democratic Front for the Liberation of Palestine (DFLP): Formation and Course of Action, 1969–2007* (n.d.).

52. Ghassan Khatib, former JCP member, interview by author, June 2013; Hanna Amireh, former JCP member, interview by author, June 2013.

53. The Popular Front for the Liberation of Palestine, *Limadha?: Darabat al-Jabha al-Sha'biyya Li-Tahrir Filastin Dud al-Mu'assasat al-Isra'iliyya Wa al-Sahyuniyya Wa al-Imbiryaliyya Fi al-Kharij* [Why?: The PFLP Strikes against Israeli, Zionist and Imperialist Targets outside the Arab World] (1969), 18–22. Cobban, *Palestinian Liberation Organisation*, 146, 288. Indeed, one former PFLP member claimed that the hijackings played a key role in his joining the group over a decade later; former PFLP Member, interview by author, June 2013.

54. Morris, *Righteous Victims*, 378.

55. The Popular Front for the Liberation of Palestine, *Limadha?* 33–36.

56. Sayigh, *Armed Struggle*, 215.

57. Indeed, the PFLP discussed this very strategy at its conference on the eve of Black September. Yezid Sayigh, interview by author, May 2010.

58. Sayigh, *Armed Struggle*, 232; former DFLP member A, interview by author, December 2009.

59. Quandt, Jabber, and Lesch, *Politics of Palestinian Nationalism*, 116.

60. Anat N. Kurz, *Fatah and the Politics of Violence: The Institutionalization of a Popular Struggle* (Brighton, UK: Sussex Academic Press, 2005), 59–60; Jamal Nassar, *The Palestine Liberation Organization: From Armed Struggle to the Declaration of Independence* (New York: Praeger, 1991), 56.

61. J. Gaspard, "Palestine: The Struggle of a People to Become a Nation," *New Middle East* 16 (September 1970).

62. Fateh, *A Dialogue with Fateh* (Beirut: Palestine National Liberation Movement, Fateh, Al-Tali'a, 1969), 13.

63. This was not the first time the Fatah leadership had to mediate. In February 1970, clashes between the guerrillas and Jordanians broke out while Arafat was in Moscow, and he had to rush home to negotiate a cease-fire. Quandt, Jabber, and Lesch, *Politics of Palestinian Nationalism*, 120.

64. Another PFLP-hijacked plane was flown to Cairo and destroyed after its passengers were released. The third of the three planes held in Jordan was hijacked after another planned hijacking was thwarted by El Al security, leading to the capture of Leila Khaled, a PFLP operative.

65. Leila Khaled, interview by author, 2010.

66. In 1969 and early 1970, almost all of the population of Jordan supported the *fedayeen*. By September 1970, only the refugees and poor Jordanians did because the reckless actions of the *fedayeen*, of which the June hostage-taking and September hijacking were paramount examples, had blackened their reputation. In previous months, a Palestinian friend of Arafat angrily told him, "This is no longer a PLO, this is guns, gangsters and guns" and "I am one of you, but if I were King Hussein I would kick your asses back to the Dead Sea!" Fakhri Abu Shaka, interview by author, September 2009. "The guerrillas may have been able to take over in early 1970, but their subsequent actions alienated the people. When the fighting came, most people stayed in their basements." Nawaf Tell, interview by author, August 2009.

67. Fatah argued that the establishment of a secure base was a central objective. Jordan largely possessed the four key characteristics described by Fatah: "a place in which the revolutionaries have complete authority and control," "it should be in contact with enemy grounds to enable the revolutionaries to undertake armed action," "it should be in the midst of the people directly connected with the revolution," and "it should be located so as to enable the revolutionaries to resist the siege and annihilation operations of the enemy." Fatah, *Political and Armed Struggle*, 27.

68. "Khalid al-Hassan, Fatah," in *Palestine Lives; Interviews with Leaders of the Resistance*, ed. Clovis Maksoud (Beirut: Palestine Research Center and Kuwaiti Teachers Association, 1973), 28–29. Adnan Abu Odeh, a Palestinian who is a former Jordanian minister and adviser to King Hussein, argued, "Fatah's toleration of the leftists was its biggest mistake. The leftists alienated the people and shifted the image of the guerrillas from those who want to liberate to those who want to rule." Adnan Abu Odeh, interview by author, 2009.

69. "Abu Iyad [Salah Khalaf], Fatah," in Maksoud, *Palestine Lives*, 44. Even when the Palestinian movement achieved a brief moment of unity in 1974 and initial UN recognition, the alliance quickly faltered due to resistance from those who had less power and therefore had accrued fewer benefits, and were backed by foreign influences that easily infiltrated the movement due to its multiple significant groups.

70. Despite the clear strategic problems resulting from the PFLP "external operations," the strength of violent competition amid fragmentation was demonstrated yet again when Fatah itself engaged in such operations under its auxiliary Black September Organization (BSO), formed in late 1971 and named after the Jordan debacle. The PFLP and Fatah had thus reversed roles in 1965–1967, when Fatah started launching what the PFLP considered foolhardy attacks, only to have the PFLP later follow suit. The operations of the group, including the attack on Israeli athletes at the Munich Olympics in 1972, initially captivated world attention and drove some recruits to the BSO. Fatah was quick to disband the BSO, however, once it became clear that its operations hurt the standing of Fatah both internationally and with large portions of the Palestinian public, putting larger organizational gains at risk.

71. Cobban, *Palestinian Liberation Organisation*, 78–79.

72. Sayigh, *Armed Struggle*, 596–601.

73. Rashid Khalidi, "The PLO as Representative of the Palestinian People," in *The International Relations of the Palestinian Liberation Organization*, ed. Augustus Richard Norton and Martin Greenberg (Carbondale: Southern Illinois University Press, 1989), 65.

74. In the Arab League summit in Baghdad in 1978, Arab governments agreed to pay hundreds of millions of dollars to the Palestinians as a result of the Camp David Accords, including $150 million annually to be distributed by the PLO in the West Bank and Gaza and another $250 million paid directly to the PLO; Sayigh, *Armed Struggle*, 437, 441, 479–81.

75. Adam Zagorin, "Auditing the PLO," in *The International Relations of the Palestinian Liberation Organization*, ed. Augustus Richard Norton and Martin Greenberg (Carbondale: Southern Illinois University Press, 1989), 197–99.

76. Aaron David Miller, *The PLO and the Politics of Survival* (New York: Praeger, 1983), 42.

77. Sari Nusseibeh, interview by author, December 2009. Nusseibeh was a Fatah strategist with the UNC.

78. Khalil al-Wazir, known as Abu Jihad, was a founding Fatah leader who had been building the group networks in the West Bank and Gaza since the early 1980s. Shabiba leaders, interview by author, June 2013.

79. Former DFLP member B, interview by author, 2010.

80. Nigel Parsons, *The Politics of the Palestinian Authority: From Oslo to Al-Aqsa* (New York: Routledge, 2005), 264–65.

81. Yezid Sayigh, interview.

82. Sayigh, *Armed Struggle*, 467, 484, 519–520.

83. Hanan Ashrawi, interview by author, July 2013.

84. Francesco Strazzari, "Another Nakba: Weapons Availability and the Transformation of the Palestinian National Struggle, 1987–2007," *International Studies Perspectives* 11 (2010), 119.

85. Al-Hout, *My Life in the PLO*, 238–39.

86. Sayigh, *Armed Struggle*, 624.

87. William Quandt, interview by author, May 9, 2015; "Memorandum from William Quandt of the National Security Council Staff to the President's Assistant for National Security Affairs (Brzezinski)," September 19, 1977, 1977–1980 Vol. VIII, Arab-Israeli Dispute, January 1977–August 1978, Document 103, Foreign Relations of the United States.

88. Qaddoura Fares, interview by author, June 2009.

89. Mia Bloom, "Palestinian Suicide Bombing: Public Support, Market Share, and Outbidding," *Political Science Quarterly* 119, no. 1 (2004), 66–67.

90. Palestinian Center for Policy and Survey Research, Public Opinion Poll #3: "Palestinian Elections," November 11, 1993; Palestinian Center for Policy and Survey Research, Public Opinion Poll #6: "Palestinian Elections and the Cairo Agreement," February 19, 1994.

91. Barton Gellman, "Arafat Likely to Prosper as Hamas Dodges Vote," *Washington Post*, January 14, 1996; Palestinian Center for Policy and Survey Research, Public Opinion Poll #7: "Palestinian Elections and the Hebron Massacre," March 20, 1994; Palestinian Center for Policy and Survey Research, Public Opinion Poll #26: "Abu Ghneim, Armed Attacks, Permanent Settlement, Peace Process, and Local Elections," March 1997.

92. Shaul Mishal and Avraham Sela, *The Palestinian Hamas: Vision, Violence, and Coexistence* (New York: Columbia University Press, 2006), 92.

93. Ahmed Qurei (Abu Alaa), interview by author, June 2013.

94. Mishal and Sela, *Palestinian Hamas*, 87; Ziad Abu-Amr, "Hamas: A Historical and Political Background," *Journal of Palestine Studies* 22, no. 4 (July 1, 1993), 16; Youssef Ibrahim, "Brotherhood of Anger—Palestinian Religious Militants: Why Their Ranks Are Growing," *New York Times*, November 8, 1994.

95. Kydd and Walter argue that Hamas was a strong challenger during this period and that its *strength* was why negotiations and the movement succeeded; Andrew Kydd and Barbara Walter, "Sabotaging the Peace: The Politics of Extremist Violence," *International Organization* 56, no. 2 (2002): 263–96. Although I agree that movement credibility and trust are important, the systematic data presented here and in online appendix A on the strength of Hamas demonstrates its relative weakness. Furthermore, Kydd and Walter's argument comes up short for the periods before and after Oslo. There were strong Palestinian challengers in the 1960s and 1970s, while Hamas itself became a strong(er) challenger from 2000 until today, yet there were no successful negotiations in any of these periods. MST thus provides a more systematic and powerful explanation for the Oslo period as well as the broader history of the movement.

96. Uri Savir, *The Process: 1,100 Days That Changed the Middle East* (New York: Random House, 1998); Yossi Beilin, *Touching Peace: From the Oslo Accord to a Final Agreement* (London: Weidenfeld and Nicolson, 1999), 269–70.

97. Moshe Ma'oz, Robert L Rothstein, and Khalil Shikaki, eds., *The Israeli-Palestinian Peace Process: Oslo and the Lessons of Failure* (Brighton, UK: Sussex Academic Press, 2004); Aaron David Miller, *The Much Too Promised Land: America's Elusive Search for Arab-Israeli Peace* (New York: Bantam Books, 2008); Jeremy Pressman, "Visions in Collision: What Happened at Camp David and Taba?" *International Security* 28, no. 2 (2003): 5–43.

98. The Oslo Accords did not give the Palestinians any control over Jerusalem, left the vast majority of refugees outside Palestine, made no agreement on the final borders of a Palestinian state, and did nothing to stop or dismantle Israeli settlements.

99. Parsons, *Politics of the Palestinian Authority*, 6.

100. Hanan Ashrawi, interview.

101. Parsons, *Politics of the Palestinian Authority*, 80.

102. The Second Intifada saw Fatah dragged yet again into strategically counterproductive violence due to the fragmented structure brought about by the rise of Hamas from subordinate to challenger; Mia Bloom, *Dying to Kill: The Allure of Suicide Terror* (New York: Columbia University Press, 2005).

103. "Meeting Minutes: Dr. Saeb Erakat Meeting with the Negotiations Support Unit," Ramallah: June 2, 2009.

104. Sayigh, *Armed Struggle*; Parsons, *Politics of the Palestinian Authority*; Gresh, *PLO*; Cobban, *Palestinian Liberation Organisation*. Interestingly, Walid Khalidi once noted seven key differences between the struggle in Algeria and the one in Palestine to explain why the latter's success might not be a good model for the Palestinians; however, the one key factor he did not mention was the structure of the movement. Yaari, *Strike Terror*, 186–87.

105. Hanan Ashrawi, interview; Qaddoura Fares, interview; Nasser Youssef, interview.

106. Wendy Pearlman, "Spoiling Inside and Out: Internal Political Contestation and the Middle East Peace Process," *International Security* 33, no. 3 (2008): 79–109.

107. Fatah pushed a common political program at the twelfth PNC in late June 1974 that all significant groups agreed to. This yielded the limited successes of the Arab League recognizing the PLO as the "sole, legitimate representative of the Palestinian people" and the United Nations granting it observer status; "Political Program for the Present Stage of the Palestine Liberation Organization," *Journal of Palestine Studies* 3, no. 4 (1974): 224.

108. For example, despite all the uncertainty today over the relative strength of Fatah and Hamas, it is undeniable that the former is the hegemon in the West Bank and the latter the hegemon in Gaza. This is a unique scenario for national movements, with different groups dominating in two noncontiguous areas of national territory, making it possible for separate balances of power to be analyzed and to affect behavior. This supplement to MST explains why Hamas has restrained rocket fire in Gaza but still attempts to spoil negotiations involving Fatah.

4. The Zionist Movement

1. Regarding the opening quotation from the Talmud, Flavius Josephus's account of the First Jewish-Roman (66–73 CE) war blames infighting among the Jews for their defeat by the Romans and the destruction of the Second Jewish Temple, an interpretation shared by many Zionists. Flavius Josephus, *The Jewish War*, trans. Henry St. John Thackeray (Cambridge, MA: Harvard University Press, 1997).

2. Benny Morris, *1948: A History of the First Arab-Israeli War* (New Haven: Yale University Press, 2008), 176; Anita Shapira, *Ben-Gurion: Father of Modern Israel* (New Haven: Yale University Press, 2014), 155–56; Ehud Sprinzak, *Brother against Brother: Violence and Extremism in Israeli Politics from Altalena to the Rabin Assassination* (New York: Free Press, 1999), 17.

3. Benedict Anderson, *Imagined Communities: Reflections on the Origin and Spread of Nationalism* (London: Verso, 2006).

4. Hovevei Zion was motivated in part by the pogroms in Russia and Eastern Europe that led to the death and displacement of thousands of Jews. Only a small number of Jews migrated to Palestine as a result, however, especially compared to the many millions that went to the Americas and Europe. Overall, 20,000–30,000 Jewish immigrants came to Palestine during the First Aliyah (immigration) in 1881–1903, although many subsequently returned to Russia or left for Europe or the Americas. Benny Morris, *Righteous Victims: A History of the Zionist-Arab Conflict, 1881–1999* (New York: Knopf, 1999), 19.

5. As Shabtai Teveth explains, "The Zionist Organization was open to all Jews over the age of eighteen. To become a member one bought the shekel, which entitled one to vote in the elections to the Zionist Congress. . . . The strength of a Zionist party was determined by the number of delegates it sent to the Congress; the number of delegates was decided by the number of votes, and only shekel holders could vote." *Ben-Gurion: The Burning Ground, 1886–1948* (Boston: Houghton Mifflin, 1987), 173.

6. Morris, *Righteous Victims*, 24.

7. The importance of relations with state powers was further demonstrated by the impact of the Turkish reaction to World War I. The Turks ordered that Jews in Palestine had to become Ottoman citizens or leave the territory. Close to 30,000, or one-third of the total Jewish population, left Palestine, dealing the immigration efforts of the Zionist Organization a significant setback.

8. Baruch Kimmerling, *Zionism and Territory: The Socio-Territorial Dimensions of Zionist Politics* (Berkeley: University of California Press, 1983), 43–44.

9. League of Nations, "Mandate for Palestine," August 12, 1922, http://unispal.un.org/UNISPAL.NSF/0/2FCA2C68106F11AB05256BCF007BF3CB, accessed September 22, 2016.

10. Yaakov Thon, *Otto Warburg: The Third President of the Zionist Movement* [in Hebrew] (Herzlia: Massada Print, 1938), 59.

11. Nathan Gelber, "Congress, Zionist," *New Encyclopedia of Zionism and Israel* (Cranbury, NJ: Associated University Press, 1994), 280.

12. Zeev Tzahor, "The Struggle between the Revisionist Party and the Labor Movement: 1929–1933," *Modern Judaism* 8, no. 1 (February 1988), 16. Other scholars agree that "after 1931, the structure of the movement changed." Yaacov Goldstein, "Mapai and the Seventeenth Zionist Congress," *Studies in Zionism* 10, no. 1 (1989): 19.

13. Teveth, *Ben-Gurion*, 401.

14. Yaacov Shavit, *Jabotinsky and the Revisionist Movement, 1925–1948* (London: Frank Cass, 1988), 43.

15. Teveth, *Ben-Gurion*, 505.

16. Kimmerling, *Zionism and Territory*, 18. I thus provide a complementary argument to Kimmerling: not only did control of aliyah and immigration help Mapai become the leader, but it was the position of Mapai as the leader that helped push it to pursue such strategic goals for organizational ends.

17. Ibid., 45.

18. Ibid., 97.

19. Yitshaq Ben-Ami, *Years of Wrath, Days of Glory: Memoirs from the Irgun* (New York: Shengold Publishers, 1983), 316. *Aliyah* is a Hebrew word that literally means "ascent," but it became the term for the immigration of Jews to the Mandate (and later Israel).

20. Ibid., 320.

21. Kimmerling, *Zionism and Territory*, 87.

22. Uri Milstein, *History of the War of Independence: A Nation Girds for War* (Lanham: University Press of America, 1996), 203. As noted before, Ben-Gurion led both the Histadrut and Jewish Agency for much of the Mandate period, and he had control over appointments to the Haganah leadership, which followed orders from the Jewish Agency in any case.

23. Shavit, *Jabotinsky and the Revisionist Movement*, 28–31.

24. Joseph Schechtman and Yehuda Benari, *History of the Revisionist Movement*, Vol. 1 (Tel Aviv: Hadar, 1970), 219–21; Yaacov Goldstein, *From Fighters to Soldiers: How the Israeli Defense Forces Began* (Brighton, UK: Sussex Academic Press, 1998), 176–79.

25. Shavit, *Jabotinsky and the Revisionist Movement*, 49–51, 98–99.

26. Kimmerling, *Zionism and Territory*, 98.

27. Joseph Heller, *The Stern Gang: Ideology, Politics, and Terror, 1940–1949* (Portland, OR: Frank Cass, 1995), 61–62.

28. "Illegal Immigration: Intelligence Reports," May 17, 1939, CO 733/396/5, The National Archives, UK (hereafter TNA); Shavit, *Jabotinsky and the Revisionist Movement*, 376.

29. Amos Perlmutter, *Military and Politics in Israel* (London: Frank Cass, 1969), 41.

30. Shavit, *Jabotinsky and the Revisionist Movement*, 88; Teveth, *Ben-Gurion*, 410–13; Goldstein, *From Fighters to Soldiers*, 178–81.

31. Goldstein, *From Fighters to Soldiers*, 198–217.

32. Ben-Ami, *Years of Wrath, Days of Glory*, 110.

33. Ben-Gurion scuttled unity talks in 1939 and 1940 on the same basis; Milstein, *History of the War of Independence*, 224.

34. Eldad Harouvi, *Palestine Investigated: The Criminal Investigation Department of the Palestine Police Force, 1920–48* (Chicago: Sussex Academic Press, 2016), 42.

35. Shavit, *Jabotinsky and the Revisionist Movement*, 37; "Le 21e Congres Sioniste [The 21st Zionist Congress]," Anglo-Palestinian Bank, 1939.

36. "The New Zionist (Revisionist) National Army," January 17, 1939, KV 5-34, TNA; Moshe Marks, "I.Z.L. and Lechi in Palestine: The Recruitment of Funds and Economic Means (1940–1948)" [in Hebrew] (PhD diss., Bar Ilan University, 1994), 24.

37. The Irgun certainly did not perceive itself as a weak subordinate. Its representatives at the Zionist Congress in 1939 declared Irgun "the most important actor in the Middle East." Meir Pa'il and Yurman Pinhas, *The Test of the Zionist Movement 1931–1948: The Authority of the National Leadership against the Dissidents* [in Hebrew] (Tel Aviv: Cherikover, 2004), 66.

38. Vladimir Jabotinsky, "Horaot leInyaney haIrgun [Directives for the Business of the Irgun]" in *Irgun Zvai Leumi* [National Military Organization], Vol. 1: *Collection of Archival Sources and Documents April 1937–April 1941* [in Hebrew] (Tel Aviv: Jabotinsky Institute, 1990), 15.

39. Meir Chazan, "The Dispute in Mapai over 'Self-Restraint' and 'Purity of Arms' during the Arab Revolt," *Jewish Social Studies* 15, no. 3 (2009), 99–100.

40. Morris, *Righteous Victims*, 147.

41. Ibid.

42. Ben-Ami, *Years of Wrath, Days of Glory*, 116.

43. Ibid., 232–33.

44. Pa'il and Pinhas, *Test of the Zionist Movement*, 44.

45. "Conversation between Yunitzman, Shimon (Hayim Lubinski) of Etzel, and Eliyahu Golomb of Hanagah, Tel Aviv, August 30th, 1938," in *Irgun Zvai Leumi*, Vol. 1, 448–53. The Irgun was also referred to as the "Etzel," which is the pronunciation of its acronym in Hebrew (IZL).

46. Avraham Tehomi, "Lama Hitpaleg haIrgun haZvai haLeumi? [Why Did the Irgun Zvai Leumi Split?]," *Yediot Aharonot*, October 17, 1958.

47. J. Boywer Bell, *Terror out of Zion: Irgun Zvai Leumi, Lehi, and the Palestine Underground, 1929–1949* (New York: St. Martin's Press, 1977), 43–44; Yehuda Bauer, "From Cooperation to Resistance: The Haganah 1938–1946," *Middle Eastern Studies* 2, no. 3 (1966): 185–87; Pa'il and Pinhas, *Test of the Zionist Movement*, 37–38.

48. "Conversation between Yunitzman, Shimon (Hayim Lubinski) of Etzel, and Eliyahu Golomb of Hanagah, Tel Aviv, August 30th, 1938"; Anita Shapira, *Land and Power: The Zionist*

Resort to Force, 1881–1948, trans. William Templer (New York: Oxford University Press, 1992), 253–54.

49. Shmuel Yavnieli argued that Mapai must "move the earth. If we do not . . . others [the Revisionists and Irgun] will." In Teveth, *Ben-Gurion*, 740.

50. One Irgun veteran noted that "In Netanya, the Etzel [Irgun] was stronger than the Hagana." "Interview with Yaakov 'Yoel' Amrami, Testimonials—Etzel, 1938–1943," 1991, 17, 2/5- עע, Jabotinsky Archive.

51. "David Raziel's Letter to Zeev Jabotinsky [Michtavo Shel David Raziel LeZeev Jabotinsky]," in *Irgun Zvai Leumi*, Vol. 1, 66.

52. Harouvi, *Palestine Investigated*, 76–80.

53. Hillel Cohen, *Army of Shadows: Palestinian Collaboration with Zionism, 1917–1948* (Berkeley: University of California Press, 2008), 122–44.

54. Tom Segev, *One Palestine, Complete: Jews and Arabs under the British Mandate* (New York: Macmillan, 2001), 414.

55. In the 1940s, "Probably no more than 10 to 15 percent of the Yishuv supported the right." Ehud Sprinzak, *The Ascendance of Israel's Radical Right* (New York: Oxford University Press, 1991), 32.

56. Robert Weltsch, "A Tragedy of Leadership (Chaim Weizmann and the Zionist Movement)," *Jewish Social Studies* 13, no. 3 (1951), 213. Norman Rose claims that, even by the late 1930s, "Without Mapai, Weizmann was powerless." "Weizmann, Ben-Gurion, and the 1946 Crisis in the Zionist Movement," *Studies in Zionism* 11, no. 1 (1990), 29. For those seeking exogenous shifts in power, the Holocaust and World War II provide a clear example that decimated movement challengers.

57. The early 1940s starkly demonstrate the difficulties of assessing the strength of armed groups; not only must we rely on somewhat vague estimates of membership in clandestine organizations, but many of those members were not active because they were either serving thousands of miles away on European battlefields or in Palestine in units commanded by the British. To deal with this issue, I provide potential challengers with every benefit of the doubt, meaning that, if they are within one-third as strong as the leading group by any measure, they qualify as a challenger.

58. In 1942, the British noted that the "majority of [the Haganah] members are serving in one or other of the forces": 10,000 in the British Army, 5,800 in regular police, and 15,400 in the special police Secret Intelligence Service. Secret Intelligence Service, "Left Hagana," March 18, 1942, KV 5-33, TNA.

59. According to Yoav Harpaz, a former Palmach member, the name *Palmach* means "the striking force" and many joined because they thought the Palmach was the striking force of the Jewish resistance; Yoav Harpaz, interview by author, August 10, 2012.

60. The Haganah and Palmach bases in the kibbutzim became even more important as the British banned weapons at various times (e.g., in 1943) *except* for the defense of settlements. This was particularly crucial given that the Palmach and Haganah were technically illegal organizations but their position as defenders of the settlements made them more legitimate than their rivals in the eyes of the British. Morris, *Righteous Victims*, 174. The British estimated that there were 600 Palmach and 20,000–25,000 Haganah in April 1943. "Palestine: Hagana," April 19, 1943, KV 5-34, TNA.

61. Trevor Dupuy, *Elusive Victory: The Arab-Israeli Wars, 1947–1974* (New York: Harper and Row, 1978), 4–6.

62. At the same time, Mapai helped prevent the Revisionists from becoming stronger by assuaging the Mizrahi (a potential Revisionist partner) about its desired future boundaries for a Jewish state. On the related Biltmore Program and its importance, see Nadav Shelef, *Evolving Nationalism: Homeland, Identity, and Religion in Israel, 1925–2005* (Ithaca: Cornell University Press, 2010), 36–43.

63. According to Jacob Eliav, a Lehi member, Lehi had around 120 members in total throughout all of Palestine in 1941. Pa'il and Pinhas, *Test of the Zionist Movement*, 96. Moshe Ben Shahar, an Irgun member, claimed that the Lehi members took many of the Irgun weapons with them, further weakening the group. Moshe Ben Shahar, interview by author, August 2012.

64. The British estimated Irgun membership at 1,200–1,500 in 1942, lower than it had been during the Arab Revolt. "Extract from Security Summary ME No. 55," June 18, 1942, KV 5-34, TNA.

65. According to Hanna Armoni, a former Lehi member, Lehi was the smallest organization in part because there were very strict rules in effect to keep it clandestine. Hanna Armoni, interview by author, August 8, 2012.

66. The Lehi committed more than twice as many assassinations as the Irgun and Haganah, including the killing of many Jews. Nachman Ben-Yehuda, *Political Assassinations by Jews: A Rhetorical Device for Justice* (Albany: SUNY Press, 1992), 397.

67. "Terror," in *Lohamey Herut Israel: Fighters for the Freedom of Israel: Collected Works*, 2nd ed., Vol. 1 [in Hebrew] (Tel Aviv: Yair Publications, 1982), 144.

68. Ezra Yakhin, interview by author, June 17, 2013. Hanna Armoni, interview.

69. Marks, "I.Z.L. and Lechi in Palestine," 81–82.

70. Yehojachin Brenner, "The Stern Gang 1940–1948," *Middle Eastern Studies* 2, no. 1 (1965), 10. The British referred to the Lehi as "the Stern Gang."

71. Eldad Harouvi, interview by author, August 9, 2012; Harouvi, *Palestine Investigated*, 85, 92–93.

72. Harouvi, *Palestine Investigated*, 83, 94–95.

73. Ezra Yakhin, interview; Pa'il and Pinhas, *Test of the Zionist Movement*, 119.

74. Saul Zadka, *Blood in Zion: How the Jewish Guerrillas Drove the British out of Palestine* (London: Brassey's, 1995), 28.

75. Marks, "I.Z.L. and Lechi in Palestine," 252–53.

76. Bruce Hoffman, *Inside Terrorism* (New York: Columbia University Press, 2006), 48–49; Harouvi, *Palestine Investigated*, 119–22, 125, 128.

77. "Intelligence Summary No. 3/44: Jewish Affairs, The Revisionist Party," February 18, 1944, 4, FO 921/153, TNA. Recall that the British referred to the Lehi as "the Stern Gang," and that the Irgun was also referred to as the "Etzel," which is the pronunciation of its acronym in Hebrew (IZL).

78. "Meeting of Regional Commanders and Staff Officers, 10/19/1944," in *Irgun Zvai Leumi*, Vol. 3: *Collection of Archival Sources and Documents January 1944–December 1946* [in Hebrew] (Tel Aviv: Jabotinsky Institute, 1994), 134–37.

79. Winston Churchill, House of Commons, "Palestine: Terrorist Activities," November 9, 1944, PREM 4/51/11, TNA.

80. "Jewish Agency Statement," November 7, 1944, PREM 4/51/11, TNA; "Active Measures against Terrorists," *Zionist Review* 4, no. 47 (November 24, 1944), 2. Although they did not act until after Moyne's death, Mapai and the Haganah had verbally condemned Irgun actions from the start, and the Haganah distributed a pamphlet in April 1944 that "listed ten reasons to condemn the terror." In May 1945, Moshe Shertok said that "terror is treason." In Harouvi, *Palestine Investigated*, 132–33, 144.

81. Pa'il and Pinhas, *Test of the Zionist Movement*, 133.

82. Zadka, *Blood in Zion*, 54–55.

83. Indeed, Begin himself saw the crackdown of the Season coming despite the fact that the Lehi had assassinated Moyne. "Headquarters Meeting No. 10, 11/9/1944," in *Irgun Zvai Leumi*, Vol. 3, 139–42. Other Irgun members clearly saw the Season as an excuse for the Haganah to get rid of the rising challenger. Ezra Yakhin, interview.

84. Pa'il and Pinhas, *Test of the Zionist Movement*, 146–48; High Commissioner for Palestine to Secretary of State for the Colonies, "Telegram No. 197," March 1, 1945, CO 733/457/12, TNA.

85. High Commissioner for Palestine to Secretary of State for the Colonies, "Telegram No. 197."

86. Criminal Investigation Department, "Intelligence Summary No. 8/45," April 24, 1945, 1, CO 733/457/12, TNA.

87. Ibid., 2.

88. "PIC Paper No. 2 (Revised): Jewish Illegal Organizations in Palestine," November 8, 1944, FO 921/154, TNA; Ezra Yakhin, interview.

89. Zadka, *Blood in Zion*, 22, 55; Eldad Harouvi, interview.

90. Pa'il and Pinhas, *Test of the Zionist Movement*, 158–60; "On Consistent War," in *Irgun Zvai Leumi*, Vol. 5: *Collection of Archival Sources and Documents January 1948–September 1948* [in Hebrew] (Tel Aviv: Ot Paz, 1999), 109.

91. Steven Wagner, "British Intelligence and the Jewish Resistance Movement in the Palestine Mandate, 1945–46," *Intelligence and National Security* 23, no. 5 (2008), 632; John Newsinger, *British Counterinsurgency: From Palestine to Northern Ireland* (New York: Palgrave, 2002), 16.

92. "Extract from War Cabinet 146 (44)," November 6, 1944, PREM 4/51/11, TNA.

93. "Extract from Security Summary Middle East No. 221," February 14, 1945, 6, KV 5-34, TNA.

94. Pa'il and Pinhas, *Test of the Zionist Movement*, 137–39, 146.

95. Yoav Harpaz, interview.

96. "Extract from Report on Interview No. 8 with KOLLEK," October 20, 1945, KV 5-34, TNA.

97. Pa'il and Pinhas, *Test of the Zionist Movement*, 160.

98. Milstein, *History of the War of Independence*, 39.

99. Pa'il and Pinhas, *Test of the Zionist Movement*, 179.

100. Even when Irgun members had expressed their opinion that attacks should be stopped, it was because they thought they should "focus all our efforts on substantiating our internal situation—recruiting men and increasing the fruit [arms and money]." "Headquarters Meeting No. 2, 8/17/1944," in *Irgun Zvai Leumi*, Vol. 3, 104–6; Mark A. Raider, "'Irresponsible, Undisciplined Opposition': Ben Halpern on the Bergson Group and Jewish Terrorism in Pre-State Palestine," *American Jewish History* 92, no. 3 (2004), 330.

101. Colonial Office, "Palestine: Irgun Zvai Leumi," February 21, 1946, KV 5-34, TNA.

102. Bauer, "From Cooperation to Resistance," 206.

103. Yoav Harpaz, interview.

104. "Extract from DSO Palestine & Transjordan Report Re Jewish Reactions to Military Operations," July 8, 1946, KV 5-35, TNA.

105. Pa'il and Pinhas, *Test of the Zionist Movement*, 161.

106. Ibid., 203–4. Of course, the Irgun faced the reverse accusation: that it wanted to overshadow the bridge-destruction operation with its own. Ironically, the Irgun later attempted to restrain the Lehi from launching an attack while the Irgun planned another kidnapping of British officers to secure the release of Irgun prisoners. The Lehi launched the attack anyway. British officers subsequently surrounded themselves with armed escorts, denying the Irgun the ability to carry out its plan. "Announcement," in *Irgun Zvai Leumi*, Vol. 4: *Collection of Archival Sources and Documents January 1947–December 1947* [in Hebrew] (Tel Aviv: Ot Paz, 1996), 26–29.

107. Newsinger, *British Counterinsurgency*, 19–20.

108. Wagner, "British Intelligence," 651.

109. "Report on Operation 'Agatha,'" July 9, 1946, 16, WO 275-27, TNA.

110. A Royal Air Force (RAF) report noted that Agatha led to the arrest of 194 Hanagah and Palmach members, compared to 14 Irgun members and 1 Lehi member. "RAF Intelligence Report," July 1946, AIR 40/2460, TNA; "Op Agatha Div & Bde Reports," July 1, 1946, WO 275-29, TNA.

111. "Implication of the Jewish Agency with Hagana, Irgun Zvai Leumi and Stern," July 1, 1946, CO 537/1715, TNA; "Notes on the White Paper of Evidence," July 31, 1946, CO 537/1715, TNA.

112. Sir John Shaw, High Commissioner for Palestine to Secretary of State for the Colonies, "Evidence against Jewish Agency," July 12, 1946, CO 537/1715, TNA.

113. Anita Shapira, *Land and Power*, 295; Pa'il and Pinhas, *Test of the Zionist Movement*, 206–8.

114. Pa'il and Pinhas, *Test of the Zionist Movement*, 209–10; Yoske Nachmias, interview by author, August 7, 2012.

115. High Commissioner for Palestine to Secretary of State for the Colonies, "Palestine Telegram No. 1038," July 9, 1946, CO 537/1715, TNA.

116. Accounts from Amichai "Gidi" Paglin, the Irgun chief operation officer, support the argument that Mapai and the Haganah wanted the King David attack to prevent the discovery

of their connections to the HRM violence. Joseph Evron, *Gidi: One Chasing a Thousand* (Jerusalem: Gefen, 2009), 103–5, 176.

117. "Illegal Zionist Armed Forces in Palestine and the Complicity of the Jewish Agency," July 19, 1946, 23, CO 537/1715, TNA.

118. Yoske Nachmias, interview.

119. "Telegram from Cairo (Minister Resident's Office) to Foreign Office," November 18, 1944, PREM 4/51/11, TNA.

120. "Jewish Agency and Haganah Anti-Terrorist Campaign," September 20, 1946, KV 2-1435, TNA; Brenner, "Stern Gang," 20.

121. "2 INF BDE 00 No 2: OP 'SHARK,'" July 28, 1946, WO 275-33a, TNA; "Suspected Terrorists Arrested," August 30, 1946, WO 275-33b, TNA; David Cesarani, "The War on Terror That Failed: British Counter-Insurgency in Palestine 1945–1947 and the 'Farran Affair,'" *Small Wars & Insurgencies* 23, no. 4–5 (2012), 648–70.

122. Pa'il and Pinhas, *Test of the Zionist Movement*, 230; Moshe Ben Shahar, interview.

123. Dupuy, *Elusive Victory*, 8–10.

124. Morris, *Righteous Victims*, 176; Raider, "'Irresponsible, Undisciplined Opposition,'" 337.

125. Pa'il and Pinhas, *Test of the Zionist Movement*, 222–23.

126. Morris, *Righteous Victims*, 177.

127. Ibid., 178.

128. Pa'il and Pinhas, *Test of the Zionist Movement*, 273–74.

129. In ibid., 240.

130. "Kol Zion HaLokhemet [The Voice of Fighting Zion]," July 6, 1947, 8.15-4כ, Jabotinsky Archive.

131. As Shelef notes, Mapai accepted partition even though it did not yet give up its claim to more territory, policies that were maintained in part to maintain the spoils of leadership. *Evolving Nationalism*, 29–30, 37–39. Begin's Herut would subsequently do the same after coming to power in 1977 (106).

132. Pa'il and Pinhas, *Test of the Zionist Movement*, 246, 264.

133. Ibid., 220–21, 291.

134. Newsinger, *British Counterinsurgency*, 28; Morris, *1948*, 39.

135. Pa'il and Pinhas, *Test of the Zionist Movement*, 273.

136. Ibid., 271–72, 285–86.

137. See Morris, *1948*, 51–74.

138. Ibid., 55.

139. Ben-Ami, *Years of Wrath, Days of Glory*, 114.

140. Conversely, Ben-Gurion also argued that the subordinate Irgun and Lehi did not take the Arab state threat seriously. Pa'il and Pinhas, *Test of the Zionist Movement*, 229–30.

141. Morris, *1948*, 86–88.

142. Ibid., 399.

143. Ibid., 90.

144. Ben-Gurion noted that, because of these arms, "the situation is radically different in our favor." "D. Ben-Gurion to M. Shertok (New York)," April 16, 1948, Political and Diplomatic Documents, December 1947–May 1948, Israel State Archives.

145. Leftist newspaper accounts of the early Irgun attacks on Jaffa "[suggested] that the Irgun was less concerned with capturing Bustros Road in Jaffa than with Allenby Road in Tel Aviv." As Begin explained, "'Allenby Road' is another name for the votes of the Jewish people." Menachem Begin, *The Revolt: Story of the Irgun* (Tel Aviv: Steimatzky Agency, 1977), 359–60; Pa'il and Pinhas, *Test of the Zionist Movement*, 323–24.

146. Morris, *1948*, 113–79, 405.

147. Ibid., 113–15, 175.

148. Ibid., 175–76.

149. Despite Zionist fears at the time and propaganda in the aftermath, the combined size of the deployed Arab forces was always a bit smaller than that of the Zionists. The Haganah thought that the Arab states had armies with 165,000 troops, but in reality, they had less and sent less, about 20,000 in total, followed by another 8,000 in first two to three weeks. Both sides

increased the size of their forces, but the Zionists always had slightly more: 88,000 Zionists compared to 68,000 Arabs by October 1948; ibid., 205.

150. Amitzur Ilan, *Bernadotte in Palestine, 1948* (New York: St. Martin's Press, 1989), 161.

151. Morris, *1948*, 339–41.

152. Ibid., 176; Shapira, *Ben-Gurion*, 155–56; Sprinzak, *Brother against Brother*, 17.

153. Yoske Nachmias, interview.

154. Irgun, "Declaration, 6/9/1948," in *Psychological Warfare and Propaganda: Irgun Documentation*, ed. Eli Tavin and Yonah Alexander (Wilmington, DE: Scholarly Resources, 1982), 247–49. The Irgun commander in Jerusalem, Samuel Katz, bemoaned the fact that "we cannot attack the Old City if the Haganah is prepared to prevent us." Samuel Katz, *Days of Fire* (Garden City, NY: Doubleday, 1968), 266.

155. The *Altalena* demonstrated the potential of opening the door to foreign intrigue. French support for the Irgun was a bet on the group becoming more powerful, providing the French with leverage in a formerly British sphere of influence; Sprinzak, *Brother against Brother*, 18–19.

156. David Ben-Gurion, *Memoirs* (New York: World Publishing, 1970), 91.

157. Ben-Ami, *Years of Wrath, Days of Glory*, 491.

158. Begin, *Revolt*, 168.

159. The tension and confused logic are clear from Begin's subsequent speech. He starts out by saying, "We place these arms at the disposal of the Government," but later notes that "Some of the precious arms must go to our soldiers. The balance we shall give you." Menachem Begin, "The Truth about the Altalena," [speech] Tel Aviv, The Voice of Freedom, June 22, 1948.

160. In 1947, Begin claimed that the Irgun, not the Yishuv leadership, spoke for the majority of the people. Pa'il and Pinhas, *Test of the Zionist Movement*, 119, 248, 298.

161. It is noteworthy that Begin rejected a return to the Revisionist Party and instead struck out on his own, later absorbing the Revisionists into his party (rather than the other way around) a few years later. He had announced his intention to form Herut on May 15, 1948, not coincidentally as a challenge to Ben-Gurion's independence proclamation the day before.

162. Ben-Ami, *Years of Wrath, Days of Glory*, 497–498.

163. "Cabinet Meeting Protocols (Irregular Meeting of Provisional Government)," June 22, 1948, 12/1/308, Israel State Archives.

164. Ibid.

165. Mordechai Na'or, ed., *Koach HaMagen Lexicon—The Haganah* (Ministry of Defense Publishing House, 1994), 33, Haganah Archives; interview with Aryeh Ben Eliezer, 1958, 6–7, 9-בע, Jabotinsky Archives. At the start of the conflict in November 1947, the Irgun had only two hundred rifles and "tens of thousands of bullets." Pa'il and Pinhas, *Test of the Zionist Movement*, 298.

166. *Altalena* [film], directed by Ilana Tsur, 1994; Ben-Ami, *Years of Wrath, Days of Glory*, 485.

167. Sprinzak, *Brother against Brother*, 24–25; "Cabinet Meeting Protocols."

168. Elad Peled, interview by author, June 23, 2013.

169. In a preview of later political battles, Yitzhak Rabin was an IDF commander at the Tel Aviv beach facing off against Menachem Begin. In his memoirs, Rabin explained that the Irgun shot at the Palmach headquarters and the Palmach returned fire. He said one of the Irgun commanders shouted, "'Why are you shooting Jews?' I told him, 'When Jews stop shooting us, we'll stop shooting Jews.'" In Amir Oren, "Defense Ministry: Altalena Fallen Were 'Murdered,'" *Haaretz*, June 19, 2011.

170. Morris, *1948*, 271; "Cabinet Meeting Protocols."

171. "Announcement of the Irgun Zvai Leumi," in *Irgun Zvai Leumi*, Vol. 5, 189–92.

172. Begin, "Truth about the Altalena"; Avi Shilon, *Menachem Begin: A Life* (New Haven: Yale University Press, 2012).

173. Office of Strategic Services, "Illicit Arming by Arabs and Jews in Palestine" (U.S. Department of State, September 30, 1943), 14, 867N.01/1946-2199, May 1943–Feb. 1944, May 1943–Feb. 1944, Record Group 84, U.S. National Archives.

174. As many Arab states correctly pointed out, Israel had conquered territory outside of the boundaries of UN Resolution 181, and it planned to incorporate rather than internationalize West Jerusalem. Nevertheless, most UN states felt this was an acceptable change given that

Mapai had accepted UN Resolution 181 long before the war, which those states blamed on the Arab countries as much as or more than the Israelis. The Provisional Government was also able to cite the *Altalena* as evidence that they would face down extremists in their own camp to uphold cease-fires. Yemima Rosenthal and Barukh Gilad, eds., "M. Shertok to P. Cremona, 6/26/1948," in *Documents on the Foreign Policy of Israel*, Vol. 1 (Jerusalem: Israel State Archives, 1984), 222–25.

175. "Application of Israel for Admission to Membership in the United Nations: Report of the Ad Hoc Political Committee (A/855)," United Nations, May 11, 1949.

176. Of course, it helped that *his* party was the strongest and that it would be *his* leadership in the new state, as MST suggests.

177. David Ben-Gurion, "Ben-Gurion Replies to Altalena Critics," *Jewish Criterion*, August 13, 1948; Sprinzak, *Brother against Brother*, 32.

178. "Letter from Commander of Etzel to Headquarters Abroad," in *Irgun Zvai Leumi*, Vol. 5, 507–15; Pa'il and Pinhas, *Test of the Zionist Movement*, 298.

179. It is not as if the weaker groups did not try to chain-gang. In the battle for Jerusalem in summer 1948, "Lehi reasoned that it was its job to initiate actions that would force Haganah to decide upon its own operations within the framework of being dragged under Lehi's initiatives." But the Lehi failed to pull the Haganah into situations it found strategically unwise, in large part because "Lehi's entire fighting force consisted of no more than an enhanced platoon of 45 men." Yitzhak Levi, *Tish'a Kavin* [in Hebrew] (Tel Aviv: Ma'arachot, 1986), 346.

180. "Broadcast from Sunday, 4/11/1948," in *Irgun Zvai Leumi*, Vol. 5, 298–99.

181. Oren, "Defense Ministry"; Matthew Bell, "Raising Israel's Altalena Ship 'A Lesson for the Future,'" *BBC*, November 27, 2012.

182. See Bruce Hoffman, *Anonymous Soldiers: The Struggle for Israel, 1917–1947* (New York: Knopf, 2015).

183. Those who suggest the hanging of the sergeants was the key factor are mistaken; the British had turned the issue of the Palestine Mandate over to the United Nations months before the hanging of the sergeants, and they did not initiate the withdrawal until after the United Nations voted for an end to the Mandate and the Haganah had conquered significant territory. Furthermore, the British were facing growing sentiment on the home front to bring their troops home before the attacks. "Situation: Internal Security Public Reactions," 1948, CO 733/477/1, TNA.

184. Anita Shapira, *Land and Power*, 295.

185. Chazan, "Dispute in Mapai," 104, 107.

186. Elad Peled, interview.

187. Pa'il and Pinhas, *Test of the Zionist Movement*, 427–28.

188. One Irgun commander noted that the Haganah had tried to arrest him three times, the British CID only once. Irgun commander A, interview by author, March 2014.

189. Anita Shapira, *Land and Power*, 249.

190. Indeed, one has to wonder whether Begin ever listened to the radio broadcasts of his own group in 1947 and 1948, which excoriated the Haganah and Jewish Agency, calling the former a "traitorous militia" and worse. At best, Begin's stance may help explain why there was more outbidding than infighting, but it did not affect the degree of competition among groups. Eli Tavin and Yonah Alexander, eds., *Psychological Warfare and Propaganda: Irgun Documentation* (Wilmington, DE: Scholarly Resources, 1982), 232–33. One Irgun commander said, "My friends in the Irgun will hate me for saying it, but Begin demanded from Ben-Gurion something that no Prime Minister in the world would agree to." Irgun commander A, interview.

5. The Algerian National Movement

1. The opening quotation is from André Mandouze, ed., "Proclamation of the National Liberation Front, November 1, 1954," in *La Révolution Algérienne par les Textes* (Paris: François Maspero, 1961).

2. I owe a particular debt to William Quandt, Robert Parks, and CEMA for allowing me to examine Quandt's notes from interviews with Ferhat Abbas, Saad Dahlab, Benyoucef Benkhedda, and many other key figures who passed away before I had the opportunity to speak with them.

3. André Nouschi, *La Naissance du Nationalisme Algérien* (Paris: Éditions de Minuit, 1962).

4. Alistair Horne, *A Savage War of Peace: Algeria 1954–1962* (New York: New York Review of Books, 2006), 30.

5. The activist Young Algerians of the World War I era were not nationalists, a label they themselves considered "injurious and unjust." William B. Quandt, *Revolution and Political Leadership: Algeria, 1954–1968* (Cambridge, MA: MIT Press, 1969), 31.

6. Ferhat Abbas, interview by William Quandt, February 17, 1967, William Quandt Field Notes, CEMA.

7. Despite government reforms supposedly designed to improve this situation, fewer than 2,500 Muslim Algerians had become French citizens by 1936. Horne, *Savage War of Peace*, 35.

8. Shoko Watanabe, "To Be Religious and to Be Political in Colonial Algeria: The Ulama and the Nationalists, Two Approaches," in *Secularization, Religion and the State*, Vol. 17 (Tokyo: University of Tokyo, 2010), 120; Malika Rahal, "A Local Approach to the UDMA: Local-Level Politics during the Decade of Political Parties, 1946–56," *Journal of North African Studies* 18, no. 5 (December 2013), 709.

9. Adria Lawrence notes that the PPA started small, probably between 3,000 and 11,000 members. *Imperial Rule and the Politics of Nationalism: Anti-Colonial Protest in the French Empire* (Cambridge, UK: Cambridge University Press, 2013), 81–82.

10. Abbas portrays the Muslim Congress of 1936 as a time when "[Algerian] elected officials, the ulema, socialists, communists, old veterans, fellahs," all united in an attempt to plead the Algerian cause to Paris. "Algeria, in its quasi-unanimity, wanted to break with the colonial status quo" but failed to do so. Ferhat Abbas, *La Nuit Coloniale* (Paris: Julliard, 1962), 128–29.

11. Mahfoud Kaddache, *Histoire du Nationalisme Algérien: Question Nationale et Politique Algérienne, 1919–1951* (Algiers: Société Nationale d'édition et de diffusion, 1980), 671.

12. This provides further evidence of the greater importance of hegemony compared to unity and total movement strength, because the latter two yielded failure at their peak despite having even greater grassroots support. Quandt, *Revolution and Political Leadership*, 50.

13. Ibid.

14. Gilbert Meynier, *Histoire Intérieure du F.L.N. 1954–1962* (Paris: Fayard, 2002), 64–65.

15. Shoko Watanabe, "Organizational Changes in the Algerian National Movement as Seen through the Muslim Boy Scouts in the 1930s and 1940s: The Struggle for Influence between the Association of Ulama and the PPA-MTLD," *Journal of Sophia Asian Studies* 30 (2012), 66.

16. By this time, the *colons* included significant proportions of Italians and Greeks, among others, in addition to the French.

17. To those who suggest that French actions were the driving force behind the Algerians' behavior, Adria Lawrence explains, "Surprisingly, violence did not erupt where French rule was most long-standing, stubborn, or cruel." "Driven to Arms? The Escalation to Violence in Nationalist Conflicts," in *Rethinking Violence: States and Non-State Actors in Conflict*, ed. Adria Lawrence and Erica Chenoweth (Cambridge, MA: MIT Press, 2010), 147.

18. Horne, *Savage War of Peace*, 73. Abbas's claim is strongly supported by other observers: Ferhat Abbas, interview; William Quandt, interview by author, February 20, 2015; Alf Andrew Heggoy, *Insurgency and Counterinsurgency in Algeria* (Bloomington: Indiana University Press, 1972), 25–27; Hamou Amirouche, *Memoirs of a Mujahed: Algeria's Struggle for Freedom, 1945–1962* (San Diego: Amirouche Publishing, 2014), 82.

19. Watanabe, "Organizational Changes," 48.

20. Jean-Louis Planche, *Sétif 1945: Histoire d'un Massacre Annoncé* (Algiers: Chibab Éditions, 2006), 182. This was the case for Hamou Amirouche's father, who was arrested and tortured despite not having taken part in the uprising. Amirouche, *Memoirs of a Mujahed*, 62.

21. Abbas did not denounce the Manifesto, but he often shied away from stressing the goal of independence until the early 1950s.

22. The PPA continued as a clandestine organization, but the MTLD was its public face and I use this label going forward.

23. See Heggoy, *Insurgency and Counterinsurgency in Algeria*, 31; Horne, *Savage War of Peace*, 70.

24. Horne, *Savage War of Peace*, 75.

25. Michael Clark, *Algeria in Turmoil: A History of the Rebellion* (New York: Praeger, 1959), 52.

26. Abderrazack Chentouf, interview by William Quandt, November 29, 1966, William Quandt Field Notes, CEMA.

27. Clark, *Algeria in Turmoil*, 75; Abderrahmane Chibane, interview by William Quandt, March 10, 1967, William Quandt Field Notes, CEMA.

28. "Declaration de Hadj Messali," *Algérie Libre*, no. 126, September 24, 1954.

29. The UDMA and MTLD ran candidates separately and captured eight and nine seats, respectively, with the pro-French Muslims capturing the far larger balance. The small percentage of nationalist victories did not reflect popular opinion, however, as is confirmed by the 58% of the Algerian vote garnered by the two groups in the 1947 municipal elections. The French went further in the 1951 elections, giving the nationalist parties only seven or eight seats *combined* in the Algerian Assembly and none in Paris due to massive vote-rigging. Quandt, *Revolution and Political Leadership*, 56–58; Horne, *Savage War of Peace*, 71–72; Hamou Amirouche, interview by author, February 25, 2015.

30. Benjamin Stora and Zakya Daoud, *Ferhat Abbas, une Utopie Algérienne* (Paris: Denoël, 1995), 180, 190.

31. Jacques Valette, *La Guerre d'Algérie des Messalistes, 1954–1962* (Paris: L'Harmattan, 2001), 24.

32. Quandt, *Revolution and Political Leadership*, 64.

33. Ibid., 90–91.

34. Zohra Drif, interview by author, March 2015.

35. Saad Dahlab, interview by William Quandt, April 13, 1967, William Quandt Field Notes, CEMA.

36. Amirouche, *Memoirs of a Mujahed*, 95–96; Meynier, *Histoire Intérieure du F.L.N.*, 114; Mohammed Harbi, *Le FLN, Mirage et Réalité des Origines à la Prise du Pouvoir (1945–1962)* (Paris: Editions Jeune Afrique, 1980), 114.

37. In Arslan Humbaraci, *Algeria: A Revolution That Failed* (New York: Praeger, 1966), 47.

38. In Slimane Chikh, *L'Algerie en Armes: Ou le Temps des Certitudes* (Algiers: Casbah Editions, 1998), 287.

39. Yves Courrière, *Les Fils de la Toussaint* (Paris: Fayard, 1968), 71.

40. Valette, *Guerre d'Algérie des Messalistes*, 29; Hamou Amirouche, interview.

41. Horne, *Savage War of Peace*, 84.

42. Omar Ouamrane, interview by William Quandt, March 11, 1967, William Quandt Field Notes, CEMA.

43. Heggoy, *Insurgency and Counterinsurgency in Algeria*, 63–65. Furthermore, the Egyptians offered no aid at the outset, telling the FLN to "Start the revolution first, . . . then aid will follow." Horne, *Savage War of Peace*, 85.

44. Amirouche, *Memoirs of a Mujahed*, xvi; Matthew James Connelly, *A Diplomatic Revolution: Algeria's Fight for Independence and the Origins of the Post-Cold War Era* (New York: Oxford University Press, 2003), 69.

45. Quandt, *Revolution and Political Leadership*, 7, 93.

46. Ali Kafi, *Ali Kafi: Du Militant Politique au Dirigeant Militaire* (Algiers: Casbah Editions, 2004), 38; Harbi, *FLN*, 135.

47. Quandt, *Revolution and Political Leadership*, 64.

48. Kamel Chachoua, *L'Islam Kabyle: Religion, État et Société en Algérie* (Paris: Maisonneuve et Larose, 2002), 256; Kafi, *Ali Kafi*, 39.

49. Kafi, *Ali Kafi*, 40; Abdelkader Guerroudj, interview by William Quandt, April 18, 1967, William Quandt Field Notes, CEMA.

50. Stora and Daoud, *Ferhat Abbas, une Utopie Algérienne*, 204.

51. Hugues Canuel, "French Counterinsurgency in Algeria: Forgotten Lessons from a Misunderstood Conflict," *Small Wars Journal* [online] (2010), 2, http://smallwarsjournal.com/jrnl/art/french-counterinsurgency-in-algeria.

52. Anthony Clayton, *The Wars of French Decolonization* (London: Longman, 1994), 115; Connelly, *Diplomatic Revolution*, 80.

53. Benyoucef Benkhedda, interview by William Quandt, February 7, 1967, William Quandt Field Notes, CEMA.

54. Even as the war went on and French intelligence improved, David Galula wrote that "the majority of cadres lived in an intelligence vacuum" and rarely received precise orders other than to "pacify" the rebels. *Pacification in Algeria: 1956–1958* (Santa Monica, CA: RAND Corporation, 2006), 57–64.

55. Robert Merle, *Ben Bella*, trans. Camilla Sykes (London: Michael Joseph, 1967), 94; Chikh, *Algerie en Armes*, 287.

56. Heggoy, *Insurgency and Counterinsurgency in Algeria*, 88.

57. Jean-Charles Jauffret, "Bulletin Politique Mensuel, October 1954, 1H1202," in *La Guerre d'Algerie par les Documents*, Vol. 2 (Paris: Service Historique de l'Armee de Terre, 1998), 523.

58. Meynier, *Histoire Intérieure du F.L.N.*, 448–49; Jacques Simon, *Messali Hadj 1898–1974: La Passion de l'Algérie Libre* (Paris: Editions Tirésias, 1998), 189.

59. Mohammed Harbi, *Aux Origines du FLN: Le Populisme Révolutionnaire en Algérie* (Paris: C. Bourgois, 1975), 145, 149.

60. In Harbi, *FLN*, 145.

61. In Valette, *Guerre d'Algérie des Messalistes*, 47.

62. Meynier, *Histoire Intérieure du F.L.N.*, 181.

63. In Valette, *Guerre d'Algérie des Messalistes*, 35.

64. Courrière, *Fils de la Toussaint*, 418.

65. Meynier, *Histoire Intérieure du F.L.N.*, 451.

66. Jean-Charles Jauffret and Maurice Vaïse, eds., *Militaires et Guérilla dans la Guerre d'Algérie* (Bruxelles: Editions Complexe, 2001), 223.

67. Abane Ramdane, "Lettre à la Délégation Extérieure du FLN du Caire de Abbane, 9/20/1955," in *Le FLN: Documents et Histoire, 1954–1962*, ed. Gilbert Meynier and Mohammed Ahmed (Paris: Fayard, 2004), 207.

68. Jauffret and Vaïse, *Militaires et Guérilla*, 230.

69. Horne, *Savage War of Peace*, 92.

70. Heggoy, *Insurgency and Counterinsurgency in Algeria*, 116.

71. Connelly, *Diplomatic Revolution*, 78.

72. The name of the city was changed from "Philippeville" to "Skikda" after Algeria won its independence. See figure 5.1.

73. Horne, *Savage War of Peace*, 122.

74. Ibid., 123.

75. Martha Crenshaw, *Revolutionary Terrorism: The FLN in Algeria 1954–1962* (Stanford: Hoover Institution Press, 1978), 46–47.

76. Chikh, *Algerie en Armes*, 289.

77. Valette, *Guerre d'Algérie des Messalistes*, 35.

78. Harbi, *FLN*, 158.

79. Jauffret and Vaïse, *Militaires et Guérilla*, 227; Meynier, *Histoire Intérieure du F.L.N.*, 450.

80. In Meynier, *Histoire Intérieure du F.L.N.*, 177.

81. Horne, *Savage War of Peace*, 135–36.

82. Benjamin Stora, *Ils Venaient d'Algérie: L'Immigration Algérienne en France (1912–1992)* (Paris: Fayard, 1992), 207–8.

83. Benjamin Stora, ed., *Algérie: 1954–1962* (Paris: Les Arènes, 2012), 107; Guy Perville, "Combien de Morts pendant la Guerre d'Algérie?" *L'Histoire*, no. 53 (1983), 89–92.

84. Harbi, *FLN*, 101; Chikh, *Algerie en Armes*, 294–95.

85. Mohammed Ali Haroun, interview by William Quandt, February 15, 1967, William Quandt Field Notes, CEMA.

86. Zohra Drif, interview.

87. Jauffret and Vaïse, *Militaires et Guérilla*, 224.

88. Meynier, *Histoire Intérieure du F.L.N.*, 124, 185; Mohammed Yazid, interview by William Quandt, March 6, 1967, William Quandt Field Notes, CEMA.

89. Saad Dahlab, interview by William Quandt, April 25, 1967, William Quandt Field Notes, CEMA.

90. Ibid.

91. Jauffret and Vaïse, *Militaires et Guérilla*, 231.

92. Benyoucef Benkhedda, interview.

93. Meynier, *Histoire Intérieure du F.L.N.*, 186.

94. Hachemi Djiar, *Le Congrès de la Soummam: Grandeur et Servitude d'une Acte Fondateur* (Algiers: Editions ANEP, 2006), 29.

95. Ibid.

96. James McDougall, "S'écrire un Destin: L'Association des Ulama dans la Révolution Algérienne," *Centre National de la Recherche Scientifique*, no. 83 (2004).

97. Chikh, *Algerie en Armes*, 305–7; Horne, *Savage War of Peace*, 137–38; Emmanual Sivan, *Communisme et Nationalisme en Algérie: 1920–1962* (Paris: Fondation Nationale des Sciences Politiques, 1976), 243; Connelly, *Diplomatic Revolution*, 107; Mohammed Harbi, *Les Archives de la Revolution Algerienne* (Paris: Les Éditions Jeune Afrique, 1981), 111–12; Meynier, *Histoire Intérieure du F.L.N.*, 181.

98. Djiar, *Congrès de la Soummam*, 87–88.

99. Omar Ouamrane, interview.

100. Belkacem Fantazi, interview by William Quandt, March 13, 1967, William Quandt Field Notes, CEMA.

101. Jauffret and Vaïse, *Militaires et Guérilla*, 227.

102. Meynier, *Histoire Intérieure du F.L.N.*, 456.

103. Horne, *Savage War of Peace*, 142.

104. Ibid., 258; Valette, *Guerre d'Algérie des Messalistes*, 153.

105. Horne, *Savage War of Peace*, 221–22.

106. "Nameless ANPA Tract," Fall 1957, 3 SAS 53, Archives Nationales D'Outre Mer (CAOM).

107. Valette, *Guerre d'Algérie des Messalistes*, 166–69; Commandement Superieur Interarmees, 10th Region Militaire, "Instruction," September 9, 1957, 3 SAS 53, CAOM.

108. In Meynier, *Histoire Intérieure du F.L.N.*, 453.

109. Ibid.

110. Germaine Tillion, *France and Algeria: Complementary Enemies*, trans. R. Howard (New York: Alfred A. Knopf, 1961), 146–47.

111. Meynier, *Histoire Intérieure du F.L.N.*, 454.

112. Zohra Drif, interview.

113. In Stora, *Algérie*, 110.

114. "Rapport du 3 au 10 Mai," 1956, 1H1430, SHAT. Mohammed Harbi agrees that the French "were not unhappy to allow this noise to continue in order to widen the fracture between the two organizations." *FLN*, 150.

115. Hamou Amirouche, interview.

116. Meynier, *Histoire Intérieure du F.L.N.*, 451–54.

117. Crenshaw, *Revolutionary Terrorism*, 14.

118. Chikh, *Algerie en Armes*, 296.

119. Horne, *Savage War of Peace*, 237; Mohammed Ali Haroun, interview.

120. Even the lowest FLN estimate of 46,000 fighters in 1958 puts the group well above three times larger than the MNA scattered hundreds in Algeria and 4,000 in France. Philippe Tripier, *Autopsie de la Guerre d'Algérie* (Paris: France-Empire, 1972), Annexe 21, 194; Jauffret and Vaïse, *Militaires et Guérilla*, 80; Horne, *Savage War of Peace*, 321.

121. Connelly, *Diplomatic Revolution*, 75.

122. Ibid., 74–75.

123. Amirouche, *Memoirs of a Mujahed*, 183.

124. Connelly, *Diplomatic Revolution*, 110.

125. Ibid., 144.

126. Christophe Gillissen, "Ireland, France and the Question of Algeria at the United Nations, 1955–62," *Irish Studies in International Affairs* 19 (2008): 151–67.

127. Connelly, *Diplomatic Revolution*, 195.

128. "List of Recognitions of the Provisional Government of the Algerian Republic (GPRA)," 1959, Dossier 33/02, Archives Nationales d'Algérie, http://digitalarchive.wilsoncenter.org/document/121604.pdf?v=f7b64692c97cd6acfed6df19bd9e2b86, accessed September 24, 2016.

129. Rabah Aissaoui, *Immigration and National Identity: North African Political Movements in Colonial and Postcolonial France* (London: I. B. Tauris, 2009), 259.

130. Jauffret and Vaïse, *Militaires et Guérilla*, 338–39.

131. David C. Gordon, *The Passing of French Algeria* (London: Oxford University Press, 1966), 60.

132. Zohra Drif, *Mémoires d'une Combattante de l'ALN, Zone Autonome d'Alger* (Algiers: Chibab Éditions, 2014), 205.

133. In *Remembering History* [film], directed by Gillo Pontecorvo, 2011, bonus DVD with *The Battle of Algiers* [film].

134. Gordon, *Passing of French Algeria*, 59–60.

135. Heggoy, *Insurgency and Counterinsurgency in Algeria*, 232.

136. Benyoucef Benkhedda, interview; Saad Dahlab, interview by William Quandt. For Drif's part, she explained, "We never thought we could defeat the French on the battlefield. The point of violence was to make Algerian independence an issue in France and internationally, then win the diplomatic struggle." Zohra Drif, interview.

137. Connelly, *Diplomatic Revolution*, 81.

138. Horne, *Savage War of Peace*, 229.

139. Kaddache, *Histoire du Nationalisme Algérien*, 617; Paul Aussaresses, *The Battle of the Casbah: Terrorism and Counter-Terrorism in Algeria 1955–1957* (New York: Enigma, 2002), 25.

140. Horne, *Savage War of Peace*, 135, 466; Crenshaw, *Revolutionary Terrorism*, 37; Benyoucef Benkhedda, interview.

141. Connelly, *Diplomatic Revolution*, 209; Alain Peyrefitte, "Salon Doré, 20 Octobre 1959," in *C'était de Gaulle* (Paris: Fayard, 1994), 59.

142. Charles-Robert Ageron, "L'Opinion Française devant la Guerre d'Algérie," *Revue Française d'Histoire d'Outre-Mer* 63, no. 231 (1976): 260–71.

143. Corps d'Armée d'Oran, "Déclaration du SNP S. Ben A," July 18, 1958, IH 1705/D1, Service Historique de l'Armée de la Terre (SHAT). See also Martha Crenshaw, "The Effectiveness of Terrorism in the Algerian War," in *Terrorism in Context*, ed. Martha Crenshaw (University Park: Pennsylvania State University Press, 1995), 477.

144. Valette, *Guerre d'Algérie des Messalistes*, 278–82; Benjamin Stora, *Messali Hadj: 1898–1974* (Paris: Hachette, 2004), 278.

145. "Bulletin d'Information No.1 de l'E.M.I/3rd Bureau," April 6, 1960, 3 SAS 87/2, CAOM.

146. Valette, *Guerre d'Algérie des Messalistes*, 272–74.

147. Ibid., 274–75.

148. Ibid., 275.

149. Ibid., 266–67.

150. Ibid., 265, 277–78.

151. Ibid., 267–68.

152. "Weekly Bulletin on the Situation of Opinion in Algeria," March 26, 1961, 1H1111–1, SHAT.

153. Tanya Matthews, *War in Algeria: Background for Crisis* (New York: Fordham University Press, 1962), 123.

154. Valette, *Guerre d'Algérie des Messalistes*, 286–90.

155. Dorothy Pickles, "General de Gaulle and Algeria," *World Today* 17, no. 2 (1961), 49; Brian Crozier and Gerard Mansell, "France and Algeria," *International Affairs* 36, no. 3 (1960), 312.

156. "Bulletin d'Information No.1 de l'E.M.I/3rd Bureau."

157. Ibid.

158. Matthews, *War in Algeria*, 120.

159. Omar Ouamrane, interview.

160. Belkacem Fantazi, interview; Abdelkader Boutaleb, interview by William Quandt, February 17, 1967, William Quandt Field Notes, CEMA.

161. Clayton, *Wars of French Decolonization*, 165–66; Connelly, *Diplomatic Revolution*, 227–29.

162. Horne, *Savage War of Peace*, 508.

163. "Note d'Information," March 24, 1961, 1H 1718/D1, SHAT.

164. Ageron, "Opinion Française," 276.

165. Ian Lustick, *Unsettled States, Disputed Lands: Britain and Ireland, France and Algeria, Israel and the West Bank-Gaza* (Ithaca: Cornell University Press, 1993); Hendrik Spruyt, *Ending Empire: Contested Sovereignty and Territorial Partition* (Ithaca: Cornell University Press, 2005).

166. Lustick, *Unsettled States, Disputed Lands*, 123.

167. Ageron, "Opinion Française," 277–78.

168. Saad Dahlab, interview by William Quandt.

169. Courrière, *Fils de la Toussaint*, 15.

170. Horne, *Savage War of Peace*, 530.

171. Kathleen Gallagher Cunningham, "Divide and Conquer or Divide and Concede: How Do States Respond to Internally Divided Separatists?" *American Political Science Review* 105, no. 2 (2011): 275–97.

172. Stora, *Algérie*, 79; Lustick, *Unsettled States, Disputed Lands*, 111.

173. Quandt, *Revolution and Political Leadership*.

174. Ferhat Abbas, interview.

6. The Irish National Movement

1. The opening quotation is found in Bernard Shaw, "The Irish Crisis," *Manchester Guardian*, December 27, 1921.

2. Harry Donaghy, interview by author, June 20, 2014.

3. Ian Lustick, *Unsettled States, Disputed Lands: Britain and Ireland, France and Algeria, Israel and the West Bank-Gaza* (Ithaca: Cornell University Press, 1993); Nadav Shelef, *Evolving Nationalism: Homeland, Identity, and Religion in Israel, 1925–2005* (Ithaca: Cornell University Press, 2010).

4. The gap in table 6.1 from 1923 to 1968 represents a shift in the focus of the movement from all of Ireland to Northern Ireland. This period involved a series of fragmented failures amid a proto-nationalist movement in Northern Ireland in which a robust movement for independence from the United Kingdom and union with Ireland took time to develop.

5. The IPP achieved a brief period of movement dominance in 1885–1886, although it did not have a history as a cohesive organization and soon after formally split apart. Nonetheless, in 1886 the national movement did get closer to achieving significant strategic success (in the form of Home Rule, which was narrowly defeated in a parliamentary vote) than in any earlier period. On the debate over Home Rule, see Stacie Goddard, *Indivisible Territory and the Politics of Legitimacy* (Cambridge, UK: Cambridge University Press, 2010), 47–114.

6. Brian Feeney, *Sinn Féin: A Hundred Turbulent Years* (Dublin: O'Brien Press, 2002), 43.

7. Ibid., 49–52.

8. Fergus Campbell, *Land and Revolution: Nationalist Politics in the West of Ireland 1891–1921* (Oxford: Oxford University Press, 2005), 196.

9. Colin Reid, "The Irish Party and the Volunteers: Politics and the Home Rule Army, 1913–1916," in *From Parnell to Paisley*, ed. Caoimhe Nic Dháibhéid and Colin Reid (Dublin: Irish Academic Press, 2010).

10. Charles Townshend, *Easter 1916: The Irish Rebellion* (Chicago: Ivan Dee, 2006), 118–21, 136–43.

11. J. Bowyer Bell, *The Secret Army: A History of the IRA 1916–1979* (Cambridge, MA: MIT Press, 1980), 5.

12. Campbell, *Land and Revolution*, 215.

13. In David Fitzpatrick, *Politics and Irish Life, 1913–1921: Provincial Experience of War and Revolution* (Cork: Cork University Press, 1998), 97; Richard English, *Armed Struggle: The History of the IRA* (New York: Oxford University Press, 2003), 10–11.

14. "GOC-in-C's Orders," May 3, 1916, WO 69/1, TNA; Charles Townshend, *Political Violence in Ireland: Government and Resistance since 1848* (Oxford: Clarendon Press, 1983), 308.

15. Michael Tierney, *Eoin MacNeill: Scholar and Man of Action, 1867–1945* (Oxford: Oxford University Press, 1980), 223–24.

16. In Dorothy Macardle, *The Irish Republic* (Dublin: Irish Press, 1951), 917.

17. Lennox Robinson, ed., *Lady Gregory's Journals* (London: Putnam, 1946), 170.

18. Bell, *Secret Army*, 12–13.

19. Liam Deasy, *Towards Ireland Free: The West Cork Brigade in the War of Independence, 1917–1921* (Cork: Mercier, 1977), 5.

20. Tim Pat Coogan, *De Valera: Long Fellow, Long Shadow* (London: Hutchinson, 1993), 97.

21. Feeney, *Sinn Féin*, 95.

22. Ibid., 67.

23. Brian Walker, ed., *Parliamentary Election Results in Ireland, 1801–1922* (Dublin: Royal Irish Academy, 1978), 184.

24. In De Valera's election in Clare, "Throughout the campaign the Volunteers played the dominant role. Uniformed Volunteers marched, held band and torchlight parades, organized church-gate meetings after Mass and generally swaggered about the constituency." Feeney, *Sinn Féin*, 63–66.

25. In another precedent for The Troubles, Thomas Ashe, the president of the IRB after the Rising, died in prison while on hunger strike. This drove further support to Sinn Féin and the IRA. Feeney, *Sinn Féin*, 93.

26. Tim Pat Coogan, *Michael Collins: The Man Who Made Ireland* (New York: Palgrave, 1990), 67.

27. The vote total for Sinn Féin would have been higher if the IPP had run more candidates against them instead of having them run unopposed, as well as if they had run candidates in the North against the IPP in four districts. Estimates of total vote support for Sinn Féin are 53% on the low end to 65% or more on the high end for all of Ireland. Removing the unionists, this translates to around 75% of the entire national movement, which clearly constitutes hegemony. Those who suggest that support for the IPP was higher overlook the fact that in the thirty-seven head-to-head contests, Sinn Féin beat the IPP candidates in thirty-five of them. Feeney, *Sinn Féin*, 109.

28. In ibid., 91.

29. John O'Beirne Ranelagh, *A Short History of Ireland* (Cambridge, UK: Cambridge University Press, 2012), 222.

30. Michael L. R. Smith, *Fighting for Ireland?: The Military Strategy of the Irish Republican Movement* (New York: Routledge, 1997), 38.

31. Michael Laffan, *The Resurrection of Ireland: The Sinn Féin Party, 1916–1923* (Cambridge, UK: Cambridge University Press, 1999), 327–29; Nicholas Whyte, "Dáil Elections since 1918," Economic and Social Research Council, Northern Ireland, 2011, www.ark.ac.uk/elections/gdala.htm, accessed September 25, 2016.

32. Campbell, *Land and Revolution*, 254–55.

33. Smith, *Fighting for Ireland?*, 35; J A Byrne, "Irish Volunteers: Scheme of Organization," March 28, 1918, WO 35/69, TNA.

34. "Dáil Éireann Debate—Debate on Treaty," December 19, 1921, http://oireachtasdebates. oireachtas.ie/debates%20authoring/debateswebpack.nsf/takes/dail1921121900003, accessed September 25, 2016. Although the final claim was a stretch, the previous ones were certainly not.

35. In Bernard Shaw, "The Irish Crisis." To be fair, Michael Collins conceived of his act as a selfless one that was good for Ireland but not for himself because it risked his life and reputation, regardless of any personal political gains.

36. The distinction between unionists and loyalists is similar to the one between republicans and nationalists, albeit on the opposite side of the issue. The two groups shared a common objective of keeping Northern Ireland separate from the Irish Republic and in a union with England, had a common base of supporters that often moved between them, and shared common enemies (the republicans, nationalists, and the Irish government). Both groups were almost entirely Protestant, just as the republicans and nationalists were largely Catholic. The distinction between the two groups is imperfect, but it is usually split along the lines of class and the use of force. *Unionist* often referred to upper-class Protestants, including most of those who long served in the government to maintain the union with England until recent times. *Loyalist* was often used for working-class Protestants who were more amenable to the use of force in the face of republican and nationalist threats.

37. Richard Rose, *Governing without Consensus: An Irish Perspective* (Boston: Beacon Press, 1971), 228; Brendan Lynn, *Holding the Ground: The Nationalist Party in Northern Ireland, 1945–1972* (Aldershot, UK: Ashgate, 1997).

38. Brian Hanley and Scott Millar, *The Lost Revolution: The Story of the Official IRA and the Workers' Party* (London: Penguin Books, 2010), 11, 13, 16, 54.

39. Denis Haughey, interview by author, June 12, 2014.

40. Stormont in East Belfast was the seat of the parliament of Northern Ireland at this time.

41. Bell, *Secret Army*, 364.

42. Hanley and Millar, *Lost Revolution*, 112.

43. In Gerald Murray and Jonathan Tonge, *Sinn Féin and the SDLP: From Alienation to Participation* (London: Hurst and Company, 2005), 19.

44. English, *Armed Struggle*, 84. Hanley and Millar, *Lost Revolution*, 114. OIRA members reject the claim that they failed to protect communities: "The proof that 'I Ran Away' was false is that we were strongest in the area of the Lower Falls, supposedly the area that was not defended. Why would the people support us there so strongly unless we defended them well?" Official IRA member A, interview by author, June 20, 2014; (Official) Irish Republican Army, "Army Council Statement," Easter 1970, P16293, Linen Hall.

45. Both groups refer to themselves as the *IRA* and dislike the added labels, which nonetheless I use in this book for the sake of differentiation. The Provisional Sinn Féin was also referred to as Provisionals or Provos, whereas the "Official Sinn Féin first adopted the title Republican Clubs, later Sinn Féin–the Workers' Party [1977] and then the Workers' Party [1982]." Sean Farren, *The SDLP: The Struggle for Agreement in Northern Ireland, 1970–2000* (Dublin: Four Courts Press, 2010), 367; Sinn Féin (Provisional), *Sinn Féin: Statement on the Split* (Sinn Féin (Provisional), 1970).

46. Ed Moloney, *Voices from the Grave: Two Men's War in Ireland* (London: Faber and Faber, 2010), 48; Hanley and Millar, *Lost Revolution*, 153–54; Joe Doherty, interview by author, June 5, 2014.

47. In Moloney, *Voices from the Grave*, 50.

48. Joe Doherty, interview; Hanley and Millar, *Lost Revolution*, 141. The draw of violence was not limited to the PIRA and may have been a regional phenomenon: "People always saw the Provos were more militant. In my area, the OIRA were more militant, and that's why I joined them." Official IRA member A, interview.

49. Bell, *Secret Army*, 374.

50. The OIRA was still dominant in Derry (three hundred members at its peak), Newry, and South Down, although this too was to change. Jack Holland and Henry McDonald, *INLA: Deadly Divisions* (Dublin: Torc, 1994), 9, 16.

51. In Moloney, *Voices from the Grave*, 67.

52. "Talking about a Lost Revolution: An Interview with Brian Hanley and Scott Millar," Indymedia Ireland, September 28, 2009.

53. To the extent we consider Fianna Fáil as part of the national movement at this time, its actions make perfect sense according to MST. Its support of the PIRA would both shore up its own credentials for defending Catholics and also split, and so weaken, its major rival for republican leadership, which also was thought to have communist ties. In fact, many in the OIRA believed that this was precisely Fianna Fáil's motivation. Bell, *Secret Army*, 369–71; Official IRA member B, interview by author, June 20, 2014.

54. Bell, *Secret Army*, 439.

55. In English, *Armed Struggle*, 122.

56. Joe Doherty, interview.

57. Hanley and Millar, *Lost Revolution*, 161, 230.

58. Official IRA member A, interview.

59. This was also true of one of the most infamous days of The Troubles—Bloody Sunday, when the British military killed fourteen Catholic civilians during a civil rights march on January 30, 1972.

60. "Meeting of Mr. Gerry Fitt MP and Minister of State," December 22, 1971, CJ 4/42, TNA. According to SDLP representatives who met with the secretary of state and his associates in 1973, the PIRA had a vested interest in keeping detention going. According to them, "the minority

community would see that the Provisionals were nothing more than wreckers if detention ended and they continued with their campaign"—to that end, the SDLP was advocating the release of detainees, "possibly with rehabilitation provisos," before the SDLP would consent to sit on an Executive. "Notes of a Meeting between the Secretary of State and Representatives from the SDLP," December 19, 1973, CJ 4/518, TNA.

61. Denis Haughey, a founding member of the SDLP, argued that, "The Nationalist Party wasn't a party at all. It did not have an organization." Denis Haughey, interview.

62. In Farren, *SDLP*, 25.

63. Murray and Tonge, *Sinn Féin and the SDLP*, 28.

64. Ibid., 11.

65. In Farren, *SDLP*, 47.

66. Ibid., 54.

67. Ibid., 38.

68. "Meeting of Mr. Gerry Fitt MP and Minister of State."

69. Murray and Tonge, *Sinn Féin and the SDLP*, 33.

70. Denis Haughey, interview. It was not just the PIRA, either. OIRA members beat up John Hume's brother. Hanley and Millar, *Lost Revolution*, 296.

71. "We saw ourselves as the strongest grouping in the nationalist movement from our founding, without peer." Denis Haughey, interview.

72. Murray and Tonge, *Sinn Féin and the SDLP*, 10.

73. Farren, *SDLP*, 47.

74. For additional efforts to compare the strength of the SDLP and Sinn Féin, see Devashree Gupta, "Selective Engagement and Its Consequences for Social Movement Organizations: Lessons from British Policy in Northern Ireland," *Comparative Politics* 39, no. 3 (2007): 331–51.

75. Denis Haughey, interview.

76. In English, *Armed Struggle*, 174.

77. As the British themselves noted internally at the time, the PIRA attacks on them had organizational benefits: "The IRA have a three-pronged strategy of upping the cost for the British; they kill British soldiers as part of their retaliation policy, they disrupt the economy and they gain popular support for this process of disruption and murder by defending the local population of working class housing estates when the British search for arms." "IRA Political Activities of Sinn Féin of Republic of Ireland," March 15, 1971, FCO 33/1593, TNA.

78. In Bell, *Secret Army*, 379.

79. In Eamon Collins and Mick McGovern, *Killing Rage* (London: Granta Books, 1997), 5.

80. The OIRA also gained many members in the early years of The Troubles, and a 1971 OSF report claimed that "Current registered membership shows an increase of almost 30% over last year." Sinn Féin (Official), *Ard Fheis Report 1971*, P1460 (Dublin: Sinn Féin (Official), 1971), 13.

81. Sinn Féin (Official), *Ways and Means: A Handbook for Members of the Republican Movement* (Dublin: Sinn Féin (Official), 1970), 14.

82. English, *Armed Struggle*, 93. For their part, the PIRA recognized that sectarianism existed but claimed that it was a creation of the British. Thus, the way to victory was to destroy the sectarian Northern Irish state.

83. Harry Donaghy, interview.

84. Hanley and Millar, *Lost Revolution*, 215–16.

85. Ibid., 171.

86. Danny Morrison, interview by author, June 17, 2014.

87. In Moloney, *Voices from the Grave*, 61.

88. Joe Doherty, interview.

89. Smith, *Fighting for Ireland?*, 88.

90. Official IRA member C, interview by author, June 20, 2014.

91. Chain-ganging dynamics were present as well. The OIRA claimed that the PIRA started the shooting that led to the Falls curfew. This forced the OIRA to get involved against its wishes and bear the brunt of the fighting, which led to it losing much of its weaponry that was stored in the area. As an OIRA member on the scene later noted, "The way we looked at it, we were not going to put up our hands and let them take the weaponry. We didn't want the confrontation,

but we couldn't surrender." In Patrick Bishop and Eamonn Mallie, *The Provisional IRA* (London: Corgi, 1988), 159.

92. Farren, *SDLP*, 56; Bell, *Secret Army*, 388.

93. Hanley and Millar, *Lost Revolution*, 176.

94. Mia Bloom and John Horgan, "Missing Their Mark: The IRA's Proxy Bomb Campaign," *Social Research* 75, no. 2 (Summer 2008): 589.

95. Murray and Tonge, *Sinn Féin and the SDLP*, 31.

96. In Smith, *Fighting for Ireland?* 121.

97. In ibid., 117.

98. In English, *Armed Struggle*, 245.

99. Joe Doherty, interview; Jim Gibney, interview by author, June 12, 2014; Harry Donaghy, interview; Denis Haughey, interview.

100. "Attitude of SDLP towards Meetings between S of S for NI and Members of Provisional IRA," June 20, 1972, FCO 87/74, TNA.

101. Adams claims to have never been a member of the [P]IRA. Regardless, it is clear he participated in the talks.

102. Brendan O'Brien, *The Long War: The IRA and Sinn Féin* (Syracuse, NY: Syracuse University Press, 1999), 169.

103. Smith, *Fighting for Ireland?*, 108.

104. To those who say that coercion would have been impossible under any circumstances, it is worth noting that "a Daily Mail poll in September 1971 . . . indicated that over 60 per cent of the British public favored the withdrawal of the British Army." Ibid., 101.

105. The SDLP, PIRA, and OIRA disagreed over whether direct British rule was a step forward or backward, and the groups could not work together the day after Stormont fell. The OIRA and SDLP wanted to institute a cease-fire, but the PIRA decided to press on with attacks because the British had not withdrawn. The OIRA was soon drawn back in, and the fragmented morass began anew.

106. The fading Nationalist Party joined in criticizing the SDLP, accusing it of "a crude bid for political power." Farren, *SDLP*, 76–77.

107. In private meetings with the British, the SDLP pushed to hold the Assembly elections before local elections, claiming that they were motivated by "the public good" but also betraying that their real concern was that "The election of even a handful of Sinn Féin candidates on to a local authority could stalemate progress because they could hold the balance of power." Of course, the SDLP would claim that the two were one and the same because it saw the empowerment of Sinn Féin as contrary to the public good. "Notes of a Meeting between Mr. David Howell and a Delegation from the Social Democratic and Labour Party," April 6, 1973, CJ 4/518, TNA.

108. *Assembly Elections Manifesto: A New North, a New Ireland* (Belfast: SDLP, 1973), 1.

109. "Notes of a Meeting between Mr. David Howell and a Delegation."

110. P. J. McLoughlin, "'Dublin Is Just a Sunningdale Away?' The SDLP, the Irish Government and the Sunningdale Agreement," Institute for British-Irish Studies Working Paper, no. 82, University College, Dublin, 2007.

111. Teachta Dála (TD) is the Dáil equivalent of the British MP; in *Irish Times*, December 10, 1974.

112. Smith, *Fighting for Ireland?*, 124.

113. Hanley and Millar, *Lost Revolution*, 293.

114. The major change involved the reorganization of the PIRA into cells to prevent the decimation of the group from informants.

115. "IRA Demands," *United Irishman* 26, no. 6 (June 1972), 1.

116. Hanley and Millar, *Lost Revolution*, 182.

117. Ibid., 181–82, 191, 194–95.

118. *Stick* is a somewhat derogatory term that refers to the OIRA and OIRA members. The term originates with the Easter Rising commemorations, for which republicans often wear pinned Easter lilies. Starting in 1967, Sinn Féin and IRA members started wearing lilies with self-adhesive, sticky backing. After the split, the PIRA returned to the more traditional pinned

lilies and referred to OIRA members as Sticks; ibid., 6. "SDLP was the 'stoops' for 'Stoop Down Low Party' and Sticks were 'Rusty Guns' so it was about the use of violence and competition in terms of perceptions." Gerard Foster, interview by author, June 12, 2014.

119. Holland and McDonald, *INLA*, 20.

120. In ibid., 22.

121. "The Way Forward," *Starry Plough*, April 1975.

122. Holland and McDonald, *INLA*, 31; English, *Armed Struggle*, 177; Hanley and Millar, *Lost Revolution*, 283. The departure of Costello saw the number of OIRA/OSF cumainn drop from twenty-five to nineteen; ibid., 275.

123. Holland and McDonald, *INLA*, 38–39; Hanley and Millar, *Lost Revolution*, 284.

124. Costello's membership claim was supported by the *Irish Press*, which suggested four hundred defections from Official Sinn Féin; Holland and McDonald, *INLA*, 35–37, 43, 108–9.

125. Hanley and Millar, *Lost Revolution*, 287, 289.

126. Ibid., 294.

127. Costello himself was killed by the OIRA in 1977, leaving his group without clear leadership. Smith, *Fighting for Ireland?* 88.

128. Official IRA member A, interview.

129. Holland and McDonald, *INLA*, 4.

130. Hanley and Millar, *Lost Revolution*, 295; Holland and McDonald, *INLA*, 343–44.

131. Danny Morrison, interview.

132. Official IRA member B, interview.

133. Hanley and Millar, *Lost Revolution*, 315–21.

134. Ibid., 314.

135. Danny Morrison, interview.

136. Official IRA member B, interview.

137. Séanna Walsh, interview by author, June 5, 2014.

138. Danny Morrison, interview.

139. Official IRA member B, interview.

140. Holland and McDonald, *INLA*, 78.

141. Hanley and Millar, *Lost Revolution*, 286.

142. Gerard Foster, interview.

143. Holland and McDonald, *INLA*, 79.

144. Gerard Foster, interview.

145. English, *Armed Struggle*, 219.

146. Gary McGladdery, *The Provisional IRA in England: The Bombing Campaign 1973–1997* (Dublin: Irish Academic Press, 2006), 114.

147. Bell, *Secret Army*, 531.

148. Fra Halligan, interview by author, June 13, 2014.

149. From this point forward, I refer to Provisional Sinn Féin simply as Sinn Féin. OSF changed its name to Sinn Féin, the Workers' Party in 1977 and to the Workers' Party in 1982, due to the increasing dominance by Provisional Sinn Féin of the brand and the desire of OSF to stress its socioeconomic objectives.

150. The INLA was worried that the PIRA would speak for all the protestors and so reap all the political advantage. Holland and McDonald, *INLA*, 177–79; Bell, *Secret Army*, 497.

151. Moloney, *Voices from the Grave*, 236.

152. Harry Donaghy, interview; Hanley and Millar, *Lost Revolution*, 429.

153. Official IRA member A, interview.

154. Jim Gibney, interview.

155. Sixty-two people died in the riots accompanying Sands's hunger strike and death. Noraid went on to raise hundreds of thousands of dollars on a U.S. tour for the relatives of the hunger strikers, including one from the INLA. Nonetheless, all of the money went to the PIRA. Holland and McDonald, *INLA*, 184; Bell, *Secret Army*, 503.

156. Danny Morrison, interview.

157. Fra Halligan, interview.

158. Jim Gibney, interview. Sean "Spike" Murray agrees. Sean "Spike" Murray, interview by author, June 14, 2014.

159. Danny Morrison, interview.

160. In Smith, *Fighting for Ireland?* 155.

161. Sean Farren, interview by author, June 16, 2014.

162. Tom Hartley, interview by author, June 14, 2014.

163. Sean Farren, interview. For their part, Sinn Féin members agreed: "We forced the SDLP to abstain in 1982; I have no doubt about it." Danny Morrison, interview; Jim Gibney, interview.

164. Farren, *SDLP*, 181.

165. Denis Haughey, interview.

166. Ibid.

167. Jim Gibney, interview.

168. Sean Farren, interview; Tom Hartley, interview.

169. Sean Farren, interview; Sinn Féin, *Hillsborough: A Failure, the Balance Sheet 1985–1988* (Dublin: Sinn Féin Publicity Dept, 1988), 30.

170. From this point forward, I refer to the PIRA as simply IRA due to the OIRA name changes.

171. Fra Halligan, interview.

172. Hanley and Millar, *Lost Revolution*, 390–91, 425.

173. Kacper Rekawek, "'Their History Is a Bit like Our History': Comparative Assessment of the Official and the Provisional IRAs," *Terrorism and Political Violence* 25, no. 5 (2013), 696.

174. Des Dalton, interview by author, August 15, 2014.

175. Tom Hartley, interview.

176. The SDLP and Sinn Féin disagree over the similarity between Sunningdale and Good Friday. Sean "Spike" Murray of Sinn Féin argued that "Issues of policing weren't addressed in Sunningdale, but were in the Good Friday Agreement." Sean "Spike" Murray, interview. Sean Farren of the SDLP responded that "Policing was different, but it was promised in Sunningdale, and the IRA and Sinn Féin helped to bring that agreement down. If that's what they were fighting about, we could have conceded that easily. That is reading history backwards." Sean Farren, interview.

177. English, *Armed Struggle*, 317.

178. As Gerard Foster noted, "Since both the SDLP and Sinn Féin supported the Good Friday Agreement, there was not much internal discussion in the movement." Gerard Foster, interview.

179. English, *Armed Struggle*, 316; Brendan O'Brien, *The Long War*, 389. The president of RSF explained, "In the early years, the Provos did try to intimidate us, but today they don't see us as an organizational or political threat. We are a reminder of what they were, what they left. We make arguments they would have made 30 years ago." Des Dalton, interview.

180. Kacper Rekawek, *Irish Republican Terrorism and Politics: A Comparative Study of the Official and the Provisional IRA* (New York: Routledge, 2011), 69.

181. Jim Gibney, interview.

182. This is a possible addition for future analysis within MST: challengers are more likely to use violence except in cases in which ceasing that violence will allow them to become the leader or hegemon.

183. Denis Haughey, interview.

184. Séanna Walsh, interview. Haughey admits that "few of us expected the electorate to tilt towards support of the Provos given their record." Denis Haughey, letter to author, July 30, 2014.

185. Gerard Murray, *John Hume and the SDLP: Impact and Survival in Northern Ireland* (Dublin: Irish Academic Press, 1998).

186. Mary McAleese and Martin McAleese, interview by author, October 28, 2013.

187. It should also be noted that many of these leaders put themselves at significant personal risk by supporting the Good Friday Agreement, whatever the political impact on their parties.

188. Sinn Féin (Official), *The Lessons of History* (Dublin: Sinn Féin (Official), 1970).

189. In Sean Swan, *Official Irish Republicanism, 1962–1972* (Lulu, 2008), 400.

190. In ibid., 317. John Horgan, *Divided We Stand: The Strategy and Psychology of Ireland's Dissident Terrorists* (Oxford: Oxford University Press, 2013).

191. In English, *Armed Struggle*, 319.
192. In a statement that echoed those of Provisional Sinn Féin to the Officials in 1970, or the anti-Treaty forces to the pro-Treaty forces, Republican Sinn Féin President Des Dalton said, "We argue that we never left Sinn Féin, they left us. We kept the constitution and the core principles, they left them for the spoils of office." Des Dalton, interview. Ed Moloney, "Now Sinn Féin MUST Break with Their Old Friends," *Daily Mail*, March 16, 2009.
193. The president of Republican Sinn Féin argued, "Fianna Fáil and the Provos have waved the green flag when they are out of power, but everything changes once they are in power." Des Dalton, interview. It is worth noting that nationalist groups were not above turning to force when their hold on power in the movement was threatened, as when John Redmond and the IPP helped build up the Irish Volunteers as a military force.
194. For more information on the many dissident factions, see Horgan, *Divided We Stand*.
195. This raises an additional issue for future research, namely that groups may be challengers to other challengers but not to leaders, and so including such strong subordinate groups in our analysis may provide further insight.
196. Victoria McGroary, "Marketing Rebellion: Explaining Choices of Violence and Nonviolence in Nationalist Movements," PhD diss., Brandeis University, 2016.

7. The Politics of National Movements and the Future of Rebel Power

1. Mancur Olson, *The Logic of Collective Action: Public Goods and the Theory of Groups* (Cambridge, MA: Harvard University Press, 1971); Herbert Haines, *Black Radicals and the Civil Rights Mainstream, 1954–1970* (Knoxville: University of Tennessee Press, 1988); Daryl Press, *Calculating Credibility: How Leaders Assess Military Threats* (Ithaca: Cornell University Press, 2005); Robert J. Art and Patrick M. Cronin, eds., *The United States and Coercive Diplomacy* (Washington, DC: United States Institute of Peace, 2003).
2. The percentages probably understate the difference in escalating violence because the percentage of challengers that escalate violence is dragged down by the fact that more than a quarter of them are Zionist political parties from a single decade.
3. The anomaly here is Fatah 1969–1986, which had to deal with the unique situation of foreign governments such as Jordan potentially negotiating for—and aiming to integrate—the Palestinian people.
4. Shimon Peres and David Landau, *Ben Gurion: A Political Life* (New York: Schocken Books, 2011), 92.
5. Robert Jervis, "Do Leaders Matter and How Would We Know?" *Security Studies* 22, no. 2 (April 2013): 153–79.
6. John McCarthy and Mayer Zald, "Resource Mobilization and Social Movements: A Partial Theory," *American Journal of Sociology* 82, no. 6 (1977): 1212–41; Doug McAdam, Sidney Tarrow, and Charles Tilly, eds., *Dynamics of Contention* (Cambridge, UK: Cambridge University Press, 2001); Sarah Soule, "Bringing Organizational Studies Back into Social Movement Scholarship," in *The Future of Social Movement Research*, ed. Jacquelien van Stekelenburg, Conny Roggeband, and Bert Klandermans, 107–24 (Minneapolis: University of Minnesota Press, 2013).
7. Erica Chenoweth and Orion Lewis, "Unpacking Nonviolent Campaigns: Introducing the NAVCO 2.0 Dataset," *Journal of Peace Research* 50, no. 3 (2013): 415–23.
8. Nils Petter Gleditsch, Peter Wallensteen, Mikael Eriksson, Margareta Sollenberg, and Håvard Strand, "Armed Conflict 1946–2001: A New Dataset," *Journal of Peace Research* 39, no. 5 (2002): 615–37.
9. Victor Asal, Amy Pate, and Jonathan Wilkenfeld, *Minorities at Risk Organizational Behavior Data and Codebook*, Version 9/2008, 2008, http://www.mar.umd.edu/mar_data.asp, accessed September 26, 2016.
10. It is also possible, as Cunningham suggests, that fragmented movements may generate a number of smaller concessions offered from states seeking to buy off parts of the opposition, while hegemonic movements are more likely to yield concessions that are larger but perhaps

less frequent. Still, this study finds little support for such an argument given that the fragmented campaigns analyzed within it had poor records of generating even limited success. Kathleen Gallagher Cunningham, "Divide and Conquer or Divide and Concede: How Do States Respond to Internally Divided Separatists?" *American Political Science Review* 105, no. 2 (2011): 275–97.

11. The only thing harder than counting the number of members in a few clandestine groups is counting the total number of members in all groups. My calculations for movement size focus disproportionately on armed groups, whose membership is often easier to find than political parties (I do not automatically count voters as party members). Therefore, although I am generally confident in the trends and conclusions here, the numbers for total movement size are less precise than I would like.

12. Robert A. Pape, "The Strategic Logic of Suicide Terrorism," *American Political Science Review* 97, no. 3 (2003): 343–61; Max Abrahms, "Why Terrorism Does Not Work," *International Security* 31, no. 2 (2006): 42–78.

13. Erica Chenoweth and Maria Stephan, *Why Civil Resistance Works: The Strategic Logic of Nonviolent Conflict* (New York: Columbia University Press, 2011), 7–10.

14. William Roger Louis, "The Dissolution of the British Empire," in *The Oxford History of the British Empire, Vol 4: The Twentieth Century*, ed. Judith M. Brown and William Roger Louis (Oxford: Oxford University Press, 1999), 330.

15. Adria Lawrence, *Imperial Rule and the Politics of Nationalism: Anti-Colonial Protest in the French Empire* (Cambridge, UK: Cambridge University Press, 2013).

16. It is worth noting that many individuals, Israeli or otherwise, dispute the notion that the Zionist movement should be considered colonialist in the same fashion as the British and French cases. Benny Morris, *Righteous Victims: A History of the Zionist-Arab Conflict, 1881–1999* (New York: Knopf, 1999), 38–39.

17. Adria Lawrence, "Driven to Arms? The Escalation to Violence in Nationalist Conflicts," in *Rethinking Violence: States and Non-State Actors in Conflict*, ed. Adria Lawrence and Erica Chenoweth (Cambridge, MA: MIT Press, 2010), 151–54; Frederick Cooper, *Colonialism in Question: Theory Knowledge, History* (Berkeley: University of California Press, 2005), 18–26.

18. Tony Smith, *The Pattern of Imperialism: The United States, Great Britain, and the Late-Industrializing World since 1815* (Cambridge, UK: Cambridge University Press, 1981), 111.

19. Hendrik Spruyt, *Ending Empire: Contested Sovereignty and Territorial Partition* (Ithaca: Cornell University Press, 2005); Ian Lustick, *Unsettled States, Disputed Lands: Britain and Ireland, France and Algeria, Israel and the West Bank-Gaza* (Ithaca: Cornell University Press, 1993); Bridget Coggins, *Power Politics and State Formation in the Twentieth Century: The Dynamics of Recognition* (New York: Cambridge University Press, 2014). It is also worth analyzing how regime fragmentation affects battlefield effectiveness. Caitlin Talmadge, *The Dictator's Army: Battlefield Effectiveness in Authoritarian Regimes* (Ithaca: Cornell University Press, 2015).

20. Jonah B. Schulhofer-Wohl, "Dynamics of Civil Wars: The Causes and Consequences of Subsidies to Armed Groups" (PhD diss., Yale University, 2012).

21. For the best argument along these lines, see Michael Woldemariam, "Why Rebels Collide: Factionalism and Fragmentation in African Insurgencies" (PhD diss., Princeton University, 2011).

22. Donald Horowitz, *Ethnic Groups in Conflict* (Berkeley: University of California Press, 1985); Jeremy Weinstein, *Inside Rebellion: The Politics of Insurgent Violence* (Cambridge, UK: Cambridge University Press, 2007).

23. Kenneth Waltz, *Theory of International Politics* (New York: McGraw-Hill, 1979).

24. Victor Asal, Mitchell Brown, and Angela Dalton, "Why Split? Organizational Splits among Ethnopolitical Organizations in the Middle East," *Journal of Conflict Resolution* 56, no. 1 (2012): 94–177; Fotini Christia, *Alliance Formation in Civil Wars* (Cambridge, UK: Cambridge University Press, 2012); Paul Staniland, *Networks of Rebellion: Explaining Insurgent Cohesion and Collapse* (Ithaca: Cornell University Press, 2014); Costantino Pischedda, "Wars within Wars: Understanding Inter-Rebel Fighting" (PhD diss., Columbia University, 2015); Lee Seymour, Kristin Bakke, and Kathleen Cunningham, "E Pluribus Unum, Ex Uno Plures: Competition, Violence, and Fragmentation in Ethnopolitical Movements," *Journal of Peace Research* 53, no. 1

(2016): 3–18; Henning Tamm, "Rebel Leaders, Internal Rivals, and External Resources: How State Sponsors Affect Insurgent Cohesion," *International Studies Quarterly,* (2016), doi: http://dx.doi.org/10.1093/isq/sqw033.

25. Virginia Page Fortna, "Do Terrorists Win? Rebels' Use of Terrorism and Civil War Outcomes," *International Organization* 69, no. 3 (2015): 519–56; James DeNardo, *Power in Numbers: The Political Strategy of Protest and Rebellion* (Princeton: Princeton University Press, 1985).

26. Stacie Goddard, *Indivisible Territory and the Politics of Legitimacy* (Cambridge, UK: Cambridge University Press, 2010); Nadav Shelef, *Evolving Nationalism: Homeland, Identity, and Religion in Israel, 1925–2005* (Ithaca: Cornell University Press, 2010).

27. Carrie Wickham, "The Path to Moderation: Strategy and Learning in the Formation of Egypt's Wasat Party," *Comparative Politics* 36, no. 2 (2004): 205–28; Jillian Schwedler, "Can Islamists Become Moderates?: Rethinking the Inclusion-Moderation Hypothesis," *World Politics* 63, no. 2 (2011): 347–76; Nadav Shelef and Orie Shelef, "Democratic Inclusion and Religious Nationalists in Israel," *Political Science Quarterly* 128, no. 2 (2013): 289–316.

28. Shafiq al-Hout, *My Life in the PLO: The Inside Story of the Palestinian Struggle* (London: Pluto Press, 2011), 56.

29. Arthur A. Stein, "The Hegemon's Dilemma: Great Britain, the United States, and the International Economic Order," *International Organization* 38, no. 2 (1984): 355–86.

30. William Wohlforth, *The Elusive Balance: Power and Perceptions during the Cold War* (Ithaca: Cornell University Press, 1993).

31. It may also be the case that perceptions linger, and so the once-challenger Irgun was perceived as a larger threat than its current strength might have dictated. Sartori would explain this as the difference between a predominant party and a predominant party system—it takes approximately three cycles of the former to achieve the latter—otherwise, something so recently gotten is not immediately assumed to last. Giovanni Sartori, *Parties and Party Systems: A Framework for Analysis* (Cambridge, UK: Cambridge University Press, 1976).

32. Pischedda, "Wars within Wars."

33. Kelly M. Greenhill and Solomon Major, "The Perils of Profiling Civil War Spoilers and the Collapse of Intrastate Peace Accords," *International Security* 31, no. 3 (2006): 7–40.

34. For some initial research on this question, see Morgan L. Kaplan, "How Civilian Perceptions Affect Patterns of Violence and Competition in Multi-Party Insurgencies," MS, University of Chicago, 2015.

35. Jeffrey Friedman, "Cumulative Dynamics and Strategic Assessment: U.S. Military Decision Making in Iraq, Vietnam, and the American Indian Wars" (PhD diss., Harvard University, 2013).

36. Hamou Amirouche, *Memoirs of a Mujahed: Algeria's Struggle for Freedom, 1945–1962* (San Diego: Amirouche Publishing, 2014), 50.

37. Edmund Morgan, *The Birth of the Republic, 1763–89* (Chicago: University Of Chicago Press, 2012).

38. William J Duiker, *The Communist Road to Power in Vietnam,* 2nd ed. (Boulder: Westview Press, 1996); Fredrik Logevall, *Embers of War: The Fall of an Empire and the Making of America's Vietnam* (New York: Random House, 2012).

39. Roy Pateman, *Eritrea: Even the Stones Are Burning,* 2nd ed. (Trenton, NJ: The Red Sea Press, 1998), 132.

40. Okbazghi Yohannes, *Eritrea: A Pawn in World Politics* (Gainesville: University Press of Florida, 1991), 272.

41. Douglas Johnson, *The Root Causes of Sudan's Civil Wars* (Bloomington: Indiana University Press, 2003).

42. Peter Krause, "Many Roads to Palestine? The Potential and Peril of Multiple Strategies within a Divided Palestinian National Movement," Crown Center for Middle East Studies Brief no. 60, Brandeis University, March 2012, 10.

43. Zuhayr Qusaybati, "Interview with . . . Mas'ud Barzani," *al-Hayat* (London), June 5, 1994.

44. In Michael M. Gunter, "The KDP-PUK Conflict in Northern Iraq," *Middle East Journal* 50, no. 2 (1996): 240.

45. Dana Adams Schmidt, *Journey among Brave Men* (Boston: Little, Brown, 1964), 201.

46. See Nawshirwan Mustafa Amin, *Fingers That Break Each Other: Political Events in Kurdistan from 1979 to 1983* (Iraqi Kurdistan, 1998), in Pischedda, "Wars within Wars."

47. Timothy P. Wickham-Crowley, *Guerrillas and Revolution in Latin America: A Comparative Study of Insurgents and Regimes since 1956* (Princeton: Princeton University Press, 1991).

48. Aisha Ahmad, "Going Global: Islamist Competition in Contemporary Civil Wars," *Security Studies* 25, no. 2 (2016): 353–84.

49. Barak Mendelsohn, "The Jihadi Threat to International Order," *Washington Post*, May 15, 2015.

50. Melvyn Dubofsky and Foster Rhea Dulles, *Labor in America: A History* (Wheeling, IL: Harlan Davidson, 2010).

51. Rufus Miles, "The Origin and Meaning of Miles' Law," *Public Administration Review* 38, no. 5 (1978): 399–403; Graham Allison and Phillip Zelikow, *Essence of Decision: Explaining the Cuban Missile Crisis* (Boston: Longman, 1999).

52. In Nathan Leites and Charles Wolf, *Rebellion and Authority: An Analytic Essay on Insurgent Conflicts* (Santa Monica, CA: Rand, 1970), 43.

53. Hamou Amirouche, interview by author, February 25, 2015. See also Wendy Pearlman, "Emotions and the Microfoundations of the Arab Uprisings," *Perspectives on Politics* 11, no. 2 (2013): 387–409.

54. The growing practice and analysis of leadership decapitation of insurgent groups are based on the idea that there is a difference between leaders and foot soldiers, although MST suggests that we should analyze whether that difference is based on individual characteristics or the incentive structure of one's position; Jenna Jordan, "When Heads Roll: Assessing the Effectiveness of Leadership Decapitation," *Security Studies* 18, no. 4 (2009): 719–55; Austin Long, "Assessing the Success of Leadership Targeting," *Combating Terrorism Center Sentinel*, November 1, 2010; Patrick Johnston, "Does Decapitation Work? Assessing the Effectiveness of Leadership Targeting in Counterinsurgency Campaigns," *International Security* 36, no. 4 (2012): 47–79; Max Abrahms and Philip Potter, "Explaining Terrorism: Leadership Deficits and Militant Group Tactics," *International Organization* 69, no. 2 (2015): 311–342.

55. Paul Staniland, "Organizing Insurgency: Networks, Resources, and Rebellion in South Asia," *International Security* 37, no. 1 (2012): 142–77; Asal, Brown, and Dalton, "Why Split?"

56. For a related discussion of wedge strategies by states, see Timothy Crawford, "Preventing Enemy Coalitions: How Wedge Strategies Shape Power Politics," *International Security* 35, no. 4 (2011): 155–89.

57. Jo Becker and Scott Shane, "Hillary Clinton, 'Smart Power' and a Dictator's Fall," *New York Times*, February 27, 2016.

58. William Zartman, ed., *Negotiating with Terrorists* (Boston: Martinus Nijhoff, 2005); Peter R. Neumann, "Negotiating with Terrorists," *Foreign Affairs* 86, no. 1 (2007): 128–38.

59. Austin Wright and Philip Ewing, "Ash Carter's Unwelcome News: Only 60 Syrian Rebels Fit for Training," *Politico*, July 7, 2015.

60. Robert Art and Louise Richardson, *Democracy and Counterterrorism: Lessons from the Past* (Washington, DC: United States Institute of Peace, 2007).

61. Zachariah Mampilly, *Rebel Rulers: Insurgent Governance and Civilian Life during War* (Ithaca: Cornell University Press, 2011).

62. Nathan Brown details a similar problem within the Palestinian Authority; *Palestinian Politics after the Oslo Accords: Resuming Arab Palestine* (Berkeley: University of California Press, 2003).

63. William Quandt, *Revolution and Political Leadership: Algeria, 1954–1968* (Cambridge, MA: MIT Press, 1969).

64. Stephen Walt, *Revolution and War* (Ithaca: Cornell University Press, 1996); Edward D. Mansfield and Jack Snyder, "Democratization and the Danger of War," *International Security* 20, no. 1 (1995): 5–38.

65. Tom Hartley, interview by author, June 14, 2014.

Index

Note: Page numbers in *italics* indicate figures; those with a *t* indicate tables.